A PSYCHIATRIC STUDY OF MYTHS AND FAIRY TALES

A PSYCHIATRIC STUDY OF MYTHS AND FAIRY TALES

Their Origin, Meaning and Usefulness

AN ENLARGED AND THOROUGHLY REVISED SECOND EDITION OF

A Psychiatric Study of Fairy Tales

By

JULIUS E. HEUSCHER, M.D., F.A.P.A.
Associate Clinical Professor, Stanford University
Lecturer, University of California Medical School
San Francisco
University of California Extension Service
Santa Cruz

CHARLES C THOMAS · PUBLISHER
Springfield · Illinois · USA

Published and Distributed Throughout the World by

CHARLES C THOMAS • PUBLISHER
Bannerstone House
301-327 East Lawrence Avenue, Springfield, Illinois U.S.A.

ISBN 0-398-02851-6

Library of Congress Catalog Card Number: 73-4267

With THOMAS BOOKS careful attention is given to all details of manufacturing and design. It is the Publisher's desire to present books that are satisfactory as to their physical qualities and artistic possibilities and appropriate for their particular use. THOMAS BOOKS will be true to those laws of quality that assure a good name and good will.

Library of Congress Cataloging in Publication Data
Heuscher, Julius E.
A psychiatric study of myths and fairy tales.
Bibliography: p. 399.
1. Fairy tales—History and criticism. 2. Subconsciousness. I. Title.
[DNLM: 1. Folklore. 2. Psychiatric interpretation. WM 460 H595p 1973]
GR550.H4 1973 398.2 73-4267 ISBN 0-398-02851-6

Printed in the United States of America
EE-11

To Ruth,
Enno Francis
and Dominic

PREFACE

We can never exhaust the depths of myths and fairy tales—of that we may be certain; but then neither can anyone else. And a cupped handful of the fresh waters of life is sweeter than a whole reservoir of dogma, piped and guaranteed.

—HEINRICH ZIMMER[188]

THERE ARE MANY tasks we would never undertake, if we were aware of all the difficulties and problems, of all the work and frustrations they would entail. Thus, while the uncertainty of the future fills us with deep anxiety, it equally emboldens us through a permissive attitude which hides many of the obstacles lying ahead. I might never have tackled the wide field of myths and fairy tales, with its manifold aspects and ramifications, if I had known beforehand what an enormous number of these narrations exist all over the world, and how excellent some of the literature concerning the subject is.

I was naively unaware of all this, like the youngest of the three brothers whom the fairy tale king sends out into the world to accomplish a seemingly impossible task. Yet, as in the case of this youngest brother, it was just this naive lack of prejudice which gave me both the incentive to meet the problems which arose out of my research and the freedom to find answers.

Some years ago, when my curiosity for the meaning of fairy tales was reawakened, I did not feel the need to scan any of the collections of myths and folk tales. On the contrary, I sensed that a few, or even only one, of the genuine folk-fairy tales would open the door to the world of these wondrous stories. Indeed, the spiritual realities, the metaphysical ideas reflected in the images of myths and fairy tales are not nearly as fragmented as our variegated material environment. J. W. Goethe expressed this magnificently when he had Faust exclaim in regard to the "world of the spirit":

Wie alles sich zum Ganzen webt,	How everything weaves itself into the whole (pattern),

Eins in dem andern wirkt und lebt!	How each part lives and works in each other part!
Wie Himmelskräfte auf und nieder steigen	How heavenly forces ascend and descend
Und sich die goldnen Eimer reichen,	Handing each other the golden vessels,
Mit segenduftenden Schwingen	Penetrating from heaven through the earth
Vom Himmel durch die Erde dringen,	Upon grace-scented wings,
Harmonisch all das All durchklingen![54]	All resounding harmoniously through all!

Thus I surmised that a completely unprejudiced, a truly *phenomenologic* approach to a single fairy tale would reveal not just a significant fragment, but a whole view of the human being.

And though, during subsequent years, I had reason to read a good many folk tales and myths, this initial, naive attitude was not all wrong. I found confirmation of my original belief in the following statement by Joseph Campbell who has written excellently and widely on the subject:

> The wonder is that the characteristic efficacy to touch and inspire deep creative centers dwells in the smallest nursery fairy tale—as the flavor of the ocean is contained in a droplet, or the whole mystery of life within the egg of a flea.[24]

An old Indian fairy tale analyzed by the prominent, late indologist, Heinrich Zimmer, reaches the same conclusion.[188] In this story, titled *The King and the Corpse,* the once prominent and self-assured king finds himself in a nightmarish graveyard-like, dark region. Here he must answer the riddles contained in the twenty-five riddle-fairy tales told to him by the spirit in the corpse which he patiently carries back and forth through the bleak night. Each one of these tales is so complete, so perfect in itself that they are universally celebrated when the king, after several more trials, has regained his throne, mightier and wiser than before. Even Shiva, "the great god, overlord of all the Spectres and Demons," does them honor. And thus the story announces in the end that, "whoever recites with sincere devotion even a *single one* (of the riddle tales) shall be free from sin."

The last quote is of the deepest significance. It points towards the intimate relationship between the tale and the one who receives the tale. On the one hand, the "truthfulness" of the fairy tale is not simply objectively given, but depends upon the ability of the listener to *perceive* the truth. The German expression for perceiving, *wahrnehmen,* literally meaning *to take the truth,* refers to this interrelationship between the objective truth and the faculties of the observer. This is largely the reason for the differing interpretations of the same fairy tale or myth by various qualified students. Rather than seeing the differing interpretations as erroneous, we may try to recognize them as the particular truths which the observer has been able to grasp among the wealth of meanings harmoniously interacting in the images of the story.

On the other hand, the intimate relationship between the tale and the listener or reader purifies the person. As he becomes able *to recite with sincere devotion* the tale, as he is led to experience the truth contained in it, he is simultaneously purified of sin. This is of utmost importance. Genuine understanding cannot be a merely intellectual process; rather, it goes hand in hand with an emotional cleansing process. The tale cleans the soul, and the purification of the soul, in turn, is necessary for the fuller comprehension of the tale. Here we must remember that, like the epos, the fairy tales were originally narrated by adults for adults. It is only during the past two centuries that fairy tales have been confined, more and more, to the children's world. And even the epos lost much of its former influence upon the adult listeners.

Yet, just as the mythic drama was seen by the Greek as a purifying, cathartic mystery and not merely as entertainment, so is the fairy tale to be viewed not just as a pastime for the child, but also as a fare which helps our young listener. In these overly rationalistic times the fairy tale and myth have remained an indispensable nourishment which can strengthen the non-intellectual soul forces, the emotions and impulses, of the growing child. All the techniques of child rearing, helpful as they may be with particular problems, cannot offer an adequate substitute for this necessary food of the child's soul.

But even to the adult, the lecture of myths, heroic epos and fairy tales may become a healthy compensation against the overly technologic and rational world in which we live. Thus James

Thurber became so engrossed in his delightful fairy tale of *The Thirteen Clocks* that he kept on rewriting it until his friends figuratively tore it out of his hands; and in a modern play we see the serious scientist periodically seeking solace and harmony in the simple cottage of an elderly couple, listening to the fairy tales spontaneously flowing from the woman's lips.[166]

By gaining a deeper understanding, a greater respect for these stories, the parent will be able to read or tell them to his child at the proper time and in a manner which, rather than creating fears, will commune the hidden meaning. Elaborating on some of the preceding remarks, we might say that the truth contained in the fairy tale is *not* relative, but that it becomes alive and operative in the *relationship* between the story, the parent and the child. And the purification of the narrator and listener, resulting from experiencing the meaning of the tale, makes them progressively more capable of perceiving ever new truths. In other words, the narration itself becomes a more and more transparent "Mask of God" which allows an experience of the invisible and ineffable.[25]

I have been digressing from the assertion that *one* single tale may open our eyes to the inner world of the growing and groping human being, as well as to the deeper meanings of human existence and evolution. Now one should add that, especially in our times, the need is felt to illuminate the various truths from *many* viewpoints. We are so thoroughly conditioned by modern natural-scientific methods which usually require numerous, repetitive observations in order to achieve statistically valid conclusions, that it becomes difficult for us to accept fully the truths which can be gathered from a single observation. This may well have been a substantial reason for my continued interest in ever new folk-narrations.

But the study of a great number of these stories not only offered new confirmation of what I had sensed beforehand; it proved fascinating for at least two additional reasons, which, in a way, are paradoxically complementary. On the one hand, one is led to recognize that the ultimate basic themes of fairy tales and myths from all parts of the world seem to converge on one and the same, all-embracing center of wisdom. Joseph

Campbell has illustrated this aspect excellently in the light of Indian philosophy which sees our variegated terrestrial existence as a kaleidoscopic reflection of the inscrutable unity in Nirvana.[24] On the other hand, one can be easily fascinated by the almost innumerable marked differences and fine nuances by which related fairy tales and myths distinguish themselves. Focusing upon these differences, we become aware that they not only are illusory mirror images of the one and only truth, but that they point towards specific, individual meanings which must be viewed and understood as such. If, for example, the French *Sleeping Beauty*[139] is attended by seven, and the analogous German *Briar Rose*[58] by twelve good fairies, we may find that this difference reflects some significant characteristics of the two cultures[124] (see Chapter XVI).

Numerous myths and tales have been added for discussion in this enlarged and revised edition. This must not be construed as an attempt to offer a historically or geographically comprehensive coverage. The selection was guided exclusively by the need to illustrate several basic perspectives. Rather than dogmatic views, these are challenges, encouraging the reader to see ever new and ever deeper aspects of the infinitely varied themes of these narrations. However, this cannot be accomplished without overcoming some of the blindly accepted presuppositions of modern Western civilization, such as radical analytic reductionism, one-sided scientific objectivism, exclusive atomism, as well as various unproven assumptions concerning the workings of the "primitive mind." Thus the person who endeavors to become aware of the more hidden dimensions of the world of myth and folklore will experience a personal growth. We shall see that such a wider awareness finds an echo in the newest endeavors of life scientists who are forced to the conclusion that the exclusive reductionist approaches of traditional natural science have only limited validity. They must be supplemented or balanced with forms of thinking that can grasp the reality of organizing, systemic forces, of *gestalts*, of Koestler's *holons*,[100] and of hierarchical organizations.

Indeed the strong challenge for change in our present world may be only dimly and confusedly reflected in the numerous sociopolitical unrests. Primarily it is a challenge for an internal growth that does not reject the fruits of natural science, but aims for a wider consciousness and a deeper experience of love and freedom. Some narrations mentioned in this book clearly allude to this need for an eventual transcendence of one-sided materialism and rationalism.

Yet we must not see such transcendence simply in terms of our conventional, technologically flavored, ideas of progress. Most of us have such an extremely limited experience of the human being that we despair over the endless and seemingly inefficient attempts of the human race to better its lot, to develop towards a fairer, happier and morally higher plane. It is hard for us to accept the innumerable failures and the unspeakable suffering that accompany these attempts; and we cannot grasp why so enormously much time is seemingly wasted for such small gains. And even if optimistically we hope for an eventual blissful denouement, we not only can barely sense its meaning, but we also lose all understanding of the significance of time subsequent to it. At best, such ruminations will lead us to question our current, limited definitions of progress, goals and time.

Myths and fairy tales do not give us rational answers to these perplexing problems. However, their worlds usually do not respect the conventional dimensions and limits of our everyday world. They are imbued with a profound conviction of the meaningfulness of human existence. This is true even of those Oriental stories that emphasize the illusory nature of the world, of Maya, and the need to lose one's identity in merging with Nirvana. Yet, though it is unusually difficult for Western man to experience correctly this philosophic orientation,[129,131] it appears, nevertheless, that *the Way* which is the way to Nirvana, is a long, arduous and meaningful development rather than a passive, weak regression to *Nothingness.*

True, attempts to recognize deep mysteries of human existence in each sample of folklore can be overdone and may bypass more obvious features or intents. Nevertheless, the need to bridge the gap between the individual's isolating consciousness and his environment by means of images and rituals that guarantee his experience of harmonious embeddedness in nature is a potent factor in much of folklore. Thus is also the wish to shape and establish viable sociopolitical structures or to convey moral attitudes and —occasionally—moralistic injunctions. And the offering of entertainment or esthetic satisfaction is an important element in all folklore: sometimes for its own sake, but more often for conveying the deeper messages to the audience.

Whereas scholarly anthropologic and folkloristic endeavors concentrate on source, transmission and original meanings and purposes, the Freudian as well as the Jungian approaches to folklore can be called phenomenological, inasmuch as they stress very little the historical derivations. Instead, they view the extant products as intrinsically significant, with little regard for the degree of change and distortion these products may have undergone in the course of the centuries and in the course of their transmission across the continents. Freudians and Jungians alike tend to view the extant product as shaped by the psyche (individual or collective) that uses the available themes freely to express its continuing and new problems, challenges and hopes. The creation of a more recent story out of the elements of earlier ones can then be likened to some degree to Freud's theory of dream formation out of various "remnants" of remembered events of the preceding day. Thus a myth or a fairy tale that is still part of a culture can be explored for its own intrinsic meaning, without deriving these meanings primarily from those of its earliest ancestors. Insight into the latter may be helpful in guiding our understanding of the recent story, but the latter has always its own structuring core that belongs to the present. This "present" is the time when the story has become fixated in written language, whether this was at the time of Homer, of Apuleius, of the Grimm brothers or of Tolkien and Sendak. We shall return to this structuring core on later occasions, since we already have exceeded the usual dimensions of a preface.

However, as we shift our viewpoints and as we move from one theme or story to another, it will become apparent to the reader that the assessment of what is most important and beautiful is not something that remains static. Rather, this assessment must be reacquired, cultivated and augmented constantly, since it may dwindle in the flows and pauses of life if we neglect it! It is something that we may gratefully cherish even if we possess it only to a slight extent; something that fills us with the purest joy when we begin to sense that it can lead us to ever broader and deeper meanings. Yet this is not a blanket endorsement for dreamers and short-cut individualists; on the contrary, the search for wider meanings places an enormous burden of responsibility upon the investigator and can progress successfully only if coupled with the most serious intent to develop continuously his own personality. A sincere preoccupation with folklore, on the other hand, will nourish this intent.

I have deliberately refrained from categorizing sharply my own viewpoint, since this would be restrictive. Rather, I would stress the validity of most if not all viewpoints, provided that the observations and conclusions are recognized as necessarily limited by the viewpoint. Some emphasis has been placed on what is commonly termed a "phenomenologic" approach, and the reader will easily recognize the influence of various existential-philosophic trends.

One thing is certain: namely, that the presentation of findings and ideas such as those contained in this volume should not be seen as a comprehensive, closed system, but as a beginning, as an opening. It may challenge us to develop our own skills in recognizing ever new meanings. As Heinrich Zimmer states:

> . . . to awaken in ourselves the old ability to read with intuitive understanding this pictorial script that at one time was the bearer of the spiritual sustenance of our ancestors.[188]

Yet, an "old ability" developed in a modern consciousness becomes a "new" ability with new qualities and purposes. Indeed it is gratifying to notice during recent years the rapid increase of interest in fairy tales and myths, especially among teachers, teenagers and college students. Though at times still somewhat superficial or overly analytical, the numerous new courses on mythology reveal the great thirst for deeper meanings, for non-dogmatic spiritual values, for experiential rather than merely intellectual growth, in the young as well as in the not-so-young. Channeled into extremely one-sided, bureaucratic, technocratic and conformist life-patterns, it is particularly the grown-up person who may be most in need of something that can still speak to the hidden, forgotten part of his personality. In a psychotherapeutic setting where he gradually feels freed from the taboos and selfconsciousness imposed by everyday life, he can gradually open himself again to the language of some myths and fairy tales and respond to it. Thus there has been recently also a growing interest in the use of mythic and fairy tale themes in psychotherapy and I shall elaborate on this briefly in the last part of this book. However, I see no sharp delineation between the therapeutic and growth enhancing aspects of folklore. The therapeutic-growth enhancing facet of the entire volume could then be seen in the continuous questioning of the limits of our understanding. Thus the preoccupation with folklore would reveal ever new facets of the world and of ourselves. Yet this process, leading to ever deeper insights, to ever wider "world-designs" is —in my opinion—a never ending endeavor.

In this enterprise I have become indebted to many authors and I hope that the numerous quotations and bibliographic references will give ample testimony of this. My preoccupation with the ideas and insights of various psychologists, folklorists, anthropologists and phenomenologists has enabled me to find the directions that made the study of myths and fairy tales such a profoundly rewarding personal experience that I desired to share some of it by writing this book.

CONTENTS

A PSYCHIATRIC STUDY OF MYTHS AND FAIRY TALES

PART I

The World of Myths and Fairy Tales

CHAPTER I

PRELIMINARY COMMENTS AND DEFINITIONS

Illustrated with Egyptian Myths and Tales

In very ancient times, Tefnut, the daughter of the sungod, Re, argued with her father. Full of rage, she left her country, Egypt, and traveled southward into the Sudan where she lived in the guise of a wildcat. But Re, gravely worried about his beloved daughter, instructed his messenger, the god Thoth, to bring her back. Disguised as a gibbon Thoth went to meet her; but all his cleverness, his entertaining dances, his delightful sorcery, and his well chosen narrations barely succeeded in calming the enraged woman who would turn into a raving lion whenever she became annoyed or suspicious. Thoth is saved only by his extreme tact and skillfulness; since as the daughter of Re, the great judge, Tefnut has also the power over life and death, and could kill Thoth even though he is a god.

We see Tefnut alternate between being fascinated by Thoth, shedding streams of tears because of homesickness, and flaming-hot rages. Yet, eventually, as they wander together northward toward Egypt, Thoth proves with his actions that one of his meaningful fables *is* true; namely that even the strong (referring to Tefnut) may need the weak (referring to himself). He cleverly saves the enraged goddess from the bite of a serpent. Now they peacefully finish their journey to Heliopolis, the city of the sungod Re, where the daughter makes peace with her father.[15]

This tale, condensed from *The Myth of the Sun-Eye,* dates back several thousand years. Its first known written version goes back to 1400 B.C., and has been transmitted to us in a more complete form through a papyrus of the second century A.D. The tale combines religious elements with elements characteristic of a nature myth. Thus it can be viewed as a portrayal of the yearly southward trip of the sun (Tefnut) and its return during spring, characterized by unpredictable weather (calmness = friendliness; heat = hot rage; and heavy rains = tears). It contains elements of fables: not only do the two protagonists appear mostly in animal guise, but the gibbon also narrates several typical, moralistic fables. And finally it has many characteristics of the fairy tale, to mention but the numerous acts of sorcery, including the ability to change oneself into an animal, or from one animal into another.

We must remind ourselves, however, that the distinction of these various stylistic elements corresponds more to a later need to categorize than to an original separation. Indeed the earliest civilizations had an experience of the integrated fullness (*pleroma*), of the unitary origin of *all*. The original narration was not religion, not nature-myth, not fable, not fairy tale, but all these four together, and more. Nowadays this feeling for the central, all-embracing meaning is almost extinct; and in the place of it we see the fullness in the numerous categories, details, varieties and shades which emerged from the original unity. Thus we are inclined to view this original unity as an empty, meaningless abstraction to which we then lend substance by subdividing and grouping. In this orientation we prove to be somewhat one-sided. I might compare it with an attitude in which I would attribute more meaning to the beautiful acacia tree outside of my window, with its hundreds of thousands of blossoms, and with its millions of minute leaflets, than to the one tiny seed remaining in the dried husk of the preceding year.

The nature of "The original, undivided Unity" is brilliantly described and richly illustrated with numerous quotations by Joseph Campbell[24] and Heinrich Zimmer.[188] Their books are based on myths and fairy tales from all corners of the world, and their conclusions are largely inspired by the philosophy imminent in the early Indian texts. They emphasize the ephemeral, illusory nature of all dividedness, of each separate ego-consciousness, of the manifold data gathered by our sense organs. Death and life, past and future, time and eternity, wealth and poverty, sickness and health, happiness and suffering, good and evil, victory and defeat, glory and despair, freedom and necessity, love and hate, soul and universe, darkness and light, etc: they all are opposites only through illusion, they all ultimately coincide in the *one*, all-creating, all-consuming, constantly evolving and yet unchangeable *Void*. This void can be experienced as negative or positive, as constructive or destructive. The Indian mystic described it as *Nirvana;* many a myth or epos see it as the hidden, eternal spring; Dante[33] experiences it in a vision of the Unity contained in the Trinity; and a fairy tale may visualize it, for example, as the *Lady of Tubber Tintye*[188] lying on a golden couch which perpetually turns around in a circle as it stands upon the rotating cover hiding the well of fire.

Campbell's hero who reappears with ever new faces is always confronted with the same task. He must gain access to the mystery of Nirvana, to the secret of the unity and nothingness of *All*. Whereas the average human being reaches this goal only in his dissolution in death, the hero manages to confront this source of *All Being* already during his lifetime. Thus the heroes seem to have the unique function of renewing the essential mainstream of life for their people, of fructifying their culture with the inexhaustible forces springing out of the void, and of imparting new (and yet always the same) awareness of this transcendental creative nothingness to the future generations. In consummating their arduous task, in going through the experience of "Dying and Becoming" (Goethe's *Stirb und werde!*[55]), they recognize their oneness with the *Self*. Yet this *Self* is but another aspect of Nirvana, of the one, all-embracing and yet spaceless void; and thus the hero loses all "ego-ness."

Campbell and Zimmer also strongly reflect some of the views of Jungian psychology, and the former makes a serious effort to give due credit to Freudian psychoanalysis. In their brilliant and scholarly discussion of numerous myths and fairy tales they touch upon several fundamental questions and problems. These must be dealt with in order to develop a proper perspective in regard to folklore.

When trying to understand genuine folk tales and ancient myths one must avoid several pitfalls. I shall discuss later the one-sidedness—if not fallacy—of the assertion that these stories are nothing but naive, fanciful explanations of natural phenomena which the "primitive" mind could not grasp, was frightened by, and tried to master. The error, here, consists foremost in making unwarranted assumptions concerning the functioning of this "primitive" mind; assumptions due partly to projecting our own ways of thinking and experiencing into the "world-view" of earlier cultures, and to overidentifying the "world-views" of present day, arrested, primitive groups with those of our cultural ancestors. In the following, we shall discuss several aspects of another pitfall which is gaining popularity today.

The natural-scientific achievements of our Western culture have been seen by some as a gigantic error. Such a condemning opinion should exhort us to return to the "unchangeable truth," to the wisdom of the most ancient cultures, and to seek these ultimate truths in the old myths, in the sagas, legends and fairy tales, as well as in mystic experiences and dreams. But we cannot uncritically abdicate our entire present civilization—frightening as it may loom off and on—without very substantial reasons for doing so. Otherwise we would be guilty of escapism and cowardice. Nor can we allow ourselves to judge previous cultures within our present conceptual framework. Rather we can try to develop greater awareness of the frame of mind with which the people of these cultures regarded themselves and the world.

Recorded Indian, Sumerian and Egyptian myths and folk tales date back well into the third millennium before Christ. These were times during which cultural change or progress was still imperceptibly slow. Self-awareness and the recognition of the value of the individual human being were only in their early beginnings. The priest, the king, the pharaoh and maybe some of the wise, powerful and wealthy in their entourage attained distinction, while the rest of the population, including the slaves, still constituted largely impersonal masses whose coming and going was of little human import. During these early, and yet brilliant, cultures the awakening of self-awareness started to lead away from the wholly natural, spontaneous experience of the world which was so naively and completely monistic that it had to be, by necessity, also spiritualistic. As primitive man experienced as real only his own feelings, impulses and ideas, he was bound to interpret the world about him in those terms. Only with the development of a clear-cut self-awareness was the stage prepared for the progressive subject-object split, for the separation of spirit and matter, of soul and body, as well as for the dreadful idea of deliberately interfering with the balance of nature.[51]

This led eventually to our scientific and technologic prowess, as well as to a degree of alienation of man from nature which now threatens to destroy him. In the early beginnings the separation was mostly experienced as a loss, as a painful condemnation. The human being, becoming aware of his *personal* suffering, longed to return to the blissful previous state when, being an unconscious part of nature (i.e. devoid of personal consciousness), he partook of the one big harmony and when, untroubled by the discriminatory activity of thinking, he experienced everything as *one* spiritually alive world.*

Soon man came to experience this original world as a void. The experience of this all-generating and all-destroying void can be seen as the expression of the hopeless longing for something irretrievably lost. Still lacking sharp discrimination, the young consciousness in those early cultures experienced that which was lost and the inner feeling of utter emptiness on account of the loss, as one and the same. Thus the lost could alternately be described as immeasurably rich and as completely empty. On the other hand, that which had been gained, the awareness of the new world of matter, of causality, of measurable space and time, was seen as the *Deceiver*, because it had led away from what once was immensely valuable. Thus the soul seemed to exist between a meaningful void and a meaningless plethora of appearances. Yet

*This does not necessarily conflict with the common explanation that the idea of a paradisiacal, blissful and painless world was a compensatory dream or phantasy of early man plagued by all kinds of evil. Nor does it postulate that, prior to the birth of consciousness, suffering did not exist at all. It does, however, imply that suffering assumed an entirely new, disagreeable connotation with the development of consciousness; and that the ability itself to portray a paradisiacal world may have grown out of the longing to return to this pre-conscious existence.

this plethora of illusions of the world of the senses could be fantastically attractive. *Shiva* would for eons of time sit in quiet contemplation of the supreme, unchanging, all-pervading source and end of being.[188] But then he would periodically take to himself a wife, *Sati* or *Paravati.* Though she may have different names, she is always the same since she is an incarnation of Maya. With her, he experiences to the utmost all the pleasures of the soul and of the senses, and after she dies, all the ravages of suffering and despair. Eventually, however, he again turns his meditative gaze inward, absorbed in the perfect void of his own being. This is the eternal cycle, the universal round of creation and dissolution.

In early cultures, when the changes from generation to generation were almost imperceptible, our present day idea of human progress did not exist as yet. Instead, the Indians, for example, saw themselves and their gods involved in an eternal, unchangeable cycle reflecting both the seductiveness of the sensuous world appearing to the young consciousness, and the longing to efface this consciousness in order to return to a previous, dimly remembered, blissful state. Viewed from the standpoint of the young consciousness, however, this return or regression is seen as dangerous, frightening and deadly.

In this respect the central problem of the earliest great cultures can be compared to the main theme of the story of *Hansel and Gretel.* In a later chapter we shall elaborate how growing self-awareness, cleverness and discrimination lead them to become aware of rejection, sadness and anxiety. They regress to the paradisiacal world of the gingerbread house and to the witch who almost devours them. In the witch's stomach, then, all would become undifferentiated darkness; maleness and femaleness would be reunited and uniform; Hansel and Gretel would be newly unconscious, unborn, in an empty void. Yet the shriveled-up witch has another center which is a precious source of constructive forces for the growing young consciousness. This center is represented by her jewels which the siblings carry back home after her death. The *Jewel in the Lotus* of the Bodhisattva *Avalokiteshvara,* the *Lotus-Bearer,* carries the same meaning. Equally, the jewels in the rotten apples in the delightful Indian tale of *The King and the Corpse*[188] point to these permanent values.

It is fascinating to find new analogies between motifs or themes of innumerable fairy tales and myths of all times and regions. One of the most profound, recurrent themes, as we have seen, refers to the ultimate, universal, undifferentiated, unitary origin of all existence. However, this insight can lead one to overlook the countless details which differentiate related narrations, or to view them as illusory and therefore insignificant reflections of the common, underlying theme. It may escape us that we are making a somewhat arbitrary decision when we give precedence to what these narrations have in common over what differentiates them. Such a decision, furthermore, implies that we are able to grasp what is meant by the words, "unitary origin of all." But it is paradoxical to assume that we can *ever* grasp it, since the very act of grasping must be a part of this undifferentiated unity. At the very best we can get a vague inkling of what the Indians meant by *Nirvana,* the Nordic races (*Edda*) by the *Creative Void,* the Greeks by *Chaos,* Goethe by *The Mothers,* etc.

Thus we may be fully and equally justified in asking, "What do these fairy tales, sagas and myths tell us, if we chose to bypass the common denominators and focus our attention upon their peculiarities?" We then will discover, as others have done, that many trivial and accidental factors have been influential in modifying these narrations from generation to generation and from one region to another. Among these factors we will find regional taboos, influences by organized religion or political trends, substitution of local scenery, unwarranted condensations of several tales, or loss of understanding for the intrinsic meaning of certain motifs or symbols. Yet, even if we could neatly eliminate the influence of all these secondary factors, we still would be confronted with countless specific differences between related tales which are of the greatest significance. An approach like Campbell's in *The Hero with a Thousand Faces,*[24] which magnificently emphasizes the analogies between many folk narrations, will be sensitive mostly to all those ancient elements in a tale which point toward the basic oneness and eternal sameness of existence. The common & the differentiated myth in understanding the world's cultures.

Contrariwise, the unprejudiced study of the variations of a motif, theme, or tale in its travels through time and across the earth will point to another, opposite and yet complementary meaning expressed in these narrations. We now find that the specific differences refer to *human growth.* This growth is no longer the illusory temporary emergence in a fictitious, variegated, material and sensuous world, but a *real* achievement. The specific features of the tale point toward the possibility of the human being to grow. Whereas the narrative at times seems to refer more specifically to the growth of the *individual* human being, it deals at other times more with the human development of the *whole cultural group.* Myths and fairy tales speak of the eternal all-creating and all-consuming source of existence, but they also point to the *growth* of the human being, which—true enough—appears mysterious in its earliest beginnings, incomprehensible in the present, and enigmatically open towards the future.

In early cultures the dimension of true human growth was barely noticed. There was, however, an awareness of the gradual separation of the individual psyche from the harmonious totality of nature. This separation was primarily experienced as error, as sin. It led to the ambivalence of wishing simultaneously to turn back *and* to maintain the newly won identity. Outward evolution proceeded at such a snail's pace, and the longing to return was so deep, that the ideal of development onward towards something entirely new took hold only gradually. It seems that it is this onward human development, which does not simply make a circular movement and end up at the origin, which underlies and determines the most meaningful variations of motifs and themes as we follow them through time and space.

Joseph Campbell[24] frequently attempts to juxtapose the two viewpoints: that of *our* world which sees a large array of different heroes who overcome by their own courage, initiative, cleverness and choice the greatest odds, and that of the *cosmos* which recognizes that the choices, perils and fortunes of the hero are nothing but innumerable reflections of the same, magnificent and inexorable game of Maya which combines all paradoxes in one point. In the end, however, Campbell would leave little doubt in us that of these two viewpoints the first one is ephemeral; that this first viewpoint, too, is but another manifestation of the only true *Being*, of the one and only *Self* which is everything and nothing, plethora and void; that it is but an illusory reflection of the all-devouring and all-creating *mother* for whom time and eternity, point and infinity, existence and nonexistence are *one*. Everything, then, birth, life and death become involuntary. But, if the cosmos is viewed as an eternal, though timeless, predetermined and magnificently balanced rainbow-circle of death and rebirth, action and reaction, and if even this perfect circle in the last analysis is *Maya*, what use would there be in writing such beautiful and scholarly books as the mentioned ones by Campbell and Zimmer? Do such authors see themselves as the handmaidens of a destiny which leads them to write about a thousand different heroes, when the description of one would not only suffice, but also be an illusion? Or do they at least implicitly acknowledge the meaningfulness of multiplicity, diversity and real growth, by the very love they have poured into their work?*

Paradoxical as it may appear, the two viewpoints *must* be juxtaposed. The less we attempt to explain fairy tales and myths by onesided and overly abstract deductions or by forcing them to conform to an ingenious hypothesis, and the more we keep our heart and mind open to what these narrations reveal by themselves, the greater will be our harvest. Thus the recognition of the ultimate unity and integration of all divergences, of all the opposites. This insight into the narrowness of our frustrations, gripes, sorrows or demands for justice, may offer us a great deal of consolation and serenity. Yet the feeling of resigned fatalism which is generated by the idea of *Nirvana* and *Maya* may lead modern man to quiet despair because of the stress upon the illusory nature of our will. We sense deeply that human growth is our mission, but we cannot conceive of growth without will. It is here that—in contrast to the universal themes—the specific

*Campbell's treatment of the symbol also reflects his basic philosophy. The symbol as such is seen as meaningless. Be it the cross, the mysterious well, the tree of life, the morningstar or the image of the deity itself, these symbols are but doors towards the oneness and undifferentiatedness of *All*. In fact he stresses, with considerable justification, that arresting oneself *at* the symbol leads to stagnation, to stoppage of the energy which rises from the *Void*, vitalizing the phenomenal world.

nuances of myths and fairy tales which support the meaningfulness of progressive individual growth will strengthen our courage.

Those interpretations of folk-fairy tales and ancient myths which focus upon the unitary source and end of everything, are not only compensatory reactions against our one-sidedly developed, natural-scientific, technologic culture, but they are also, in some respects, analogous to the ultimate conclusions of this present culture.

Radical materialism is bound to lead to the idea that more complex forms can evolve spontaneously from simpler forms. In biology this would occur mostly by the way of accidental mutations leading to the natural selection of the superior or fitter forms of life. Extrapolated to the extreme, such a viewpoint would bring forth this sort of reasoning: (a) man is an animal, highly developed as a result of the process of the survival of the fittest; (b) by the same process the more complex animals have very gradually evolved from the lowest forms of life, such as the viruses which resulted accidentally from complex, organic, inanimate molecules; (c) these, then, derive from fortuitous combinations of various atoms; (d) yet even these evolved from combinations of infra-atomic, more and more uniform units which ultimately become so ephemeral that they cannot be grasped either by our sense organs or by our intellect; (e) eventually we are forced to surmise an utter void in which size, space and time become quite relative, a void out of which *Everything* evolved in the course of innumerable cosmic years.

To what degree natural science has come to a formulation of existence which is analogous to that of some of the most ancient explanations of the cosmos can be seen from the following quotation taken from a recent *New York Times* article based on a paper by Dr. Sandage concerning the nature of the universe:[152]

> A preliminary examination of the (*new*) evidence . . . suggests that the universe is not infinite, but rather a closed system that pulsates. . . . This would mean that the present expansion of the universe will ultimately be reversed to be annihilated in an explosion from whose promethean fire a new universe—and ultimately new life—would be born. . . . The clues indicate that our universe pulsates (explodes) once every 82 billion years. . . . Space is curved

in upon itself, limiting the expansion (*of the universe; . . . and thus one must postulate*) a cycle of repeated expansions and contractions. (Italics mine.)

This, though less poetical, corresponds exactly to the idea we find expressed in the *Kalika Purana*, the *Romance of the Goddess*, where the goddess or *maya* would represent the new universe born out of the one that was annihilated:[188]

> This, then, is the goddess who sprang from the incubating, world-creative self-contemplation of the Creator Brahma. But that was not properly the creation of her; that was simply the story of how she stepped into manifestation. There can be no description or discussion of her creation; for it is out of her that everything has come into being, and it is in her spell that everything must remain captive, and it is back to her that everything must return.

Myths from early cultures and the natural scientific myth thus share the belief that continuous human evolution is ephemeral, that the spiritual independence of the ego is an illusion, and that the universe is constantly created and destroyed. In early cultures it was the longing to return to a "pre-ego-consciousness" state as well as the despair of ever reaching a self-assured identity which fostered this belief. In our epoch it is the fascination with modern natural science* and the degradation of the value of the immediate experience which supports it.

The phenomenal world, the immediate experience was shunned in early cultures, since it fostered ego-consciousness which was associated with insecurity and suffering. Today, the

*Natural science has gained a reputation of certainty and reliability. This is due partly to the unique predictability of the majority of phenomena within its scope, and partly to its tremendous practical achievements. The scientists themselves are largely aware of the many significant gaps in our knowledge. However, the popular belief in science will frequently influence even the expert to underestimate the meaningfulness of these gaps, among which the lack of an adequate explanation of gravity (or, in atomic theories, of the mechanism of the attraction between the proton and the electron) is paramount. What happens in the nothingness between the proton and the electron—or between two heavenly bodies? How, to use a metaphor, does the one communicate to the other that he must draw near? Thus, it is important to keep in mind that the fundamental laws of physics describe *relationships* between items pertaining to a hypothetical system; and that our materialistic world view has contributed little towards an understanding of what *mediates* these laws.

reality value of the immediate experience is shunned on account of our natural scientific, analytical orientation which aims to objectivate everything including the human being, to reduce everything to measurable items interrelating in complicated causal chains. Thus materialism has split our world in two; one world which is real because it is measurable, and one which is illusory because it is *only* subjective. Finally, as we have shown, even this real material world comes to resemble the world of *Maya* described in the *Romance of the Goddess.*

Without denying the greatness and significance of these transphenomenal views, one must question their exclusive validity. There is good reason to complain that by doubting the phenomenologic data as such, one creates a (fictitious) dichotomy. Are not *being* and *phenomenon* one and the same? Is not the real meaning *in* rather than in some assumed entity *beyond* the phenomenon? Analyses and abstractions bypass the beauty and uniqueness of each phenomenon or experience and lead to general laws. On the other hand, focusing on the phenomenon itself, letting the phenomenon reveal itself, will bring forth those meaningful facets of existence which are related to identity and development. Since myths, legends, fables, epos, fairy tales and ballads have always been genuine portrayals of deepest human experience, the focusing not only on their universal, common meaning, but also (and especially) on their specific details, will reveal them as portraits of the particular levels which the constantly growing human being has reached in his quest for identity —portraits which are painted against a universal, unchanging background.

In the *Kalika Purana* we constantly see this background of *Maya,* of the self-creating and self-consuming goddess. In the Egyptian myths of *Hathor,* the *Eye of Re,* who aims to destroy all the human beings because they have rebelled against and separated from their creator, we find again an allusion to the same cycle of creation and destruction. Yet *Hathor* only partially accomplishes her mission. Eventually the human beings find a new level of conscious relationship to the Godhead. Returning to the story with which we started, we find that Tefnut, the sungoddess, related to Re, still executes the wide, circular movement of life and still looms potentially destructive. But Thoth, the messenger between the gods and the human beings who represents cleverness and wit, demonstrates beautifully that the still frail and inferior consciousness has the possibility to withstand the destructive power of the irate goddess.

Thus we see that, very slowly, the variegated world which developed out of Chaos, out of Nirvana, out of Re's Eye, begins to assume its independent meanings. Therefore we can find an inexhaustible *real* treasure in the innumerable variations of themes and motifs which appeared through the years in countless myths, fairy tales, legends, and epos from all corners of the earth.

After these preliminary glimpses into the richness of these narrations, and before considering in the next chapter the proper approach to their understanding, we must offer a few definitions of the most frequently mentioned types of folklore.

There is considerable flexibility in the usage of terms such as "myth," "legend," "fable," "epos," "fairy tale," "folk tale" and "saga." Some confusion may derive partly from inaccurate usage and from overlapping of the terms, partly from the fact that there are all kinds of intermediary forms of narrations. The following classification, though somewhat rigid, reflects the prevalent usage of these and related terms.

- (Saga) EPOS (Epic Poem)
  - popular
  - artistic
    - of Gods and demons: myth
    - of heroes: heroic epos or saga
    - of saints: legend
    - smaller epic tales:
      - ballad (heroic, sung verses)
      - fable (animals, mostly)
      - idyl (romantic)
- FAIRY TALE (Folk Tale)
  - popular (e.g. Grimms' tales)
  - artistic (e.g. Andersen's tales, Wilde's fairy tales, Hauff's fairy tales, etc.)

The two terms that most easily give cause for confusion are "saga" and "folk tale." The term "saga" refers primarily to a specific type of Icelandic narratives in prose, with a unique, concise style, covering epic themes as well as fairy tales. However, the term "saga" (in German, *Sage*) is also used almost synonymously with "epos." Quite often, however, the term is used in contradistinction to "epos," denoting somewhat simpler narrations that originated within small, local groups. The term "folk tale" has a slightly broader scope than "fairy tale." "Folklore" is an even broader term, including not only myths, sagas, fairy tales and ballads, but also numbskull tales, merry tales, some proverbs and riddles that are often found enclosed in fairy tale collections.

In this volume we shall use primarily the following terms:

1. Fairy tales or folk-fairy tales, the prototype being some of the classic folklore narrations of Western civilization, orally transmitted until they were collected by Basile,[8] Perrault,[139] the brothers Grimm[58] and Lang,[103] to mention but a few. It must be noted, however, that not one of these collections is limited to typical fairy tales, since they also contain fables, numbskull tales, etc.

2. Art-fairy tales: analogous to the above in content, but committed directly to the written word by their authors. They usually differ considerably in style from the orally transmitted fairy tales, and address themselves frequently to the adolescent and grown-up, rather than to the preadolescent child.

3. Myths (or religious epos) usually deal with deities and semi-deities. However, we also follow the broader use of the term that includes other types of epos.

4. Epos include both narrations of super-human beings and of heroes. Often, however, the term is used synonymously with

5. Heroic epos.

6. Sagas or folk sagas designate a type of epos that is closer to the experience of the common people. They represent a local, semi-historical folklore which reflects the human being's concern, awe and terror in regard to numinous regions.

7. Legends are *written* glorifications of lives and deeds of saints.

8. Folklore: a quite comprehensive concept embracing all types of prose and poetic narrations that were transmitted orally within a certain cultural group, before being written down by the authors of the great epos or by modern collectors.

9. We shall touch only tangentially upon narrations related to the above, to wit: ballads, nursery rhymes, science fiction stories, comic strips or comic books, riddle or numbskull tales, merry or witty tales, fables, trickster tales and proverbs.

CHAPTER II

A CRITIQUE OF SOME INTERPRETATIONS OF MYTHS AND FAIRY TALES

WHEN WE EVALUATE other cultures as sadistic, barbaric, neurotic or inferior, we either focus upon decadent remnants of formerly superior civilizations, or we blindly apply both our own values and our materialistic thinking to the beliefs and workings of foreign ethnic groups which thereby are grossly misunderstood. This is particularly the case in those innumerable instances where the mythologist automatically interprets the colorful and marvelous images of ancient or primitive people as resulting from the transformations of ordinary phenomena of nature. He assumes that these transformations are an expression of the unusually lively fantasy of these "simple people," or that they are due to their need to explain naively those processes of nature for which scientific knowledge was inadequate. Furthermore, he assumes that these explanations are necessitated by fear of the unknown: A fantastic explanation is better than none, and it tends to place the helpless human being into the center of creation, thus substituting self-worth for weakness and insignificance. Ultimately then, these fantastic images and explanations can be arranged into an orderly structure and when they are accepted by the group and its leaders, they become their religion.

But in all this we move from one unproved assumption to another, and worse: We look at all the transmitted mythic and legendary treasures as if we ourselves had created them right here in the framework of our present culture. And then we ask ourselves how we arrived at creating them. Finally we take our answer and conclude that the ancient or primitive people arrived at their images in the same way. Thus we superimpose some of our cultural patterns upon another culture rather than understanding this culture. Yet, understanding this culture would be highly beneficial in making us sensitive to the limiting patterns of our own culture.

The more we are able to grasp the dimensions of the world of people in early civilizations or the world of contemporary primitive man, the more we will recognize that fantasy (as we experience fantasy) was (or is) an insignificant element in their imaginative view of their existence. What they saw, felt, experienced and described were realities to them; and if these realities appear grotesque, odd, illogical, childish or silly to most of us, there may be a number of reasons for this reaction. There is, however, little doubt that this connotation of strangeness, exaggeration and irrationality characteristic of the world of our ancestors as well as of most contemporary primitive civilizations is at least partly due to our inability to experience their world the way it was experienced originally. We are confounded and impressed by Indian descriptions of eternally recurring periods lasting over 600 trillion years, where each period represents the passing of one Brahma or the blinking of the eyes of Vishnu. Yet we find it nearly impossible to experience the meaning of such descriptions.[189]

We are caught millionfold in the narrow, rationalistic framework of our advanced epoch—we cannot free ourselves from it fully even for a moment; therefore, we can never immerse ourselves totally into a world where measurable time and space, causality and materiality were experienced only dimly as secondary attributes, as shadowy abstractions of a wider existence. The originators of myths and fairy tales had no propensity for abstract thinking. As long as symbols are misunderstood as metaphors or some other sort of abstractions, it is erroneous to say that these narrations use symbols to explain various aspects of the world. Equally it is misleading to speak of plays on words in regard to the multiple meaning of some of the terms in myths and fairy tales. Plays on words in our culture are usually clever, abstract constructs, whereas in these stories the multiple meanings of a term or the similarity of terms refer to experienced, meaningful realities. This can be illustrated with one of the most beautiful tales from Brunner-Traut's excellent collection of Egyptian folklore,[15] to which we referred in the preceding chapter.

The story of the partial destruction of the human race by God (Re) and of the separation of heaven and earth contains motifs which we find not only in the Old Testament (Adam and Eve, Noah) but also in narrations from all parts of the world.

As the human beings become stronger and more arrogant, Re grows weaker. Who is Re, the god who now sends his Eye in the form of Hathor to destroy the human race? He is the son of Nun, of Chaos or of the Formless All. Re is equally the god who—like the uroboric serpent—created himself. He is the first formed entity, and his form is concentrated in his Eye. The iris of the Eye—like the Chinese Wu-Gi—is the perfect round out of which all that *is* germinated, and which can again consume everything. This Eye of Re is alternately and simultaneously sense organ and sun. As sun it is the source of all life, but as sun it also can destroy the life of the people in the desert. The creative aspect of this perfect round is also apparent from the similarity, in the Egyptian language, of the words "creating," or "making" and "eye." These are not plays on words.[15] They only seem plays on words to us for whom the terms "eye," "create," "circle" and "god" are sharply different concepts. To the original storyteller the images of the god Re, of Re's eye, of the goddess Hathor as the revenging eye, of the sun, of creating, must have been confluent if not identical. This was so, not because of an unbridled fantasy of the storyteller, but because of his viewpoint which led him to the immediate conviction that these images were interchangeable, just as our modern, entirely different frame of reference compels us to group and to distinguish the physical data as well as the abstract concepts of our world in certain ways.

In the old Egyptian language the terms for "human being" and for "tear" were almost the same. Yet, again it was not a play on words when the human beings were called "the tears of Re." To the original narrator the human being was the self-created God's tear. Indeed, what an overwhelmingly beautiful image, rich in meanings, is this! The human being, separated from the eye of God like a tear, soon becomes God's sorrow. At first, Re, living among mankind, wants to preserve his all-pervading power; therefore, when the human beings strive toward independence, he wants to use his eye to consume them again. The heat of his sun-eye would dry up all the tears and restore the former strength of the god. Yet, while the tears separated from the eye, god became divided within himself. Now his wish for self-contained perfection battles with his pity for the human beings. This leads to the division of everything. God now dwells no longer on earth, but—having outwitted Hathor (who has become his feminine counterpart)—he assumes a throne upon the heavenly cow, which becomes the sky. Day separates from night and the people on earth separate into two inimical factions.

The experience of meaningfulness which this drama of creation kindles in him who hears it without bias may well exceed that aroused by an advanced natural-scientific explanation of the universe. We saw this drama begin with Nun, the unformed Chaos from which the all creating, all embracing, all-consuming Re emerged. At first, as Sun or as the perfectly round circle of the Iris he is self-contained. Yet, as the creator and self-creator, this perfect circle splits and the resulting harmoniously and creatively interacting darkness and light, above and below, left and right, are best portrayed by the Chinese Yin and Yang.

Another magnificent story from ancient Egypt will illustrate a different facet of primitive thinking; namely its peculiar experience of time, of space, of causal relationships and of identity. This is the tale of *The Two Brothers* (Bata and Anubis), the basic theme of which recurs in many variations in most nations. Bata, after having been falsely accused by his older brother, Anubis, of incestuous desire for his sister-in-law, separates himself from his brother as well as from his heart. Only after being again and again betrayed by the woman he loves, is he born again to this very woman. Later he reigns as king for thirty years. Then he is succeeded by his older brother, Anubis. The mythic tale cuts across all logic. How, for example, could the older brother be expected to live long enough to succeed the younger brother's son? Identities are treated most liberally. The oldest brother's wife, Bata's wife, the Pharaoh's wife, all become one: sister-in-law, wife and mother, lover, consoler and traitor. Distances are transcended: Bata lives on while his heart is removed and nourished by the sap of the Umbrella-Pine; Bata's brother, though far away, receives by magic a prearranged sign indicating Bata's extreme peril. Parts are identified with the whole: Two drops of Bata's blood regenerate him in the shape of two Umbrella-Pines; and a mere splinter from these pines, flying into the woman's mouth, regenerates him anew in his own child.[15]

This ancient and very elaborate tale contains many motifs which we recognize again in a host of later fairy tales (such things as the creative power of blood drops, the gift of understanding the voices of animals, and the treacherous woman wishing to eat the liver of the protagonist). And, perhaps more clearly than many other fairy tales, this story can be seen as portraying three main periods in human development:

1. *Early Childhood:* At first Bata, naively open to the voices of nature, innocent and devoted, freely serves his older brother who is married and who is simultaneously a father to him. Through the actions of the brother's wife, Bata becomes unwillingly involved in an oedipal conflict solved only incompletely with the onset of

2. *The Latency Period:* He has escaped into a far away region. He has cut his heart out of his chest and has placed it into the crown of a tree; he has become sexless since, in his anger (or guilt for hidden desires?) over being accused of incest, he has cut off his genitals.

3. *Adolescence:* His heart is found by his brother who places it back into Bata's chest and thus rescues him from death. Near-death and rescue from death are common motifs of adolescence. Finally, his virility is fully restored and he now meets the treacherous woman-wife in the form of a bull. He is repeatedly betrayed, but after many trials he emerges victorious when his ego is born and he can become King. The fact that after a reign of thirty years his older brother, Anubis, succeeds him, is a subtle portrayal of the deepest nature of the ego, of its transcendence of measurable time.

In an Egyptian version of the story of *Solomon and the Queen of Sheba,*[15] gravity and distance are transcended when the king orders his "winged spirit" to bring from the queen's country a large column upon which is engraved everything known in the world. The winged spirit brings the column within the space of time between inhaling and exhaling. The storyteller experienced the speed of the winged thinking—which transcends all space and which can appropriate all that is known, the durability and the power of the thoughts—in the image of the rapidly transported column. The latter, again, was not used as a metaphor. The inner experience of the Egyptian confronted by a majestic column with inscriptions was identical to that produced when he considered the nature and power of thinking. Thus both would be given the same designation. Such an image may seem to contradict our natural-scientific logic; however, it corresponded to, and elicited an experience more genuine than most of the abstract formulations of the thought processes which have been advanced by modern philosophers and psychologists.

In his comments on the collection of ancient Egyptian tales, Brunner-Traut insists that originally the cosmos was experienced in "Pictures and Events," the interpretation of which remained unconscious. This is slightly inaccurate, since it seems more likely that these "Pictures and Events" did not call for any interpretation (much less so than modern "Pictures and Events" such as "The Superego," "The Animus," "The Cathexis," or "The Oedipus complex"). However, he then describes excellently how, during the earliest Egyptian history (about 3000 B.C.), identifications such as "King-Lion" or "King-Falcon" were still experienced as absolute realities. Gradually, these animals were seen more and more as symbols, though the immediate experience of the interchangeability of the animal and the corresponding supreme being or god persisted to a large degree. With the classification, grouping and naming of things the world became fragmented more and more.

What was once a grandiose mythic drama became a moralistic narration. The struggle between Horus and his uncle Seth, at first solely an experience of cosmic happenings, became—by gradual categorization and by moralistic abstractions—the tale of *Truth and Lie*. Still beautiful, this story left its reflections in fairy tales from all corners of the world. Originally, Seth and Horus were beyond truth and lie, beyond good and evil. Similarly, Adam and Eve's deed was beyond good and evil, for these concepts could assume validity for them only after they had eaten of the forbidden fruit. In the Egyptian *Truth and Lie* tale we may recognize remnants of this transcendence of the opposites in the fact that "Truth" lies at times while "Lie" often tells the truth.[15]

The fable of *The Argument between the Parts of the Body* dates its first Egyptian version to 900 B.C. Here the trunk, the arms, the head and other parts of the body argue as to which is most important. Brunner-Traut points to the fact that moralistic, metaphoric versions of this common tale are always secondary to a version in which the ranks and interdependence of the body parts are not used as illustrations of a thought or with a moral intent. Rather, in its primary version, the fable must have been the expression of an immediate (or intuitive) experience.

The progressive fragmentation of the world has been pictured in many myths and fairy tales. The young hero may cut to pieces the uroboric serpent (as Seton Chaemwese does in another tale of ancient Egypt) or the original Giant (for example Ymir in the *Edda*). The abstract intellect can no longer conceive of the meaning of the whole; it can only find meaning in the divided. At one time man had still a feeling for the reality, for the significance of the undivided totality in the beginning of time, and experienced it as person. In Finland, for example, it was the original giant Wipunen, as in Egypt the god Nun. The loss of the sense for the fullness of the original unity is impressively shown by contrasting two corresponding verses from two manuscripts of the *Edda,* one stemming from the eleventh, the other from the twelfth century A.D. In the earlier version the reference to the beginning of time reads: "Once was the time when *Ymir* (the original Giant) *lived.*" A hundred years later the analogous verse reads: "Once was the time when *nothing existed.*"[123] Already a more modern intellectual viewpoint prohibits the personalization of the Chaotic Nothingness.

Fragmentation and specialization go hand in hand with a loss of appreciation of the intimate connections between things. This has had its effect also on recent interpretations of myths and fairy tales. Thus the one-sided interpretation of myths as fanciful portrayals of natural phenomena—rather than as descriptions of fundamental human problems—is a direct result of the waning understanding of the intimately meaningful integration of Nature and Man. Myths have expressed this integration as it existed in the "beginning." In the *Kalevala,* for example, we are at first mystified to read of two creations of the world. Twice heaven and earth are separated and twice the land emerges from the water. This must be so, because the Finnish Laulaia (singer) still sensed the basic relationship between the forces creating the Universe (Macrocosm) and those creating Man (Microcosm). Nor does the *Kalevala* separate the historic, political meaning of the struggle between the Finns and the Vikings from the meaning which this struggle between culturally quite different ethnic groups had for the development of the Finnish soul or character.

It may appear incongruous if not contradictory to us when we find the same mythic or fairy tale theme interpreted once as political parody, then as portrayal of the evolution of mankind, then as reflecting stages in individual human development, then as moral parable and finally as primitive attempts to explain some mysterious phenomena of nature. Whatever multiple meanings we do see are all too easily explained as accidental or as ingenuously created correlations. It is difficult for us to see them as intimately related expressions of a unitary idea.

And yet the longing for such a holistic experience persists deep inside of us. Perhaps like the great Finnish singer, Wainemoinen, this longing hides at the horizon of our world. It waits for the right time to become manifest again, while we are engaged in sharpening our intellect (like the Finnish hero Ilmarinen) and in exploring the sensory data of the material world (like Lemminkainen).

Wainemoinen, the first and greatest Laulaia, longs with all his heart for the beautiful virgin on the rainbow. "Singing is older than speech!" In singing, the human being has always expressed his relatedness with the forces, with the totality of life. In his speech he expresses his relationship to things. Song is the primeval communion of all, the ancient amicable-inimical closeness to nature whose pulse educated its rhythm.[18] The *Kalevala,* therefore, indicates that the union with the beautiful virgin on the rainbow can no longer be obtained by simply reverting to the early times when the subject-object split had not yet occurred. Ilmarinen, the blacksmith who has suffered and toiled, also strives for her. He succeeds in forging the axe which is sharp enough to split hairs, but while he works on it the poison of a wasp, unnoticed, gets mixed into the iron. We thus are confronted by a beautiful image of the human being who has developed the keenest intellectual forces which, however, do not suffice to retain the ideal virgin once she has been reached.

The attempt to grasp myths and fairy tales—as much as possible—phenomenologically does not in the least imply an exhortation to regress toward the unitary world-experience of earliest cultures. In fact it is the *Kalevala* itself which stresses that such a regression is not feasible and that only the refined skill of Ilmarinen can prevent the destruction of the world by firestorms and lead us out of utter darkness into a new light. But he cannot forge this new light which eventually will create a new rainbow bridging the whole human existence and carrying the beautiful virgin.

Yet, while the earth is in great turmoil, the powerful songs which Wainemoinen left behind keep alive our hope that the great Laulaia is waiting behind the horizons, and that in a distant future he will return to partake with his younger brothers of a new, harmonious and meaningful experience of our world. (See also Chapters VI and VII.)

CHAPTER III

THE ORIGIN OF INDIVIDUALITY

Comments on an American Indian Myth

IN THE TRICKSTER CYCLE of the Winnebago Indians collected some sixty years ago by Radin[141] we have one of the most integrated collections concerning a being with human, divine and animal characteristics. Jung[86,87] has likened this being to what he calls the *Shadow:* a most significant Gestalt, System, or dynamic complex of specific forces which emerged in his study of the individual and collective (group-) psyche.

Here we shall focus upon this cycle from one particular vantage point which will show that the series of episodes of which it is composed reveals a profound understanding of the earliest emergence of human consciousness.

On the surface the cycle contains a collection of entertaining stories concerning a typical American Indian trickster figure. Between his extreme connotations of culture hero and animal spirit (coyote, spider, raven, etc., depending on tribe and geographic location), Trickster is primarily an alternatively cunning, outwitting and outwitted, taboo-breaking but not maliciously evil being that finds itself in—and creates all kinds of—embarrassing, painful and funny situations.

In the Winnebago cycle Trickster appears first as the chief of the Thunderbird clan. Within the first few episodes he is divested—or divests himself—of all attributes of status and humanness. This divestiture can be likened to that in Western myths and fairy tales. To mention but Ulysses who, after breaking the Sun God's taboo on Thrinakia, loses his last men and earthly possessions, and is washed on the shore of Calypso's island; or the self-divestiture of Grimms' girl with the star-ducats (see Chapter XXIII). Wakdjunkaga, the Winnebago trickster, seems to break the most sacred taboos partly deliberately and partly unwillingly. Since he continues to do so when on the war-path, all his men are deeply shocked and leave him. Only now that he is utterly alone, he reveals himself fully as the Trickster. His existence is so inchoate that he is nameless and unaware of his own body to the extent that one hand starts to fight with the other. Totally uncommitted, he is incapable of any feelings of responsibility. Eventually he is reduced to a frightened being, loses contact with the firm ground of the earth, and drifts—just like Ulysses—helplessly in the large ocean that surrounds the Winnebago earth. It is significant that the very fear that led him to seek refuge in the ocean (both Ulysses and Wakdjunkaga flee from a powerful god-man whose injunctions they disregarded), becomes the beginning of self-awareness.

Finding himself subsequently imitating a tree-stump that has a single branch, in the belief that it was a man pointing, he begins to identify himself: "Indeed it is on this account that the people call me *The Foolish One;* they are right." Then follow a series of episodes during which Wakdjunkaga gradually recognizes and accepts his anus, his intestines, and finally, also his genitals, which he carries in a satchel, as integral parts of himself:

> . . . Suddenly he heard someone singing: "Trickster, what is it you are packing? Your penis it is you are packing!"
>
> "My, what an awful thing he is saying, that contemptible person! He seems really to know what I am carrying (on my back)." On he went. Shortly after this, and from a definite direction, he again heard singing. It was as if it was just at his side:
>
> "Trickster, what is it you are carrying? Your testicles, these you are carrying."
>
> "My, who is this that is mentioning these things? He must indeed have been watching me. Well, now I will carry these things correctly." Thereupon he emptied his box and threw everything out. Then he placed his testicles underneath next to his back. As he was doing this again, suddenly, he heard someone singing right at his side:

"Trickster, what is it you are packing? . . . Your testicles underneath, your testicles underneath!"

"My, what a contemptible person it is who is thus teasing me! He must have been watching my pack." So again he rearranged his pack. He now put the head of his penis on top. Then he went on but soon, unexpectedly, he heard the singing at his side again:

"Trickster, what is it you are packing? Your penis you are packing! The head of your penis you have placed on top, the head of your penis you have placed on top!" . . .

The singing voice is then identified as Chipmunk who disappears in a hollow tree. As Trickster probes for him with his enormously long penis, Chipmunk gnaws off piece by piece. Trickster is disconsolate finding that he has left only a short member. Yet now that he has gradually acquired his physical identity, his "body-ego," Trickster can develop along novel lines. His limiting his genital sexuality* leads to the possibility of creativity on a broader scale, and he is now on the way to becoming a culture hero, giving origin to many useful plants. The parts of his chewed-off penis are thrown into water and turn into various species. On the one hand this can be seen as a dramatic illustration of the Freudian sublimation concept. On the other hand we may stress the fact that at this point of his development, Wakdjunkaga becomes *aware* of his sexuality which in previous episodes was detached from his Self and thus proceeded in an uncontrolled way. This greater awareness of his body goes hand in hand with the growing awareness of the surroundings, of the plants and their usefulness. As he is able to define himself, he is able to *name* and thus to bring into being the various species of plants.

Wakdjunkaga also tries now to develop himself by imitating the skills of others; and though he blunders terribly in most of these attempts, he nevertheless becomes more and more versatile and capable of settling in a respectable home and position in the village (social integration). No longer the naively tricked and trickster, he assumes moral roles, first by taking revenge on some

*Indeed, the singing voice that is right by his side, commenting about his body, is the constituting force of the Self that gradually determines and becomes aware of the "body-ego."[38]

of his former tormentors, then in ordering the world. (Thus he reminds us of Heracles who eventually also takes radical revenge against all those who had tricked or slighted him, who is less than human in his periods of insanity, who has animal connotations when dressed in his lion-skin, but who is also a semi-deity and culture hero. See Chapter XVII.)

It appears strange, at first, that this Trickster seems to "exist" for quite a considerable period (through eleven episodes to be exact) before he becomes vaguely aware of himself and begins to identify with the essential parts of his body. However, the cycle reveals a keen intuition of basic facts concerning *human* consciousness. Indeed—contrary to most animals who are physically independent almost from birth—the helpless child during the first three months is in a *preconscious* state,[38,39] and this is followed by another three months of *primordial consciousness* which is not yet characterized by any identification with, or of, the body, nor by any distinct awareness of a separate, outward space. Elkin,[37] who has brilliantly integrated the empirical observations of Spitz,[164] Hartmann,[61] Klein,[159] Fairbairn and others, shows us that a nonspatial consciousness with temporal connotations precedes the *constitution* (i.e. the infusion with ego-qualities and the assigning of roles to various parts) of the body. His conclusions based on the observation of infantile development coincide largely with those of the phenomenologist, Edmund Husserl,[80] who tried to establish the foundation for understanding how the human being arrives at experiencing himself and the world. Seeking a presuppositionless approach to human consciousness, Husserl showed that what we ordinarily or naively decree or assume as belonging to *ourselves*—feelings, impulses, sensations, body-image, etc.—is not automatically given as part of the *Self*, but is *constituted* by an organizing system that he designates as *transcendental ego.* This transcendental ego corresponds to Elkin's *primordial consciousness;* it is pure consciousness prior to any split into object-subject, body-soul, etc. It is Wakdjunkaga's nameless state, prior to his immersion in the ocean, when he does not yet experience his hands as parts of himself so that they can fight with each other as if they were not related to a central organizing system. His sense of self is aroused only in fearfully *recognizing* the pursuing individual whose injunctions he ignored. This primordial consciousness is temporal rather than spatial, inasmuch as it has to do with *re-cognition.* In the infant the awakening of primordial consciousness is linked to the *re-cognition* of a—usually parental—face which indicates an awareness of the continuity of a primordial *Other* which is not yet experienced as spatially separate, inasmuch as "body-ego" and spatial awareness have not yet developed.

Early cultures were more immediately aware of ordering systems or *holons* which regulate the life of the world, and they pictured them in their divine and semi-divine beings. On the other hand they ignored largely the other, mechanistic pole of life. We shall see, for example, how Wainemoinen, Ilmarinen and Lemminkainen in the Finnish *Kalevala,* how the three artisans in Grimms' *The Juniper Tree* or how the Kings in Goethe's *The Fairy Tale* can be viewed as concrete portrayals of the forces that regulate basic organizing systems, Gestalts or Holons that make up the human being. From a Jungian viewpoint they would often appear as Archetypes. Thus Jung has likened the Trickster figure to the archetypical figure of the Shadow. In terms of the above remarks concerning the development of human consciousness, however, Wakdjunkaga can be seen as portraying the individual's primordial consciousness that gradually establishes a personal body and a more complex and socially integrated psyche. What is neglected, denied or pushed aside in this process, remains back as *Shadow,* as a complex of forces that are hindering but that could become useful if the individual were able to face, accept and enjoy them as unavoidable counterparts of his established conscious personality. Not only the American Indian, but cultures from all parts of the world have been aware of the *Shadow* as a basic part of all human beings. In the telling of the Trickster tales, in the stories about Shamans, in the confrontation with the shadow in carnivals and the like, the hidden aim was to reach this complex of forces that thus could contribute to the further growth of the individual. Only as the Trickster fulfills his function, can other aspects of the individual's psyche—such as intuition and awareness of feelings, clear thinking, and capacity for genuine commitments—manifest themselves as harmoniously operative Gestalts or Systems.

We shall run into the Trickster again, especially in the guise of Ping, Pong and Pang, the ministers of Turandot who have to be faced by Calaf, the unknown Prince trying to overcome the cruel coldness of the princess (see Chapter XXVI).

CHAPTER IV

BRIEF HISTORICAL NOTE CONCERNING THE ORIGIN OF MYTHS AND FAIRY TALES

THE GREAT MAJORITY of our contemporary fairy tales originated as folk tales transmitted by word of mouth for many generations until they were finally written down. While a more pictorial experiencing or thinking is common to all early cultures, there can be little doubt that the most significant folklore productions are the work of pedagogically outstanding leaders, since they reveal such a profound insight into human nature and such assured guidance of the hero's inner development towards future goals.[124] Other stories rightfully deserving the designation of fairy tale were the direct literary product of the creative and intuitive fantasy of such writers as H. C. Andersen (*Thumbelina*),[3] O. Wilde (*The Fisherman and his Soul*),[183] W. Hauff (*The Stone Heart*)[62] C. L. Dodgson (*Alice's Adventures in Wonderland, or Through the Looking Glass*),[27] Lorenzini (*Pinocchio*),[111] de Saint-Exupéry (*The Little Prince*),[151] M. Sendak (*Where the Wild Things Are*),[161] J. Thurber (*The Thirteen Clocks*),[173] I. Tolkien (*The Hobbit*),[174] etc. These art-fairy tales frequently amalgamate the joys, sorrows and vicissitudes common to all men with those peculiar to the narrator. It is said that *The Ugly Duckling* represents not only our common wish to liberate ourselves from all that we sense as imperfect in us, but also Andersen's own life, where the poor, ugly, ridiculed youth turned into the admired and beloved storyteller.[5]

Along very general lines we shall find broad agreement that these tales represent various efforts to explain and to deal with the phenomenon of human existence; that they not only express the ways people think, feel, hope, desire, believe and behave, but also reinforce these ways along idealistic lines; that they satisfy and further man's basic emotional needs, while simultaneously strengthening faith and morality.[5]

Most religious and heroic epos were recorded quite early. Thus we find that the most complete version of one of the oldest myths, namely that of *Gilgamesh and Enkidu*,[52] dates back almost three thousand years, while fragmentary themes and illustrations of it are found dating as far back as five thousand years. The large myths probably resulted from the intuitive combination of simpler or briefer themes; but it is also true that many delightful stories assuming fairy tale characteristics derived from mythic fragments.

Many of the basic plots and themes of myths and fairy tales can be found all over the world. For example, there must exist several hundred variants of the Cinderella story among the fairy tales from Egypt, India, all parts of Europe, and even North America.[113,135] Related to these is the Zuni story of *The Turkey Girl*[79] which will be mentioned later on. While the best known Cinderella stories are based on the Grimms' *Aschenbrödel*, we may but mention the Italian *Cenerentola*,[95] the Swiss *Aschengrübel*,[167] the Scandinavian *Aschenpeter*,[85] the Russian story of the golden haired *Fair Vasilissa*,[35] and the American Indian *Cinderella*.[113]

The similarity of such tales has been explained in two ways. (1) Merchants, adventurers, migrants and mariners carried these stories from land to land and in the process they changed gradually, adapting themselves to the particular culture of various tribes, races and nations. While it has been possible to follow accurately the geographic and historical path of some fairy tales, this first explanation gains further support from the fact that there is greater similarity between related stories where the transmission was across an ocean than where it was across land (which usually involved a much greater number of passages from narrator to narrator). This first explanation has grown in importance as we have gained more knowledge of the considerable geographic mobility of earlier civilizations. (2) Nevertheless, the similarity of basic themes and plots is also due to the fact that these tales express deep experiences, problems and challenges facing people everywhere in their collective as well as in their individual evolution. This explanation of the relatedness of epic or fairy tale topics indicates sublimated, distorted, partial or symbolic expressions of the basic, and fairly universal, conflicts and hopes which are not allowed direct expression or acting out, but which can be mitigated by indirect, veiled, permissible outlets. Thus they resemble dreams which are explained by Freud as disguised fulfillments of frustrated or forbidden wishes, and by Jung as outlines of not yet realized potentials.

The psychoanalytic emphasis would partly explain the frequency in folklore of primitive, destructive and cruel events. It would also be in keeping with the so-called prelogical thinking[107,145] that we encounter in many folk tales and which is still characteristic of some of the mental processes of primitive tribes. Without necessarily conflicting, the Jungian emphasis is on the transpersonal character of some basic psychic configurations. "The archetypes of the collective unconscious are *intrinsically formless* psychic structures which become visible in art."[131] Any one archetype will manifest itself in quite different forms or styles, as it is shaped by the canons of the particular culture and by the individual psychological constellations of the person experiencing it. It is often difficult to recognize the deep relationship between motifs and images that superficially appear quite different. In many tales, for example, elements of pre-Christian beliefs and traditions can be discovered along with Christian motifs. Thus it has been shown that deities revered in ancient times reappear in later folk tales as well as in paintings under the guise of their favorite animals.* We must not see this as a deterioration of

*The beautiful amalgamation of early Egyptian and Christian symbolization of the *great mother* in Leonardo's painting of *Saint Anne with Virgin and Christ Child* was pointed out by Pfister.[140] Here the Virgin's dress is in the shape of the vulture which was discussed by Freud in his analysis of a most important childhood recollection of Leonardo. Both in this recollection and in the painting, the vulture, symbol of the Egyptian great goddesses, is an archetypical image analogous in meaning to Saint Anne and the Virgin.[131]

the ancient symbol because of the introduction of Christianity in the Western world, or as curtailing of genuine Christian beliefs. The inclusion of fragments of ancient myths in later folklore was a constructive use of the old imaginative language which was still able to activate the mentioned formless psychic structures, thus stimulating the production of new, additional symbolic figures. Combined, the new and the old images become effective in depicting the spiritual problems facing humanity since the advent of Christianity and since the subsequent gradual establishment of natural science and technology.

The myth whose own evolution is shrouded in the darkness of prehistoric times,[5] also tends to give way to organized religion. The latter, however, while offering definite values and moral guidance, is less able to light up with its language a bright spiritual world within the soul of the common man. Thus the child—as well as some hidden realms that have retained a child-like perceptiveness in us adults—remains responsive to and hungry for the language of the myth which became that of the fairy tale. The narrations changed in the course of time and during their migrations across the earth; but these changes originated largely in those psychic depths of the storytellers from whom the keen apprehension of the meaning of our changing world poured out in an imaginative language* This applies also to a great extent to the modern art-fairy tales as well as to some science fiction works and existential plays or novels (see Chapter XXX).

Information concerning the early historical development of the folk tale and epos will always remain vague and fragmentary. However, I agree with Frankl[48] that beyond the wish for security, for love, for achievement, the human being is endowed with a

---

*In some tales (e.g. *Jack and the Beanstalk*) many themes are said to be borrowed from the then contemporary political situation. In such cases, the events of the day are chosen only to the extent that they simultaneously offer suitable images for the wider and deeper meanings of the tale. One recognizes in this a clear analogy with the structure of the dream as explained by Freud. Our dreams commonly make use of various occurrences of the preceding day in order to illustrate long-standing conflicts or in order to express, in disguised form, intense, forbidden wishes which may date back to childhood. To see in a tale only the expression of current political events and moralistic attitudes, or to see in the dream only a disorderly reverberation of happenings of the preceding day, would be to overlook their central meaning.

"will to meaning." And I believe that it is this will to meaning that is one of the strongest forces underlying the creation of fairy tales, epos and myths. It is a force that seems to originate simultaneously with the first awakening of human consciousness. We must ask ourselves whether this desire for meaningfulness is an illusion, a desire for something we project into our environment, or whether it corresponds to objective values. Most important, this will to meaning always includes the wish to *share* this meaning (along with love, security and accomplishments) with our fellow human beings; this will to meaning gains its very strength from this encounter with a close human being, with the "thou."[16]

The external history of the fairy tale or myth is not nearly as important as the fact that ever and again its pictures become living words expressing what goes on in the hidden parts of our soul and in the deepest recesses of our culture—even now in the present, fateful evolution.

In order to illustrate and support some central ideas concerning the meaning of myths and fairy tales, we shall select stories from many cultural groups, emphasizing in particular several epos and a few of the best known Grimms' tales. The latter are so familiar and so easily available that they need not be retold in detail. Even after reviewing folklore collections of various nations or regions, I find that the Grimms' tales are, all in all, the most authentic and moving portrayals of the numerous, multilevel vicissitudes of the human beings. This opinion is supported by the remarks of W. H. Auden, the American poet, who reviewed a recent edition of *Grimms' Fairy Tales:*[58]

> . . . among the few indispensable common property books upon which Western culture can be founded . . . these tales rank next to the Bible in importance. . . . It will be a mistake, therefore, if this volume is merely bought as a Christmas present for a child; it should be, first and foremost, an educational "must" for adults; . . . for the reader who has once come to know and love these tales will never be able again to endure the insipid rubbish of contemporary entertainment.

This in no way proves that the Grimms' tales are the most beautiful or finest fairy stories. It is indeed difficult to weigh the excellence of fairy tales, since any judgment will always depend on one's preference for style, structure and wit. It will depend on our cultural background (my Swiss-German origin undoubtedly influenced the selection of many tales mentioned in this book), as well as on our ability to sense the deeper significance of certain stories. Some people may find more charm in the Russian fairy tales[35,181] which depict with a great deal of warmth, kindness and humor a natural wonderland rather than a fairyland. Others may prefer some of the Irish tales[5,32a] which are imbued more thoroughly with a fairy atmosphere. Many Scandinavian tales compiled by two scrupulous scholars[85] compare favorably with the Grimms' tales, often surpassing them in buoyancy and wit. Those who love excellency in style, polish, logical development of the plot and delicacy will appreciate the *Contes de ma mère l'oye,* even though Perrault's[139] recasting of the stories robs them of some of their deeper meanings.

While basic plots tend to recur in innumerable variations, the total number of folktales is enormous. There are many thousands of Irish, American Indian, Indian and Russian tales. Of the hundred-thousands of lyric, epic and magic *runos* collected in Finland, most are still in archives, while Loennrot's *Kalevala*[91] (see Chapter VII) has reawakened some of the ancient power of many of these verses. Add to these the American Negro, the English,[103] the Czechoslovakian, the Norwegian, the Swedish, the Spanish, the Hawaiian, the Swiss and many, many other tales (including the Oriental tales hardly touched upon in this book), and you begin to gain a faint idea of the wealth of fairy tale lore in existence.

In size these stories vary from half a page (e.g. one of the Grimms' tales) to booklength. The latter are usually art fairy tales such as *Alice in Wonderland,*[27] *The Little Prince,*[151] or Tolkien's *The Hobbit* and *The Lord of the Ring.*[174,175] In style they may vary from crude, folksy narrations to refined court tales. In content they may border on the myth, the ballad, the legend, the nursery rhyme, the jingle, the witty tale, the fable or the heroic epos; and they may change from a fairyland to a wonderland to a more naturalistic atmosphere which may bring it close to the symbolical novel (e.g. *Don Quijote*).[137] Their structure varies from perfect, harmonious beauty to marked, at least outward, incongruity; and their meaning ranges from superficial, narrow-minded moralism to unfathomable spiritual depths.

The myths we focus upon are principally the story of *Heracles*,[158] the *Kalevala*[91] and the *Winnebago Trickster Cycle*.[141] Each lends itself to illustrating particular aspects of human development. They will be supported by the more casual mention of other religious and heroic epos which, additionally, will reveal other significant aspects of human existence.

The stories mentioned in this book represent but a coarse sampling guided by the desire to bring into perspective the scope, meaningfulness and usefulness of these narrations. They depict concretely and realistically the basic psychologic and spiritual structures of the human being and his society, as well as the dynamic interactions between these structures. Again and again we shall notice how the storytellers from disparate parts of the world perceived these structures in similar ways. Differences will result not so much because of their errors in observation, but because similar basic themes develop in diverse directions in various cultural groups. Furthermore, the psychologic or spiritual structures (systems, or holons)[100] are themselves in a process of continuous development and appear differently at different stages.

In Chapters XXX and XXXII we shall discuss briefly the significant relationships between folklore on the one hand, and Westerns, science fiction, existential plays as well as novels on the other hand. Meanwhile, I hope that these cursory notes may give an inkling of the wide range of the world of myths, heroic epos and fairy tales, so that our subsequent remarks may be seen in a wide perspective.

CHAPTER V

RELATIONSHIP BETWEEN FOLKLORE AND OTHER PRODUCTS OF THE SOUL RELATED TO THE UNCONSCIOUS

Hallucinations, Dreams, Visions, Jokes, Art

FROM A PSYCHOLOGICAL point of view, the fairy tale and myth, inasmuch as they portray preconscious apprehensions, longings and aspirations, deserve a significant place amongst other, at first apparently irrational, productions of the human soul. Such are psychotic experiences and utterances, many jokes, dreams, visionary experiences of saints and most art. They all contain something which loses in beauty, richness, depth or effectiveness whenever we attempt to express it in the terms and thought-patterns of our everyday rational or practical life. We sense that such experiences and productions extend reality beyond the material and moral confines of our—often quite narrow—daily world.

Any extensive discussion of these phenomena would lead beyond the scope of this book. However, pointing out some of their characteristics may be helpful in understanding what place and role fairy tales and myths have among them.

While hallucinations can be described as sensory experiences, the source of which lies entirely within the person, the term "vision" usually implies that what is experienced is outside the person. Both vision and hallucination are generally not shared by nearby people. The vision is not experienced by others because it is believed to be something of a spiritual nature which speaks only to the seer whose soul is prepared for and open to it. The hallucination is not shared by others, because it is the result of abnormal psychological processes or of disorders of the nervous substance (or both). Visions are usually seen as attributes of prophets and saints; hallucinations as symptoms of mental illness. In a similar way dreams can equally be divided into hallucinatory and visionary dreams; most of our present-day dreams would have to be classified as the former. They are sensory experiences, occurring during sleep, originating within the person. Visionary dreams, mentioned in innumerable myths and fairy tales, as well as in religious texts (*cf.* the Pharaoh's dream interpreted by Joseph) are seen as caused by external spiritual influences. A similar distinction can be made in regard to art, and we would then have productions which are essentially the expression of inner turmoils and longings, and those which attempt to express or paint objectively beauty and spirituality:

Ich sehe Dich in tausend Bildern
Maria, lieblich ausgedrückt,
Doch keins von allen kann Dich schildern
Wie meine Seele Dich erblickt . . .

I'm seeing Thee in thousand paintings
Maria, lovingly expressed,
Yet not a one can so describe Thee
the way my soul has Thee beheld . . .[134]

This poem by Novalis not only shows the poet's attempt to describe what he has experienced as objective spirituality, but also reveals the close relatedness between the seer and the artist as well as between the poet and the painter. One finds in the majority of artistic creations a mixture of expressions of objective truths, beauty, values on the one hand, and of personal feelings and problems on the other hand.

Finally we mention jokes simply because much of their appeal is based on elements which are beyond the confines of our daytime consciousness. They usually lack the prestige of art and visions, or even of dreams and hallucinations. Mostly they afford socially acceptable outlets to wishes which are more or less taboo, but occasionally they may transcend that scope.

Just as there are dreams with all the earmarks of a fairy tale (see Chapter XXVII), and visions which are expressed in art, so there are hallucinations and dreams which have many of the characteristics of the joke. A patient suffering from procrastination had a recurrent dream in which she received a mysterious phone call. Whenever she asked the caller to identify himself, he would reply, "This is *Tom Morrow.*" Finally she understood and woke laughing, realizing that this *is tomorrow.*

The joke, myth, fairy tale, dream, vision and hallucination have in common the ability to view everyday existence in a new way, from a different angle, or with some detachment. While one can see transitions between all these productions, each one has some outstanding features.

It is not as easy as one might think to establish the salient features which clearly distinguish our dreaming from our waking existence. In fact, while we dream we are largely unaware that it is only a dream, and while we are awake we may have moments when we ask ourselves whether we are dreaming. In the dream our world is often rich with experiences, feelings and interests which we considered ourselves incapable of when awake. And from the waking viewpoint many dreams appear illogical, disconnected and absurd. Yet, these are characteristics which are not present in *all* dreams. I am inclined to agree with Boss[12] who sees the basic difference between our waking and our dreaming existence in the dream's lack of any "continued evolution of existence." He points out that the dream can be likened to a "mirror experience" where the dreamer comes face to face with himself, his problems, his wishes, his total life situation. Our dream of tonight does not continue an evolving process of yesterday's dream, while our waking life always continues the life process of the previous day. Dreams, therefore, can only change in their basic meaning when there have been significant changes in the individual's makeup during his waking life.

Hallucinations can be viewed as waking dreams. They reflect hidden conflicts, wishes, potentials, drives and fears. Usually the patient cannot separate them from the sensory experiences coming to him from the outside world. Their meaning is similar to that of the dreams, but as they become part of waking life, the latter becomes dreamlike. Now the growth of the personality tends to stop, unless the patient can profit from the challenges inherent in his hallucinations. This is most dramatically seen in the perpetually rigid catatonic patient, or in the patient who, innumerable times, repeats the same mannerisms and stereotypies. While life evolution has stopped, the revealed *potential* existence of some of these patients may be so rich and fascinating that their normal, restricted and adjusted existence, before or after their illness, appears narrow and drab in comparison.

Visions, defined as perceptions of objective spiritual realities, seem to have an opposite effect upon the seer. The growth, the life purposes of the individual are not hindered but enhanced. Saints, such as Francis or Augustine, have been pushed into a more active and creative existence by visions and by visionary dreams. While hallucinations have distinct sensory (visual, auditory, etc.) qualities, the pictorial descriptions of visions largely are attempts to convey spiritual experiences that are not distinctly sensory, that are formless. Formerly visions were seen as coming from heaven, while hallucinations were thought to be due to devilish influences; and careful evaluations were made to distinguish one from the other. While this reasoning led to a misunderstanding of, and some extreme cruelties to, mentally ill persons, it nonetheless contained a truth which nowadays one might express thus: the seer has developed an inner harmony and strength which allows him to recognize the spiritual background of his world and to apply what he has seen to the shaping of his life. The hallucinated individual seemingly has a similar inner perception, but because of the disharmony of his personality structure and the intensity of conflicting, inner drives, he only gets scattered glimpses of the spiritual significance of the world around him, while mistakenly seeing his own wishes, hopes, fears, conflicts and guilts (which prevent any objective vision) as outward realities. The distinction between visions and hallucinations holds true regardless of one's position concerning the exact nature of visions, and concerning their correspondence to an objective spiritual reality.

The comparison of the attitudes of a healthy student and of a schizophrenic individual towards a complicated mathematical problem can be used as an analogy. While the student, proceeding calmly and securely, following a harmonious scientific process, will eventually reach the solution of the problem, we may see the schizophrenic patient write abrupt, disconnected formulas, often interspersed with weird drawings and odd notations. These he takes as pertaining to the solution, but in fact they are reflections of unrelated experiences within himself which overwhelm him while he tries to deal with the problem. And while he may steadfastly assert that he has found a very meaningful solution, the latter appears utterly absurd to anyone else.

In trying to experience or to understand the non-material, psychic or spiritual aspects of existence, we encounter two worlds: on one side we meet our own inner world of drives, instincts, ambitions, feelings, goals, needs and wishes; on the other side we find the meaningfulness, purpose, beauty of the outer world. If he rejects, on theoretical grounds, any objective significance of existence, the psychoanalyst is bound to see everywhere only the first, subjective world. Then the beauty, meaning and purpose of outward reality is viewed as merely an extension or projection of this subjective world. The psychoanalyst may well be justified in restricting his interest to this inner, instinctual world of his patient. However, unless he supports by his own attitude the patient's need for meaningfulness, for values, the analyzed patient may eventually find himself disconsolate in an empty world. On the other hand, only when our drives, wishes or instincts are harmoniously channeled can we hope that they will not, at times, grievously distort the understanding of our world and values.

Applying this to art, we can now state that the more the artist has developed the ability to confront his own feelings *freely*, at least for short periods, the more he can use them to experience and to express what has meaningfulness and beauty to all human beings. Freely acknowledged feelings could be likened to spiritual sense organs. This can be illustrated with the poems of the ailing Giacomo Leopardi,[106] from which we quote several times in this book. Some of them (*cf.* "The Infinite" and "To Himself") are perfectly structured pure gems within which the fundamentally subjective theme is completely and harmoniously integrated. In others, the compositional beauty contrasts sharply with the expression of blind adolescent ambitions and neurotic complaints. Whenever the poet succeeds in detaching himself from his neurotic sensibility and suffering, whenever he transcends momentarily his neurosis and his physical ailments, this extraordinary effort allows him to express ideas and feelings which find an echo in the heart of everyone. In the folk-fairy tale and myth we find this appeal to everyone to the highest degree, because here the frequent oral transmission has helped to eliminate anything which might have had only a narrow, personal meaning.

In the artistic fairy tales, created and written by a single individual, one finds personal elements intermixed with those having universal significance. At the pole of extreme subjectivity we would find an amalgamation of images or symbols characteristic of schizophrenia. This, however, is not real art but rather an unadulterated outpouring of disorganized soul contents which may help the therapist to understand the patient. The writings and drawings of the individual suffering from schizophrenia do not aim primarily at communication of meanings to other human beings, but express only the inner situation of the person who—since his day has become dreamlike—is stuck in his development. True human development and creativeness, however, are tied to meaningful communication with fellow human beings.[66] This may be illustrated by the following witty story:

> A successful businessman consults a well-known psychiatrist. He unfolds his tales of woe and the psychiatrist, grown increasingly bored and impatient, suggests, "I have many things to attend to; why don't you continue and dictate your story into this dictaphone." The businessman seems agreeable, but when the psychiatrist, a few minutes later, steps into the elevator, he runs into him. "I thought you were still in my office?" "Well," the businessman apologizes, "I, too, happen to be hurried; and since I have seen other psychiatrists before, I made a careful recording of my story. So I took the liberty of calling my secretary asking her to bring over my tape and dictaphone, so that my dictaphone can tell the story to yours."

This tale shows how the joke can give a meaningful message. On the one hand it allows some outlet for feelings and drives which are taboo. In this joke such feelings are the rather sadistic rejection of a suffering human being by the psychiatrist, and the getting even with a resented authority by the businessman. On the other hand the joke bares the emptiness of a "busy" life in which emotions and true human communication are relegated to the machine; and it points to the need for experiences that must be based on healthy human relationships.

The differences between fairy tales, myths and heroic epos are discussed elsewhere. Along with any other true art, they have in common the characteristic of being visions. While the creators of the fairy tales and myths may not have experienced the reality of their wonderful images as overwhelmingly and vividly as the seer, they nonetheless transgressed the confines of their everyday world. Detaching themselves, they penetrated behind the superficial appearances of things and discovered a marvelous, significant, harmonious world. This harmony is frequently expressed in the structure of these narrations of which the number three is often an integral part. This number has always and everywhere been expressing spiritual entities, to mention but the Holy Trinity, or the structure of the *Divine Comedy* consisting of three books with thirty-three cantos each, made up of verses grouped by three.[33] We see this number three return in innumerable ways especially in fairy tales: as three brothers, three challenges, three suitors, etc. Further meanings of numbers in fairy tales will be discussed later.*

Let me end this chapter with a beautiful example of a three-times-three harmony in fairy tales. In *Little Brother and Sister* (Grimms' tales), the children flee from the bad stepmother, but the boy succumbs to her third attempt to bewitch him and becomes a deer. He now lives with his sister in the woods and enjoys the challenges of the king's hunt. The king marvels at the deer, follows it the third time he sees it, finds its home and marries the sister. When she gives birth to a child, the jealous stepmother kills it and substitutes her own one-eyed daughter.

*In Hindu mythology the threesomeness of the godhead is ubiquitous. Ancient Indian religion furthermore recognized a threesomeness of the levels of human consciousness, analogous to the waking, dreaming and sleeping stage. However, beyond this threesomeness, Indian thought recognized a fourth, ineffable member. It is the nothingness between destruction and rebirth, it is the silence following the three-lettered syllable AUM that expresses the three levels of consciousness.[188] In American Indian tales the number four tends to predominate over the number three.

But at night the young queen returns to rock her baby; in the third night the king recognizes her as his true queen and speaks to her. With this the spell is broken; the stepmother and her daughter are exposed and receive their deserved punishment.

CHAPTER VI

THE LANGUAGE OF FAIRY TALES AND MYTHS

HARDLY ANYWHERE do we find a more thorough denial of truth than among those people who under the banner of non-denominationalism, non-partisanism or agnosticism attempt to portray an unlimited amount of tolerance. By stressing the relativity or subjectivity of all convictions, and by pointing out that most of these convictions cannot be proven or disproven, they tolerate condescendingly all the truths, which to them are subjective values devoid of general meaning and strength. Yet, strangely enough, this pretended, diffuse tolerance is often associated with a hidden, extreme intolerance towards any philosophy, religion or political orientation which asserts its convictions positively. It is true that agnosticism, or better skepticism, has a significant place especially in our times; it has stripped us of traditional beliefs, convictions, customs and moral attitudes to which we clung out of a need for protection and security rather than because they remained meaningful to use. Thereby it not only opened an unlimited scope to natural science, but also prepared the ground for a new spiritual awakening. The agnostics' condescending tolerance of fairy tales and myths, for example, challenges us either to relegate them to the role of second rate entertainment for small children, or to rediscover more and more their true and powerful meaning.

The rather frequent assumption that tolerance and conviction are mutually exclusive is incorrect. In fact, rather the opposite applies. Only when we are capable of deep convictions ourselves, does our tolerance of other convictions carry weight. If we have no convictions, our tolerance towards everyone is not true tolerance but diffuse skepticism. The more sincere and earnest we are in our quest for truth, the more humble and tolerant we become. This tolerance is born of the following insights:

1. Recognition that we cannot effectively force our convictions upon someone else; that while we may offer him opinions that become food for thinking, his—as well as our—growth towards new insights is always an inner process.

2. Recognition that almost any insight is limited by the viewpoint from which it is obtained, and that many convictions are branded as untrue simply because the critics view the problem from a different standpoint. In that sense, truth becomes untruth only when the point of view is not properly considered. This does not diminish the objective value of any conviction we arrive at. For example, the recognition of the one-sidedness of the viewpoint from which the picture of a mountain is obtained would not make us question in the least the existence of that mountain. In fact, the more we become aware of the relationship of our views to definite standpoints and the greater our tolerance enabling us to see other views as derived from other standpoints, the more valuable become our own insights and the greater become our skills to synthesize apparently contradictory truths into deeper convictions. Similarly, if we recognize two different photographs as those of the same mountain, we are thereby enabled to develop a three-dimensional image of the mountain.

Ortega y Gasset,[137] the Spanish philosopher, has expressed magnificently this necessary limitation of each person's view, by depicting that the combined image derived from all the individuals' viewpoints can be sensed as God's view of creation. While involved in or committed to the tasks of our lives, we must, again and again, muster the courage to limit our viewpoint in order to be effective. Only in rare moments of detachment from our everyday ego and from our everyday commitments, may we have glimpses of a wider view that approximates—slightly—that of God. These are indeed peak experiences, moments of *unio mystica,* of satori. In terms of Husserl's phenomenological philosophy, we then move away from our narrow, empirical ego towards a transcendental ego state. If properly accepted, these experiences (very varied in degree or intensity) can lead us to modify constructively our being-in-the-world, thus promoting our individual growth.

In order to begin to understand the language of fairy tales and myths, the foregoing remarks should be remembered. To presume to describe the significance of these narrations fully is like believing that by taking one snapshot of a mountain we have a complete record of its configuration, geologic structure and flora. While it is plausible that fairy tales and myths have one ultimate meaning of which all the various interpretations are smaller or larger reflections, our present day language would be inadequate to describe this ultimate meaning, even if we were able to catch a glimpse of it. We therefore must content ourselves with partial views, hoping to be able to synthesize them to a certain extent into a more profound understanding.

The Oedipus myth, for example, has been explained in different ways by Freudians, existentialists, neo-Freudians, Jungians, Adlerians, anthropologists and others. A composite of all these views, taking full account of the difference in viewpoints, would give us a more complete understanding of this myth.

Each language is constantly adapting itself to the current needs or trends of a culture. Consequently, modern languages are pragmatic, useful in business and in the natural sciences, but ill-suited to conveying values, shades of feelings, ideals and the experience of ethereal beauty. Thus Medard Boss complained that only ancient Greek and Sanskrit were well suited to the communication of the richness of experienced meanings, which is the main focus of his existential psychiatric orientation.

Selecting just one important term, namely *understand,* which is frequently used in this book, and comparing it with the connotations of its translation in a few other languages, we can recognize better that a language is not something static, abstract, but that it attempts to convey a meaning which is slightly different in each of various translations, by conjuring up various pictures. If you *understand,* you stand under the thing as if you could see the hidden aspects of the studied item. In the French *comprendre* the picture is that of collecting and embracing all the details of the item; in the Italian *capire* (as in the English expression "grasp") we are given the feeling of holding on tight to the thing. *Verstehen* in German is slightly more complex, inasmuch as it suggests the idea that by standing at an unusual *ver*-place, the item may reveal its significance which remains hidden to the one standing in the ordinary place.

The Greek *katanoeo* is made up of *kata,* meaning "against, over, under, around, near, towards, in through, according" and *noeo,* meaning "perceiving, thinking, knowing, to hold in one's soul." Here, again, we have a reference to the person's position in regard to the thing to be understood. But this position is an all-embracing one which, together with the width of the meaning of *noeo,* gives an indication of the richness of this concept, showing thereby the greater awareness the Greeks had of the fundamentally spiritual nature of understanding, and of the meaning of *Being* (for the new apprehension of which Heidegger[63,64] has struggled so valiantly in our century).

The more rigidly a language is adapted to the material world, the more expressions and verbal images it must group together in order to convey ideas dealing with values and qualities. These verbal images, when seen together, allow an understanding that is broader than the specific meaning of each term. Furthermore, in myths and fairy tales as in poetry, each term, each symbol is affected considerably by its context with other images and events of the narration.

A beautiful example of the difficulty and of the need of several expressions in conveying the richness of the ancient Greek when translating it into modern language, is given in Goethe's *Faust,*[93] where we find the despairing doctor sitting in his study and struggling with the translation of the first sentence of the Gospel of Saint John: "En archei en ho logos." He recognizes in *logos* more than the mere "word" as commonly valued in our times; he sees in it also "meaning," "force," and "action." Yet as he struggles to grasp the full significance of *logos,* the spirit-denying devil, Mephistopheles, comes forward and interferes with Faust's meditation. He appears first as a stray poodle who accompanied Faust to his home, but becomes uncomfortable and swells up when Faust begins to recognize God's son and the Trinity as being contained in the "word." Cynically he sneers at the doctor who loses his hold on the deeper significance of "logos," and sees in action alone the original and ultimate meaning of existence.[66] *Kynos* means dog. The cynic sniffles around along the ground, ignoring everything else. Thus the cynicism of the materialistic epoch turns us away from values, from spiritual beliefs, just when we seem to be close to them. Similarly, Mephistopheles is able to lull Faust's mind into pleasant dreams, turning him away from the *logos,* thus hoping to conquer his soul.

Indeed, more than ever before the word has become abstract; that is abstracted from a real, meaningful, powerful, efficient content. The word has become a means to hide rather than to reveal truth; a means to hide rather than to reveal genuine feelings and honest commitments. The word has become something accepted in the head, instead of something experienced in the heart. The speaker and the hearer distrust words more and more. Thus words leave no imprint and are forgotten. One then either continues to prattle aimlessly, hoping to find meaningful experiences in a sensory-instinctual-emotional realm; or one starts using words *quantitatively,* hoping to create some impact by innumerable repetition, drowning out opposite views by propaganda rather than by quality. Already fifteen years ago, in *The Search for Meaning,* Rollo May offered an excellent analysis of the pathological weakening of the power of words, of language, concluding that, "along with the loss of the sense of self has gone also a loss of our language for communicating deeply personal meanings to each other."[121]

Meaningful language and sense of self are mutually related. Without a sense of self we have no experience of world. Therefore, our ability to develop at least an internal language would be a prerequisite for experiencing any sort of meaningful, ordered world. Thus Saint John was not too far off when he stressed that everything came into existence through the "word," that without it not one thing originated.

Therefore we must not lightly dethrone language in favor of nonverbal communication or of sensory encounters. The latter are to be seen partly as a healthy compensation for excessive rationalism, and partly as a symptom of the failure of this rationalism. Yet, and this cannot be stressed sufficiently, language is *not* to be identified with rationalism. Language, taken seriously, honestly and experienced deeply, conveys personal meanings that nothing else can convey. However, this requires not only two intelligent individuals with sound ears and tongues, but two human beings who are sincerely trying to be open and committed to the dignity of man; who furthermore are able to sense the creative potential in the word and who thus believe in the perfectibility of man.

In our days the word has often become more and more prostituted, serving the opposite of creativity. Certainly the publications explosion is a questionable human achievement; in politics words are frequently used to delude the populace; and in many families we find that words are in the service of the establishment of double binds that hamper normal growth. Thus let us attempt to experience more and more profoundly the personal meanings of the words, of the language we use. Awareness of our language is indeed the highest form of sensory awareness we may achieve. Such an awareness will always be articulated harmoniously with the awareness of our feelings, of our sensations, of our impulses and of our actions.

The Grimms' tale of *The Three Languages* touches upon the same theme: The son of a count is rejected by his father because he cannot acquire the traditional knowledge. Its language has become meaningless to him. As a wanderer he spends the night in a deep cave with ferocious dogs which have regularly demanded human sacrifices. Since, instead of school knowledge, he has learned the language of the dogs, he can tame them. By also understanding the language of the frogs and then of the doves he is so successful in meeting all the seemingly impossible challenges that he ends up as the new head of Christianity, celebrating a Mass inspired to him by the white doves. Here again, as in *Faust,* we find a human being who severs the rigidified connections with the past and who has to face, understand and tame the subterraneous forces of materialism (the dogs in the depth of the tower) before he can gradually ascend to a newly meaningful world.

Dramas like *Faust,* myths and fairy tales tend to give sweeping outlines of basic human problems and goals. The struggle against our own cynicism, against the mephistophelian forces which deny any depth of meaning, continues from day to day in different ways. At times we think that we recognize the purely mechanistic, natural-scientific world as senseless; at other times we look at our finest insights into the significance of our world and find them sterile and abstract. How often has our heart rejoiced during a quiet moment of thinking at the recognition of a new, live idea, or at the discovery of a meaningful relationship; and yet, when we try to formulate the same thoughts at a later date, what appears a precious new acquisition, has shrunk to a few miserly crumbs. Only the *memory* of the first happy revelation may prevent us, at times, from rejecting these crumbs entirely. Humbly we should acknowledge, then, that the defect lay not in what was discovered, but in our own inability to hold on to the richness of the original experience.

Our own character has to develop so that whatever we comprehend remains living reality and so that we can conduct our lives according to this new knowledge. Numerous fairy tales deal with this problem of being worthy of not only receiving, but also of keeping the newly found treasure. Let me mention three, all taken from the Grimm collection. In *The Presents of the Little Folks* only the man whose character is kindly, unselfish and open-minded is able to retain the gifts from the good spirits, whereas the greedy, intolerant and unloving man finds his pockets full of coals instead of gold. In the story of *The Gold Children,* the fisherman again and again catches the wonderous fish who helps him to exchange his poor little hut for a splendid castle. But each time, his wife (namely his soul) is unable to control her curiosity; and because of her weakness the fisherman and his wife find themselves again in their miserable hut. Finally *Cinderella* is the individual who is able willingly to restrict her enjoyment of the prince's palace and feast, until she has grown sufficiently, until the slipper fits perfectly.

Our ability to retain what we have gained in our search for a meaningful existence (the splendid castle) is threatened not only by the cynicism of our times which has infiltrated all of us to a certain extent, but also by those uncontrolled instinctual drives and desires which can becloud our thinking. As long as the latter is focused upon the natural-scientific realm, it cannot lead us too far astray, since any error is quickly manifested by the experiment or by the material situation to which it is applied. Such a double check upon the accuracy of our thinking does not exist when it deals with values, spiritual principles and esthetic concepts. In the nonmaterialistic realm we are much more on our own with our thinking, and only strictest self-discipline prevents us from erring. The frequent careful application of thinking to natural-scientific problems may gradually strengthen its accuracy. But only when we have freed ourselves from the cynical influences of the one-sided materialism around us, as well as from compelling instinctual drives and desires within us, can we discover a new solitude in which the world of ideas loses the paleness of abstractions. Then it becomes a source of a colorful, rich life that no longer slips away easily, and in which our unique individuality finds itself at home as in a splendid castle. The dog in myths and fairy tales, therefore, represents not only the earth-sniffling cynic, but also the impulsive, barking, instinctual drives which disturb and disrupt our search for the truth (*cf.* Cerberus confronting the heroes willing to face the mysteries of the Greek underworld).

The fact that thinking if not constantly confirmed by the experiment so easily goes astray, has been used as an argument against the reality of values, thoughts and ideals. Maybe this skepticism exists also because the structure of the thought-world seems qualitatively so different from that of the physical world that each one, seen from the viewpoint of the other, appears empty, monotonous and senseless. Each would appear, at first, to exclude the other one.* To learn to accept both in spite of their seemingly paradoxical aspects and to integrate them, may well be

*We can compare the difficulty of retaining spiritual insights with the ease of forgetting dreams. Psychoanalysis stresses that dreams are forgotten mostly because of their reference to unconscious forbidden wishes. This may occasionally be true also of spiritual insights. However, in addition, both the content of dreams and of our ideas and ideals may be quite different from what seem more urgent and practical daily concerns. Therefore, they are pushed aside towards our taboo desires and memories, become associated with them and share their fate of repression. Finally, one may also conjecture that our insights into values and ideas are even further repressed, since our preoccupation with them detracts from more immediate, permissible, seductive, sensuous satisfactions.

the real challenge of today. It is what Kierkegaard[96] envisioned in *The Sickness unto Death,* showing that authenticity or freedom from despair is attained as human consciousness evolves between poles that are often experienced as paradoxical, maintaining some distance from both and recognizing their reflection in the Self.

The above statement that natural-scientific thinking cannot lead us too far astray is correct only in a narrow sense. True, the results of experiments will prove whether our hypotheses are correct or not. But what about the choice of the type of hypotheses. We may very scientifically figure out that a certain megaton blast will cause only this or that damage, and the experiment will confirm—or lead to a modification of—the thinking underlying the hypothesis. But what about the numerous implications of even considering and testing such a hypothesis? It is here that a more encompassing kind of thinking is imperative if we are to prevent some natural-scientific approaches from getting out of hand like the famous broom of the sorcerer's apprentice. The testable accuracy of natural-scientific thinking must be an example to the more encompassing phenomenologic thinking; yet the latter must assign to science its proper range.

As we cultivate this encompassing thinking, we must simultaneously acquire a new, deep experience of language. The words of folklore may still find a receptive soul in the child; and if as adults we no longer understand or misunderstand these stories, we must recognize our culturally conditioned inadequacy to foster in our soul an open and receptive attitude. Yet, the less we become perceptive to the qualitative aspects of the world portrayed in myths and fairy tales, the less suited does our language become to describe them. We thus find ourselves in a vicious circle, with seemingly no way out.

Dramas like *Faust* and the *Divine Comedy,* religious texts and many folklore narrations, however, offer hope that there *is* a way out of this dilemma. Just when we seem to have lost forever the inheritance carried down from the "Golden Age," just when we forget our paradisiacal origin and become hardened by cynicism, our soul, alone and solely dependent on itself, may start to become aware of those spiritual forces which can free it from its captivity in the material world. In the above-mentioned story of *The Gold Children,*[58] the fisherman and his wife become parents of two golden boys. While one of the sons stays with the parents, the other storms out into the world. After many an adventure he ends up in a wood, where he is turned into a stone by a witch whose barking dog he tries to defy. His golden brother becomes aware of his fate, overcomes the witch and frees him from this incarceration in the mineral world. Even when we seem lost in the depths of the wood, and when we seem hopelessly bewitched by devilish and cynical forces, we find that we carry deep inside of us a brother who never left the paternal home and who can help us towards a new, free and more consciously meaningful life. The Yugoslav story of *The Three Eels,* for example, is one of many similar tales. Here, the third of three eels give to the poor fisherman twin sons, twin colts and two golden sabers. The one twin, who decides to go out into the world and gains the beautiful princess and a palace, is eventually turned into stone by the old witch on the magic mountain. His brother senses his distress, comes to his aid and revives him: now it is the nefarious witch who turns forever into stone.[32]

In epic form, the story of Percival beautifully stresses a similar idea. He leaves his mother Herzeleide and pure, but inexperienced, arrives at the castle of the Holy Grail. Unable to comprehend the suffering of the king, born out of sinfulness, and not ready to ask the right question, Percival is chased away; and only after years of erring through the world can he find the castle again in the mysterious woods and prove himself worthy of the guardianship over the Holy Grail containing Christ's blood. This blood flowed in order to reverse the trend of man into materialism and perdition. Yet only the one who has faced the material world with its sorrows and sins is ready to protect the Holy Chalice in the wondrous castle.

In order to find the way to our true Self, to the hidden castle with the Holy Chalice; in order to harmonize Self and World, we must develop *new* qualities of hearing and asking questions.

Some of our cultural ancestors had an intuitive awareness of the close relationship between the origin of words and the decline of man's selfless integration in nature. The word was seen as capable of controlling all the secret powers of heaven, earth and netherworld. The early scribes held insights into deepest mysteries, but sensed that such insights could be dangerous. In the tale of Seton Chaemwese,[15] referring to the reign of Ramses II and recorded about 50 B.C., the famous scribe acquires a booklet with magic formulas by means of which he gains insight in, and power over, the realms of the gods and of the dead. However, the possession of these magic words obtained by dividing the uroboric serpent protecting the elaborate casket in which the booklet was hidden, brings misfortune. Seton and his time experienced the knowledge of powerful words as admirable, but felt also that the human being must not yet cross certain limits in his quest for the deepest mysteries. Seton Chaemwese is brought close to insanity and death through the greedy possession of the booklet which he finally is willing to return.

With the growing dominance of rationalism this early experience of the power of words faded rapidly. Man became aware of himself as a separate individual in an unfeeling environment that was his to control, and language became a practical tool. But now our own epoch is growing old and a new period is dawning, a period in which we are freed from the extreme rationalism that began to trespass its own legitimate domain and to lead the human being away from his true essence. Dürckheim, in a wonderfully written booklet *The Breakthrough to Our True Being*,[36] experiences this innermost, true being as a hidden partner of our present-day ego; a partner who—like the twin brother who stayed home—can become our redeemer, as soon as we learn to listen to his voice. Rather than a regression to a former, selfless state, this is the willingness to find a newly alive language that does justice to the spiritual *and* to the material realms, to the soul *and* to the body, to the Self *and* to the World.

CHAPTER VII

MYTH, FAIRY TALE AND FOLK SAGA

Some Comments Concerning Stylistic Distinctions

A. We shall introduce this subchapter with a few remarks concerning the Finnish epos, as it provides a transition from the preceding chapter to the consideration of stylistic qualities in folklore. Maybe nowhere in folklore do we find as magnificent a portrayal of the meaning and of the power of the *Word* than in the *Kalevala*. This epos is both the creation of a people and the work of an individual, since Elias Loennrot (b. 1802), the last of the great Finnish bards or *laulaias* united or reunited into a large epos the songs he collected during his long wanderings.[91,123]

It is particularly true for the Finns that singing is older than speaking. The predominant figure in the *Kalevala,* Wainemoinen, has the power to move and create almost everything with the words of his songs. While song is man's relation to the powers, to the wholeness of life, speech—appearing later—is man's relation to things. It is more indirect and expresses the acquired separation between man and nature, while song expresses the elemental community with nature.[91] Thus while song relates to magic, beauty and ultimate meaning, speech focuses upon causal connections between particulate things.

The songs, made up of four trochee verses, can be grouped into lyric, epic and magic ones. While the lyric songs take on and transform almost any event or occasion, the epic *laulaia* presents his *runes* at banquets, assisted by an aide and accompanied by a five-stringed harp. The aide and the *laulaia* sit facing each other, and while the first repeats each verse, the second prepares the next one. Rhythmically proceeding, they can thus go on for hours relating the tales of heroes. The magic or sorcerers' songs, in contrast to the lyric and epic, have special powers. It is the power of the word, of the word that is master over the elements. The knower of the word knows the origin of all things (*cf.* "In the beginning was the Word and the Word . . .") and thus all things become his subjects. He speaks in *ecstasis,* becomes a *haltia,* a demon, appealing in everything to *physis,* to the "ground of Being."[91,123] His songs are his possession; and unless he drops from them three words to render them powerless, he will not give any of them to an outsider.

This distinction between magic and non-magic songs is common all over the world. We find an identical separation in the American Indian Winnebago where the sacred *Waikan* is distinguished from the epic or entertaining *Worak*[141] (see Chapter III).

Words become magic. As the Egyptian god carries the things as words in his body and creates them in throwing them as sounds from his mouth, so the Finnish sorcerer creates the things he sings.

The *Kalevala,* in which all three types of songs are harmoniously interwoven, can be seen as a magnificent portrayal of the human being's struggle for a new or higher consciousness.

Kalevala is the land of the giants from which the Finns descended, and the epos describes the origin of their world and the vicissitudes of their greatest representatives—half gods and half heroes—who are also the sons of Kaleva, the giant. While superficially these vicissitudes reflect some of the fights between the Ases (or Vikings) in the North and the Jotunes (or Finns) in the South, one soon senses that underneath the external events, there is a struggle for a higher consciousness. The latter develops as a result of the confrontation between the more coldly rational Nordic tribes and the more intuitive, experiential, feeling Finns.

Wainemoinen portrays excellently this non-reflective, feeling consciousness, a consciousness that arises as soon as the *giant* stage of development is being left behind. In fact, Wainemoinen, Kaleva's son, has not fully separated himself from the dull consciousness of the giants. When he is in despair, he tends to regress toward it.

We can distinguish four basic themes of the epos: first, the creation of the world and of Wainemoinen. Here we find expressed in grandoise images the interdependent, simultaneous creation of the universe (macrocosm) and of the individual (or microcosm).

Kerényi[88] has shown that the ancient mythologem of the birth of the primordial human being passed over into the philosophy of the early Ionian thinkers: "The cosmic content that forms the nucleus of mythology passes over into Greek philosophy." Again we find the mythologic image of the primordial human being born out of an egg. Just as in the *Kalevala* Wainemoinen, so in Greek mythology Eros, Anadyomene or Aphrodite, and among the Hindu Parjapati emerge from an egg floating in the cosmic ocean. Heaven and earth are formed from the two halves of the egg shell: beyond the limits of the egg there is but non-being. The mythologic experience of this emergence, of this creation of consciousness that confronts the creation of the world is then succeeded for the first time in Greece, by rational explanations viewing water as the ultimate reality, as the source of all things and living beings. Yet, the myth conveys more vividly the interpenetration of self and world. Only with the birth of a conscious self can there be world, and only with the emergence of world can there be self.*

Kerényi puts it beautifully, saying, "The primordial child is hatched out of an egg which came into being in the waters of the beginning—hatched, that is to say, out of the void. . . . It is the primordial child in the primordial solitude of the primordial element; the primordial child that is the unfolding of the primordial egg, just as the whole world is his unfolding."[88]

Here we recognize especially well the difference between myths and the analytic, objectifying orientation of science. The mythic image of Wainemoinen born after eons of time to Ilmatar

*In our times we encounter this again on a new plane in Heidegger's philosophical notion[63] of the constitutive function of *Dasein* (or self) which stresses that there cannot be a primacy of self or of world, since self (or *Dasein*) must be viewed as being-in-the-world.

impregnated by the cosmic winds and floating on the ocean, of Wainemoinen gradually setting foot on firm land and singing all things into existence, is about as far removed as possible from a Darwinian description of the origin of *Homo sapiens*. Unhampered by a one-sided objectivation of a material world viewed as determined by the strict laws of causality, the originators of the myth were able to describe in meaningful images the very birth of consciousness.

However, the Finnish myth does not view consciousness as a homogenous thing. The intuitive, feeling-consciousness of Wainemoinen is not sharply separated either from the dull preconscious existence of the giant, or from the sharp, analytic cunning consciousness of the *thumbling*. Early in the epos this sharp, rational consciousness emerges as the little copper man who alone is able to fell the oak grown beyond all proportions and planted with the help of the giant. Later, it is portrayed by the smith Ilmarinen. And beyond Ilmarinen, we are told of young Lemminkainen, impetuous and irresponsible, but representing a dawning consciousness, the characteristics of which are a keen self-awareness, independent commitment and unique creativity. Oversimplifying and making compromises in favor of our everyday language, we can say that Wainemoinen, Ilmarinen and Lemminkainen represent the feeling, the thinking, and the acting, intending or willing spheres of consciousness: spheres that are seen as organismic systems, interacting and overlapping, yet having their own independent qualitative centers. They are not fixed, static, but constantly evolving. This evolution, in the *Kalevala*, is portrayed primarily in the heroes' quest for the beautiful virgin of the Northland, sitting on a rainbow and spinning her dress of silver and gold. This quest which is the second main theme is intimately related to the forging of the magic mill, of the Sampo, that yields on one side flour, on one salt and on the third coins.

Of all the mythological images this third main theme, the forging of the Sampo by the smith Ilmarinen, is one of the most delicately mysterious ones, and dispels any lingering belief that myths are simply an attempt to explain—by whatever metaphors are available—that which the primitive mind is not yet able to grasp. Overcoming all kinds of obstacles and failures, Ilmarinen eventually accomplishes the task, using as materials the tip of a swan's feather, the milk of a sterile cow, a grain of wheat, and a tuft of a sheep's wool.

Four times he fails, obtaining products that turn out to be harmful: first on the anvil he produces a golden bow that always wants to kill; then he produces a golden boat that always wants to go to war; then he forges a cow that always loses her milk; finally, he obtains a plow that keeps ravishing the farmland. Only he who can forge the Sampo will be able to marry the beautiful virgin.

We have in this a profound intuition in the evolution of man. The trips to the Northland not only have a parallel in the exploits of the Nibelungs, but are reflected also in the innumerable motifs of the golden-haired princess or virgin who is only won at great risk by the right (that is by the properly matured) hero. It is the quest for the eternal feminine, for the true, higher nature of man. The forging of the Sampo, then, has to do with the formation of these forces or systems in the human being that must attain certain qualities before the marriage, the *unio mystica,* can take place.

Recognizing that the Sampo and its functions refer primarily to nonmaterial aspects or needs of the human being, we may sense that the flour (in analogy to bread that is transformed within the body into strength) alludes to the ability to transform sense data into perceptions. The salt, used by the Finns largely to preserve their foods, refers to the human capacity of preserving perceptions in memory; while the coins (in analogy to money's function in trading, in changing hands) refers to the coining of concepts, expressed in words, that can be traded between human beings. Meyer,[123] in a beautiful small volume dealing with the *Kalevala,* has further indicated that Ilmarinen's four preliminary failures allude to the gradual transition of the human race from hunters (bow) to seafaring people (ship) to pastors (cow) to farmers (plow). In other words, the human development must go through all these phases, each one contributing toward an inner structuring that eventually leads to a degree of perfection of esthetic, mnemonic and communicative skills required for a viable union with the hidden higher soul, with the anima portrayed by the virgin on the rainbow. Each phase, however, turns destructive if it becomes rigid, arrested. It must be transformed into or integrated within the subsequent phases.

Even Ilmarinen, though capable of forging the Sampo and though obtaining the mysterious bride, cannot hold her. Uncouth, powerful, giant-rooted, coarse and violent impulses, portrayed by Kullervo, kill the young bride. Or, from a different viewpoint, the young bride is not yet able to accept properly and to use the Kullervo forces within her. She feeds them stones instead of bread, and with this she is consumed by her animal instincts turned ferocious.

Meanwhile the Sampo has remained hidden deep in the rocky mountain in the Northland. There it has grown three powerful roots (imagine a mill growing roots!) that nourish it, each one referring to one of its functions, perception or esthetic qualities, memory, and language or communication. After the loss of the mystic bride, the three heroes, hearing of the great boon bestowed by the Sampo upon Northland's people, decide to undertake an expedition to bring it to Finland. Great battles ensue and during the pursuit of the victorious heroes, the Sampo shatters as it crashes into the ocean. However, some splinters of it are driven as new fertile seeds to Finland's shore, thus continuing their boonful influence.*

However, the struggle with the ever more deadly cold forces from the North continues, and the events become more and more apocalyptic. The old woman of Pojola (Northland) steals sun and moon, and locks them into the stone mountain. The fire which Ukko tries to forge into a new sun and moon goes out of control, devastates the entire landscape. The world becomes dark and the forces that the intellect (Ilmarinen) tries to manipulate become dreadfully powerful as well as uncontrollable. Ilmarinen makes a moon out of gold and a sun out of silver, but they will not shine. However, Louhi finally does release sun and moon. And though the son of Mariatta—in a barely disguised parallel to the events in Palestine—escapes the persecution of Ruotus

*This fourth theme has many significant parallels with the Greek myth of Jason and his companions in quest of the golden fleece.

(Herod) and is crowned king of Karelia, the world is in disarray. Wainemoinen, unable to recognize the significance of the new Christian impulse and having lost his powerful cantele, growls and departs on a ship to the edge of the horizon, there to wait for the time when his people are again able to receive the full meaning of his songs and for the time when he will forge them a new Sampo. We may surmise that then the beautiful virgin of the Northland—alive again—will be able to unite herself with him who has attained the highest consciousness. Only when Lemminkainen (who previously was considered too immature to be invited to the virgin of the Northland's wedding) has attained his full potential, and only when the oldest consciousness represented by Wainemoinen has fully severed its ties with the giants, integrating his powers with those of the Sampo, only then the *unio mystica* and the birth of the higher self—foreshadowed by the birth of Christ—can occur.

After losing the beautiful virgin of the Northland, Ilmarinen first tries to forge her likeness in gold, but he cannot warm himself at her side. He then hopes to woo his dead wife's sister, but she is reluctant to marry him; angered, he bewitches her into a seagull that flies along the seashore and whose melancholy cry contains a vague hope or hunch of eventual deliverance. The same longing is evoked by the new cantele given to his people by Wainemoinen before his departure. It is no longer endowed with the full power of the one that was made of the jawbone of a giant fish and the golden hair of the horse from the underworld. That cantele was lost in the battle with the wrathful people from the Northland. The new one is made of birchwood and the hair of a virgin. The once magic power of song manifests itself now in the melodious poetry that again reflects the predominantly intuitive-experiential-feeling aspect of the Finnish soul. Yet this melodious song not only is a reflection of the original magic power of the word, but it also helps us surmise that somewhere in the future the word, emerging from a more self-reflective consciousness, will again manifest its profound effectiveness. Just because the Finnish soul is still more deeply rooted in the intuitive-feeling realm, it has access to those prophetic visions that can rekindle the hope of all of us who often find ourselves trapped by the despair of a cold, dark and seemingly meaningless materialistic world.

Lemminkainen represents both our anxieties and our hopes. He reminds us so much of today's here-and-now youngster, attempting to be free and to act entirely on his own. He has no respect for tradition and causes confusion wherever he goes. Thus, at first, he appears lawless and selfish; but he also has a captivating beauty in his openness and in his potential for human freedom. He evokes our concerns and may lead us close to despair; shaking up our values, he will undermine complacent feelings of security; and overlooking our one-sided rational attitudes, he may anger us as he did anger the old man without eyes in the Northland. We must not let the critical, cold, narrow rationalism which is blind to the spirit destroy this new, dawning consciousness. We must not only try to assist its harmonious development in the young, but we must recognize it in ourselves. The words of the myth indicate to us that in this endeavor the three spheres of consciousness must work together, penetrating the finest aspects of our organization so as to create a "Sampo" making us worthy of the *unio mystica*. Yet as we are willing to find the proper path, we risk death again and again. Thus Wainemoinen, Ilmarinen and Lemminkainen, each in a different way, must confront the underworld.

The *Kalevala* makes it quite clear that we are but on the way, and its songs underline in various ways the central significance of the word, of the *logos*, in guiding us.

B. We have touched but a few highpoints of this grandiose epos that emphasizes and exalts so magnificently the powers of song and word. Because of this emphasis we can be sure that its rhythm and style are equally significant. They convey a profound message centering upon the need for bridging the apocalyptic divisions that have risen out of the development of human consciousness.

The songs of the *Kalevala* celebrate the confrontations, sometimes peaceful, often violent, between the intuitive, feeling Finns and the predominantly cold, rational people of the North. These confrontations seemed necessary for the development of new states of consciousness. Yet these songs also convey, especially in their style, the continued awareness of the need for bridging the gaps and for reestablishing the harmony between man and man, between man and world and between man and God. We mentioned in the beginning of this chapter that the original style of these runes required more than mere language. It included the use of the five-stringed harp or cantele, in whose music the human soul and the soul of the cosmos were experienced as merging; it included also the rhythmic interaction between the Laulaia and his assistant which conveyed equally the bridging power of song; and it finally included the time, place, occasion and participants of the celebration.

In the written epos we still recognize the cosmic, unifying music in the absolutely even meter of the verses that are made up of four trochees each. In the very frequent repetition of the same basic images or ideas in pairs of verses, we still find a reflection of the harmonious interaction of the Laulaia and his assistant (*cf. Runo* I, writing of the virgin's, Ilmatar's conception):

> Then a storm arose in fury,
> From the East a mighty tempest,
> And the sea was wildly foaming,
> And the waves dashed ever higher.[91]

Though the runes that make up the Finnish epos date back at least to the Middle Ages, they dwelled and grew among the Finnish people and were transmitted orally until the first half of the nineteenth century when they were frozen into written words by Elias Loennrot. Having thus remained responsive to basic cultural changes in the Finnish population until recently, they may be able to speak to us more immediately than the Sumerian, Greek or Egyptian myths that were committed to the enduring form of the written word twenty-five to thirty-five centuries ago. The latter thus belong to a cultural realm removed from us in time. Similarly, some of the African, American Indian and Oriental myths find less easy access to our psyche, since they belong to a largely different cultural orientation.

The extent to which verbal rhythm and style are supported by nonverbal features (dance, music, drums, masks, ritual actions, symbolic drawings, etc.) varies enormously. While on the one hand we note that the styles of the *Odyssey* or *Iliad,* of the *Divine Comedy* or the *Edda,* or of the average Western fairy tale are largely confined to language (implemented at best with some illustrations), we find one of the richest stylistic implementations of portrayals of mythic events in the American Pueblo Indian ritual dances. Here the interaction of earth, plant, animal, human being and God becomes an expression of cosmic harmony. The human performers, clothed in their Kachina costumes *become* Kachinas, that is powerful spiritual beings. At the right moment and at the right place they emerge from the world-navel, the Kiva, and they reestablish with their ritualistic dress, walks, dances, songs and words, with their sandpaintings and paho sticks the peace and unity with rain, sunshine, bear, serpent and fire.[178]

An entirely different mythic portrayal that transcends the verbal style is the opera, where image, music and word are combined. In the *Ring of the Nibelungs,* for example, Wagner[31] makes use of ancient Nordic themes in order to portray the tragedy of the human being (Siegfried) who loses his link with the cosmic forces. He forgets Brunhilde, his wife, daughter of Wotan, and loses his ability to understand the language of the birds. In the process of delevoping his self-awareness he becomes freer, but he also becomes susceptible to the deadly influence of Hagen, Alberich's (a Mephistophelian being's) son. His ring, beautifully symbolizing the newly awakened, self-contained wisdom, escapes the diabolical forces and is guarded by the Rhine daughters for a future epoch. Thus, at the very height of the tragedy of the Twilight of the gods (Goetterdaemmerung), a note of hope triumphs. In Wagner's music that so vividly supports the word and is in turn supported by the word, we find again a style carrying the hidden message, that myths, poetry and song will lead—on a higher plane of consciousness—to an experience of cosmic harmony that has been lost.

In passing it is interesting to contrast the Wagnerian style and message with that of Tolkien's trilogy[175] that treats, I believe, the same theme: the theme of the power and danger of a too one-sidedly developed human self-awareness symbolized by the ring. In the middle of the twentieth century, Tolkien can no longer accept that a positive purpose is served by the retention or by an eventual recovery of the ring. This type of consciousness that is portrayed in Frodo's (or Sauron's, or Gollum's) ring can at best offer temporary help—but only if this help is sought unselfishly —and even then it tends to corrupt the best of the best. The only meaningful goal is the permanent annihilation of the ring. Tolkien's prose is of the finest, and its effectiveness is manifested in the elaborate, rich and powerful descriptions of scenery, of events and of internal psychological stages. Believing that they would but detract from the reader's freedom to portray the events in his own inner images elicited by the words, Tolkien clearly rejects any mixture of various artistic media such as illustrations, music, etc. Thus he would not even condone illustrations in fairy tales or in the classical myths.

But let us now turn somewhat more systematically to the question of verbal style in myths, epos, saga and fairy tales.

C. It is far beyond the scope of this book to enter into all the innumerable stylistic differences in myths, epos, sagas and fairy tales of various epochs and cultures. However, in order to convey an idea of the importance of style in folklore, we shall briefly enumerate some of the salient characteristics of the typical Western folk-fairy tale, noting in passing some of the similarities and differences in myths, epos, sagas and art-fairy tales.

Rather frequently the fairy tale has characteristic introductory and/or terminating sentences that set the tale off against the everyday world. They may be as short and simple as "Once upon a time . . ." and "if they haven't yet died they are still alive," or as bizarre as "There is no if and no why, the tripod unquestionably has three legs," and "Were you also at the wedding? Yes I was; my headdress was of butter and I came into the sunlight and it melted; my dress was a spiderweb and I walked through thornbushes, and so it tore off; my slippers were of glass, and I stepped on a stone and they broke."[109]

In the folk saga, epos and myth introductory and terminating phrases are usually less bizarre, serving simply as formal beginnings and conclusions:

I am driven by my longing
And my understanding urges
That I should commence my singing
And begin my recitation.

Now my mouth must cease from speaking
And my tongue be bound securely,
Cease the chanting of my verses,
And my lively songs abandon.
—From the beginning and the end of the *Kalevala*[91]

Quite characteristic of the true folk-fairy tale are rather short, direct sentences. Indirect sentences and quotations are almost completely avoided:

> It is not long ago, quite two thousand years, since there was a rich man who had a beautiful and pious wife; and they loved each other dearly. They had, however, no children, though they wished for them very much; and the woman prayed for them day and night, but still they had none. Now there was a courtyard . . . in which was a juniper tree; and one day the woman was standing beneath it, paring herself an apple. . . . she cut her finger. . . . "Ah," said the woman, and sighed right heavily, "ah, if I had but a child as red as blood and as white as snow!"
>
> —Beginning of the tale *The Juniper Tree*[58]

This is predominantly also the style of the folk saga and many epos (see quotes from the *Kalevala*), whereas that of the art-fairy tale often departs from it.

> It was the night before the day fixed for his coronation, and the young king was sitting alone in his beautiful chamber. His courtiers had all taken their leave of him, bowing their heads to the ground, according to the ceremonious usage of the day, and had retired to the great hall of the palace, to receive a few last lessons from the professor of etiquette; there being some of them who had still quite natural manners, which in a courtier is, I need hardly say, a very grave offence.
>
> —Beginning of *The Young King*[183]

The concise, rather brief, direct sentences contribute to the sharpness of design in fairy tales. This sharpness is heightened by maximal simplicity of description, leaving the filling in of any accidental details to the listener: A "horrid looking witch"; a "beautiful house in the center of the forest"; a "Troll with three heads"; a "girl with golden hair"; a "big wolf"; a "boy the size of a thumb"; a "slight tailor"; "beautiful flowers"; "cake and bread"; an "old woman"; a "tall tower"; a "large giant"; etc. It is this appeal to the reader's or listener's imagination that largely influenced Tolkien[176] to oppose pictorial illustrations of narrations dealing with what he calls the "secondary world."

Wherever we find details of description (*cf.* description of the witch's features in *Hansel and Gretel*), we may suspect that they were added by the collectors of the tale, or that the narration belongs more to the folk saga group which tends to focus upon the outward, concrete, historical and physical details.[112]

Thus the images in fairy tales seem frequently abstract or stylized. The hero, for example, enters a town where the houses are painted black indicating that the whole city is in mourning. An analogous theme in an art-fairy tale or in a folk saga would more likely consist of a careful description of the subdued atmosphere in the town and of specific evidences of mourning. Thus in Western folk-fairy tales a brief signalization may suffice in place of a detailed picturing of scenes and events.[112]

While descriptions of the features of the outside world are held to a minimum in this genre, internal, psychological processes as well as interpersonal relationships tend to be expressed, visualized, by external conditions or actions.[112] The close bond between two persons is frequently expressed by means of a token or material object. In a beautiful Grimms' tale concerning two brothers, for example it is a golden lily, in an analogous ancient Egyptian tale it is a filled beer mug that indicates the condition of the relationship between the siblings; and in *The Goosegirl,* it is a handkerchief that represents a sustaining link with the young princess' past.[124] Or the feeling of intimacy is expressed in action, such as delousing, whereby the loving partner eats the lice, thus even taking in the blood of the beloved—which naturally is a very universal theme. In the Greek tale of *Mister Smigdali or the Man Made of Flour,*[112] the young princess' first longings are graciously portrayed in her inability to love any suitor until she finally creates her own lover by kneading him into shape after mixing two pounds each of sugar, flour and almonds. In the epos—and even more in the saga—

feelings of the protagonists are described more directly. In other words, one might see the world of the fairy tale (to a degree also that of myths), as an outwardly projected portrayal of subjective experiences, while the saga and epos attempt an introspective description of subjective experiences.

The fairy tale carves the powerful images of this soul-world: (a) by means of contrasts, (b) by extremes of exaggerations, (c) by preference for the formed and structured over the diffuse, soft, malleable, unclear, (d) by sharply isolating sequences of episodes, and (e) by presenting rarely at one time more than two interacting individuals.

This imaginative portrayal is further enhanced by repetition (with marked emphasis on threefoldness), by stylized variations and by potentiation.

The isolation of episodes may be so pronounced as to lead to logically impossible psychological events. Thus, in a Swedish tale,[112] we find one and the same servant to three princesses confronting the same hero three times on three succeeding days, each time assuming that he is the monster or troll which each time emerges subsequently from the ocean. Only among some of the classic Western fairy tales do we find this sharp chiseling and stylizing in its full beauty. Most art-fairy tales do not aim for this extreme clarity and simplicity. Myths have these qualities in attenuated form, and in the heroic epos they are even less predominant. The folk saga focusing, as indicated above, on an objective description of the protagonist's turmoils in confronting the numinous world, lacks most of these stylistic characteristics, except for the elements of potentiation through repetition.

The absence of historical time and place is again most pronounced in the Western fairy tale, while myths and heroic epos often do refer to actual geographic places or regions and to a certain past that is not simply a remote historical past but one that retains a fairly constant distance from the present, whether this present is that experienced in ancient Greece, or that of today.[138] However, the myth and heroic epos can easily switch from the worldly to an otherworldly geography. In the *Odyssey*, for example, the hero after leaving burning Troy, soon finds himself traveling through a world of imaginary islands, before eventually returning to the concrete geography of his native land. The saga, contrariwise, is clearly placed in historical time and objective geography.

The fairy tales's images describe a world in which things are meaningfully arranged in a far more profound sense than we ordinarily assume; and from this diaphanous world it brings joy and strength and health, as well as the message that it *is* meaningful to trust. In the myths we find some, in the epos a few elements of this; in the saga hardly any.

For a long time—and without final conclusion—there have been debates as to whether the great myths of mankind were assembled originally from simpler, folk-fairy tale-like narrations, or whether the latter are to be considered as fragments of ancient, great myths. As a matter of fact, fragments of folklore have been recombined in modern times into new myths or epos by later bards. Sam Blowsnake helped Radin[141] to recombine the *Winnebago Trickster Cycle;* Wagner[31] used ancient Nordic themes for his operatic *Ring of the Nibelungs;* or Loennrot traveled for many years through the territories of the Finns and Lapps in order to combine splinters of ancient folk-runes into the magnificent *Kalevala.*[18] The question concerning the ultimate origin of myths, epos and fairy tales is all the more difficult to answer, as the limits between these various genres become indistinct in ancient and primitive folklore (see Chapter IV). There can be little question, however, of the great similarity between many essential qualities of myths and fairy tales, the latter being often more crystallized, diaphanous portrayals of the world of the soul and spirit.

Especially in the Western fairy tale we may encounter Kierkegaard's *knight of faith.*[96] Like Abraham he is engaged in a quest that has its main motivation not in the external environment and its moral laws, but in his inner world. His undertaking may appear not only burdensome and hopeless, but also absurd. Yet in the face of the absurd he believes. Guided by an inner voice, he is truly authentic. Kierkegaard's *knight of infinite resignation,* or the tragic hero of the epos (*cf.* Agamemnon or Theseus) is called on to take desperate risks. However, these are never absurd and are accepted since the common good is seen as superseding ethically the good of the individual and his family. The heroic epos—at times—straddles the line toward the myth and fairy tale, at times that towards the folk saga. In the latter case it focuses on man's dilemma rather than on his eventual victory. It then has a somber mood and usually ends tragically.

In the fairy tale the stylistic element is such an integral part that it helps to reveal much of the significance of the story —not unlike a well-chosen dress which can manifest many characteristics of its wearer. In the folk-fairy tale the esthetic principles have not been applied deliberately to the structuring of the story; they are a spontaneous outcropping of the intrinsic meaning which they help to convey. Thus, in addition to verbal concepts and images, many nonverbal cues speak directly to our emotions and sense of harmony. Like symbolic images, stylistic elements become a dialogue with those vast areas of our psyche that are not fully comprehended by an intellectual analysis. The alliterations and rhythmic reiterations so powerful in the Nordic runes, the veiled and profound meanings of various numbers in epos and fairy tales, as well as all the other above-mentioned stylistic elements are an expression of this broader, richer and more colorful realm of human consciousness, whether we label it extended consciousness, personal unconscious or collective unconscious. The most articulate messenger between the world of meaning, or Tolkien's secondary world, and the earthbound human being is the *word* with its conceptual and pictorial content. However, it gains much of its effectiveness from many nonverbal elements associated with it. It is also inclined to associate itself with artistic media capable of addressing directly our innermost sensibilities. Such are the colors of paintings, the intervals between music notes, the gestures in rituals and the graceful movements of dancers and actors. The spiritual world, source of values, beauty and meanings, source of myths and fairy tales, often appears drab when clothed in the words of our modern, overly abstract and pragmatic language. Yet its reflection in various artistic media can give an inkling of its infinite variety and wealth.

So we find that myths, epos and fairy tales have lent themselves in various ways to further artistic elaborations. Many have become subjects for operas, to mention but: *Faust, Mefistofele, Tristan and Isolde, Salome, Lohengrin, Orpheus and Euridice, Parcifal, The Flying Dutchman, La Cenerentola, Hansel and Gretel, The Ring of the Nibelungs, Turandot, The Magic Flute, Ariadne on Naxos, Les Contes de Hoffmann, The Woman without a Shadow, The Fisherman and his Fru, Rumpelstilzchen.*[31] Some have been used for ballets, such as *Giselle, The Beauty and the Beast, Sheherazade, Swan Lake, The Nutcracker Suite, Daphnis and Cloé, Don Juan* and *Sleeping Beauty.* Sophocles, Euripides, Corneille and Racine, Schiller and Goethe, as well as many other great writers, have used mythic and epic narrations for dramas or tragedies; but also fairy tales have become the prime material for plays: *Greensleeves, Alice in Wonderland, Turandot, Aladdin and the Wonder Lamp, Midsummernight's Dream,* etc. The puppet theater lends itself well to the portrayal of some folklore themes, and the cinema has had some successes with well known fairy tales (*Cinderella, Snow White and the Seven Dwarfs*). When clothed as dramas, ballets or operas, myths as well as fairy tales address mostly the grown-ups, as if the heaviness of the dramatic form, the subtlety of the human movement in the ballet or the sophisticated spirituality of music metamorphosed them into adult fare.

Contrariwise, there are relatively few paintings of fairy tales that intend to address the grown-ups, in spite of the innumerable illustrations of varied quality in fairy tale books. On the other hand there are numerous famous paintings depicting epic or mythic themes (The *Birth of Venus* by Botticelli, *The Parnassus* by Mantegna and Raphael, the *Sybils* by Michaelangelo), prophetic dreams (for example Raphael's *Dream of the Knight,* Giotto's *Dream of the Pope*) and visions (*Temptation of Saint Anthony* by Gruenewald and by Parentino, *The Vision of Saint Bernard* by Lippi, or *The Stigmatization of Saint Francis* by Giotto).The reason for this difference lies probably less in the fact that fairy tales used to dwell among the common people and later addressed themselves mostly to children, than in the fact that the subtle, transcendental, transspatial and transtemporal qualities can too easily be destroyed and distorted. In the heroic and religious epos we find a greater integration of the story in the geographic and historical realities of the people, which makes it somewhat easier to illustrate their themes without doing injustice to their deeper meanings.

Though most fairy tale book illustrations are of poor quality, overly sophisticated, too realistic, or incongruous with the deeper contents of the narration, we find that with the growing awareness of the importance of the psychological development of the child and of the educational value of folk tales, there are some suitable illustrations that guide the reader or listener toward a finer understanding of the stories. The use of ill-suited illustrations may have an adverse effect not only upon the child's comprehension of the story, but upon the child himself. If, for example, the picture is too photographic, it will lead the child to see in the story primarily the entertaining and moralizing features. He will not respond to the finer, hidden messages, and he will misunderstand those parts that are illogical or overly cruel when taken at their face value.

Even more detrimental are exaggerated caricatures in which any deeper significance and much of the delicacy in feelings is radically destroyed by ridicule and by macabre or surrealistic features (*cf.* Disney's *Snowwhite and the Seven Dwarfs*). Indeed, Tolkien[176] is of the opinion that any illustration of secondary-world tales is likely to diminish rather than enhance their effectiveness, by interfering with the spontaneous imaginative activities of the reader. While I believe that this opinion may be too radical, it nevertheless imposes upon the illustrator of folklore the very difficult injunction to expedite a fuller comprehension of the narration without interfering with the reader's or listener's own creative imagination. Maybe Gustave Doré's famous illustrations of the *Divine Comedy*, or Maurice Sendak's illustrations of his beautiful tale *Where the Wild Things Are*[161] come close to meeting this criterion. Some of the best fairy tale illustrations, internalized by the young child, can become lasting, helpful and harmonizing forces in the psyche of the developing youth. In our times this may be of very particular importance, since on account of television, comic books, etc. there are so many dulling forces that impede or disrupt human development.*

In an effective illustration the choice of colors, shades, forms and details results directly from a keen understanding of the theme. The data of our everyday world are not neglected or distorted (as in abstract paintings), but—whatever the artistic style—we sense an interpenetration of the physical with the psychological and spiritual realms. Frequently we find a simple, ethereal, and somewhat stylized beauty which speaks primarily to the heart and which allows the viewer to mingle into it his own delicate perceptions. An effective illustration certainly does not result from the deliberate grouping of symbols; and yet much of it can be interpreted symbolically. In the illustration of Rumpelstilzchen, for example, we recognize the large but shriveled intellect (the dwarf, old and all head) dancing around the meager fire he has lighted in the night. Thoroughly oriented toward the earth, he looks away from the heavens with their moon and stars. His house, like his body, is small and shabby; and he seems unaware of the tall, strong mountains which point toward the sky. Most of the shading is dark, and the dwarf's gaiety appears fake in this bleak surrounding where even the weak little flame is devoid of the warmth of love. The fact that there is beauty in both composition and form helps the child experience good as well as evil as indispensable parts of a meaningful world.

Always keeping in mind that the children's emotions must be helped to mature before excessive emphasis is placed on intellectual achievements, it becomes self-understood that symbolic and other analyses of tales and tale illustrations would only interfere with their intuitive capacities. Any but the simplest explanations of fairy tales to children are likely to be rather harmful. Even the adolescent and adult should allow himself to experience fully and repeatedly the themes or images of epos, myths and folk tales before cautiously proceeding with some intellectual uncovering of symbolic and other meanings.

*A secondary fringe benefit of illustrations is that they familarize the child or adolescent with items or people no longer existing in his everyday world: Weavers and Grinders, spindles and mills, etc

While most adults have no longer the child's intuitive capacity for the themes and images of folklore, they often are able to sense in the musical interpretation of myths, epos and fairy tales that their truths transcend intellectual understanding, though the latter may indeed enhance some people's experience. It is this greater intuitive openness for music that makes myths and especially fairy tales, dressed in the cloak of an opera or of a ballet, more acceptable to adults.

CHAPTER VIII

UNDERSTANDING AND ANALYZING

Wär nicht das Auge sonnenhaft	Was not the eye alike the sun
Die Sonne könnt' es nie erblicken,	The sun it never could behold;
Läg nicht in uns des Gottes eigne Kraft	Was not within us God's own force
Wie könnt uns Göttliches entzücken.	How could we cherish what is godly.[55]

In what is childlike we see only predominantly primitive, instinctual drives, as long as we look at it with the eyes of a grown-up steeped in materialism, whereas we can find in it a long lost meaningful, spiritual world, if we succeed intuitively to re-enter our own early childhood."[77] Myths and fairy tales which have their origin in the childhood of human history are often judged primitive, barbaric, heathen, silly and worthless, because they are not based upon our contemporary scientific knowledge and because they often employ a type of logic which is foreign to our modern, more abstract thinking.

Already early in this century Lévy-Bruhl has shown that this primitive logic refers constantly to an invisible, spiritual world as the primary cause of all happenings; those events which we would nowadays consider as causes are, to the primitive individual, only a means through which the spiritual world expresses itself. A man may die of an organic illness, a snake bite, being hit by a tree or devoured by a crocodile; but the tree, the illness, the poison, the crocodile are only tools. A secret power, a sorcerer used any one of these tools to kill that man. Furthermore, a causal relationship between things is frequently blindly accepted merely because of their proximity in time or in space: a person passes a house just when someone inside dies. This proves to the primitive individual that the pedestrian was the murderer. The pedestrian is made to drink a lethal potion. If he dies, this demonstrates his guilt; if he vomits the poison and lives, this reveals his innocence. This prelogic thinking often admits intolerable contradictions and it seems quite anthropocentric: everything, good or bad, happens for or against the human being. It excludes the possibility of accidental happenings and is irrefutable, because it takes care of its own apparent contradictions, which are either given new meaning or ignored. The primitive's desire to explain all phenomena with this prelogic, anthropocentric thinking is usually seen as a result of his hope to be able to influence, mitigate, propitiate nature whose language he understands and which is not deaf to his voice, thereby lessening his numerous fears. His beliefs in forces behind the phenomena become his myths and his attempts to deal with these spiritual forces become rituals and ceremonial sacrifices.

The presence of beneficial *and* malevolent supernatural beings in almost all myths as well as the complexity of the rituals allow the explanation of failures of propitiating ceremonies. Either the malevolent spirits or an error in the performance of the ritual can be blamed; the myth and the value of the ritual, however, is never doubted in the least, since they are the main defense against otherwise overwhelming anxieties. One can point out that such defenses against anxiety can only be weakened by the introduction of better defenses and that the natural-scientific view of the world offering logical, mechanistic explanations for what is considered of mystic origin is, or seems, a more effective defense. Yet, whenever the first enthusiasm for these new explanations subsides, the human being finds himself in a merciless world. He cannot maintain a thoroughly objective, scientific, materialistic view without falling into despair. He may then try to make natural science and dialectic materialism into a new religion, but falters because of the inherent contradictions in this undertaking. Thus he looks back longingly to the illusions which at one time enriched his life and which were destroyed by the cruel new truth.

A young Italian, Giacomo Leopardi, has probably felt and expressed this conflict as well or better than any other poet:

Dalle mie vaghe immagini	From all illusions which I loved
So ben ch' ella discorda:	I know that nature differs;
So che natura è sorda,	I know that she remains deaf
Che miserar non sa.	And that pity she cannot feel.[106]

And he senses that our most noble values and feelings become equally illusions in a natural-scientific world:

So . . .	
Che ignora il triste secolo	I know that this sad century
Gl'ingegni e le virtudi	Ignores the wise and virtuous,
Che manca ai degni studi	That truly worthwhile studies
L'ignuda gloria ancor.	Receive no praise at all.
E voi, pupille tremule,	And you, oh trembling pupils,
Voi, raggio sovrumano,	You, superhuman glimmer,
So che splendete invano	All your brightness is futile,
Che in voi non brilla amor.	From you does not radiate love.[105,106]

Inasmuch as civilization has a beginning, its first (primus) chapter may be called primitive, without thereby implying any value judgment as to superiority or inferiority. A culture which has remained stagnant, whose beliefs or values are no longer understood by its own people and which attempts unhealthy compromises with other civilizations, often can be called primitive *and* decadent. Yet many past civilizations such as the Sumerian, Assyro-Chaldean, Egyptian, Greco-Roman as well as the Mayan, Inca, Pueblo-Indian, Celtic and ancient Nordic cultures impress us with a grandiosity in art, in mythic concepts, in moral ideas, in feelings for nature, which in many ways appear so far superior to what we are practicing nowadays.

Before we begin to analyze a culture, we must try to understand it; we must humbly and without prejudice stand under that culture, look at its various manifestations without jumping to conclusions; we must learn to think and to experience in its own unique way. It is only then that the culture starts to speak to us, that we slowly begin to comprehend its language. Only then can we expedite our insights by comparisons with other cultures, by psychoanalytic and symbolic interpretations and by deductive reasoning. Thus myths, epos and fairy tales appear crude, silly and barbaric when seen from our present day natural-scientific viewpoint; but they begin to reveal their riches as soon as we learn to let them speak to us without constantly injecting our own prejudices and analytic models.

We must keep in mind that the prelogic thinking of early or primitive cultures was operative only in certain contexts.[107] The ideas, the concepts in these cultures were not abstract thoughts such as ours, but were experienced as concrete things. Yet prelogic thinking did not precede logical thinking. In fact, causal thinking, including the recognition of contradictions, was part of all those activities which dealt directly with the procurement of the vital material necessities. Furthermore, we can also ask ourselves why, contrary to animals, human beings developed a "fear of the unknown" leading to supposedly childish attempts at explaining the world. If we follow the psychoanalytic trail, this question will lead us to the problem of the formation of social groups which suppressed certain instinctual strivings (development of taboos and totems). Such suppression may give rise to conflicts and anxieties which in turn are projected into (blamed upon) the events of the outside world.

Yet this ingenious theory does not necessarily satisfy fully, because it hides the likely fact that the creation of social groups with their taboos and the investment of the world with purpose are both the result of what is most characteristic of the human being, namely his ability to seek his own and the world's meaningfulness. The meaning of things is not measurable, and I already see, therefore, a paradox in those attempts of natural science which would explain ideals, values, spiritual beliefs as products of a human brain conceived solely as a complex computer.[182] Only when we recognize that natural science is the product of a limiting hypothesis ("How does the world appear, if we assume that it has no meaning?"), can we begin to integrate its fruits in a newly significant conception of the world.

Even materialism searches for meaningfulness, but because of the above limiting hypothesis it is compelled to turn around in circles as it tries to explain the world as devoid of meaning. As an ubiquitous human experience, the need to explain, the need for meaningfulness, is frustrated by the natural sciences, including Freud's view of psychic mechanisms. No wonder that the void encountered in a thoroughly demythologized world furthers the wish to regress to a period when existence was experienced as blissfully meaningful. This regressive longing is expressed by

Giacomo Leopardi who felt awed by the great ideas of the new age of enlightenment, but who was also filled with the most delicate feelings, ideas, hopes and fantasies which he had to accept as illusions. In him, the wish for meaningfulness had to turn into a regressive desire for death whom he sees as a beautiful, kind, accepting virgin:

Null altro in alcun tempo	Nothing else ever
Sperar, se non te sola;	Desiring but you;
Solo aspettar sereno	Only waiting serenely
Quel di ch'io pieghi addormentato il volto	For the day that I lower my face, asleep,
Nel tuo virgineo seno.	Upon thy virginal breast.[106]

Leopardi was born shortly after the French revolution. Impressed by the writers of the enlightment, he loved—as an outstanding scholar of the Greek culture—the eternally beautiful images of its mythology which at one time had been part of everyday human life. Here the animal, the half-animal half-human (for example the sirens or the centaurs), the human, the half-god and the hierarchy of gods formed one continuous whole. But in the later periods of this Grecian culture the foundations were laid for modern natural science. Plato separated a perfect world of ideas from the world of the senses, and Aristotle distinguished matter and form. This led, via physicists such as Archimedes and Newton and philosophers such as Descartes and Kant, to the division of all things experienced into two basic categories: (a) measurable matter, considered real, and (b) everything nonmeasurable (values, morals, spiritual qualities and beings), considered illusory. Yet this artificial division or dichotomy, this dualism seems only to enhance man's longing to be part of an undivided cosmos. With all our knowledge about atoms and distant stars we sense that the Greeks' concept of the earth as a big saucer across which Phoebus flies with his horse-drawn sun carriage conveys a more concrete experience than the most advanced astronomic theory of the universe. I am sure that the Greeks were fully aware of the mechanistic illogicity of their belief, but their search for meaningfulness overshadowed by far any mechanistic considerations.

Among psychiatrists it was Jung who experienced and emphasized most powerfully the human being's longing for a new wholeness.[82] Thus his views on individuation stressing the integration of unconscious and conscious elements, the harmonization of *animus* and *anima* and the eventual coincidence of opposites. He recognized that this longing often led to inappropriate solutions. He was clearly against an uncritical espousing of oriental philosophies that could prove detrimental in the West; and he believed that one significant feature of space exploration was the wish to escape from the impasse of Western civilization leading to a perverted quest for wholeness.

So-called prelogic thinking should not be looked at as immature or barbaric, but rather as an early all-encompassing thinking, striving for what is significant, of which logical thinking is only a special branch. It extends beyond causal relationships between tangible, measurable items. It is more intuitive and is sensitive to simultaneousness, propinquities and analogies. We might liken it to an unusually refined sense organ which seeks, feels, or experiences the wisdom of and the inner connection between things. Though we cannot simply regress to it, we must see in it the original source for a new way of experiencing the world and ourselves.

Jung was deeply imbued by the experience of a necessary harmonious relationship between significant events within a human being and in his environment. As if to prove this, the old tree in front of his home was split by lightning on the night Jung died. Jung called this *synchronicity*.[162] In these views he is closely related to Goethe of whom legend saw him as a great-grandson.

If the eye can see the light of the sun, there must be a common force in the sun and in the eye. If we can think of a God, if divine things can delight us, then God's own strength must dwell in us.

CHAPTER IX

CONSCIOUSNESS VS. THE UNCONSCIOUS–THE "UNDERWORLD"

Signs and Symbols

WE DISCUSSED THAT a broader view of understanding and analyzing helps us in entering the world of myths and fairy tales. Equally helpful is a flexible grasp of the concepts "unconscious" and "conscious," as well as of the related concept "symbol."

Theories and opinions concerning an unconscious psychic activity have existed long before Freud.[40] With the advent of psychoanalysis, however, the role attributed to the human unconscious has grown in importance and is almost generally and blindly accepted even by the most unsophisticated. Expressions such as "doing something unconsciously," "unconscious feelings" and "unconscious reason" have become part of everyday language. It is said that our choices of friends and marriage partners, our leanings toward specific ideals, religious and political issues, as well as our following this or that profession are influenced or dictated more strongly by unconscious needs, impulses and conflicts than by rational deliberations. And we learn that we are living in the perpetual illusion that our thoughts, feelings and actions are essentially the result of our own, free, conscious decisions, since we are, at best, only vaguely aware of the unconscious conditioning influences.

C. G. Jung was convinced that the conscious life-situations plus the repressed experiences or impulses in the personal past of the individual cannot explain all his longings and dreams, his rational and his irrational behavior. He therefore concluded that beyond a personal unconscious there is an even more powerful collective unconscious. In this he sees the precipitation of all the preceding cultures which constellate in manifold ways the individual psychic activity, not unlike the Internal Release Mechanisms (IRM's) genetically embedded in the brain, that help a little chick to flee from the image of a hawk right after hatching, or which induce the newborn sea-turtles to precipitate themselves into the ocean.[25(I)] Because of the common origin of various cultures, their collective unconscious would contain similar archetypical images, IRM's, or symbols.

On the other hand, some existential philosophers and therapists[10,12,13,154] began to question radically the relevance of the concept "unconscious psyche." In view of their stress of the phenomenologic method this appears justifiable. Since *phainos* means "apparent" or "shining," and since *menon* means "remaining," one could say that phenomenology is the science which focuses on what is and remains apparent. Indeed, the possible nature and workings of the unconscious has to be inferred. Conclusions are drawn from dreams, from the fact that seemingly forgotten things can suddenly be remembered, from various psychogenic or psychosomatic symptoms. The unconscious, then, is often seen as a storehouse of memories and reaction patterns inaccessible to awareness mostly because of repression necessitated by various taboos, but still exerting indirectly manifold influences upon the human being.

For the existential psychiatrist and philosopher such a view is overly mechanistic and lacking in logical rigor. Rather than seeing the unconscious as the crowded basement of a house, they are inclined to see consciousness as an extended surface on which, for reasons of economy and effectiveness, only a certain area is clearly illuminated. This is, at any one time, the individual's world-design.[10,74] In this view of consciousness the analogy with the visual field is often used. The items beyond our visual horizon are not unconscious, they simply are not there for us at a certain moment. They may enter our visual horizon, however, as the latter enlarges, or as we are willing to shift our gaze.

A person remembers, re-experiences, is aware of certain data because they fall within his current world-design. Human growth, then, can be seen as a widening of this world design. In addition it can be seen as progressive freedom to illuminate with our consciousness various existential realms.

Dreams—amongst other psychologic manifestations—can be seen as permitting a surreptitious, modified expression of repressed, unconscious psychological or instinctual drives. The phenomenologic view, however, sees in them much more the meaningful and honest portrayal not only of the patient's everyday world-design, but also of the border areas that he may be inclined to ignore. Medard Boss,[12] for example, tends to reject the idea of an unconscious, hidden dream-story behind the manifest dream, identifiable only with special psychoanalytic techniques including the understanding of symbols. The dream of a withdrawn, narrow-minded spinster in which a soldier approaches her with a gun is not, he states, adequately explained by "an unconscious wish for sexual relations, wherein the gun would be interpreted as a phallic symbol." Rather, the gun and the uniformed soldier are more meaningful in their phenomenologic, nonsymbolic significance. He explains the dream on the basis of the world of this spinster who has not developed the capacity for a loving relationship with a man. Since she is unable to view any man as a unique individual, all men are the same to her (uniform!). And a man's approach cannot, therefore, be experienced as loving; it is felt in every aspect, including the sexual one, as aggressive, destructive.

The Freudian, symbolic interpretation, though often expedient and convenient, would thus represent a moderate distortion and a marked narrowing of the full meaning of the dream. And the term "unconscious," as used by Freudians and Jungians, would be viewed by existential philosophers and therapists as an operational hypothesis depleting somewhat the substance of the dream. Such narrowing or depletion occurs inevitably whenever a phenomenon (whether it is a dream, fairy tale, myth or hallucination, an object of art or of nature) is approached by means of a preconceived theory.

The phenomenologic and the analytic approaches differ both

in their explanation of therapeutic effectiveness and in their evaluation of the process of meaningful disclosures in folklore studies. Thus existential psychiatrists[13,83,119,121] are inclined to say that the recovery of old memories (historical insights) is not so much the *cause* of growth, of improvement, or of a widened world-design, but its *result*. The effective phenomenologic elucidation of folklore is similarly facilitated by the wholehearted participation on the part of the explorer. Nevertheless, the judicious application of analytic viewpoints can expedite the phenomenologic exploration, while the latter, in turn, throws a clarifying light upon the meaning of historic, analytic interpretations.

Another important point can be illustrated with a saying of Maurice Chevalier: "Girls used to blush when they were ashamed, now they are ashamed when they blush." Cleverly this illustrates the increasing tendency to disparage almost any emotions we become aware of and to deny their intrinsic value. But if shame—and all other feelings—are seen in this light, then the ultimate, universal aim is a world without either shame or blushing, without responsibility for or appreciation of feelings. The belittling of conscious experience in favor of a hypothetical, mechanistically operating unconscious diminishes the significance of human existence and impoverishes the world. Ideals, beauty and the most delicate feelings, at best, are accepted in the role of concealing primitive drives and of thus furthering group and social interactions necessary for the survival of our species and for continued technological progress.

Boss's emphasis on the wealth and variegated richness intrinsic in conscious experience, be it in waking life or in dreams, represents a very needed restoration of a neglected reality. Yet the emphasis on the value of conscious reality does not wipe out the significance of reductionist interpretations.

To let the things themselves, the phenomena, speak without our injecting any preconceived notions, without applying any of the theories about nature, body or soul which we grew up with, is a nearly impossible task. We are—for example—so thoroughly conditioned to the natural-scientific concepts of measurable time and space, of the ubiquitous cause and effect relationship between things, that any viewpoint considering these concepts as one-sided or restricted will at first be judged farfetched or unrealistic. Yet an unprejudiced analysis of the facts of consciousness shows that the *experience* of time and space precedes, exceeds and encompasses *measurable* time and space: A person who is a thousand miles away may be closer to us than a person in the same room; and minutes may seem a lifetime. Space and time, furthermore, have experientially many varied qualitative features that are never apprehended by measurability.[75] Similar reflections apply to cause and effect relationships, especially as pertaining to biology and psychology. A beautiful example is this: Instead of simply assuming that the light rays cause an image on the eye's retina the way a picture is produced in a camera, one may grow to see the sun, the light, the eye, and the image as an interrelated whole. Goethe described this in the beginning of the stanza with which we introduced the preceding chapter: "Was not the eye alike the sun, the sun it never could behold . . ."[55] Cause and effect, subject and object, environment and individual, soul and body become again, and in a new way, part of *one* world which, especially as an initial consequence of Descartes' philosophy, was rent in two.

The problem of the unconscious requires some additional discussion of symbolism. The term "symbol" has been used in many different ways.[28] Thus, whenever feasible, I tend to circumvent it with more precise expressions. Also, most symbolic interpretations tend to have overly restrictive connotations. Erich Fromm[50] rightly points out that symbolic language pertains to a sphere other than our everyday existence with its measurable space and time, and with its thinking based on causality. While he distinguishes accidental symbols which are personal reminders of some past happenings; conventional symbols which simplify communication by means of *signs* (including letters and words); and universal symbols, it is usually only the latter which psychiatrists refer to when speaking of symbolism. However, even then their use of the term will vary in meaning from:

1. The designation of one physical object by another. (Examples for this would be the various phallic symbols of the

psychoanalysts, or Fromm's description of Little Red Riding Hood's red cap as a symbol of menstruation); to

2. Designating an idea, impulse or feeling by a concrete thing (such as seeing wild animals as symbols of aggressive impulses, or the cross as a symbol of Christianity); and to

3. Expressing something which cannot be otherwise expressed as accurately and concisely (such as the triangle as symbol of the Trinity, the Chinese Yin and Yang (Fig. 2), or the ancient

swastika symbol). It is this last category that best deserves the term "symbol." Here the image stands for something that is beyond the sensory realm; it becomes the door to the experiential rather than intellectual comprehension of the suprasensible. The symbol then becomes the mask of the god, necessary as long as we cannot see the gods face to face.[25*]

Erich Fromm rightly stresses that a symbol may have a multiplicity of meanings, but he nevertheless tends to restrict this meaning in individual situations. Medard Boss tends to dispense completely with the term, stressing that the full richness of an image, usually designated as a symbol, can best be understood not by seeing in it the representation of something else, but by a scrupulous phenomenologic exploration (*cf.* the above dream of the spinster). His reasoning is *ideally* valid. However, he tends to overlook the *practical* advantage to the patient, in terms of expediency and comprehensibility of symbolic interpretations, and the mysterious power inherent in many symbols.

---

*Yet eventually, as our vision develops, the symbol and the symbolized may again be experienced as *one*. The primary and the secondary world merge.[176] Thus, after ever-renewed doubts and struggles, Kazantzakis[94] experiences our variegated world no longer as a mask that hides the deity, but as an immediate manifestation of God.

In psychology and elsewhere it is thus hard to achieve a harmonious synthesis between natural-scientific, analytic, reductionist approaches and the phenomenologic approach. Therefore, in the subsequent discussion of folklore, I shall frequently let various approaches stand side by side, hoping thereby to convey an inkling of their ultimate interrelatedness.

Accidental symbols, originating in the personal life experiences of the narrator, can be presumed to be largely eliminated from folk-fairy tales and myths, because these were originally transmitted through numerous bards before someone wrote them down. Thus many images in folklore can be treated as universal symbols. However, even these images get their *specific* meaning only from the context of the entire narration, whereby quite seemingly trivial details may turn out to be of great importance. While a thorough acquaintance with universal symbols allows a quick grasp of the probable main themes and meanings of a narration, it is the ability to experience the story with as few presuppositions as possible, that introduces us to its qualitative richness. We shall return to this when comparing various tales with a similar, basic plot, and when focusing upon the meaning of the differences of these stories. We shall also recognize cultural taboos which determine the choice of the elements that are allowed to become part of the story. In the artistic fairy tale and epos created largely by just one person (Andersen, Hauff, Thurber, Wilde, Sendak, Dante, Virgil, Tolkien and many others) the introduction of elements from the author's personal life experiences complicates the understanding of the meaning of the story. These personal elements can be analyzed separately if we know the author's personal history. In discussing Puccini's opera *Turandot* we shall notice how the basic problem and destiny of the composer became integrated with an old fairy tale.

Returning to the discussion of the unconscious, we may note that only in our present century the idea that there are inner, unconscious psychological processes for which the human being was *not* responsible has been broadly accepted. Even when psychiatry became a respectable medical specialty in the nineteenth century, it held on to an ambivalent attitude concerning disorders of the psyche, fearing lest the moral-spiritual core of the soul be ignored. Thus it distinguished true mental illness which was presumed of organic origin from other emotional disorders. These, psychoneuroses, character neuroses, etc., were relegated to the moral field was excluded from scientific endeavors. But then came Freud, and shortly it appeared that all aspects or expressions of our psychic life would be gobbled up by the instincts whose complex interaction with social demands could explain everything. The study of the human psyche with all its vicissitudes became only now an exclusive branch of the natural sciences. We were told that our feelings of love, of freedom, of will, as well as our ideals, were illusions. Especially Jung,[82] the son of a minister, as well as Binswanger[10] and Jaspers,[69] the first existential psychiatrists, rebelled against this extreme position. Later on, Laing,[102] Boss,[13] Minkowski,[126] Frankl,[44] Maslow,[116] May[121] and many others worked at bridging the subject-object gap created in psychology through the rigid application of the standard natural-scientific method. We are still far from what could be the finest goal of Western culture, from a true integration or marriage of spirit or soul, and matter.

There was a time when the division between spirit and matter did not yet exist. In Genesis this paradisiacal epoch ceased with the expulsion of Adam and Eve into the world of death and suffering which, however, offered in turn the promise of greater self-awareness and knowledge. Through the prophets, shamans and the deep experience of mythologic events and rituals the spiritual world still reached for quite a while into this world of sin, death and pain. This is discernible clearly in the early Greek epochs where the gods fought and loved side by side with the human beings. Gradually the contact with the gods above and with those of the underworld was lost, and only the all-pervading feeling for beauty and freedom as well as the more and more decadent oracles were left as reminders of the original harmony between man, earth and God. As this alienation of God and man progressed, the underworld, netherworld or Hades assumed greater prominence. Half gods such as Castor and Pollux, or Demeter's daughter Persephone, still alternated living on Mount Olympos and in Hades. But the division became more complete as the early Mylethian philosophers began a rational explanation of the traditional beliefs, and as humanity moved towards Roman pragmatism and modern natural science. In fact, the development of the underworld in which the souls sadly long for the life on earth, the increasing interest in natural science discounting human subjectivity, and the formation of the unconscious seem to go hand in hand. The world of the shadows, Hades, is the lost heaven, Nirvana, to which the Buddhist wishes to return by surrendering self-consciousness, selfishness, ego, which are seen as Maya, as illusion. In Western cultures hell, to a large extent, is but what is seen in this world of shadows, of matter, of suffering, when we lose all contact with the spiritual world. It is for this reason that Freud, looking into the human unconscious, could only see sinful, harmful, bad impulses. Jung, Boss, Fromm and others, attempting to go beyond a strict natural-scientific orientation, again see helpful as well as hindering, superior as well as inferior forces in all the manifestations of the unconscious, and particularly in the dream.

A beautiful tale of the Hopi Indians showing the development of the underworld, is that of the origin of the Kachinas,[34] demonstrating how in the remote parts of Arizona man experienced his fate similarly as in the culturally highly advanced Greece:

> The Kachinas were beneficent spirit beings who came with the Hopis from the Underworld (corresponding somewhat to the Garden of Eden of the Genesis), whence came all people . . . . With their powerful ceremonies, the Kachinas brought rain for the crops . . . and all the blessings of life. But eventually the Hopis came to take the Kachinas for granted, losing all respect and reverence for them. So the Kachinas returned to the Underworld. But . . . they taught some of their ceremonies to a few faithful young men and showed them how to make masks and costumes. When the other Hopis realized their loss, they remorsefully turned to the human substitute Kachinas, and the ceremonies have continued since that time.

It is admittedly an oversimplification to reduce the basic challenge to our evolution to three stages: one, progressive feeling of loss of unity with our (spiritual) origin; two, gaining awareness of our identity in the course of our contact with the material world; and three, eventual synthesis on a higher plane.

This path is at least as rich in variety, in depths, and in colorfulness as our everyday environment. The process of extricating one's self from a one-sidedly materialistic world in which only the measurable is acknowledged and in which determinism prevails, implies a gradual reorientation toward life which involves our entire subjectivity. This effort is constantly endangered in two ways. One may slide backward into exclusively materialistic and deterministic ways of thinking, or one may lose one's self in too lofty, abstract, subjective or mysterious thoughts which have no real impact on the conduct of our life and cannot be communicated adequately to our fellow human beings.

The challenge is to face our lower material world without becoming imprisoned by it and without fleeing from it regressively into vague, lofty daydreams in which we lose our identity. Before his resurrection, Jesus Christ—of whom our "higher ego," "Self," or "Transcendental ego"[99] is a reflection—descended into the Netherworld. Maybe once our higher ego* is able to penetrate safely our own underworld, our unconscious, it may turn at least part of it into paradise. The lower world became hell or Hades only when the ego no longer could find ultimate dissolution in Nirvana (in Indian mythology the souls of the dead do not, like in Greek mythology, retain a specific identity). And the lower world remains an evil hell or a realm of blindly compelling forces as long as the ego tries to maintain itself by avoiding any confrontation with it.

The Revelation of Saint John portrays in magnificent images the two seemingly evil powers that must be confronted and dealt with if the human being is to fulfill his mission on this earth. From the two spots—one on the sea and one on the solid ground—upon which the powerful angel had placed his feet, thereby creating a door towards a new world, we see emerge two dreadful animals. One has seven heads and ten horns, the other is a seemingly harmless, lamb-like, two-horned hard and cruel creature. In the Old Testament these two beings appear as Leviathan and Behemoth, in the Germanic saga as the serpent Midgar and

*In the German language the letters JCH, initials of Jesus Christ, become the world for ego!

the Fenris-wolf; and they are reflected in our language in the terms "devil" and "satan." The first is often associated with the more fluid, the second with the solid, rigid elements. In the Odyssey (see Chapter XXXI) we see them represented as Charybdis and Scylla, the rocky cliff and the whirlpool that threaten to disrupt Ulysses' mysterious, initiatory voyage. The two animals in the 13th chapter of the Apocalypse are two aspects of the dragon in the preceding chapter. They are complementary like the diabolical and satanic, the luciferic and ahrimanic aspects of Goethe's Mephistopheles who first appears to Faust as a seemingly harmless poodle.

In the Revelations we read that the *sign of the animal* appears on the forehead and the hand of those who fall under the spell of the animal emerging from the earth. We can see in it what appears the greater peril in our times, the power of the cold, detached, abstract thinking that studies man exclusively in a physical and biological context and thus becomes satanic. Man becomes more animalistic as he is studied as exclusively animal. At first the link to the animal realm may seem to be limited to the forehead, to the way man thinks about himself. But it spreads soon to the hand, to the field of his actions.

The most beautiful picture of the conscious human being trying alone to find his path between heaven and earth is that of the sungod's son Phaëthon[57,158] who tries with youthful courage to lead the sun carriage across the earth. Unskilled, he scorches first the sky and then the earth. Let us avoid his fate; we have not arrived yet; we are still on our way.

CHAPTER X

THE SIGNIFICANCE GIVEN TO FAIRY TALES AND MYTHS IN OUR TIMES

HARDLY ANYONE WOULD QUESTION that living in Western civilization, he has to adjust, to make concessions to a materialistic way of life. If not by the words and attitudes of our parents, this is taught in our schools, by our companions, by the mass communication media, and by the every day necessity of coping with innumerable technical aspects of modern life.

We have become more conditioned to the physical, natural-scientific, sensual and sensuous sides of our world than to its ideas, ideals and values. Our ability to think has, therefore, largely limited itself to the natural-scientific exploration and exploitation of the world. This analytic thinking—focusing on measurability and causal relationships—cannot grasp the contents of fairy tales without impairing their beauty as well as their meaningfulness. Though abstract, cold and preferring shadowy outlines to the copious qualities of things, this analytic thinking with which we are familiar allows an initial opening of the door to the understanding of fairy tales and myths. What we see through the gap may be enough to make us aware that a wider exploration of the hidden treasures will be worthwhile. Thus Goethe in his story *The Fairy Tale*[53] has the sharpwitted will-o'-the-wisps devour the golden lock to the door of the mysterious temple underneath the ground. Their critical faculty, their ability to move in abstractions, initiates the resurrection of the temple and the new millennium.

The careful application of natural-scientific thinking to the evaluation of folklore will reveal the interrelatedness of many stories from various cultures, their characteristic features, their harmonious structure and their type of reasoning. Furthermore, the use of psychoanalytic concepts can reveal the reflection or expression of fundamental instinctual needs, fears and conflicts in many of these stories. However, while our intellectual curiosity may derive some satisfaction from psychoanalytic interpretations, we sense that the narrations lose most of their lively charm when we explain them solely with this approach.

When we interpret a patient's dream, we are greatly helped in our analysis by the remarks and by the associations the patient can offer in regard to the various things that occurred in the dream. In psychoanalyzing myths and fairy tales this is obviously not possible. The acceptance or nonacceptance of our dream interpretations by the patient, his emotional reaction toward them and his corrections of them, will help us evaluate their correctness. Since this is not available in psychoanalyzing these stories, we cannot gain the same degree of assurance in regard to their exact meaning in terms of unconscious impulses and problems. Freud[49] pointed out that it is difficult to discover the true hidden significance of dreams without additional information obtained from the dreamer, because dreams express a great many things in a distorted paradoxical way. This is certainly true also of the unconscious fears and drives which may seek a mode of expression in fairy tales and myths. Let us take, for example, *Little Red Riding Hood* who has been seen, psychoanalytically, as the sexually tempted young girl, suffering from conflicts over menstruation, intercourse and pregnancy.[50] The warning by her mother not to break the glass with the wine by deviating from the accepted path is seen as a symbolical admonition not to lose her virginity; and the wolf is viewed as the expression of animal (male) sexuality. The red cap has been explained as representing (by displacement from the genital region to the head) the blood of menstruation which indicates that the girl has reached the age where she could get pregnant. Then, by some tricky maneuvering, the wolf with the two live human beings in his stomach demonstrates the fearfulness, danger and sinfulness of a pregnancy which ultimately kills him. The confusion is enhanced by the wolf's masculinity and by the appearance of another male individual, the hunter with his gun. Dangerous because of this weapon, he is at the same time a savior because, instead of using this weapon, he delivers the grandmother and the girl with a pair of scissors. With some facility for "brainstorming," these events can be given numerous other psychoanalytic interpretations. Especially when discussing the tales of *The Juniper Tree,* and *The Dragon in the Black Wood,* we will find further evidence for the validity and flexibility of psychoanalytic interpretations of folklore.

By selecting or emphasizing only a part of the elements of the story and aligning them according to a somewhat preconceived theory, a fairly consistent psychoanalytic interpretation becomes usually possible. Yet this can afford at best a one-sided and incomplete understanding of a tale, and we hope that our study will show the feasibilty of a more comprehensive explanation which takes into account each and every detail of the narrative. We shall begin to recognize the importance and specificity of the choice of a particular symbol, and to appreciate that what we first looked at as displacements and distortions has an independent meaning. This meaning is frequently far more weighty than its (simultaneous) usefulness in expressing surreptitiously taboo material. We will come to the conclusion that forbidden instinctual processes and conflicts play only a minor or secondary role both in the production and in the message of a story.

Let us remember that instincts, as Freud has shown, are integrated in our *human* existence only with difficulties. They seek indirect release whenever and wherever possible. Therefore, since fairy tales deal primarily with the problems of human existence, it is quite plausible that repressed desires, taboo wishes and the anxieties caused by these, seek an opportunity for acceptable expression in the colorful images and events of these stories. However, since the true fairy tale as well as the myth focuses primarily upon the spiritual nature of man and on the development of his unique individuality, it will adapt to the tendencies seeking instinctual wish fulfillment only to the extent where this does not interfere with its primary aim. In fact, these narrations often illustrate how drives can be refined and transformed into human qualities. The magic mill (see Chapter VII) is a profound symbol for this. In the average dream the primary aim is different. While the dream, like the fairy tale and myth, can be viewed as portraying the existential problems of the individual, it would be hard to deny Freud's contention that it aims largely at preserving sleep by affording disguised, distorted or sublimated release of instinctual pressures.

Whereas accurate analytic thinking may indeed open the door to a broader understanding, one runs into numerous casual and superficial remarks from nonanalytic sources concerning the significance of folklore. These explanations clutter the access to a deeper comprehension, since they either miss the main point almost entirely, stress secondary aspects as if they represented the principal purpose and meaning, and often consist of rather vague and empty phrases. A few brief quotes[165] will illustrate this quite adequately:

> "Since . . . fairy tales have come up out of primitive civilization, they contain a good deal that is unnecessary."
>
> "It will be admitted that there is some value in the doctrine of the purgative effect" (of the violent scenes of fairy tales).
>
> ". . . free play of fancy . . . loosens up the mental machinery . . ."
>
> "Like play it releases pent-up powers."
>
> "There is wholesomeness in the 'just for fun' tales."
>
> "Children can laugh away a lot of foolishness that the rude tools of serious thinking fail to uproot."
>
> "Facts . . . are dead until the fancy with its magic wand quickens them into life."

Entertaining, moralizing, offering instinctual abreaction and escape from the dreary everyday surroundings, are facets of folklore which are secondarily derived from their basic purpose which is to portray, to rekindle the awareness of, the purpose of human existence. The latter, however, can be understood only if we gain some insight into the basic features of the history of the human race as well as of the problems in the development of the individual human being. The evolution of humanity is expressed in the struggle for proper understanding, for control, and for the sharing of the material world. Similarly, each individual in his own development is challenged to come to terms, not only with the surrounding physical world, not only with his fellow human beings, but also with his own instinctual drives. While (unlike the dream) the fairy tale's primary role does not consist in offering *indirect* release for instinctual drives, the problem of the human being's relationship to his physical needs and desires and to the physical surroundings becomes the tale's paramount concern. Each person's struggle with his problems is intimately interwoven with the history and the attitudes of the society he lives in. Therefore, we shall find that the individual's problems in development also overlap in folklore with themes dealing with the problems which the human race faces collectively. For the sake of clarity, however, we have separated chapters based on tales which refer to phases in the *development of the child* (Part II) from subsequent chapters of folklore themes dealing primarily with more *general problems of human existence* (Part III).

PART II

Human Development

CHAPTER XI

INTRODUCTORY REMARKS

During the child's so-called formative years (zero to six or seven) we notice the gradual differentiation from a stage in which the psyche experiences itself and the world as *one* undifferentiated whole, toward a stage when this same psyche can see itself as a separate entity among other human beings. The individual has grown to appreciate that these human beings are not only related to himself, but also have relationships among each other which have *nothing* to do with himself. This first, formative period is considered as lasting approximately six to seven years, coinciding largely with the preschool period and made up of several phases which can be described as follows.

The initial task of the newborn is to learn to distinguish between himself and the outside world. Only later the awareness develops that his various bodily parts belong to him and that outside objects are separate from him.* However, even after this awareness occurs, he still experiences everything as existing only for himself, the infant—that everything is there for his satisfaction. This may be likened to a period of megalomania, when he is the absolute king, the ruler of his world. Soon the growing child is faced with the gruesome realization that not everything brings him pleasure, but that there is pain, hunger, cold, etc. As a result of this he structures his world so as to maintain a feeling of wholeness and power. He distinguishes in this world what is pleasure-producing from what creates discomfort. He

*Indeed, it appears to be a crucial characteristic of the human infant that his very earliest consciousness is not spatial, but temporal. Elkin,[39] basing his data on Spitz[164] and Klein,[159] clearly shows that this temporal consciousness arises in the third month, as a result of the *re*-cognition of a face by the infant who is still totally unaware of the spatiality of his body and of his surroundings.

tends to identify himself with what gives pleasure and to consider as part of the outside world whatever produces pain. Only much later the concepts of pleasure and pain are linked with the connotations of good and evil. On numerous occasions the grown-up returns to this early structuring of his world. We often fail to see this in ourselves, but we easily observe it in another whenever he tends to give credit to himself for everything that brings him praise, happiness and success, while he blames others for all failures, displeasures and mistakes.

Soon, however, this world picture proves inadequate, and the child realizes that pain can arise from the *inside* of *his* body, and that pleasure can be derived from the *outside* environment. While still grouping all the experiences in his world as pleasurable and uncomfortable, good and evil, the child is compelled to develop his rapport with the outside, the non-self, in order to procure pleasure and dispel displeasure. Still, there is only one axis of relationship, namely "world" (which is essentially mother, as everything else is seen as in her service) and "child." The outside world assumes powerful and ambivalent features: on the one hand kind, feeding, comforting and lulling, and on the other hand threatening with total destruction. The divine mother is supplanted by the diabolical mother. From being a powerful ruler of the universe, the child has turned suddenly into a completely helpless center of the universe, at the mercy of *another,* of his mother, and of his world. Eventually, in an accepting, supportive, loving environment the child succeeds in coping with this terrifying ambivalence, largely by learning to repress his most violent responses to the threatening world around him. This is facilitated by his repeated experience that his *real* mother, the *other,* will not destroy him. Yet another intense fear arises, namely the fear of being abandoned. This fear is the result *not* of the recognition that the outside world can be painful or cruel, but of a necessary, new, radical rearrangement of the child's world.

The infant turning child begins to realize that the world does not consist in a simple, unidimensional, exclusive relationship between himself and mother, but that mother—and all other people—are engaged in various human relationships which have nothing to do with him. It is this insight which leads to feeling the threat of abandonment; consequently there is, in the helpless child, an understandable wish to do away with whoever threatens the original, more secure, unidimensional relationship. In the boy this leads to the well-known triangle relationship which Freud has described as the oedipus complex, where the boy experiences a fierce rivalry with father in order to keep mother all to himself. In the girl this triangle relationship is more complex, inasmuch as the wish for retaining an exclusive relationship with mother yields to the wish for an exclusive possession of father. A part of these feelings and conflicts becomes manifest outwardly, whereas another part evolves toward structuring the inner world of the child. While these triangular competitive relationships with the parents are paramount, all the other competitive jealousies with brothers, sisters and playmates, are but additional expressions of this unwillingness to abandon the unidimensional mother-child world, and to acknowledge the existence of equivalent relationships between other persons. That few ever attain a full resolution of this conflict is well attested by the innumerable petty jealousies, self-overevaluations, self-depreciations, over-dependencies, etc., which we recognize in ourselves and in our fellow human beings. In the mature person, the exclusive unidimensional dependence is substituted by a healthy self-preservative drive which combines with a deep respect for the feelings and rights of other people. Unidimensional relationships now become freely chosen commitments.

It requires considerable empathy to sense the depth and drama of this evolution of the child's psyche from the zero-dimensional state, where no distinction exists between outward and inward reality, to the egocentric unidimensional, and eventually to a "bidimensional" world:

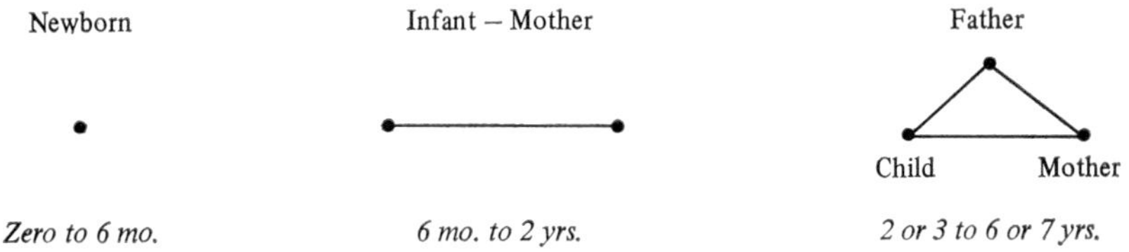

Certain attitudes and the acquisition of various skills (in terms of body function) characterize these three stages even in the child's physical or organic development. Because of this, the three stages have been designated by the psychoanalysts as oral, anal and oedipal. This is justified, though often one-sidedly overemphasized. In many ways during the early oral phase, the infant and his mother are almost one. The infant experiences the mother (or rather, at first, only the mother's breast, the "other") as part of himself, and so there is *no* dimension between child and mother. His world is zero-dimensional, though a primordial form of consciousness, without spatial features, develops during this period. Some attempts to maintain the zero-dimensional world are seen beyond this period in such habits as thumbsucking and carrying a blanket.*

Only with successful toilet training does a clear-cut spatial separation between the parent and the child develop, inasmuch as the latter is now put in a position to do something—not just for his own sake or satisfaction—but for someone else. The earliest forms of giving, of frustration tolerance, of self-control, of pride and of enjoying the parent's gratitude are connected with this toilet training. This relationship is still only unidimensional, namely parent vs. child. With his growing ability to regulate his eliminations (*cf.* comments concerning Wakdjunkaga, Chapter III), to consider the wishes of the parents, the child's objectivity increases. He becomes aware not only of the immediate meaning of things to himself, but also of his and his actions' significance to others, and eventually of the meaning of people outside of

*Noteworthy, here, is the identity of the Latin word for breast, *mamma,* and the almost identical term for mother. I have observed a little boy whose terms for his blanket and for his mother were indistinguishable "mammam" for quite a while until gradually the blanket became "namnam" and the mother "mamma."

Even the so-called narcissistic and homosexual periods of early development, roughly corresponding to the oral stage and early toilet training, can be viewed as attempts of the child to maintain a zero-dimensional world by denying that there are other people. He only sees himself (narcissism) or he loves people only inasmuch as they are seen as identical to him. Later in life we find reflections of this clinging to the earliest world in some of our most immature reactions and in some of the more severe neuroses.

himself to each other. As we said, this poses a severe threat of abandonment. Since up to now satisfactions have been to a large extent physical, the jealousy born of the fear of abandonment implies also a loss of sensual gratification. By this time the child's ability to experience some genital gratification has biologically developed, and it is therefore likely that this oedipal jealousy is, as Freud postulated, at least partly, a genital jealousy.

However, many of the alleged oedipal memories and fantasies of the adult are probably a mixture of these early feelings and conflicts and later, sexual, interpretations and deformations of early childhood experiences and problems. Therefore, it is usually feasible to de-emphasize the sexual aspects of oedipal conflicts, and to stress that the basic development during this oedipal period is the growing ability to live in a triangular (and therefore bi-dimensional) human relationship. The child learns to use aggressive feelings and impulses constructively, rather than for the purpose of eliminating the third person in order to re-establish the previous unidimensional parent-infant relationship. The genital aspects of this conflict are secondary and due to the particular biologic phase which becomes a medium for expressing the more basic problem. Fromm[50] sees primarily in the oedipus drama the conflict with the "third" person, experienced by the small, weak child as "authority," rather than the portrayal of the guilt over incestuous desires.

Existential philosophers (Heidegger,[61] Buber[16] and others) and psychotherapists (Boss,[13] Binswanger,[10] May,[119] Jung[87] and others) have beautifully and convincingly shown how our existence as individuals depends on the relationship to another person. Without a "thou," they point out, there is no identity. The indispensable pillars of our feelings of selfhood are the affirmation of our experiences (or of our "world") *and* the openness to genuine human relationships. We cannot exist alone. This does not conflict with what we have outlined briefly in regard to the psychoanalytic concepts of early childhood development.

The very beginning experience of an outward reality (the transition from a zero- to a unidimensional world) is the recognition of the parent ("other" or mother) as a "thou," as separate from one's self, and as alternately absent and present again.

When the mother who at first is *one* with the infant is recognized as separate, she is experienced predominantly in her depriving, frustrating aspects. She becomes the source of all disagreeable feelings, since the child still considers all his pleasurable experiences as originating in himself. Later he gradually realizes that displeasure can arise in him, and that the outside world, which *is* mostly mother, contains "bad" *and* "good." As the child grows, this mother-outward-reality, this "thou" extends and proliferates into the rich and varied world we know as adults. The essence of this "thou" consists in our meaningfulness to it and vice versa.

Later on in life, the individual, who for whatever reason loses or refuses any experience of relationship to a "thou," finds himself back in a zero-dimensional world. There is no inside and no outside. Voices originating in his own psyche seem to come from without, and the true meaning of the outward reality and its voices is lost. This psychotic world is essentially a frustrating attempt to return to a zero-dimensional world.*

If the individual manages to retain a limited relationship at least to the physical aspects of the outside world, some sense of self is retained while a genuine relationship with the "thou" is lost. Lonely in a world which is meaningless to him, he is depressed and hopeless. He cannot love and be truly considerate of the feelings of others; and the kind help proffered by fellow human beings hardly touches him. No one can have a positive sense of Self without a "thou." We need the abiding presence of someone to whom our existence means something and whose existence is meaningful to us. Indeed, even the hermit can main-

*Such regressions are not necessarily always negative. They may include desperate, heroic attempts at unstructuring a personal world that has become suffocating. Whether such unstructuring leads the individual toward a rebuilding of a better world or leaves him in a dreadful, confused or empty world where he feels controlled by external forces (delusions), depends on a variety of factors. Most important among these is the presence or absence of a friendly guide who accompanies the individual on his—drug induced or spontaneously occurring—"trip." Just as a far-out tale or myth might prove harmful when told without love to an insecure child, and wholesome if told with affection and understanding, so a *mind-expanding* experience can lead to impoverishment or to growth depending on the environment in which the individual finds himself.

tain his experience of existence only in feeling a deep, real, purposeful relationship with his God.

Myths and fairy tales stress this in manifold ways. The development of a loving relationship between the hero and the princess brings a happy kingdom and true riches. The Western fairy tale, especially, describes the quality of love of which the quantitative, technical and sexual elements are but one side. Today, children learn early about this side. They know how, but they often do not apprehend the deepest qualities of a true intersubjective relationship.

Feeling unloved can lead to depression, psychosis and self-destruction. Thus Ajax, feeling degraded by his fellow Greek, lapses into a depression followed by a delusional psychosis, and finally ends his own life. Heracles becomes psychotic when his pride overcomes him or when he feels spurned. Hybris (excessive pride) and rejection may thus undermine our identity by shattering its necessary pillar of human relatedness.

According to psychoanalytic theory, the early formative period is followed by the latency period which roughly corresponds to the grammar school years. The expression "latency period" was derived from the observation that intense feelings and conflicts of the previous years become latent or repressed, only to emerge in a new form at the end of this period. Now the child is primarily involved in (a) acquiring the academic and physical skills which will enable him to develop experience in a trade or profession; and (b) expanding toward satisfactory friendships and group-relationships the skills in interpersonal relation acquired within the family setting during the oedipal confrontations. During the latency period the child learns to live—at least a good part of the day—away from home and family. The sum total of taboos, rules, habits, warnings and conditions acquired during the early formative years now guide him, keep him out of trouble and danger, and give him needed self-assurance and strength. The normal child still accepts this guidance blindly, identifying with it rather than rebelling against it, as he does in the following period. Not that the conflicts of the formative years are completely silenced. Occasionally they break through with little distortion. More often they are manifested only in disguises such as nightmares, phobias, tics and psychosomatic disorders.

With the advent of adolescence we first notice a modified, rapid recapitulation of the formative years. Increased selfishness and self-centeredness with lack of consideration for others may alternate with close friendships with one's own sex and rejection of the opposite sex. Then love turns again either toward mother or a mother substitute, before the adolescent's longings for companions of the opposite sex awaken. In the normally maturing adolescent the integration of the greatly intensified erotic impulses with his ability to relate to his family and to deal adequately with the world at large requires a number of years, outwardly ending with his becoming of age. My thirteen-year-old boy expressed this quite succinctly, earnestly and naively when he declared, "You know, I have now a school life, a home life and a romantic life; and it is real hard to harmonize them."

During these turmoils the teenager must also overcome, sublimate or repress the strong wishes to return to the earlier world-designs of the formative years. In early cultures adolescent initiation rites were often given extraordinary significance (*cf.* J. Campbell's excellent analysis[25(I)] of the male adolescents' initiation into adulthood among the Australian Arunda). In more advanced cultures they have only occasionally retained their effectiveness. The Jewish bar mitzvah, for example, in which the thirteen-year-old boy is the center of a ceremony in which the whole community participates, remains a powerful experience. In the various Christian denominations the analogous confirmation has largely become a rather weak ritual retained by tradition. Thus the redirection of early instinctual drives accomplished in intense initiation procedures where the young individual is firmly introduced to and linked with the mythological past of his tribe, gives way to a more gradual and lengthy transition period. The latter does not guarantee as consistent results as the former; but it opens the individual to a more flexible future in which he can explore more freely his creative potentials.

In our culture the adolescent usually lives with his parents and completes his schooling or learns a trade. However, he is inclined to question, change or reject many of the rules, beliefs and taboos which he received in the formative years and which he fancied—almost—to be his own during the latency period. This rebellion seems to stem from two sources. On the one hand the superego is in conflict with the intensified erotic and aggressive drives; it is fought fiercely, both in order to allow some outlet for these drives and to lessen the guilt aroused by them. On the other hand, the adolescent's growing awareness of the forthcoming need to assume responsibilities without relying on his parents, challenges him to strengthen his own evaluation and manipulation of external reality. This independent evaluation and manipulation has the advantage over the guidance by the superego of being much less rigid, more timely and more adapted to the real needs of both the subject and his actual environment. Rollo May[120] has repeatedly pointed to the danger resulting from overlooking some intense inner turmoils of the adolescent by blindly supporting, condoning or abetting all and any intense self-assertions and demands for freedom, without simultaneously recognizing hidden insecurities, dependency needs or anxieties. The insecure youth clamoring for less restrictions (both because of his own natural rebelliousness and because this clamoring may bring considerable approval from his peers) becomes frequently even more restless and anxious if all his demands are satisfied. Yet, instead of recognizing his need for limits and controls, he tends to blame his increased dissatisfaction on whatever limits he still finds in his way. Thus he is caught in a progressively vicious cycle.

Much of the adolescent's rebellion is not yet a free, realistic and truly moral self-assertion, but rather a blind reaction against the superego in a rash attempt to gain independence. Only at the end of normal adolescence is the beginning of true freedom born. With this arises the possibility for more objective evaluations, wisdom and tolerance. The maturing individual no longer relies on establishing his identity by saying *no* to external demands. He becomes increasingly open to his inner experiences (thoughts, feelings, impulses) as well as to the environment; and he can agree or disagree, like or dislike, comply or resist more independently in the face of any blind outward or instinctual pressures. This capacity for detachment, for responding rather than reacting blindly, is a lofty, never fully attained goal.

The distinction between the terms reaction and response, reacting and responding, reactivity and responsibility, is of utmost importance. Referring with *responsibilty* to an inner experience of choice between various alternatives, the difference between the two sets of terms can be illustrated with the theme of the eager young page who tries to please his king. When the king longs for a roast duck, the young man promises to hunt a dozen ducks: when the king desires a rabbit, the page insists that he will shoot ten. Blindly he wants to please. Yet the king is wise and is neither flattered nor satisfied by the mere eagerness of his servant whom he orders jailed. Yet eventually the young page awakens to the fact that he had been a slave to his impulse to *react* pleasingly to his king. He becomes free. He becomes open not only to his master's request, but also to the totality of his own situation. Now he *responds* to the king's wish, as well as to the awareness of his limited skills as a hunter and to the recognition of inalterable or unpredictable factors in the outside world. Thus he responds to the king's longing for a faisant with, "Your Majesty, I shall try my best to get one."

In this context *reaction* and *response* are opposites. The failure of a reaction is experienced as imposed, unfair. In his jail the young page can blame fate. Contrariwise, a genuine response cannot truly fail; and therefore the responsible person will not suddenly find himself in a jail. Certainly his modest response did not guarantee the success of the page's hunt, but it seemed to favor it by *not* predicting it. Yet even if the hunt had been unsuccessful, the young man would not have failed since his response, his life project fully accepted the possibilty that the hunt, meaningful in itself, might lead to nothing.

The above psychoanalytically oriented subdivision of childhood development can be compared with (a) Eastern philosophies which envision the periodic acquisition of ever new, essential human qualities; these are usually seen as emerging at the end of seven-year cycles; (b) biologically oriented views which describe human development as the emergence of neuro-psychologic functions and skills; (c) phenomenologic viewpoints seeing development as a sequence of important changes of man's relationship to the world going hand in hand with periodically widened world-designs. All these views seem to indicate that human development is not something continuous and gradual, but occurs in phases. Each phase may show its early origins in the preceding one and contains the seeds for the following one; yet each phase has its own distinctive characteristics. Each has its own purpose, and if this purpose is not fully attained, the human being may be crippled in some respects. It is often impossible to complete or correct fully at a later date that which has been neglected or bungled at the proper time. The laws of human development which prescribe the fulfillment of certain tasks at specific times are as intransigent as the cruel but wise king who sends the exuberant youth out to meet three challenges, each one offering the possibility of completing a new step in his personal growth.

Fairy tales, which seem to deal primarily with childhood development, also distinguish the three mentioned periods, often assigning to each one a span of approximately seven years. While sometimes covering the entire span from early childhood to adulthood, they frequently focus on one of the three periods: early childhood, latency period or adolescence. In the following five chapters we shall illustrate this with the stories of *Hansel and Gretel* and of *Little Red Riding Hood* which deal mostly with the early childhood period; *Snow White and the Seven Dwarfs, The Wolf and the Seven Goats* and *The Juniper Tree,* which are concerned with the latency period; and *Sleeping Beauty, Tredeschin* and *The Dragon in the Black Wood,* which center on adolescence.

While illuminating specific periods and conflicts of childhood, all these tales reflect simultaneously not only various aspects of cultural development, but also local customs, ethical precepts and metaphysical orientations.

Epos, sagas, legends and myths, on the other hand, do not focus to any degree upon the problems of childhood development. Their emphasis is upon the challenges confronting the grown person, challenges which reflect both the hero's and his environment's need for expansions that alone can preserve and enhance the meaningfulness of life.

CHAPTER XII

HANSEL AND GRETEL

"IN FRONT OF A LARGE WOOD there lived a poor woodcutter with his wife and two children . . . ."

In attempting to gain access to the meaning in and behind the story of these two children, we will first try to view this fairy tale with the help of the previously discussed psychoanalytic concepts of early childhood development, supplementing this with some illustrations taken from other tales, from sagas and from poetry. Then we will expand upon this by adding various thoughts based upon a fairly detailed phenomenologic analysis.

It may seem arbitrary to assume that the story deals with the earliest childhood or formative years, when there is no direct reference to the age of these children (contrary to *Snow White and the Seven Dwarfs* and *Briar Rose,* discussed later on, where the age of the girls is mentioned). However, the general tenor of the story, the fact that Hansel and Gretel are not yet able to work and to share (like Snow White), and especially the fitness of the hidden meaning will support our assumption.

The little family's problem consists in their not having enough to eat. They are poor. It is during the night when the children experience the greatest anxiety over this, since their hunger (psychoanalytically expressed: their oral frustration) leads to their feeling threatened with complete annihilation. They hear mother (the rejecting-frustrating mother who first had fed them well) persuade their father that for her and his own good the children have to be abandoned in the *forest.* The oral frustrations inherent in early childhood training lead to an emotional interaction between child and parents in which the latter (at least unconsciously, at night) are experienced as unloving, selfish and rejecting. Since they need their parents desperately, children attempt to counteract, to deny this rejection. In fact, Hansel succeeds in finding the way back from the forest, in which they were abandoned the followed day, by trailing the moonlit pebbles he had collected as soon as he heard of the parents' plan, and which he had strewn on their way to the woods.

The wood is a common symbol for the human being's loss or abandonment of previous values and securities. Dante starts his *Divina Commedia* with:

Nel mezzo del cammin di nostra vita	Just in the middle of my life's endeavors
Mi ritrovai per una selva oscura,	I found myself deep in a darkened forest,
Che la diritta via era smarrita.	Because the correct path had been forgotten.[33]

We shall see Snow White wander through a dark and perilous forest and Little Red Riding Hood deviate from the path in the woods. Percival could not find again the castle of the Holy Grail deep in a forest after he was expelled, because he missed asking the right question of the king; and in the depths of forests of Thrace, Orpheus spent his last years after he had tried in vain to rescue his wife Eurydice from the shadows of the underworld.

Hansel and his sister Gretel seem successful at first. But the frustrations at home continue. The mother seems to become more shrewd in her plans for rejecting the children, finally convinces the father again to abandon them, and prevents Hansel from collecting during the night the white pebbles. A desperate attempt to still mark the way home out of the forest, by sacrificing the very bread which was so scarce, fails when the birds eat all the crumbs he has strewn. Therefore, this last defense against the frustration fails and *regression* takes the place of *repression.* The children are lost in the woods. Guided, finally, by a white bird, they arrive at the gingerbread house of the witch who is clearly a regressive image of the frustrating mother.

The confrontation with the *physical* world and its deprivations has helped Hansel and Gretel to experience the beginning of an individual psychologic and bodily existence. Yet, to the small child the frightening frustrations of everyday life become intolerable. They long for a return toward an earlier existence, when food was unlimited, when to the children the house was almost equal to food and to mother, when their existence consisted of eating and of sleeping in nice little beds. And so, after wandering three days in the dark forest, they are led by the white bird to the gingerbread house. They arrive in the evening and proceed eagerly to eat the roof and the window. In spite of this discourteous behavior, the old witch treats them at first quite well, offering them the most exquisite foods and then bedding them in two nice little white beds. "They felt as if they were in heaven." In psychoanalytic terms: *total regression!*

But the witch built the gingerbread house only in order to catch the children. In other words, there is a catch in this regression to the earliest, heavenly, childhood stage. The catch is that this regression carries with it the loss of whatever experience of physical and psychologic independence the children had acquired through their previous frustrations. This threat to their independent existence is well expressed in their gradual realization that the witch's ultimate aim is to eat them up.

Psychodynamically this realization implies a process of *projection,* since, in a healthy family, the mother does not *really* have a desire to destroy the child's identity, and since the child's fear of being gobbled up by the mother-witch is mostly a direct result of his own wish to return to an early existence when he and mother were still one.* Thus in this tale the struggle begins between the two young individuals and the witch (or between the child and what his projection of his wishes has made out of mother). It lasts four weeks and ends with Gretel pushing the old woman into the big oven which had been prepared to roast the girl. We can see in this, symbolically expressed, the alternative of incorporating the witch instead of being destroyed or eaten by her. The fact that the children then turn to her home and collect her pearls and precious stones seems to bear this out: the child deals with the earliest image of mother which has become threatening, by incorporating and repressing what is too frightening to the young ego. At the same time he retains as a

*Granted that this is an oversimplified version. Even good parents have hidden needs to reject the child or to consume it with their love. Thus projection—as most projection—is not entirely upon "Nothing," but upon some features that correspond to the projected fears and wishes. And *un*satisfactory parents *are* often witches and sorcerers.

permanently helpful gift the pearls and precious stones (we might also say the love and security) which keep nurturing the child in his subsequent course through life. Comparing this introjected mother to the psychoanalytic superego, we can distinguish a threatening, witchlike aspect of this superego from its helpful, precious aspect. In our analysis of *Snow White and the Seven Dwarfs* we shall see these two aspects re-emerge in the witch-stepmother who again tries to destroy the girl, and in the seven dwarfs who are helpful and bring gold and iron ore from the mines in the mountains. A forest separates the gingerbread house and the parents' home. Similarly, seven forested mountains lie between the stepmother-queen's castle and the dwelling of the dwarfs to which Snow White flees.

Having overcome the witch, the children return home, and with the help of a white duck they cross the "large water." Then the surroundings become familiar. The mother has died during the "four weeks" (which psychologically makes sense) and they display the pearls and precious stones to their father, anticipating a happy life. (Little do they suspect that the witch may return and hound them again.) The crossing of the large water, leaving the witch's forest behind, indicates a final process of successful repression of the negative aspect of the ambivalence toward mother. This ambivalence had been created by the early frustrations as well as by the beginning assertion of an independent ego.*

*We are inclined to view this repression (analogous to the one later described in our interpretation of *Snow White and the Seven Dwarfs*) as completed only toward the age of seven. However, this is open to debate as one may be inclined to see in the story only the vicissitudes of the *earliest* childhood, namely of the child's attempts to recognize himself as separate from mother. If we interpret the story in this way, the working through of the oedipal problem would have to be seen as a separate, later phase, leading to the ability of seeing one's self as a well-functioning part of a group. Only this second phase, then, would terminate around six or seven, with the repression of those feelings which are incompatible with a satisfactory group relationship. Finally, if with Erich Fromm we see the oedipal conflict as a struggle with the authoritarian parent, then the two phases of early individuation and of making peace with authority become almost one continuous overlapping process. The fact that the children share with a third person, father, the pearls, would point to a fairly adequate solution of the oedipal conflict understood in this sense. This was described in more detail in the previous chapter.

So far we overlooked the mentioning of various animals, other than the white duck and white bird, in the story. By focusing on these animals we find an opportunity for viewing the story from a slightly different vantage point.

The other animals in the tale are a white kitten, a dove, the threatening wild beast in the forest, the birds which ate the bread crumbs, and the mouse mentioned in the somewhat bizarre terminating sentence of the narrative.

The white kitten and the dove are mentioned in connection with Hansel's dropping at one time the pebbles, another time the bread crumbs in order to mark the path back to the house. He does this by turning and gazing toward his home. Both times he is caught looking back by the father. The first time he pretends that he is looking for his white kitten, the second time that he is looking for his dove. The first time it is the mother, the second time the father who corrects him, saying: "It is only the sun shining upon the chimney, you fool!" It would be a great mistake to dismiss such small episodes as meaningless details; in fact, why did Hansel have to turn around to drop his markers, and why did he use the excuse that he saw these particular two animals? The parents obviously see only the most material aspect of the home, the chimney. To Hansel the home is a much more dynamic, live concept. In the kitten he experiences his home as something you *have to* stay fairly close to, whereas the dove already represents an animal which can separate itself from the house by long distances, without forgetting from where it came. And so looking back is an additional expression of the intention to return to the home after the journey through the forest.

Furthermore the dove, invisible to the parents, may remind us of the more ethereal forces that surround the small child like a helpful spirit, such as we also find portrayed in the good fairy and the guardian angel. The white bird—first a dove, then a snow-white bird, and finally a white duck—seems to accompany Hansel and Gretel in their vicissitudes, reappearing in those moments of despair in the woods, when the path is lost. It is as if the young child, emerging out of his earliest world (which is one of unity with mother) would certainly get lost in the dark forest of life with its voracious animals, if it were not for this helping spiritual force which comes to his assistance whenever the need is greatest. With the loss of blissful fusion of child, mother and home, the world becomes dark and confusing, and the instincts are experienced as dangerously threatening, like devouring beasts. Now the snow-white bird leads the wandering children to the witch and the gingerbread house. After the grueling re-experiencing of the relationship with the early mother (witch), it is the white duck which will carry the children back into a more familiar world.

We are reminded of Goethe's[54] verses:

Ein guter Mensch, in seinem dunklen Drange,	A good person, ringed by his dark urges,
Ist sich des rechten Weges wohl bewusst.	always remains aware of the right path . . .

The fearsome arousal of the ambivalent child-mother union is not simply a regression in the sense of a complete return to an earlier mode of functioning. The children have become more aware of what is going on and their experience has a purpose. They are now able to take a stand toward this terrifying situation: they can salvage what is valuable in it, and they can destroy or repress what is threatening them. Thanks to the precious stones, and with the temporary help of the white duck, they can hope to meet the world more happily and successfully.

We have not yet commented about the fact that there are *two* children, a girl and a boy. The way the story goes, it is Hansel who usually is the active one, except during the crucial period of his captivity at the witch's place, when Gretel takes the initiative, kills the witch and frees the brother. Representing the more conscious, intellectual aspect of the soul (*animus*), he leads the development of the individual; but he is equally the one most immediately threatened (though the witch is planning to also eat Gretel), when the path toward individuation demands an active reappraisal of the earliest mother-child period. Less directly threatened, the feeling aspect of the soul (Gretel, *anima*) is that which can prevent the destruction of the barely emancipated individual (Hansel-Gretel). In numerous other fairy tales the brother-sister theme refers also to the harmonious relationship of *animus* and *anima* (to use Jung's terminology), or (to use less technical terms) to the more intellectual, ego-aspect and the more feeling, emotional aspect of the human being. In the story of *Little Brother and Sister* (Grimms' tales), for example, we find several analogies with *Hansel and Gretel.* The two are rejected from home by the bad mother or stepmother. The little brother succumbs to her power and becomes a deer, while the sister succumbs to that which almost killed Gretel, namely suffocation by heat. However, eventually she resurrects and with that the bad mother comes to an end and the brother is freed. In the form of a modest fairy tale we see here pictured the themes we also find in sagas and dramas, such as Amor and Psyche, Faust and Gretchen, Orpheus and Eurydice, Dante and Beatrice, to name but a few.

Digressing just for a moment, we may ask ourselves whether these pictorial representations of the two aspects of the soul (*animus* and *anima,* intellectual and emotional life, sometimes also referred to as spirit and soul) are symbols, metaphors, fantasies or abstractions. If we try to be completely unbiased, however, we come to the conclusion that these images often portray reality better than most of our more abstract, natural-scientific, psychiatric concepts to which we have grown more accustomed nowadays. In fact, I would say that Hansel and Gretel and other beings in the story portray as accurately as possible, in a language which is adapted to the physical world, something which is not primarily physical. We have grown to accept phrases such as "conflict between ego and superego," "id-forces emerging from the unconscious," "introjection of the mother image," "multiple personality" and others, as if they described realities. They have become more familiar to us than witches and dwarfs, so that we do not realize that, in many ways, they are far more abstract and theoretical constructs than our fairy tale images which have the decided advantage of showing the richness, colorfulness and depth of various aspects of our personality.

But let us look at our story from still another vantage point which need not conflict with what we discussed so far. Returning to the three white birds which we encountered in the narrative of *Hansel and Gretel,* let me elaborate upon the so-called subjectivistic view which holds that the main objects of the story represent various facets, parts and problems of *one* individual. We then can equate not only the dove on the chimney of the parent's home with the snow-white bird which sets down on the roof of the witch's house; we can also see Hansel and Gretel's and the witch's house as one and the same, both located near the wood. However, when the children were abandoned the first time in the forest, the pebbles led them back to the home which they remembered; the second time their home appeared changed, bewitched. As the human spirit and soul are emancipating themselves from the all-protective, good mother, they come into direct contact with the material world full of frustrations which is experienced as a bad mother. And while this materialistic mother feeds the spirit (Hansel) only for its own selfish end, it keeps it captive; and the soul (Gretel) hungers and gets only potato peels (*Erdapfel* = earth apples): an excellent description of the soul's starvation, because of the exclusively materialistic, one-sidedly intellectual nourishment. But in his attempt to find the way back home Hansel has been feeding the birds by sacrificing his own bread; now, in this predicament, the white birds lead the children through and out of the bewitched forest. The bird is beyond the power of the hardened old woman's witchcraft, and may be viewed as that part of our soul and spirit which transcends the interaction of our biological nature with the environment.

Such a transcending aspect of the human being can be compared with the concept of a "nonacquired ego-function," discussed by Jung,[87] Ferreira[47] and others. Psychiatry, progressing on the "natural-scientific path through the wilderness" begins to recognize that the ego cannot be conceived of solely as an "intersection of various psychic activities" (Bleuler[11]), or as a complex of metamorphosed id-forces. According to Freud these instinctual forces are transformed into ego-forces because of the necessity of achieving a compromise, a balance, between the demands of the social or parental environment and the demands of the biological drives. To my way of thinking, the white bird is a much more meaningful description of this nonacquired ego-function, of this untouchable aspect of the ego. It may not always be visible in the bewitched forest, but it can come to our aid when we are completely lost. (Analogous events in tales mentioned in this book are the arrival of the eagles in critical situations in Tolkien's *Trilogy*[175] and the arrival of the hawk at the decisive moment in Goethe's *Fairy Tale*.[67]) This white bird which sets itself upon the witch's gingerbread house is the heavenly child, spiritual like the wind. It disturbs the materialistic witch who inquires as to who is shaking her house, and Hansel replies: "The wind, the wind, the heavenly child!"

In the end, the psychoanalytic, natural-scientific view may find itself in harmony with the view of the narrator of the fairy tale who created his picture through an intuitive insight into the drama of the human being. And by finding the way back to this more alive, concrete picture of the human individual we actually follow the paths of Hansel and Gretel who, bewildered by the material reality of the world and frustrated by it, found themselves first in a bewitched world. But this bewitched material world, this witch-mother, is not all negative. It yields treasures which will be most valuable when the white bird, grown now to a white duck,* leads the children back to their original home.

With this we recognize a very different slant in the meaning of the story. Not only does it refer to the small child's vicissitudes in coping with the material world, but it refers more generally to the drama of the modern human being who has to cope with the problem of material existence and who has to find his way back to his real home which is in the spiritual realm. To what is truly human in us, to speak with Goethe, all that is perishable, all that is material, is but a parable, a symbol ("*Alles Vergängliche—ist nur ein Gleichnis*"), and the unattainable is attained only in the realm of the spirit ("*Das Unzulängliche, hier wird's Erreichnis*"). This is the ultimate conclusion Faust reaches when, after his death, he enters a spiritual world (Goethe, *Faust II*).[54]

The passage through the materialistic, natural-scientific era

*The water which separates a purer, undistorted reality and a reality of untruths, distrusts and hatred, is nowhere more beautifully described than in *Lohengrin*. Across this water the white swan carries the knight of the Holy Grail back and forth from the sublime castle to the turbulent world.[31]

is not useless, senseless or Maya, as many Eastern philosophies would see it. It is part of a necessary human evolution which can be furthered only by a successful passage through the bewitched forest. In subsequent tales we will also recognize themes that refer both to individual and collective human development. Not without justification we think of ontogenesis (individual development) as a recapitulation of phylogenesis (evolution of the species). Equally, we think of earlier stages of human development as primitive forerunners or stepping stones for the later, more advanced or mature stages. However, we can also view them as the grandiose images, blueprints or matrices existing only as subjective hopes or longings. Never completely effective, they reassert themselves again and again until individuals and cultures achieve their conscious integration and actualization. As portrayals of these potentials and goals, myths and fairy tales thus continue to be effective blueprints for our future.

In the child's first acquisition of a conscious self and of a meaningful relationship to his surroundings we find rich challenges for possible later conscious developments. Only because both in early individual development *and* in myths or fairy tales are formulated these grandiose, not yet fulfilled, blueprints, can correspondences be found between the two. Elkin, in a paper dealing with the phenomenology of the development of infantile consciousness, was able to show how the blissful Nirvana or satori experience, the experience of heaven and hell, of the virgin-bambino relationship, of the fight with the dragon, and other important imaginative experiences correspond to critical levels in the development of early consciousness. They are primordial experiences of goals to be eventually attained in the course of our later vicissitudes in the world.[39]

In the stories dealing with the end of the latency period and with adolescence we shall see *dying* as the result of the interaction between the adolescent and stepmother (or matter). In *Hansel and Gretel*-themes the threat is that of being devoured. It represents a much more radical annihilation than death itself. This danger is experienced mostly in the early formative years. We see a quick reference to it also in *Snow White and the Seven Dwarfs* when the witch-queen-stepmother thinks that she is eating at least a part, the heart and the liver, of the seven-year-old beautiful little girl. This threat of being devoured is the central theme in the story of *Little Red Riding Hood* which we shall discuss in the following chapter.

In its first confrontation with the stark realities of our physical existence, the young Ego with its budding emotional and spiritual forces, the *anima* and the *animus,* or Gretel and Hansel, is jeopardized. The frightening material restrictions and deprivations are visualized in the witch who simultaneously portrays a diabolical force that would reabsorb the young ego. Especially in our days we observe a simultaneous threat to our subjectivity by the objectivation required by science and by the trends aiming to avoid the despair of materialism by escaping into ego-less nothingness.

In conclusion we may say that, phenomenologically, the story of *Hansel and Gretel* refers to two events which in our culture are interrelated: (a) the vicissitudes of the young child in his earliest contacts with the material world, and (b) the danger, ever present to all of us, of being swallowed up by a one sided, materialistic, natural-scientific, technological concept of the world which overlooks the primacy of our existential experience.

The terminal sentence: "The story is ended, here goes a mouse; who catches it can make himself a big big fur cap," not only separates the content of the story from our daytime reality by an apparently irrational remark, but seems to refer to the story itself. Who kills the quick life of the spirit can succeed in creating therefrom a cap which shields his head from the heavens above, and he becomes oriented exclusively toward the materialistic aspect of the world. This meaning of the cap will be discussed in greater detail, and its mention here offers a smooth transition to a story related in meaning to the one of *Hansel and Gretel.* A succinct analysis of *Little Red Riding Hood* may further our understanding of the small child.

CHAPTER XIII

LITTLE RED CAP

or Little Red Riding Hood

As a young medical student in Lausanne whenever I was tired of my studies and the manifold frictions of everyday city life I would hike up to the forest of the Signal, a quiet hill stretched out behind the town. And while, a few years later, the eucalyptus-covered Sutro Heights behind the University of California Medical School may not have had all the charm nor the peaceful variety of foliage trees and ferns of the Signal, it afforded equally well an escape into almost complete tranquillity. Here one could forget the shrill sounds of the streetcars and automobiles, and the chatter of people was no longer ever present. Here there was only the scent and welcome shadow of the trees, the gay song of birds and the friendly greetings of the numerous wild flowers. Within a span of ten minutes I had left behind me the noisy everyday reality of San Francisco and entered a new world. There was a refreshing feeling of freedom: one could relax and explore. Time even assumed a different meaning, and one felt at liberty to choose one's own paths. To be sure, I had to return—sometime—to the former world, but I came back to it enriched by the experience of the forest!

Picture for yourself a similarly beautiful forest into which a little girl wanders one day, neatly dressed, with a red cap on her head, and carrying cake and wine for her weak and ailing grandmother who lives in a house under three large oak trees. How different is this wood from the one in which Hansel and Gretel wandered around, or from the one through which Snow White flees to the little home of the dwarfs! It is full of charm, and even when the girl meets the big wolf, he does not appear fearsome, since she does not know what a wicked animal he is.

Little Red Cap is not the rejected, hungry child of poor and selfish parents, barely having a piece of dry bread to her name; she is the nicely dressed girl who, from the abundance of her home and with the blessings, admonitions and protection of her mother, carries food to the grandmother. The forest is not a horrible place with frightening, wild animals, in which one gets lost: the child does not have to mark a path. A good path leads from Little Red Cap's town to grandmother's home, and mother warns the girl not to stray from it, lest she fall and break the glass (of the wine bottle). The mother also admonishes her to greet the grandmother rather than peek immediately into all the corners of the room, since she knows the daughter's readiness to look at the seductive physical world around her.

The wolf meets her on the path in order to tempt her, to point out to her the charms and pleasures of the material surroundings: the pretty flowers, the lovely songs of the birds, and the merry sun rays dancing through the trees. As the wolf speaks to her, the girl lifts her eyes to all the rich beauty around her, convinced that it would be foolish to go on directly to grandmother, and justifies leaving her path by deciding to pick a bouquet of flowers for the dear old woman. While Little Red Cap wanders deeper and deeper into the forest, the wolf runs straight to the grandmother's house, gains entrance by pretending to be the girl, swallows the woman, puts on her clothes, dresses himself in her cap and lays himself in her bed waiting for the young child's arrival.

When comparing the story of Red Cap with that of Hansel and Gretel, we notice that the framework is quite similar: there is (a) a home; (b) a need for a path through the woods; (c) a period of getting away from the path; (d) the children finding a little house in the woods. While in *Hansel and Gretel* the house is inhabited by a cruel, devouring witch who barely pretends to be kindly, Little Red Cap comes to the house of the grandmother in which she finds the disguised wolf. In the story of *Snow White and the Seven Dwarfs* we shall again see a similar basic structure,

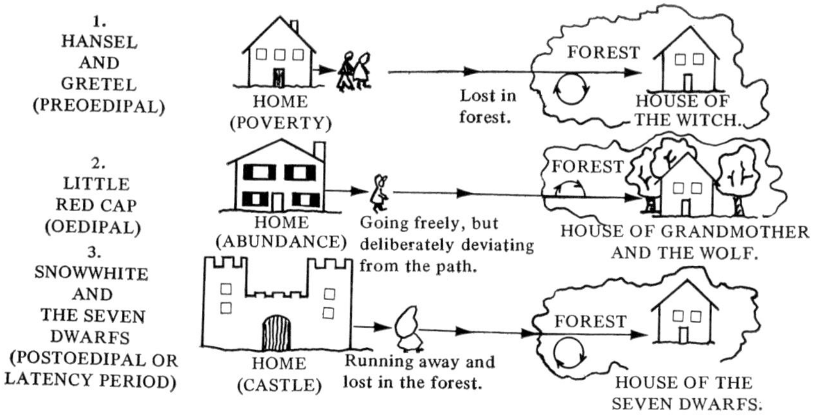

except that the house in the woods is not occupied by an all-bad witch, nor by a bad wolf and a good grandmother, but by seven benign dwarfs, the bad witch-stepmother only making an occasional appearance. In *Hansel and Gretel* the children are pushed out of a simple, poor house; in *Little Red Cap* the girl leaves her nice home willingly, while Snow White has to flee from her palatial home.

House, home, castle and hut also represent the bodily dwelling of the growing individuality. At different times it is experienced as too large or too small, as protective or bewitched, as fitting or foreign. The aim is to acquire an appropriate, homey dwelling.

We view the trials of Little Red Cap as a stage in the early development of the child, and we can find several reasons for placing the story chronologically between these two other fairy tales. We first notice that the little girl is much less frightened by the sensory world around her, that she even ends up reveling in its beauty. The physical environment is rich in gifts which appeal to the senses: cake, wine, flowers, songs and sunshine. The girl is described as a small child, needing careful instructions to stay on the trail and to greet her grandmother. One would ordinarily be inclined to treat a four- or five-year-old child in this way. While she is trusted to walk alone the half-hour-long, familiar footpath to her grandmother's home, she is still too young to help with household tasks such as the baking of the cake (unlike Snow White who has passed her seventh birthday when she becomes a good helper at the home of the seven dwarfs). These hints in regard to Little Red Cap's age find stronger and deeper support in our forthcoming discussion of the oedipal elements in the story.

At first we notice that the ambivalent relationship to the witch-mother described in our study of *Hansel and Gretel* repeats itself here in regard to the grandmother who is seen as kindly, giving, accepting and—when the wolf appears in her guise—as ferocious, hateful, sensual, devouring. In one story the witch, in the other the wolf, threaten to destroy, to devour, the young child. But there is one essential difference: the witch, bad as she may be, has still clearly a supernatural connotation; the wolf is a thoroughly physical being guided by pure greed. Hansel and Gretel shrink away from the frustrating physical world, from its hunger, poverty and voraciousness, as well as from the wild animals in the woods. They risk losing what self-awareness they had developed by returning or regressing to the witch-mother.

With Little Red Cap the situation appears to be almost reversed: now there is a danger that the child will be so infatuated with the world of the senses, that she will willingly though passively deviate from the straight path that leads to the good, giving grandmother. This is also quite different from Snow White's attitude whom we shall see dealing *actively* with the duties the physical world imposes upon the growing child. Little Red Cap passively succumbs to the world of the senses, and when she arrives at grandmother's home, only the physical sense organs of the individual in the bed are noticed by her:

> "Oh, grandmother, what big *ears* you have!"
> "The better to hear you with . . . ."
> "Oh, grandmother, what big *eyes* you have!"
> "The better to see you with . . . ."
> "Oh, grandmother, what large *hands* you have!"
> "The better to grab you . . . ."
> "Oh, grandmother, what a horrible *mouth* you have!"
> "The better to eat you with!"

We experience here a crescendo of the sensory functions, from hearing to seeing to touching to tasting, which ultimately leads to the disappearance of the girl, including her red cap, inside the bad wolf who swallows her. The passive reveling in the world of physical sensations becomes just as dangerous to the young human individuality, as the regression to the witch-mother. In the story of *Snow White and the Seven Dwarfs* we shall encounter a third equally deadly threat to the ego that approaches adolescence. It becomes *actively* involved with the chores of this world and attempts to deal constructively rather than by repression with the intensified physical longings.

In *Hansel and Gretel* the children are at the mercy of a rejecting mother and a seemingly weak father. Their first contact with the frustrating realities of life leaves them lost and confused. But as they regress to the witch-mother, she no longer is the sweet, protective, spiritual mother, but a cannibalistic monster, since she threatens their young self-awareness with destruction. Only now does Gretel rebel and, successful, the children carry the witch's treasures home, where they start a happier existence.

It appears that the story of *Little Red Cap* starts, as far as the child's development is concerned, where the story of *Hansel and Gretel* finishes. This is borne out even by the odd remark about the fur cap at the end of the latter story. The red cap is sent to the child, now living happily at home, by the grandmother. We shall explain in a later chapter that the cap in various motifs and rituals represents the shielding off of direct intuitive experiencing, of "inspiration from heaven" in favor of strengthening the ego by the individual's attention upon the everyday physical world. Furthermore, the cap is the color of blood, "the very special juice" required by the devil Mephistopheles for a signature when he attempts to trap the human soul. In departing from the link or direct path to the "Great Mother" or grandmother, the soul seeking greater independence is at first threatened by the wolf (symbolizing a diabolical, mephistophelian influence) as soon as it becomes fascinated with the sensory pleasures of this earth. It begins to fail in the attempt to experience its uniqueness between its origin in chaos and the powerful physical surroundings confronting it. This time an outside force, the huntsman, has to come to the rescue.

Note however, that the grandmother who had sent the red cap to Little Red Cap also wears a cap which the wolf later puts on. This may allude to a partial identification, to a similarity between Red Cap, the grandmother and the witch-wolf-grandmother. One may see here a parallel with what happened to Hansel and Gretel. After burning the witch, they obtain from her home something that is precious for their development.

In contrast to Erich Fromm's opinion we see in the huntsman a strong father image.[50] His careful and intelligent concern helps to deliver the girl and grandmother from the wolf's stomach. The child's red cap is the very first to appear through the opening, as if to indicate the salvation of the strong young ego. The grandmother, the huntsman and the girl thus wind up as a happy threesome. The hunter gets the wolf's skin, the grandmother the strengthening wine and cake, and Little Red Cap gains the inner conviction that she will never again deviate from the path in the woods, if mother prohibits it.

As you see, the story takes on a moralistic coloring at the end. Some simple didactic intentions such as "See, if you do not obey your mother, something terrible is likely to happen to you!" may well have helped to shape the tale. However, it would be an unfortunate mistake to overlook, because of this moralistic patina, the deeper meanings of Little Red Cap's achievement. Just as Hansel and Gretel gained the pearls and precious stones after overcoming the witch, our girl re-establishes a valuable communication with the mother against whom she rebelled. She recognized that there *is* wisdom in the good mother's teachings and that the conscious, free, willing acceptance of this wisdom will help her in her further development. Deviating from the path, in defiance of mother, of the superego, was temporarily quite essential for the establishment of the girl's young ego. Not only does she thus learn to accept and appreciate beauty independently, but by deviating from the path she also acquires the ability to gather *her own* gift (the flowers) to share with others. Added to the ones mother gave her (the inherited gifts), this gift is offered entirely on her own initiative. Thus is introduced the theme of sharing, which is again stressed at the end of the story and which is an essential characteristic of the successful solution of the oedipal conflict.

While Erich Fromm* also relates the story of Red Cap to the Oedipus myth, he sees in it the opposite outcome, namely the ultimate victory of the matriarchal principle. I cannot, however, understand how he ends up describing the huntsman as a "conventional father-figure without real weight." Is the huntsman not the one who liberates the women and who carries off the skin of the wolf! The oedipal theme can be seen reflected throughout the narrative: the girl rebels against mother and meets the seductive wolf who points to exclusively sensory pleasures; but this becomes dangerous, as the great-mother or grandmother, the one who can carry human beings in her abdomen, appears now with the wolf's characteristics. True enough, for a while the woman, the early-mother figure, appears more powerful than the libidinous male. Only later, when the man appears in the shape of a human being, considerate, forceful and helpful, this threatening bisexual aspect of mother is destroyed and the grandmother, the child and the huntsman-father form a harmonious threesome. The huntsman who carries off the wolf's skin combines the human and sexual aspects of the male without being threatening. He shows that instead of being driven by greed and violence he has control over his impulses. Instead of using the all destructive gun to

*E. Fromm[50] offers a clever interpretation of the wolf's swallowing the grandmother and the girl. He feels that the wolf is representing the man who suffers from "pregnancy envy" and who tries to play the role of the woman. However, the greedy wolf, naturally, fails and ends up with a belly full of stones which symbolize sterility. He also sees the wolf's appetite as sexual hunger and he feels that the story shows the woman's antagonism against men and sex, causing her to see the sexual act as a cannibalistic attack. Finally, by viewing the redness of the cap as symbolic of the blood of menstruation, he combines the oedipal meaning of the story with the problem of beginning adolescence, when the earlier oedipal problems are reactivated for a short time. By sticking to a strict symbolism which "can be understood without difficulty," Fromm weakens the significance of the story. Yet, in spite of the one-sidedness and narrowness of the viewpoint, his interpretation does have some validity. For a while, in fact, the wolf-grandmother, the maternal principle, appears to be victorious; but it finally yields to the huntsman.

kill the wolf, which would also have harmed Red Cap and the grandmother, he wisely and selectively uses his ability to be aggressive by opening the wolf's abdomen with a pair of scissors.

But the witch, the wolf-mother, or the bad mother never dies completely. We shall have glimpses of her again in the stepmother-queen of *Snow White,* in Turandot's ancestor Lio-u-ling, in the bad fairy of *Briar Rose,* etc. She is a seemingly negative force that indirectly promotes human growth.

The story of *Little Red Cap,* like that of *Hansel and Gretel,* can be viewed not only as a portrayal of stages in the development of the individual child, but also as a description of a stage in the historical evolution of human consciousness. The grandmother, or great mother, becomes the original mother out of whom all is born, the Nordic *Edda,*[169] the Finnish Ilmatar,[123] the Sumerian Thiamat,[52] the Egyptian Isis, the Germanic deity in the shrine under the tree sacred oaks, or the Indian Kali, to whom the human being used to return regularly to offer sacrifices and to gain spiritual strength. Having the potential of creating and of devouring, this revered ancestor has endowed the human soul with the ability to develop his sense of individuality, his ego, in his contact with the physical world.

In the story of Red Cap she has sent him the red cap which shields his head from the stars and heavens and focuses his attention upon the things of this earth. But these things can become overwhelming temptations. When the human being tries to find himself as part of the physical world, when he relinquishes his spiritual origin and looks into his own depth, he enters a mysterious forest, deviates from the path and discovers instead of the great mother the ferocious animal, all sensual and gluttonous. Dante, for example, lost in the dark forest, having wandered from the correct path, encounters three wild animals, and the wise poet-philosopher Virgil must become his guide, leading him through hell and purgatory to the entrance of paradise. Like Dante, looking into the depths of our souls, we find at first only cruelty and lust in the place of ancestral wisdom.

Sarro[153] rightly points out that the Oedipus myth may have a meaning beyond Freud's "incest-conflict" and Fromm's[50] "authority conflict"; that it may point to man's willingness to "quit the shelter into which he has settled his life and to sacrifice an illusion for a quest for a truth which can be . . . inhospitable." Oedipus' first quest for knowledge, when he confronts the riddle of the sphinx (a being half woman and half lion, daughter of a serpent-shaped nymph), was crowned with success. His second quest, when he persisted in finding out the truth about himself and his mother-wife Jocasta, led to long hardships. Oedipus and the man-eating sphynx, Perseus' victory against the shark-monster which is about to devour Andromeda and Saint George's fight with the dragon represent the ordeals and victories of a maturing ego. The *earthworm* (or dragon) who periodically demands a victim already shows in his name the threat of destruction of the human being by the seductive power of the physical senses which tend to tie him permanently to the earth. Yet this *earthworm* is but another, opposite aspect of the original great mother.

One could characterize Western culture as looking at the physical world as something worthwhile (not as nothingness or maya), and as an attempt ultimately to find a place where the individual is in harmony with his spiritual origin and physical surroundings. Though the *earthworm,* the wolf and the shark-monster are overcome, the victor carries off something that enriches him, be it the fur of the wolf or the golden fleece guarded by the dragon.* The aim is to be able to face the material world without shying back and being consumed by the transcendental, spiritual world, and without being absorbed by the earth. The magnificent myths of *Daedalus and Icarus* flying between heaven and earth on their self-made wings, or of Phaëthon leading the sun wagon across the sky beautifully show the aims and the dangers of human evolution. Both Icarus and Phaëthon deviate from the path, coming alternately too close to heaven and too close to earth; and therefore they perish.

While in *Hansel and Gretel* the earth is dangerous because

*In the myth of Jason, the conquest of the golden fleece was to give him a kingdom as reward. However, Jason's ruthless cruelty made him lose the kingdom. Giving in to forbidden sexual desires led to his destruction. The woman whom he loved and who loved him and who helped him to get the fleece became a horrible witch who engineered his and his children's deaths and then returned through the air to the faraway land from which she came.[158]

the children shy away from it and might be consumed by the fire of the supernatural witch, the earth becomes a peril in *Little Red Cap* because it threatens to absorb the individual completely. We are seeing repeatedly that the devilish forces, the witches, have two aspects (one with supernatural, one with physical connotations). While opposite in some ways, these two aspects cooperate in leading the human being away from its true mission, from the correct path. In order to achieve the true goal of Western culture, in order to develop our ego in unison with a mature acceptance of both spiritual and material values, we cannot be arbitrary or impulsive, but we have to follow a path even though we can achieve this only through erring and through being rescued. We must develop self-control, self-discipline, patience and courage. Without learning to commit himself to a meaningful path, the seeker of the truth may only find the seductive wolf and be swallowed by him.

Unfortunately, the quiet walks through a wood which an individual sought in order to find or restore himself have been almost completely supplanted by fast car rides aiming to lose one's self. We are swallowed up by the weekend traffic, by social obligations, by economic competitiveness, by advertisements, etc. We already seem to be in the wolf's stomach as we tread willfully our own path, often guided only by sensory pleasures and stimuli. The latter still offer an ongoing challenge to strengthen our ego, yet they tend to overwhelm it. Then, instead of seeking quiet recollection, all too many rush blindly in the opposite direction, hoping to overcompensate the dreadful Western influences by losing their identity in some fashionable Oriental cult that offers Nirvana.

Let me finish this chapter with a few additional verses of the Italian poet Leopardi—verses of which I would often think on my own walks to the Signal and to the Sutro Forest. (Incidentally, this forest is presently being razed for more buildings and for a gigantic television tower.) Thus he writes of the wooded hill to which he escaped when the narrowness of his little home town Recanati and the shallow pettiness of his family became too oppressive:

Sempre caro mi fu quest'ermo colle
E questa siepe che da tanta parte
Dell ultimo orizzonte il guardo esclude.
Ma sedendo e mirando, interminati
Spazi di là da quella, e sovrumani
Silenzi, e profondissima quiete
Io nel pensier mi fingo; ove per poco
Il cuor non si spaura. E come il vento
Odo stormir tra queste piante, io quello
Infinito silenzio a questa voce
Vo comprarando: e mi sovvien
l'eterno . . . .[106]

I always loved this solitary hill,
This hedge as well, which takes so large
a share
Of the far flung horizon from my view.
But seated here, in contemplation lost,
My thought discovers vaster space beyond,
Supernal silence and unfathomed peace;
Almost I am afraid; then, since I hear
The murmur of the wind among the leaves,
I match that infinite calm unto this sound
And with my mind embrace eternity . . . .[105]

—GIACOMO LEOPARDI, *L'Infinito* (1819)

CHAPTER XIV

THE LATENCY PERIOD IN THE FAIRY TALE; SNOW WHITE AND THE SEVEN DWARFS

THE STORY OF THE INFINITELY BEAUTIFUL GIRL whose early deceased mother had wished for a child as white as snow, as red as blood and as black as ebony, the story of Snow White who grew up with the seven dwarfs beyond the seven mountains, has become and has remained one of the most treasured and heart-warming fairy tales. This suggests that we not only appreciate the colorful fantasy, the fine artistic structure and the healthy moral aspects of the story, but that we also respond more or less unwittingly, to deep wisdoms hidden in the tale, hidden by our predominantly natural-scientific orientation toward the world.

Few stories distinguish quite as neatly as this one—in fairy tale fashion—between the three periods of childhood development (formative years, latency period, adolescence), while placing the major emphasis on the latency phase.

The tale begins with a very brief description of the first seven or early formative years of Snow White. The opening scene, in midwinter, can awaken in us the feeling of anticipation of Christmas. The mother-queen, hoping for a child, longingly looks through the window, gazing upon the snowy landscape. But after the birth of Snow White, the good, quasi-virginal mother passes away, and shortly we see in her place the cruel, heartless, witch-like and coldly beautiful step-mother. However, the vicissitudes between the child of one to seven years and the devouring witch-mother that are so splendidly narrated in such stories as *Hansel and Gretel* or *Little Red Riding Hood,* are totally ignored. Instead we find here the controversy between the cruel, jealous and rejecting stepmother and Snow White *after* the latter has reached her seventh year. In anticipation of some later comments, let me digress here in order to point out that this bad mother can be viewed in at least two ways. Analytically, we can see in her the negative aspects of the various ambivalent relations between the mother and the small child (see previous chapters). Phenomenologically, we may recognize in her a personality given entirely to the pleasures and beauty of the material world and threatening to destroy the spiritual life and beauty of the still ethereal small child who is about to seek her place in the world around her.

Oedipal and pre-oedipal conflicts with the mother are never fully resolved during the early formative years. When the child becomes somewhat more independent from his immediate family in the early years of grammar school, the previous conflicts tend to be reactivated in the form of various comparisons between parent and child. During the formative years the child's individuality is largely submerged under that of the parent; the mother's aura, so to speak, surrrounds the child; and even the little girl's beauty does not yet carry the stamp of individuality which could enter it into clear competition with mother's looks. However, while the mother-child conflict threatens to flare up in a new form around the seventh year, it is now coped with by means of forceful repression.

The fairy tale often depicts this repression as separation in space from the home, from the castle, from the parents. In our story the acute danger is signalized to the stepmother by the mirror, to the child by the hunter who, at the request of the queen, threatens to kill Snow White. It is interesting to delve into the meaning of this mirror at some length,* comparing it to analogous features in other tales such as Wilde's *The Picture of Dorian Gray,* Strauss' *The Woman Without a Shadow,*[31] or

*See Chapter XXIV dealing more broadly with the symbolism of reflection.

Hauff's *Stone Heart.*[62] We then see that the dialogue with the mirror can represent an attempt of the individual who has lost contact with true spiritual and moral values to face the truth or the voice of the conscience. In Jungian terms he is challenged to face his shadow. Just as Dorian Gray has to return to the attic again and again to see his true picture, and just as Hauff's hero has to return to the cave of the evil one to see his flesh heart tick, so is the queen repeatedly drawn toward the mirror to ask: "Who is the most beautiful in the whole country?" She attempts to suppress the answer which she cannot bear, by sending her hunter to kill Snow White. He, however, takes pity on the girl and instead brings back to the cruel queen the lung and liver of a deer.

It is easy to recognize in this last scene an echo of the earlier oedipal triangle, with the father figure (hunter) in a conflicting situation between the young girl and his wife (stepmother). The queen eats the lung and liver, and Snow White escapes death and oral incorporation, by fleeing through the dark forests and across the seven mountains.

The process of repression in the girl who barely has turned seven is marvelously described by the story pointing out Snow White's great fear of the wild animals which, however, cannot harm her any longer. With her arrival in the evening at the little house of the dwarfs, the process of repression seems to be successfully completed. The beds covered with white linen, the tasty food on the table, and the daintiness of it all may remind us of the small gingerbread house in *Hansel and Gretel.* There, however, the arrival after wandering three days in the dense forest represents a return, a *regression* to an early, oral stage, where the witch-mother manifests herself as feeding, controlling and devouring. In our present story the witch-mother is now seven mountains away. Instead of *regression* we deal with a process of pushing threatening things away into the distance or unconscious, namely *repression.* The role of the parents is then taken on—to a certain extent—by the dwarfs who are kindly, warm and willing to share.

In the image of the seven mountains an allusion or relatedness to the Apocalypse can be seen. In the Revelation of Saint John the *Whore Babylon* sits on seven mountains which also indicate a separation of two worlds: a onesidedly material world symbolized by Babylon that eventually disappears in the fiery depths, and a new world to come symbolized by the heavenly Jerusalem, the bride that descends from above (Rev. 17:9).

The theme of *sharing* is beautifully developed in the story. Snow White shows her ability and readiness to share as soon as she arrives, hungry and tired, at the little house to which the dwarfs have not yet returned from their daily work. Not wishing to deprive any one of too much, she eats just a little from each of the seven plates and drinks just a drop from each glass (how different from Hansel and Gretel who, rather disrespectfully, start eating the gingerbread house). When the dwarfs come home they are surprised to find Snow White in the one little bed which fits her; and they show *their* desire to share by letting the dwarf who lost his bed sleep with each companion for one hour, until daylight. Finally, the dwarfs and Snow White share with each other, when the former offer the girl full hospitality in return for her cooking, sewing and cleaning.

The ability to share willingly and happily is a result of the harmonious completion of the seven formative years, during which the child learns to accept and respect the rights of others and the relationships between them. During the latency period this acquisition is put to a test when the children are given the opportunity to acquaint themselves with the world around them and to develop whatever skills may be necessary to be able to live independently and self-sufficiently. While for Snow White these skills consisted in taking care of a household, for our children they consist mostly in acquiring that knowledge in the elementary schools which later will enable them to be on their own. During the day they are separated from the parents who still support them; yet at night the family is together and the child is protected. The elders offer advice and admonitions for the daytime, when the child must learn to cope alone with various temptations.

The first period of life can be characterized as the, often stormy, process of recognizing one's self as a *human being* among other *human beings* who share and with whom we have to learn to share. The latency period then can be seen as a somewhat quieter process of growth, during which we become acquainted with the material world around us. We learn to deal with it intelligently and to our advantage, without becoming a slave to it, while practicing and refining our previously gained ability to share. The fact that many of our biologic and psychologic drives have not yet reached their adolescent intensity and that repression keeps them under fair control, supports this learning process. Snow White's primary interest in the chores connected with our everyday material existence is underscored by the work of the dwarfs who mine iron ore and gold in the mountains. This viewpoint recognizes the dwarfs as an aspect of the growing young lady. Whereas the pearls and jewels in the tale of *Hansel and Gretel* would represent the precious heritage which we salvage from our earliest, celestial mother, the gold and ore symbolize what we ourselves can gain in active relationship with the mother-earth.

There are many ways to view the significance of the seven small men. While in some fairy tales the dwarf is maleficent (*Snow White and Rose Red*), in others half benevolent and half harmful (*Rumpelstilzchen*), we find the dwarfs in our story to be thoroughly helpful spirits, hidden in the mountains in the daytime, close to Snow White at night. We can compare them to processes, images and experiences during sleep. They can be seen as subconscious entities or forces which the soul becomes aware of during the night, and whose influence wanes when the preadolescent is interested in the diurnal material surroundings. They are pictured as guiding spirits who cherish the live spiritual beauty of the child, who are strongly integrated in the mineral world, who warn the child against succumbing to the seductiveness of material things and who come to the child mostly at night. They appear to her when she is seven and return to her every night until she is fourteen. Similarly, even today the nightly offering of suitable fairy tales and myths provide forces that mitigate the one-sided rationalistic and materialistic influences upon the preadolescent child.

The temptations of the physical world find their strongest ally in the disguised stepmother whom Snow White again and again does not recognize. She is able to find the girl across the seven mountains, and by offering external material devices to augment beauty, she attempts to destroy Snow White's inner, ethereal beauty. The corruption by the stepmother penetrates ever deeper. The comb referring to the head poisons the thinking, the narrow vest tied too strongly around the chest strangles the finest emotions, while the poisoned bite from the apple permanently paralyzes the actions or the will-impulses, when it reaches the stomach. Twice the force of the dwarfs who return at night to find Snow White overcome is strong enough to counteract these attempts. But when, on the third try, the stepmother succeeds in making the young lady eat from the poisoned apple, Snow White dies and the dwarfs cannot revive her. They must resign themselves to bed her in a glass casket, to place it on top of a mountain, to stand watch over it and mourn.

In terms of playing a role in the decision as to who is the most beautiful, the apple reminds us of the one Paris gave to Venus on the mountain of Ida; in terms of causing loss of spirituality in favor of material knowledge, it makes us think of the seduction of Adam and Eve by the serpent. The forbidden fruit carries two promises both of which imply the danger of losing the awareness of what formerly seemed spiritual realities. One is the promise of intellectual maturation and rational knowledge, while the other is that of sexual maturation and awareness of erotic pleasure. The red of the apple from which Snow White eats is no longer the red of pure, unselfish love; such were the blood drops of her longing mother which fell into the white snow outside the black-framed window, when the queen stung herself with her sewing needle, or such were the cheeks of the young, innocent cheerful girl. It is the redness of poison, desire and—just as in the *Sleeping Beauty* stories—of menstruation. The red and white halves of the apple do not represent the harmony for which Snow White's mother longed, but only a treacherous union of the deceitful red and the indifferent, ice cold white. The austere, threatening *black* spectre of death is contained in them. One-sided sexuality and one-sided intellectualism will deaden the spirit of the human being.

White, red and black can be viewed as referring to spirit, soul and body. The ideal is the eventual integration of the three.

Where this is lacking, dangerous events take place that call for such a harmonious integration. Thus we see in the Apocalypse (6:1-6) three riders appear on a white, a red and a black horse. The original, pure, non-reflective, intuitional thinking yields to a onesided, egoistic type of thought that leads to strife but is necessary for the development of consciousness. This is followed by the rider on the black steed carrying a balance referring to the deadliness of a onesidedly materialistic, quantitative orientation of the human being.

The reawakening or harmonization of the soul of the red, white and black Snow White is made possible only with the arrival of the prince who gains the hand of the beautiful girl not through his wealth or power, but by convincing the dwarfs that he can no longer live without her.

In abstract psychological terms we might describe the dwarfs as supporting, helpful superego forces. Contrary to the stepmother who represents the inhibiting, punitive, cruel, rigid aspect of the superego, they are in harmony with the early ego of the child. While necessary and useful during the latency period, they are reduced to almost helpless guardians during Snow White's deathlike sleep, and finally they are willing to withdraw in favor of a higher ego as soon as the right prince arrives.

Just as in *Sleeping Beauty* or in *Briar Rose,* the latency period of the girl ends with death. Our story emphasizes this by thrice repeating that Snow White *was* dead: "No breath came from her mouth"; "She was dead"; "The good child was dead and stayed dead." Instead of the sleep of Briar Rose lasting one hundred years, we have here "the very long time" Snow White was in the glass casket. The prince who finally revives her is not just representing the birth of the mature ego at the end of adolescence, nor is he just portraying the highest expression of a young man's love for a woman. He symbolizes both. In the *Sleeping Beauty* fairy tales which primarily center on the "hundred years of deathlike sleep" of adolescence, this double role of the arrival of the prince is expressed most beautifully: The correct timing of the blossoming of the rose bushes around the sleep-filled castle, the awakening of the princess and the arrival of the right prince illustrate the fact that only a harmonious evolution of inner and outer events can lead to the magnificent awakening of a mature individuality capable of true love. Macrocosmic and microcosmic events are seen as synchronized.[162]

The reawakening of Snow White and the arrival of the prince are heralded by the visit to the casket of the reddish-brown owl, symbol of the Greek goddess Athena; the black raven, friend of the Nordic god Odin; and thirdly the white dove, symbol of the Holy Spirit. These three birds which have been seen as the expressions of consciousness, wisdom and love seem to bring from the heavens something that will aid the spiritual growth and the eventual awakening of the beauty who "died" at the end of the latency period because of the stepmother's poisoned apple. The material world we have to familiarize ourselves with during the years of the latency period is often but a stepmother; during these years our beliefs in Santa Claus, in an Easter Bunny, in a good fairy and many other previous "illusions" (or masks of realities only mediately accessible) come to nothing. Yet with the ressurrection of Snow White and her marriage to the prince the stepmother-aspect of the material world comes to its ultimate destruction; the bad queen must dance in the red hot metal shoes until she dies. The rigidity of a soulless material world and of the cruel, negative aspects of the witchlike early superego seem both to find their exponent in this stepmother.

Finally, it is not too difficult to sense in the Snow White story reverberations of basic Christian motifs. The various stages of the tale parallel the Christian events between the pre-Christmas season and Easter. We may experience the joyful, anticipating atmosphere of the Advent period in the scene of the virginal queen hoping for her child while looking out into the wintry countryside; then comes the birth of the beautiful, pure, good, loving child (Christmas). The stormy, sometimes gay, sometimes turbulent, irresponsible pre-Lenten period (early formative years) is followed by the more sober, down-to-earth Lenten period (latency period) leading to the passion on Good Friday (corresponding to Snow White's death); finally we see the grave (or the casket on the mountain, with the guardians and the glorious resurrection on Easter.[124]

In a way, each child renews the course of humanity, losing

his early paradise. Gradually overcome by the deadening rigidity of material knowledge and temptations during the latency period, the child (under favorable circumstances) develops during adolescence those forces which eventually lead to the awakening of a mature ego and to the free acceptance of true spiritual values. We can see the mature ego as thought grown into self-reflection or consciousness, feelings grown into the capacity for deep love, and will becoming the source of wisdom. We can easily see that this has many implications as far as our responsibilities as parents, as psychotherapists and as human beings are concerned.

Very briefly, I wish to add here a comment in regard to Grimms' story of *The Wolf and the Seven Little Goats.* This is a fable-fairy tale which also seems to refer principally to the latency period. Here the seven goats can be viewed as representing the first seven years of life, so that the littlest, seventh goat portrays the seventh, youngest year. As in the above Snow White story, we find at the outset a separation of the parent (mother) from the children (in the seventh year). The seven goats are asked to care for themselves in the daytime during the parent's absence; but in spite of mother's warnings they succumb (the third time) to the disguised, treacherous wolf. He corresponds in many ways to the above stepmother and represents materialism whose seductiveness is beautifully portrayed by his white paw and his falsetto voice, and which, in the end, moves to its own destruction. This self-destruction of materialism is excellently portrayed by the wolf's stomach full of stones which leaves him thirsty and which leads him to the well into which he falls, drawn by his own greed and heaviness, landing deep within the earth. The wolf ends up with a belly full of stones because, in spite of his cleverness, he has not been able to swallow all the goats. The youngest goat succeeds in hiding in the big clock. The clock may be viewed here as representing the orderly, protective, helpful aspect of the superego, somewhat analogous to the protective seven dwarfs. And so the seventh little goat, quick and clever, and protected by the clock, becomes the savior of his six siblings.

Summarizing we may conclude that the story of *Snow White*

and the Seven Dwarfs is a fairy tale of which the central theme represents the latency period of childhood development. At the age of seven Snow White has to leave her home and lives with the seven dwarfs until she is about fourteen or fifteen. The intense instinctual urges and conflicts of the early, formative years have been partly resolved, partly relegated to the unconscious. Now the child, less deeply involved with the parents, gets to know the world about her and to learn the performance of tasks which later will enable her to become truly independent. While Snow White becomes a little housemother for the dwarfs, the conflicts with the witch-like stepmother still flare up occasionally, reaching once more a critical point with the beginning of adolescence, when the young lady almost succumbs to the poisoned apple. We have tried to see from different viewpoints the implications of some of the events in this beautiful fairy tale, finally adding a brief comparison with the story of *The Wolf and the Seven Little Goats.*

Because it represents analogous problems of the preadolescent boy, I am inserting here a chapter dealing with the Grimms' tale of *The Juniper Tree.* At the same time this tale lends itself well for discussing the meaning of seemingly atrocious cruelty in fairy tales and myths.

CHAPTER XV

THE JUNIPER TREE

Vom Machandelboum

THE GRIMMS' TALE of *The Juniper Tree*[58] can be adduced as the best evidence for the argument that many fairy tales are an overly sadistic fare for children and must, therefore, either be withheld from them or be carefully expurgated.

The story begins in a perfectly peaceful, beautiful wintry setting. We see a young wife standing under a juniper tree near her home and paring an apple for herself. She cuts herself, red drops fall into the white snow as she wishes for a child as red as blood and as white as snow; and her wish is granted. But then the tale produces in rapid succession dramatic and seemingly cruel images until an extreme peak is reached.

The mother's death in childbirth is made somewhat easier by her joy over her newborn son. However, the latter is scorned and slapped around by a mean stepmother. Eventually jealousy and rage take complete possession of this woman. She decapitates the young boy, treacherously shifting the blame and guilt for the crime upon her own small daughter, Magdalen. Thus Magdalen, terrified and desperate, becomes only too willing to side and cooperate with her monstrous mother. Together they chop up the boy's body, making black puddings out of the pieces. When the unsuspecting father returns home, he devours all of them greedily, throwing the bones under the table.

Then follows a brief, harmonious episode, after Magdalen—profoundly saddened by all that happened—places her half-brother's bones, wrapped in her silken handkerchief, on his mother's grave under the juniper tree. Handkerchief and bones metamorphose into a miraculous, colorful bird. He emerges from the foliage of the tree that—for a moment—has the semblance of burning. Suddenly Magdalen feels consoled and absolved.

The tale now switches to a melancholic, yet expectant and hopeful note, as the marvelous bird travels to the goldsmith's, to the shoemaker's and to the miller's workshops, singing repeatedly and beautifully the tale of his gruesome fate. This leads to another, rapidly reached, dramatic peak when the bird returns to the front of his family's home, carrying the gifts of the craftsmen: a golden chain, slippers and a millstone. The stepmother, hearing his song, is internally consumed by all the tortures of hell before she is squashed, annihilated and burned when the giant millstone is dropped upon her. With her death the miraculous bird regains his human form; father, Magdalen and boy can now return happily and peacefully into their home in order to share their meal.

What may appear to us, initially, as intolerably sadistic events *always* transcend the ordinary, common-sense implications of physical suffering and aggression. Thus they portray deep meanings, intuitively perceived by the original narrators—meanings for which we no longer have all the required *experiential* capacity.

Let us, for example, focus upon the theme of the hero who is cut up into pieces (which are either scattered across the land, or eaten). This theme is found in many parts of the earth and in various epochs. Among them are Osiris,[15] Pelops (son of Tantalos),[57] Orpheus,[57] Ymir (the giant in the *Edda*),[123,169] Lemminkainen (in the Finnish epos),[91] the sons of Nidhod (in the *Wieland* saga)[179] and the uroboric serpent in Goethe's *The Fairy Tale*.[67,146] We can recognize more and more that this theme refers to the fragmentation of what once was a harmoniously functioning totality, caused by an overemphasis of the objectifying intellect or of abstract thinking. Tantalos' audacious cleverness leads him to cut up his own son whom he then offers defiantly to the gods for dinner. Only Demeter, the goddess of the earth lacks the unifying vision of her immortal companions and is temporarily deceived; and while Pelops is reborn more beautiful, the fate of Tantalos can be likened to that of the stepmother in our tale. He suffers the pains of hell, hunger, thirst and never-ending frustration; and he is in permanent dread of an enormous rock precariously balanced above him.

His developing intellect leads Tantalos, the mortal human being, to such an intense feeling of selfhood and independence that he becomes an *evil* or *step*father, that he spurns the gods and simultaneously destroys what once was most precious to him, his son Pelops. Now he finds himself in a condition where he can no longer reach the water (of life) and the beautiful fruits (of knowledge), while his lonely, selfish existence is continuously threatened with total annihilation: Indeed, the fearful awareness that we may die at any moment is a direct and necessary consequence of setting ourselves authentically against the old gods. Pelops, however, through the kind efforts of the Olympians, is reborn in spite of the damage inflicted by Demeter. His ivory shoulder stands in odd contrast to Siegfried's unprotected shoulder that renders him vulnerable to the sword of Hagen revenging the betrayal of Brunhilde.[57,179]

Siegfried, son of Sieglinde and Siegmund, portrays a human being who has achieved a considerable degree of shrewdness and independence—overcoming the dragon and the evil dwarf—while still able, like Tantalos, to relate to the spiritual powers of Brunhilde, the Walkyrie, daughter of the gods. Eventually, however, the independence gained in the course of developing an ever sharper and more rational awareness of the challenging and seductive sensory world leads him to forget Brunhilde and to marry Gutrune (or Kriemhilde). His soul becomes earthbound. It is indeed the fate of the intellect to separate the human being from a harmonious, paradisiacal world, and to furnish a feeling of uniqueness, with the knowledge of good and evil and with the awareness of death. Both in the German epos (*Sagas of Theoderic*) and in many fairy tales we find veiled promises that the individual *will* find a new link with the paradisiacal garden, the Garden of Eden, or Laurin's garden that he has left behind; that he will find his way back without losing the fruits earned through his involvement with the world of the senses, with the material world.[186]

The human individual, relying solely on his intellect and lost in the variegated material world becomes lonely, fragmented and hopeless; eventually a resurrection toward a new wholistic understanding will take place: a vision of God that will not deprive us of the genuine uniqueness, of the reflexive consciousness that we have acquired. First, however, in the process of "relating our self to itself and of becoming willing to be this self"—to paraphrase Kierkegaard—we fall into despair, as we lose our groundedness in God, "in the power that constituted the self."[96] The Gospels offer the glorious, hopeful, archetypical image of the deity who becomes flesh, whose power penetrates the body so thoroughly that he can resurrect it. Simultaneously His body and blood are carried into all the parts of the earth in order to be consumed by us and to help our own resurrection.

The one-sided emphasis on the abstract intellect, on rationalism (where ratio refers to a type of reasoning that focuses on the parts = ratae) which is portrayed in the aforementioned and other stories may lead also to the depreciation of fairy tales and epos whenever it pretends to be able to explain them fully. The purely rational approach to the heroic epos, myth and fairy tale leaves us with a series of interesting, thoroughly interpreted and classified fragments; but the "spiritual bond," to quote Goethe,[54] holding them together and imbuing them with their deepest meaning, is lost. Thus these narrations fall prey to the very fate of human evolution which they depict as unavoidable. Yet they know of a future, new synthesis. They know that the fragments will be put together again, that Osiris, Lemminkainen, Pelops—or the young son in our fairy tale—will be restored and become an even more beautiful whole.

Psychoanalysis became the first powerful modern effort to evaluate the irrational in human existence. Thus came its interest in dreams, in seemingly senseless symptoms, in seemingly accidental mistakes and, finally, in myths and fairy tales. The psychoanalytic approaches to the latter brought forth a large amount of highly interesting correlations with insights into the nature of the human psyche gained during psychotherapy. Yet, psychoanalytic theory adheres strictly to the methodology and to the presuppositions of modern science based exclusively upon measurability and determinism, thus postulating that consciousness (meaning by this the subjective appreciation of sensations, feelings, values, etc.) should be kept out of the field of investigation.[128] Ultimately the latter—namely, consciousness—remains but an epiphenomenon of instinctual, biologically rooted and chemically controlled, often "unconscious" mechanisms. Therefore, the psychoanalytic investigations of myths and fairy tales may be extremely fascinating; yet the analyzed stories often lose in depth, width and charm.

Indeed we find that the less we inject theoretical presuppositions or prejudices into the experiencing of these narrations, the more they will reveal their deepest meanings. Even the Jungians' methodology, though more phenomenological, is not entirely presuppositionless.[71,76] The stress on archetypical images in this approach, for example, favors the universal over the individual meanings of myths and fairy tales.

One may question to what extent a totally presuppositionless approach *is* possible in our times. The methodology itself for such a radically empirical, phenomenological procedure is relatively new. Edmund Husserl's admonition to "go back to the things themselves," to learn to let the things speak for themselves and to listen, may seem ridiculously simple at first.[70,127] To follow this admonition turns out to be so difficult that it should be viewed as a desirable yet never completely attainable goal. Indeed the removal of presuppositions and prejudices is possible only hand in hand with profound changes in the observer which will affect not only his conceptual store, but also some of his basic emotional, volitional and epistemologic orientations. To start with, a phenomenologic approach may consist largely in rendering oneself again and again aware of the *meaning-matrixes,* the presuppositions by which we achieve some limited insight. If the combination of several such limited insights can open up new perspectives, there should be no objection against taking into consideration the results of the most varied approaches to folklore.

One's view of myths, epos and fairy tales is bound to be influenced by one's own philosophy of man. This, in the phenomenologically oriented researcher will be an existential philosophy. The latter, while recapturing the dignity of man, is not setting itself against other—biological, behavioristic, mechanistic, deterministic—studies of man, but has as its highest aim the proper integration of their contributions.[76] Thus you may discern insights from different sources in the following, more specific comments about *The Juniper Tree.*

It was especially Jung who stressed that in viewing a dream, a hallucinatory experience, a myth or a fairy tale, the various personages occurring in them can be seen as different aspects or qualities of the protagonist.[82,87] This idea which does not exclude other, simultaneous views, is eminently applicable to our tale. Here the father portrays the ultimate, persistent identity, what might have been called by Goethe,[53] *Entelechy;* by Husserl,[80] the *Transcendental Ego;* by Heidegger,[63] the *Dasein;* or by Kierkegaard,[96] the *Self.* His inner counterpart, his soul, or in Jungian terms his *anima,* appears as his first wife who is still harmoniously immersed in the experienced, lived world, in nature. In midwinter she stands under the juniper tree which, in Druidic times, was a place for initiation rites.[124] The once variegated, warm and lively landscape is covered by a quiet and cold blanket of snow. It is a time when human beings can more easily turn inward and become reflective.

Though they can look back upon a paradisiacally blissful existence, the father and his wife are consumed by the longing for a child. We may already vaguely sense that the eventual birth of the son refers to the development of a new faculty in the human being, of a new ego that is reflective, free and aware of itself. Yet the birth of this son leads to the disappearance, to the death of the original mother, to the loss of the feeling of harmonious—though only dreamlike and unselfconscious—embeddedness in nature. The apple that the mother is paring and which reminds us of the one that led Eve and Adam to self-consciousness and to the knowledge of good and evil, points both to the eventual birth of that higher or new ego, and to the loss of the ancient, intuitive soul forces that experienced in magnificent pictures a harmonious, paradisiacal world. They are now replaced by selfish, sensuous and jealously ambitious soul forces: the mother turns into a stepmother. However, the stepmother gives also birth to a child, to Magdalen, to the soul that unwittingly goes through the depths of guilt and despair, eventually emerging purified and in harmony with the new ego, her reborn half brother.

The harmonious, paradisiacal but sterile relationship of father and wife or *animus* and *anima* is replaced by the dynamic triad of the young son, the stepmother and Magdalen. In this dramatic triad, the stepmother and Magdalen begin by being allies. They share the guilt of killing the young boy, of dismembering him, of baking him into black puddings and of finally offering the latter to the father. But then a separation occurs gradually, as the stepmother persists more and more rigidly and stubbornly in her pride, hatred and lovelessness. Magdalen emerges now as that aspect of the soul that through sorrow, guilt and penance finds peace and consolation under the juniper tree where the original mother is buried and where she brings her brother's bones wrapped in her own silken handkerchief. Magdalen is not accidentally a namesake of Magdalena who sins, loves Jesus, mourns under the cross and finally finds peace and redemption.

The human being of early cultures is in total harmony with nature and experiences himself exclusively as part of a larger group whose traditions and myths he accepts without questioning. He therefore will not experience any conflict with his soul forces that serve solely this blissful, passive integration. His feelings are spontaneous; his actions quasi-instinctive and guided by his biological makeup as well as by the accepted traditions; and his intelligence is merely in the service of these traditions. However, once he becomes reflective, once he becomes able to abstract himself from his surroundings and to use his reasoning to shape various ideas by which he tries to understand and order the world rationally, the individual sets himself apart from nature (or from what the Greeks called *physis*, or Heidegger[64] "Being"), from his fellow human beings and often even from himself. Objectivation becomes estrangement. Objectivation becomes universal doubt. The experience of anything in its immediacy is no longer accepted; knowledge becomes confined to the ability to dissect everything into its ultimate particles or components, and we are eventually left with innumerable sensory data without any meaning, or with ideas produced by our reasoning. We do not know whether these ideas truly represent the real world or life. Thus the one-sided development of the rational aspects of our soul leads on the one hand toward greater self-awareness, and on the other hand toward a feeling of alienation, loneliness, meaninglessness and unaliveness. Commonly we see this in the normal development of the child when the intellectual endeavors of the early school years seem to kill much of his unselfconscious spontaneity. The reference, then, in our story to the young boy coming home from school before being led to the apples in the deadly, decapitating trunk, is of subtle significance.[124]

The one-sided exercise of rationalism fragments our world, but leaves ourselves also fragmented. Rationalism becomes selfish, an end in itself, overlooking or denying the broad area of irrationality in which it must be rooted and from which it receives its nourishment. Rationalism, as Ortega y Gasset[143] has pointed out, sooner or later leads to disillusion and to self-destruction. The ego that has become self-aware *must,* however, go through this experience of isolation, rejection and disintegration in order to become alive on a higher plane.

The rebirth of the young son reminds one of the phoenix that renews himself in the fire, or of the burning bush wherein God handed Moses the ten commandments, revealing Himself as the "I am that I am." His admonishments that we carry personal responsibilities and that, being made in His image, each one of us is a self-relating individual, contain the promise and challenge for an eventual, radical renewal. Transubstantiation (alluded to in the father's cannibalistic meal), metamorphosis and rebirth are all implicit in the image of the young boy's death and transformation which leads to his spellbinding song that always ends with "Oh, what a beautiful bird *am I.*" Fairy tales often seem to underline their themes with easily overlooked allusions, such as the mention of Magdalen's handkerchief enveloping her brother's bones. The silk of this handkerchief which transforms itself along with the bones into the beautiful bird points by its very origin to metamorphosis, as it brings up the association of the cocoon changing into a colorful butterfly.[124]

It is a basic, though frequently overlooked, rule of any real progress that it must learn to distill and to include all that was valuable in the past. We may try to apply this principle in the interpretation of the flight of the wondrous bird from the juniper tree to the goldsmith, to the cobbler and to the miller. The three craftsmen represent three epochs, each one having contributed in shaping the present human being: first, the golden age where man, lacking self- and other-awareness is open to the spiritual world and its messages; then, an epoch in which growing awareness of oneself goes hand in hand with a firmer grounding in the physical world, with a gradual loss of spiritual vision, and with a growing appreciation of one's relatedness with the people that are close to us; and finally, the age of technology and materialism.

The marvelous bird, the new ego, the "I am that I am" or, in terms of the Christian tradition, "Christ-in-me" appeals to all of us and addresses the various levels of our personality. Thus the resplendent bird is first noticed by that aspect of ourselves which, rooted in the golden age retains some sensitivity for spiritual values and is able to work gold (which in fairy tales refers usually to spiritual rather than material treasures) into jewelry. The archetypical goldsmith has preserved this type of power and intuitive sight; and in return for the bird's fascinating message he offers the beautiful chain that is later dropped as a gift around the father's neck. The goldsmith's spiritual wisdom reaches back the farthest, and thus his work is most fittingly bestowed on him whom we described as the ultimate, persistent identity of the human being. The golden chain symbolizes the meaningful continuity of our world, from link to link, from epoch to epoch, from generation to generation, from father to son to marvelous bird to reborn son and back to father.

The cobbler's main interest is to help the human being walk upon the earth with comfort, ease and grace. While no longer able to perceive directly the highest spiritual principles, he represents a stage in human development characterized by greater awareness of the objective world, of oneself and of one's fellow human beings. The story alludes to this by mentioning both the cobbler's needing to shield his eyes against the brightness of the bird, and his eagerness to share with others his fabulous experience. His gift in return for the bird's song is a pair of slippers that eventually are given to Magdalen. The properly fitting slipper—and the most famous story illustrating this is that of Cinderella—

allows a harmonious balance of the human being between his erect posture that points upwards and the horizontal earth which he must not ignore. When the slipper fits, the soul—the *anima*—is ready for the marriage with the prince.[69] Again it seems most appropriate that Magdalen ends up dancing and leaping in her new slippers. Is not she the soul that has neither stayed behind in a paradisiacal world, as the young boy's mother, nor become totally immersed in the world of matter, as her own mother—the soul that has found the perfect balance after having had to share, unwittingly, her mother's guilt.

One may add here that the goldsmith's openness for spiritual values is underlined subtly by not having to shield his eyes; yet his footing on the earth is not yet perfect: as he runs out of his shop to see the colorful bird, he loses a slipper!

Fairy tales are astonishingly sensitive to the trends of their times. We find that during the most modest beginnings of technology some stories, including ours, sensed its potential effect upon the human being. Thus we hear that the goldsmith and the cobbler respond *immediately* to the song of the marvelous bird. The millers and their millstone, however, represent the beginning of technology; they portray the most recent aspects of the human personality which are deeply involved in the laws and workings of matter. Therefore, the millers hear the otherworldly message of the bird only very gradually.

The tale depicts excellently the slow emergence of the miller and his twenty men out of their absorption in their work on a millstone. First just one, then two, then four, then eight, then only five and finally—with the very last words of the bird—the last one stops and listens to the song. Some sooner, some later, learn to hear something that is beyond the deafening noise of the mechanical tools; thus they become willing, individually, and as a group, to give the bird the millstone they were working on. They are now ready to subordinate technology with all its advantages and promises to what appears more meaningful and spiritually satisfying. Unless this happens, technology and materialism defeat themselves. Thus the heavy wheel, the millstone, symbol of technology, is bound to destroy the stepmother who represents those aspects of the human being that have become severed *permanently* from the ability to experience freedom, beauty and meaningfulness, and that have become totally subservient to a deterministic—mechanistic or instinctual—view of life that must lead to total despair. The tale depicts quite dramatically how the stepmother, not unlike the queen in the tale of *Snow White and the Seven Dwarfs,* experiences herself as more and more unfree, possessed by diabolical forces—as driven. She thus represents that aspect of the human being that has learned to objectify everything, including itself. Thus the person, having lost all subjectivity, becomes the passive executor of external demands and internal promptings.

Our tale, however, indicates that human wholeness is not achieved by simply avoiding the material world and what the intellect has created in this material world in terms of objective science and technology, in terms of understanding man as a biological, instinctual organism. Other Western fairy tales (often, for example, those speaking of twin brothers) equally allude to the *necessity* of integrating the knowledge gained by objectivation and analysis, the advantages gained by technology and natural scientific advances, within a new view of human existence. Here the individual becomes maximally aware of the range of his freedom and of his self-chosen responsibility to himself, to his fellow human being, and to his world.

In *The Juniper Tree* tale the little boy is the image of the new ego that is born or that awakens in order to accomplish a new synthesis. One could also say that he is the child that Christ urges us to become. Yet, feeling so "grown-up" for being well adjusted to our everyday mechanistic-collectivistic world, we often treat this child in us the same way the stepmother treated the little boy. The decapitation of the boy and the destruction of the stepmother allude, indeed, to the biblical passage where Christ warns that whoever would truncate (*skandalizo,* usually translated as "scandalize," originally meant truncate) one of these children would be better off if a *millstone* were put around his neck.[124] And in the Apocalypse (18:21) a giant millstone is thrown by the angel into the sea: "Thus will be toppled with one storm the great city Babylon and will never be found again."

When at the end of the tale, father, Magdalen and the young

boy enter the home to eat their meal, this is not to be seen as a callous ignoring of the dramatic events they just experienced. Rather it is an allusion to the communion that eventually will make whole that which had been divided.

The fairy tale not only retains an inkling of a world full of meaning; it not only recognizes the danger as well as the necessity of the human being's descent into a purely sensory-mechanistic world; it also knows of an eventual, enriched and more beautiful reemergence of the new ego into a newly meaningful world. Yet, in our times, the fairy tale itself is undergoing a descent into a fragmented, gray world. With all the numerous analyses of folklore, quite scholarly, subtle, fascinating and valid in many respects, the intrinsic meaning of many of these tales is all too often no longer—and never fully—experienced.

The reemergence into a newly meaningful world, seen in the tales of *Snow White*, of *The Wolf and the Seven Little Goats* and of *The Juniper Tree*, finds a most beautiful portrayal in *Briar Rose* or *The Sleeping Beauty*.

CHAPTER XVI

BRIAR ROSE

The Sleeping Beauty

For a long time a king and a queen had vainly been hoping for a child. "Then it happened that—while the queen was sitting in the bath—a frog came from the water upon the land and said: 'Your wish will be granted . . . .' "[58]

This seems, at first, a rather weird introduction to a story! It strikes us as unusual etiquette when frogs start to announce the forthcoming birth of a child to a queen sitting in a bath. It is one of those startling sentences which we find occasionally at the beginning or at the end of a fairy tale, reminding us that the story to be told is dealing with events beyond the immediate, contemporary and everyday reality. But this weird introduction also contains, or hides, a message: What is going to be told has something to do with the relationship, with the interaction between the life in the more fluid psychic world and the firm physical or material world. The frog is an amphibian (*ampho* = both; *bios* = life; he is an animal with two types of life, fishlike as a tadpole and (predominantly) land-bound as a frog. He, therefore is an excellent symbol for the metamorphosis from one world to another; he is the messenger from the sphere of the more fluid psychic world to the solid, material world.*

*Mermaids, sirens and fishermen can portray the same force lingering or communicating between the aquatic and the earthly existence. These beings may long for the shore and they may try to seduce the earthbound human to enter into their fluid realm. (Examples are the mermaid in O. Wilde's *The Fisherman*

We might remain quite skeptical of such an interpretation of the role of this frog who prophesies the pregnancy of the queen, if we did not rediscover almost throughout the entire tale various themes pointing to the interaction between spiritual or soul processes and the material world. In fact, when the promised beautiful child is born, the twelve good fairies are invited to celebrate. These, as well as the thirteenth fairy (who arrives in great anger, since she was not asked, because there were only twelve golden plates in the castle) are called the women of wisdom. Meyer[124] likens them to the twelve constellations of the zodiac whose influence upon the birth of each human being was highly respected especially in ancient times. Their spirituality is underscored both by their being served with the golden plates, and by their ability to confer upon the child such spiritual qualities as friendliness, courtesy, beauty and understanding.

In former epochs, the preciousness of gold did not consist primarily in its purchasing power. Its nobility was due to its durability, its sun-like color and its rarity. We are reminded, thus, of the golden age, a paradisiacal age, when the heavens were still open and man was able to converse directly with the gods. In those times the human being was not as consciously aware of his solid material surroundings. Like the frog, he was *amphibios* as far as his consciousness was concerned. In our story this is clearly alluded to by the remark that the queen was in

---

and His Soul,[183] the sirens in Homer's *Odyssey*, Wainemoinen's wife turned into a seductive mermaid in the *Kalevala*, or F. Schiller's poem "The Fisherman."[156]) Equally there are ethereal beings who share air and earth, and who usually refer to an intercommunication between a spiritual world and the human being. While it may be unwise to accept a rigid scheme, one can recognize here a certain parallelism between the solid material world and the body, of the water and the soul, and of the air and the spirit. In *Snow White and the Seven Dwarfs* we saw the birds whose element is the air (the owl, the dove and the raven) as life-sustaining messengers from a spiritual world. And there are numerous mythical figures, half human and half bird, who assume similar roles (to name a few examples: Mercury or Hermes, sylphs, fairies, angels, etc.). Whether they are maleficent or beneficial depends largely upon the epoch, upon the stage of development, during which they enter into relationship with the human individual.

the bath when the frog, hopping from the water upon the land, spoke to her.*

But the golden age of humanity—and of childhood—comes to an end. Humanity, and each individual in his own development, faces the loss of contact with the spiritual world, faces spiritual death and the immobility or rigidity of material existence. The twelve good fairies who bring virtues from the esoterically conceived zodiacal constellations are joined abruptly by the diabolical thirteenth woman of wisdom who may remind us of the paradisiacal serpent, or of Pandora. Vengeful because of her exclusion from the golden festivities, she promises that the beautiful girl will die upon her fifteenth birthday. Fortunately, the twelfth fairy has not yet offered her gift; and while she is unable to void completely the dark fairy's wish, she can commute the death sentence to a hundred-year-long sleep after which there will be a new awakening.

We may see a parallel between this commutation of the death sentence and God's offering redemption through his Messiah to the progeny of the condemned Adam and Eve. Similarly there remained hope in Pandora's box out of which all the evils had escaped in order to torment humanity, while Prometheus, son of the old gods and benefactor of the human race, was to be chained for thirty thousand years to a rock in the Caucasus.[59,158]

As the evil fairy's wish is fulfilled, everything becomes rigid in the realm of the castle. Not only the king and the queen, the princess and servants fall asleep, but also the leaves on the tree, the fire in the fireplace, the animals and even the roast on the stove lose all motion and become part of the death-like sleep which represents the end of the golden age. Nothing can depict this loss of the golden age more beautifully than the image of the thornbushes which grow and grow until they completely cover and hide the castle, including even the flag on its top. Only legends keep mentioning the existence of a castle with a charming, sleeping princess named Briar Rose.

In the stories of *Snow White and the Seven Dwarfs, The*

*This transition from water to land, from the foggy realms of Suomi to the cold and clear outlines of the Northland is a basic theme in the birth and life of Kalevala's hero, Wainemoinen (see Chapter VII).

Juniper Tree, Hansel and Gretel and *Red Cap* we mentioned how the fairy tale can often refer to individual human development and to humanity's collective history, the first being—in a certain sense—a repetition of the second. This holds true also for the *Sleeping Beauty*, though this story more specifically focuses upon the growth of the young girl.

During his first seven years the human being lives—figuratively speaking—in the palace of the king and queen. He has to cope with intense conflicts such as are reflected in the *Hansel and Gretel* story or in *Red Cap*, at times making the castle seem like a dreary hut. Yet he is still in the golden age or in a paradisiacal world inasmuch as he does not meet directly and with self-awareness the tasks and challenges of the physical surroundings. The latency period, subsequently, becomes the training period during which these tasks are met. Now the child has broken away from the castle, but—at least half the time, namely during the night, or subconsciously—he maintains his contact with a spiritually conceived world. In the *Snow White* tale it is the seven dwarfs who represent this live link with a nonmaterialistic world. This relationship is gradually throttled by the witch-stepmother-queen. The child learns to deal effectively with the material world during the latency period, but loses thereby his former link with a live spiritual world. In our present story, the Sleeping Beauty stings herself at the distaff when she turns fifteen and succumbs to the sleep which is to last one hundred years.

Let me quickly mention that the portrayal of the preschool child as belonging to a paradisiacal world and as not being yet actively in touch with the physical world is—like other imaginative descriptions—true only from a certain viewpoint. Obviously, even the preschool child already deals with many of the pleasant and less pleasant aspects of our material surroundings. However, some salient characteristics stem from basic laws of psychic development. We notice that the healthy preschool child plays happily at everything without any conscious plan to prepare himself for the tasks of the physical world (in fact, kindergarten represents an attempt to facilitate the transition from such play activities to utilitarian learning activities). The child of the latency period, on the other hand, wavers between an orientation toward the practical tasks which he will have to face and a child-like openness for any spiritual guidance that is offered, as well as a sometimes unrealistic dependence on the adults around him.

Finally we can recognize that the adolescent, in his rebellion, in fighting off dependency needs tends to throw off the beliefs and codes given him. Simultaneously he is bewildered by the intensity of his instinctual drives. In his basic gnawing, often subconscious doubts concerning his ability to cope eventually with life as an independent adult, he tends to value material things too highly and too selfishly. In his beautiful but changeable ideals and in whatever questions and opinions he may have in regard to the meaning of his life, he frequently displays poor integration with the rest of his personality and some lack of depth. His ideals, though noble, delicate or princely, are still immature and brittle and cannot yet become a fully effective part of the adolescent's real life. They perish at the contact with the rude aspects of reality, just like the young princes who came too early to Briar Rose's castle and were caught in the thorny bushes covering the bewitched building.

Nothing, not even the king's painstaking efforts to remove all the distaffs from his kingdom, was able to alter his daughter's fate. The phase of the loss of early spirituality, which coincides with the onset of adolescence, is just as inescapable as the menarche witch, from a psychoanalytic angle, is seen symbolized by the blood brought forth by the sting of the distaff. The king's burning of the distaffs was as ineffective as the warnings of the dwarfs in the story of *Snow White*. And—-another similarity with this tale—the temptation and downfall of the Sleeping Beauty occurred when her protectors—here the king and the queen—were not at home: a further indication of the end of the latency period, when the child is experiencing a further challenge to break away from the parents. The king and the queen return too late to be able to stop the girl's fate and, instead, become part of the great sleep which pervades the whole castle.

It is justifiable to see a symbolic meaning in the place where the temptation of the princess occurs: high up in the castle's tower, in a little cubbyhole behind a little door which can be opened with a rusty key. Is it not up in the belfry, in the head, where we spin the intellectual threads which are deadening our feelings and deep beliefs, especially if the mental processes in the brain are shut off from the rest of our soul for such a long time that the key to the door (between heart and brain) has become rusty?

It must be added that in the German language "spinning" refers not only to the mechanical operation of a spinning wheel, but also to a type of reasoning which is detached from active life, as well as to the thought processes of the mentally ill. The old woman in the room high up in the tower (she may well be the bad fairy for whom there was no golden plate) tells Briar Rose: "I'm spinning." And as soon as the girl wants to try her hand at spinning and gets stung by the needle, the thorny bushes outside spin their branches across the castle until it is completely hidden. "The spinning wheel keeps on working!"

An interesting variation of the spinning wheel theme is found in the Swiss tale of *The Fairy Godmother* who gives a spinning wheel to the fourteen-year-old girl. But here the golden-haired godmother and the spinning wheel which can spin the thread into gold represent the ability to produce live thoughts which render the soul richer.[43] This is the spinning wheel of the beautiful virgin of the Northland sitting on a rainbow and spinning silver and gold dresses that will clothe her, the *anima,* when she is ready to descend and unite herself with the ideal male, the *animus.*

Psychoanalytically, the sleep of the Sleeping Beauty has been viewed as a seduction.[163] We may do well to view it also from this angle. But seduction is not enough. The princes who arrive too early, namely before either they themselves or Briar Rose are ready, perish in the thorns. Exclusive instinctual arousal, corresponding to the luciferic* seduction in *Hansel and Gretel,* and intellectual spinning, analogous to the ahrimanic* temptation in

*We have chosen throughout this book the biblical term "luciferic" and the Persian term "ahrimanic" to distinguish two aspects of destructive influence: one toward sensuousness and selfishness, the other toward a one-sided materialism which ends up denying any moral, esthetic or spiritual values. While in many

Red Cap, lead to human death. And when the remembrance that once there was more than spinning and thorns is almost vanished, then only the old man who heard from his grandfather about the hidden castle, can tell the prince of the beautiful young lady who has already slept a hundred years. In our analysis of the story of *Turandot* we shall again observe the conflict between this old man, who tries to dissuade the young man, and the fearlessness and love of the prince who is not discouraged by the knowledge that all the previous suitors perished miserably. In *Turandot* we shall also see how and why this conflict indicates the young man's struggle between his dependence on his parent and his desire for true independence.

In myths and fairy tales the struggle of the adolescent male always carries the danger of death (see: Brunhilde's castle surrounded by a wall of fire; the numerous episodes in which the suitor has to perform three dangerous tasks; the solving of the riddle of the sphinx in the Oedipus saga; the three riddles of *Turandot;* the freeing of the maiden by Perseus; the trial of going through water and fire in various myths, etc.). The adolescence of the woman on the other hand is often depicted as the death-like sleep (*Sleeping Beauty, Snow White* and *Amor and Psyche*). The woman and the man overcome the dangers involved in adolescence in ways which are considered characteristic of them, namely passively or actively. Only when all the various forces join together harmoniously can the ideal, the mature love relationship between a spiritually live man and woman be attained. A broader discussion of the meaning of death in myths and fairy tales will be found in Chapters XXIX and XXX.

A subjective view of the story may further illustrate its meaning: if we see the castle as the *total* human being to which the old man, the fairies, the king and the queen and everything

---

ways opposite to each other, they usually work conjointly and may be portrayed by one being which can alternately assume one or the other role. In Goethe's *Faust* we see Mephistopheles quite clearly manifest these two aspects. While Ahriman, according to Zoroaster "the destroying spirit, source of all evil," and Lucifer, "the light carrier, temptor and giver of self-knowledge," seem to be suitable to portray the two kinds of influence, no specific reference to the Persian and biblical religions is implied in the choice of these terms.

appertains, then we can recognize in the prince the *animus* aspect of the individuality. If and when he completes his maturation at the right time, the thorn webs covering the beauty of the castle blossom forth and open up a gate to allow him to fulfill the integration with the reawakening Briar Rose *anima*. When his intellectual spinning matures and changes into wisdom, the thorny thought webs are no longer blocking the communication with the soul. They become beautiful and allow an open passage to the heart. With this, the possibility of movement, of action, is restored. This is excellently portrayed in the Grimms' tale of *The Frog King*. When the princess awakens from her childhood world and is able to confront the frog prince, the spell placed on him is dis-spelled. Now the three rings placed around the heart of his faithful guardian break with the expansive joy he experiences, and the couple ride into a new world in which they can be effective as grown human beings.

The helpful spiritual forces, the twelve fairies, who accompany, protect and guide the individual after birth have helped to ripen Briar Rose's forces of courage, unselfishness and love. In due time these forces transform into a cloak of flowers the thorny web which, at the end of the latency period, covers the spiritual values. From the little room up in the tower, the *animus* and the *anima* jointly climb downstairs, and everything comes alive. The harmony achieved by this integration of the *animus* with the *anima* pervades, animates everything in the human being, from the intellectual functions down to the animal, vegetative and physical features. The animals reawaken, the leaves on the trees move again and the fire in the fireplace resumes burning. Even the apparently most trivial things in this castle (still seen as representing the total person) are influenced by this awakening: the doves on the roof, the flies on the wall and the roast on the stove.

In such ways the story admirably conveys the knowledge that any real human growth cannot be measured one-sidedly by focusing only on what an abstract intellect can spin. Real growth reflects itself in all phases and aspects of an individual's activity, sublime and modest, and encompasses along with the intellectual and emotional also the instinctual and the vegetative functions.

With the advent of greater self-awareness and with the increasing knowledge of the physical world, sexuality assumed its first shameful and ugly connotations. Because of this, the early, paradisiacal, carefree and innocent existence was followed by a period in which the human being maintained his stability and developed his feeling of individuality by creating a split between the conscious and the unconscious. The latter, then, contains the reminiscences of an almost forgotten "paradise" as well as those aspects of instinctual life which are in too severe a conflict with the current social order. Stories such as that of *Briar Rose* express the hope that the thorny branches hiding the castle will not permanently conceal its beauty. When the human being matures to the point where his values, feelings and ideals penetrate his whole person, then even sexuality will be so well integrated that it must lose any disagreeable connotations which would require its partial repression. He would retain the fruits of his overinvolvement in material existence consisting mainly in a strengthened consciousness or individual identity. As the lost paradise is found again, the separation between conscious and unconscious becomes superfluous.

Eventually, the psychoanalytic and phenomenologic interpretations of the story complete each other in full harmony. Whether we see in the prince only a charming seducer, or whether we see in him also the successful birth of a higher ego, depends in a large part upon our own ability to hope for a spiritual reawakening of mankind.

Let me introject here a comment concerning some significant differences between *Briar Rose* and Perrault's *Sleeping Beauty*. While the brothers Grimm mention twelve good fairies (corresponding to the number of zodiacal constellations) and a bad one, we find that Perrault[139] speaks only of seven fairies, corresponding in number to the classical planets which were thought to be related to the human *soul* with its intellectual and feeling aspects rather than to the human *spirit*.* This difference is also expressed in the polished, delightfully witty, delicately sophisticated style Perrault uses and which contrasts sharply with the

*In Germany the emphasis is on the ethos, in France on the esthetic.

plainer, simpler frank style in *Briar Rose.* When Sleeping Beauty awakens and has met the prince, "she did not wait to dress for dinner, being already perfectly and magnificently attired, though in a fashion somewhat out of date. However, her lover had the politeness not to note this, nor to remind her that she was dressed exactly like her royal grandmother, whose portrait still hung on the palace walls."

Perrault's narrative gains in charming sophistication, but loses depth by creating a portrait of everyday life in the eighteenth century rather than of basic developments of the human being. However, the brothers Grimm did not lack a sense of humor. A handwritten notation was found in an early edition of their tales explaining that the prince eventually became bored with Briar Rose and started philandering with other sleeping princesses whom he had awakened with his kisses just to see the color of their eyes; however, he became tired of this game and returned to his wife. Yet, the trifles of everyday life of which she kept talking were so boring to him that gradually his eyes became heavier and heavier and he succumbed to a hundred-year-long sleep.

Viewing the story of Briar Rose in its broadest phylo- rather than ontogenetic meaning, we can say: a long time ago the human being was under the beneficial influence of twelve wise women. The soul was integrated in the cosmic All represented by the twelve constellations of the zodiac. But, influenced by an evil spirit (the thirteenth wise woman, the devil, Lucifer, who set himself in opposition to the All, etc.), this soul lost his early paradise. And while nowadays his former spiritual life (the king, queen, servants, etc.) appears to be asleep under the thorny branches of the spun thoughts, and while the soul is isolated in the little room high up in the tower (so often we equate brain and soul!), the human individual is being prepared for a re-awakening. This will combine a conscious awareness of himself with a new recognition of the wisdom in the world and in our existence.

Each child reflects in his own development this course of human history, where adolescence is the critical period in which the reawakening of a spiritual conception of the world, thanks to the birth of a higher ego (corresponding to the arrival of the prince), is longingly anticipated.

And now let me stress the justification of a harmonious synthesis of this subjective view of the story (seeing the castle and everything connected with it as *one* individual) with an objective interpretation (seeing in the tale the blossoming love between a boy and a girl). We have mentioned before that human maturation, true human existence, is possible only in the deep interaction with another human being (Buber: "Without thou there is no existence";[16] Goethe: "A person begins to know that he exists when he finds himself again in others."[53]). Therefore the prince is both the "Thou" in the relationship with whom the human being experiences his existence *and* the birth of a mature, higher ego which effects the awakening of Briar Rose. She awakens from the sleep into which the intensified instincts and the spinning of the intellectual threads have plunged her by separating her from the live, paradisiacal world of earlier childhood, from a world which she had experienced in a carefree way but without much self-awareness.

The charming story of *Tredeshin,*[21] taken from the Swiss-Engadin fairy tales, contains some of the developmental mysteries illustrated in *Briar Rose,* but deals with them from the boy's side. When the fairy tale or myth describes the striving human being, the seeker for his own innermost nature, the student of a deeper wisdom, it will almost always speak of the young hero. The predominantly passive qualities of modesty, tolerance, compassion, humility, gentleness and kindness tend to be described as attributes of the young woman or princess.

The protagonist's name (*Tredeshin* = the thirteenth) indicates not only that he was the last of the brood, but it implies two other things: his parents, after so many children, could not think of another conventional name for him; in a way he is nameless and he must go out into the world to make a name for himself. His being nameless makes him appear rejected or orphaned like so many other heroes, but it also offers him more freedom to become truly himself. His pseudo-name also refers vaguely to his age: he has passed his thirteenth year when he starts out into a period of his life which eventually, after three dangerous trials and several years, brings him the longed-for reward—a princess and a kingdom.

Many other tales touch upon the same adolescent problems. We mentioned this one briefly because it is a delightful story from a small, little known cultural group. It views adolescence from the masculine side, gives another example of the clever way in which fairy tales use numbers, and it points out the role of the name in connection with the development of a mature ego. Quite similarly we saw the clever use of a number to designate the age in the story of *The Wolf and the Seven Goats* and we shall see in the chapter on *Turandot* a similar meaning of the number thirteen (indicating both the age of the princess and the number of heads of former suitors). We shall also see in the *Turandot* story the important significance of the namelessness of the prince. Because of its great significance in myths and fairy tales, a special chapter will be devoted to the topic of the "name."

In the following, last chapter of this part we shall discuss the arch-hero, Heracles. We insert these considerations at this point, since this famous myth also illustrates human growth. However, it views human growth way beyond adolescence, thus underlining the fact that human growth is a never-ending process.

CHAPTER XVII

FREEDOM, GROWTH, EXPANDING WORLD-DESIGN, ROOTEDNESS AND INSANITY

Some Reflections Based upon the Myth of Heracles

THE HERACLES OF MY ADOLESCENT MEMORIES was brutal, short tempered, unfairly powerful and not too bright. Only recently could I bring myself to look into this myth again. Reading it several times, I became more and more fascinated with several facets that are intimately related. They reflect basic insights into human nature, into human growth, and into failures in human growth. Since these insights are as valid today as at the time of Hesiod, I shall use the myth to illustrate them. We shall find the following themes closely interrelated:

1. Characteristically, the hero's birth is unusual.[143,144a] He is the son of Zeus and Alcmene whose mortal husband—not unlike Joseph in regard to Jesus—is seemingly devoid of jealousy and willing to take on the role of father. Characteristic, also, are the predictions by a seer concerning Heracles' life, deeds and death.

2. The circumstances of the hero's childhood commonly prevent an intimate, nonambiguous relationship with the parents. Most frequently (*cf.* Oedipus, Theseus, Moses, Jason, Siegfried) the infant is orphaned or exposed. Later he may find his parents again. What is unusual in the Heracles myth is the combination of the theme of exposure with the extremely ambivalent role of the mother-figures (Alcmene, the physical mother, and Hera, the step-

mother). Alcmene, loving her son but fearing Hera's jealous wrath, exposes the infant. Had Hera and Athene not discovered him accidentally, he would have died of exposure. Unaware of whom she is feeding, Hera lets the starving child drink from her breast, thus conferring upon him through her milk eventual immortality. Once Athene has returned Heracles to his mother, Hera becomes aware of his identity. Now she tries to kill him by sending two large serpents to his crib. Later in his life, she strikes him twice with insanity.

3. In confronting the world with its challenges and dangers, the hero's personality keeps growing. The boon he brings to his people is a reflection of his own increasing strength, and vice versa. Probably no other myth conveys this as concretely as the story of Heracles in whose life three groups of journeys can be distinguished. In the first group his point of departure and return is *home*. In the second group—the twelve famous tasks executed at the behest of Eurystheus—the point of departure and return is Mycene, some eighty miles away from home; whereas in the third group the starting point is on another continent, over 250 miles from home, where Heracles acts as the slave of Omphale.

It is quite clear, especially in the first two groups, that each separate journey reaches out farther than the previous one. The only exception to this rule is quite meaningful and proves the rule. We shall furthermore try to show that not only the distance of the journeys and their point of departure, but also the nature of the progressive tasks indicate the hero's struggle to widen his world-design.

4. Other myths, epos and fairy tales show that growth is a discontinuous process that can be lost again. Regardless of what was promised him initially, many a hero does not attain either kingdom or princess after completing the first impossible task. He usually must complete at least two other feats. While the fairy tale tends to portray and underline the glory of eventual achievement, the epos and myth are more inclined to stress the difficulties, hardships and failures in the quest for a lofty goal, as well as the ever open nature of human growth. Many are the shortcomings, the periods of proud overconfidence (hybris), and

the failures of Heracles. Few myths or epos, in addition, also portray insanity as a periodic feature in the vicissitudes of the hero's development. Thus we hope that the study of Heracles' psychotic periods will help us shed additional light upon the meaning of human growth.

5. The maternal ambivalence toward the hero will furthermore lead to a discussion of Heracles' relationship to the opposite sex. Since the development of this relationship goes hand in hand with his coming to terms with his own contrasexual side, with his *anima,* its analysis will also broaden our view of human development. Thus we shall consider Heracles' relationship to Megara, to Jole, to Omphale and to Deianira. In addition, his role in rescuing Alceste from death will aid us in understanding his oedipal problems.

6. This will lead to a discussion of oedipal features in the hero's growth, and particularly of his relationship to his father, to Admetos and to Zeus.

7. Finally we shall evaluate the meaning of Heracles' death, immortalization and marriage to Hebe in the light of the foregoing. His death on top of a mountain and his disappearance into an other-worldly realm is again characteristic of heroes of many myths. In discussing these seven themes, I will place particular emphasis on the third.

1. Hare, the culture hero in the Winnebago Trickster Cycles, Castor and Pollux, Aeneas, Achilles, Heracles, Romulus and Remus, Siegmund and Sieglinde as well as Jesus—to mention just a few—were the offspring of a mortal and of an immortal being; and they themselves could be mortal or immortal. Whereas in the birth of Jesus the profound significance of the divine progenitor is unmistakable, we tend to underrate the motivations of deities such as Wotan and Zeus who quite often—and to the chagrin of their wives—amuse themselves with another woman. Yet even here the somewhat mundane façade hides a deeper, serious meaning. The true role of the deity consists in instilling something special into the child about to be born, something that will enable him (or her) to accomplish a qualitatively new, important task that will advance him, his people and usually also the gods. Other

heroes such as Theseus, Oedipus, Orestes or Siegfried, while not having an immortal parent, nevertheless can always trace their genealogy to a god, and thus they possess to a very special degree the creative powers of their ancestors. They are born with a bright spark of authenticity and freedom.

Yet even the greatest do not have blind, unrestricted freedom; even the greatest have a personal fate to live. This is a message that is conveyed to us in innumerable narrations, and most clearly in those where a seer prophesies the essential features of this fate. Freedom and authenticity have two poles: creating one's own life spontaneously, and being sensitive to one's particular fate. Living this fate, freely accepting it, is a special aspect of the hero's authenticity. Just as the indwelling deity points to the hero's freedom, so the prophecies uttered at his birth point to the need to fulfill a particular fate. Maybe it is only our restricted, terrestrial vantage point that sees a paradox in the tension between living one's fate courageously and the willingness to follow —with "fear and trembling"[96]—one's own creative and ethic impulses even though these may infringe upon the socially accepted norms which may have grown inappropriate, stale and narrow.[78] This polarity of authenticity—and of most aspects, contents or qualities of human consciousness—is reflected even in seemingly contradictory existential philosophic views, from Sartre preaching that man is God creating freely his own world, to Ortega y Gasset stressing the faithfulness to one's fate as the hallmark of authenticity.[155,136]

2. The hero's unusual infancy is directly related to his special birth. Its purpose is to offer an environment wherein the spark of divinity, freedom and authenticity is not overshadowed or spent by the stable values, unambiguous commitments and quiet satisfactions of a balanced and secure family. Thus, often as a result of a prophecy, the infant is exposed on a mountain (Oedipus, Paris), in a boat (Moses, Perseus) or in a cave (Ion). He may be placed with foster parents (Oedipus, Siegfried, Hare) or nurtured by animals (Romulus and Remus). His mother may raise him alone, far away from father (Percivale, Theseus, Orestes, Telemachus), or he may be educated by a centaur (Jason). In fairy tales his mother often dies at birth and is succeeded by a

rejecting stepmother. With Heracles we find—as previously indicated—the very peculiar situation where he is exposed by and then returned to Alcmene. The latter thus becomes mother and foster mother, just as Hera, his stepmother, is his loving life-giving mother inasmuch as she fed him her milk that eventually was to insure his immortality.

Heracles grows up in his parents' home, but the confusion created by his two mothers' conflicting behavior (in psychology we would speak of double binds) prevents him from developing the secure rootedness that ordinarily comes with the satisfactory resolution of the oedipal situation. He is offered by his stepfather, Amphitryon, all the educational opportunities; yet in his later adolescence he kills—in a fit of self-defensive rage, or because of the seeming irrelevance of the subject—Linos, one of his tutors. Heracles was not the intellectual type and Linos, his writing teacher, must have seemed to him to be a nagging schoolmaster.

The question can be pursued as to whether or not this homicide was a misdirected, patricidal impulse. Be that as it may, it had the practical result of separating stepson and stepfather (the latter, scared of his son's temper, sends him out in the country), and of directing Heracles eventually on his path. We can speculate further about the hero's continued ambivalent feelings toward father figures: Eurystheus who becomes his mentor in the second group of journeys; Eurytos whom he eventually slays for refusing him the daughter, Jole, he had rightfully gained in contest; Admetos to whom he returns the wife who had offered up her life for her husband's; the two kings who refuse to give him absolution for his murder of Iphitos, etc. The analysis of psychodynamic patterns also points toward bisexual problems, resulting both from the double binds imposed by his two mothers, and from his unresolved feelings for father. Thus his near-murder of his close friend Jolaos* (Heracles eventually turns his psychotic homicidal rage against his three sons), and the murder of his friend Iphitos. Most clearly the sexual ambivalence is shown in the effeminacy of the hero at the court of queen Omphale.

*Later, Heracles lets Jolaos marry Megara and almost marries Jole. Note the similarity of names and the peculiar exchange of partners.

Omphale (feminine form of *omphalos* = umbilicus), however, throws an additional light upon Heracles' struggle. In discussing below the hero's relationship to his four wives and to Jole (who was promised to him and whom he eventually gave to his son in marriage) we shall examine the meaning of his feminine identification during his three-year serfdom to Omphale.

3. Man's quest is to broaden his outlook, to elevate himself, to become more profound, to widen his horizon, to have an independent viewpoint, and most of all, to be on the right path. The *way*, the *path*, the *Tao* is foremost. Without it, without the willingness to commit himself to a basic philosophy of life, anything else becomes valueless.

As an infant he overcame the smothering serpents sent by his stepmother. Later he absorbed all the skills and knowledge offered by his stepfather and his teachers. He asserted his authenticity by killing his surly teacher Linos.* Finally Heracles finds himself as a foster child among some herdsmen. Totally alone now, he must make a commitment to a path. The central alternative is to avoid suffering and pain, or to confront them. The struggle, as in any genuine commitment, is intense. Not only must he discard temptations that are inauthentic, but in order to become the true hero, he must also be willing to sacrifice some genuine, real potentials. And now begins the first group of journeys. The starting point is in or near his home town Thebes.†

The confrontation and overcoming of various perilous, wild animals and of robbers is a common theme in the heroes' journeys, both in myths and in fairy tales. Honest confrontation with oneself reveals first all the untamed, selfish, destructive powers that interfere both with personal growth and with a genuine, loving

---

*Authenticity, from *authenticos,* originally referred to "doing with one's own hands," to "murder," as well as to "suicide." On his own almost from birth, Heracles asserts his identity against the type of teacher who would mold him into something he is not. This self-assertion is—according to the judge of judges, Rhadamanthys—"justifiable homicide." But it still alienates Heracles further from his family as he must move away from home.

†Thebes is Heracles' but not his stepfather's original home. King of a nearby city, Amphitryon had moved the Thebes to establish a home. Maybe this made him, the first mentor of Heracles' growth, more open to the latter's need to develop beyond the secure limits of a traditional family.

relatedness to others. Rooted in his own country, Heracles overcomes these powers easily, not suspecting that he may have to face them later on a much deeper level. Having freed the land of these perils, he now faces the universal fact that being good, having control over one's impulses, is not enough; that identity wanes unless we are willing to re-expand our world. The foreign king who insists upon a regular tribute is basically our own environment to which we must make concessions and which diminishes our self. This environment, the influence of which must be consciously fought, is both external and internal. Athene, the goddess sprung from Zeus' forehead, offers the arms. Yet, in assisting in the defeat of the external king, Heracles' stepfather is killed. Now the hero seems to have achieved independence, maturity and integration, and he is ready for greater feats.

After marrying Megara, the daughter of Thebes' king, Kreon, he joins the gods in their battle against the giants. Inasmuch as the latter can be killed only by a mortal, and inasmuch as Heracles—though destined for immortality—is still a mortal, the gods need him desperately to overcome the threat of these dragon-tailed, powerful creatures. Only the mortal human being, the self striving for authenticity, can decide the battle within his deepest sources of strength, between light and darkness, God and devil, good and evil. The battle in which all the Olympian, terrestrial, oceanic and netherworldly deities participate is one of apocalyptic proportions. Yet the giants' doom is never in doubt; and Heracles, easy victor in all confrontations, can settle into a pleasant domestic life with Megara who bears him three sons.

This entire first group of journeys is but a colorful foreplay. In spite of experiencing himself as the hero who has made his country safe and whom even the gods need for protection, he is still far from being a truly authentic person. He has neither gained independent self-esteem, nor has he found peace with Hera who, in Jungian terms, would be designated as the *magna mater* or the archetypical *anima* figure. The lack of independent self-esteem is clearly evidenced in his inability to swallow his pride when his barely older cousin Eurystheus is declared rightful head of all the descendants of Perseus. Hera, in cunningly promoting the premature birth of Eurystheus, expressed her jealous hatred for her stepson. On a different level, she simultaneously challenged him toward further growth. Yet this growth could take place only after much of Heracles' earlier, rapidly erected, world crumbled: despondent over having being slighted, the hero becomes insane. First he wants to kill his best friend, Jolaos; and, when the latter escapes, he shoots his own three sons. His marriage to Megara—a reflection of the unresolved relationship to the *magna mater* who protects marriages—is doomed and ends up sterile.

Returned to sanity, Heracles is finally willing to accept the gods' ruling that he must perform ten important deeds for his cousin Eurystheus in Mycene. The starting point for this group of journeys is now some eighty miles from his birthplace.* Without unnecessarily delving into details of these journeys, we notice that the first four (the overcoming of the Nemeic lion, of the Hydra, of the deer Kerynitis, and of the Erymatheic boar) are again a confrontation with powerful animals. The animals are no longer common beasts as those encountered in the hero's home country; they all have some unusual, supernatural properties. The Nemeic lion is so utterly invulnerable that after he has been strangled his skin can be cut only with the aid of his own claws; the Hydra's nine heads, when truncated, grow back two-fold, and in addition one of the heads is immortal; the deer has golden antlers; and to reach the boar, Heracles must confront the mysterious centaurs. The fifth journey is important not only because of the radically different nature of the task, but also because it underlines both the requirement for absolute openness in the performance of a task and Eurystheus' role as the hero's mentor overshadowing that of the role of jealous cousin. Hera's or Eurystheus' jealousy seen as weakness from a restricted viewpoint becomes a virtue fitting a divine plan.

Until now each journey led the hero to a task farther and farther away from Mycene: approximately six, twenty, forty and then sixty miles. The stables of Augeas that Heracles was to clean

*One might speculate here about the symbolic significance of the fact that Megara, a township named after his first wife, is about halfway between Thebes and Mycene.

of years of accumulated manure were some eighty miles from the point of departure. This challenge—somewhat similar to the menial tasks in fairy tales (*cf. Cinderella* or *Amor and Psyche*)—is not exactly a noble one; and as if to offset his having to swallow his pride again, Heracles asks Augeas for a substantial reward. As a result of this flaw, the hero's gradually broadened world shrinks again. Eurystheus refuses credit for this fifth journey; nor can he accept the subsequent one in which Heracles chases the Stymphalides to a faraway country, since these metal-feathered birds were located but thirty miles from Mycene. His world having narrowed as a result of the imperfect fifth journey, Heracles must retrace some of his steps. Only the next task that leads him beyond the sea and more than one hundred miles away from Mycene can again be given credit. Thus Heracles makes twelve rather than ten journeys under the mentorship of Eurystheus. His world continues to expand, and with the tenth journey he reaches the very borders of the physical world. Here he plants the *Pillars of Hercules*.

The last two tasks lead him beyond the limits of measurable space. In fact, when he departs for his eleventh excursion, he no longer knows what earthly direction to take. Only by powerfully confronting Nereus (analogous to Proteus, the everchanging god of the ocean and source of everything), he finds the secret of the way. From now on he deals primarily with various gods. He frees Prometheus from the rock to which he was chained by Zeus' order; and Atlas steals the golden apples of the Hesperides while the hero in the meantime sustains the universe. He is able to be useful to the gods and to use gods; and the danger of hybris again looms near. The universe has become his world; only the netherworld is not yet under his control. This is his last task: to bring the very Cerberus in chains from this world of the shadows. When this is accomplished, Eurystheus, convinced and satisfied, declares Heracles to be totally free of any bonds of obligation to him.

Yet is our hero now truly free? He makes another attempt to relate to a woman. Having married off his understandably estranged wife Megara to his best friend Jolaos, he woos Jole, Eurytos' daughter. Though he proves his worthiness by winning an archery contest, he is told to wait. While his world-design has spanned beyond the universe, the hero has not learned to tolerate the uncertainty, the frustration and the pains of waiting. Thus his world must crumble once more. As he becomes psychotic, his paranoid misperception of reality induces him to kill Eurytos' son, Iphitos, who had been his faithful friend.

During the period of frustration preceding his second insanity the hero gives battle to death himself. Since this episode relates to his ambivalence toward parental figures, we shall discuss it below. Eventually he recovers from the subsequent psychosis. Only the third king he asks to cleanse him of Iphitos' murder accedes to his wish, whereupon the oracle of Delphi demands as penance that he serve again. He becomes not just a faithful servant of a king, but the slave of a queen. For three years a woman becomes his mentor. As her reign is in Asia Minor, the starting point for the tasks he is to perform for her is across the sea, three hundred miles away from his original home. The significance of Omphale herself will be discussed below.

In regard to his life in Asia Minor, two striking aspects should be noted briefly. First we find that the hero no longer must begin with confronting ferocious animals. Instead he is primarily preoccupied with rectifying or avenging various human injustices. Second, after being successful in these humanitarian tasks, and after marrying Omphale, he turns into a rather weak, effeminate person who enjoys the luxuries of his mistress' palace and performs various feminine tasks.

As soon as the three years are up, Heracles becomes "himself" again; soon he will woo Deianira. The three years are clearly a nonmeasurable-time indication; an indication of the proper time, when the protagonist, through inward growth, has become ready for a new phase in his development. We find many analogous time indications especially in fairy tales where, for example, the young queen must maintain absolute silence for three years if she is to rescue her seven bewitched brothers.

4. Let us inquire a bit further into the meaning of Heracles' two psychotic periods between his three groups of journeys. There is one vantage point from which turning insane can be seen as an expression of incongruity or strain between the in-

dividual's world and the world around him. Of the various factors leading to such incongruity, an important one is the individual's neglect of some basic features or parts of his own personality in the endeavor to develop others rapidly. At one point he becomes unbalanced, and the lofty structure he has built disintegrates temporarily, since it cannot tolerate the strain created by the neglected aspects of the personality.*

In the first series of tasks Heracles did not consider sufficiently how much of his success was due to his being rooted in his "fatherland," how superficial his confrontation with himself was, and how little he was ready for true fatherhood and marriage. In the second series of tasks the confrontation with himself was thorough and led to his being integrated in the universe, but he still needed a father-figure as guide, and he still ended up incapable of tolerating the frustration of having to wait for his bride.† After his second psychotic period, he had to develop his humanitarian side. By identifying with the feminine role, he became capable—almost—of being a satisfactory husband and father. Psychosis, from this vantage point, is seen as a challenge to recognize what has been neglected, to develop it, and to work toward integrating it in one's personality. What has been

*Though the strain can be viewed also as due to the unbalanced development of the cultural environment, the hero's task is to deal responsibly with whatever external world he is confronted with. While Laing[102] may be right in stating that insanity is a mode of living in a crazy world, Sartre[154] is also right in stressing that we can never abdicate the responsibility toward the situation we find ourselves in without becoming more inauthentic.

†In Jungian terminology one might say that the first group of journeys dealt with the confrontation and integration of the hero's *personal shadow*. The second group of journeys dealt with the *collective shadow*—only then a confrontation with his *anima* could be in any way successful. Prior to the confrontation with Omphale, the hero's relationships with Megara and Jole ended tragically. Subsequently he had a somewhat successful marriage with Deianira and eventually a blissful life with Hebe.

While in the first two groups of journeys the growth of the hero is expressed largely in spatial terms and eventually transcends measurable space, subsequently a temporal dimension seems to enter the hero's life. This is at least alluded to by: (a) his inability to *wait* for Jole; (b) his defying the inexorable, time-conscious death in his rescue of Alceste; and (c) the commitment to slavery for a period of three years. Thus the shift from the exploration of the shadow to the confrontation of the *anima* has parallels in the development of a qualitative spatial and temporal consciousness.

called the psychotic or psychedelic "trip" would then largely correspond to the hero's attempt to become more and more himself by letting exaggerated or one-sided structures be deconstituted in the hope of building eventually a harmonious whole or "self."[82,96] Heracles did not achieve this fully in his lifetime. His marriage to Deianira was a rather stormy one and eventually led to their violent deaths. Neither had achieved the necessary "unconditional positive regard" for the other.

Uncontrolled or poorly controlled impulses—short of psychosis—had plagued Heracles all his life: from his angry homicide of Linos, to nearly killing a close friend in front of Troy because of envy, to his impulsive killing of a boy waiting on him, to his irrational slaying of a faithful messenger shortly before his painful death. Maybe it is his marriage to Hebe, the goddess of youth, that symbolizes his continued need to strive further. Heroism, probably, is not measured by how close to the goal you come, but by how valiantly, how desperately, and how far you travel. And the boon that the hero—or the schizophrenic traveler—can bring back to his people is largely contained in the message that there are new worlds, and new aspects of our psyche to explore.

5. When the beloved king Admetos was doomed by fate to die, his wife Alceste was the only one willing to offer her own life for his. Just when Lord Death, Thanatos, came to her grave to drink of the sacrificial blood, Heracles wrestled with him and forced him to return her alive. Empathy for the profound meaning of marriage, in addition to his friendship with Admetos and his sympathy for Alceste's generosity, led the hero to act in harmony with his stepmother, Hera. Thus he is later able to enter the realm of Omphale, though only after breaking down again.

Placed into an ambiguous situation in infancy, Heracles continues to be plagued by his *anima* which is jealous and challenging, and searches for an harmonious integration with it. The early marriage to Megara, ending in tragedy and separation, proves that this integration is not as simple as we often think. With Jole the attempt remains in suspense, as Heracles' son, Hyllos eventually marries her. With Alceste the hero reveals his readiness to face the deeper aspects of his *anima* that first appear in the darkness of Thanatos. Later he encounters these deep feminine secrets in the image of Omphale, the navel-woman, the mysterious source of life: queen, mentor, partner, lover and mother.

Heracles must break with any tradition and return to the very origin of his existence in order to learn what genuine humanitarianism and femininity are. It is primarily within himself that he must find this harmonizing source. We can truly understand "the Others" only when we can identify with them. Thus it becomes plausible that after his stay at Omphale's court, Heracles can enter a marriage that produces a viable offspring, Hyllos. However, his impulsive jealousy of the centaur Nessos, and later Deianira's jealousy of her husband's relationship with Jole, lead to a catastrophic end. Neither internally nor externally has the proper balance and relationship between the masculine and feminine principle been fully achieved. Only beyond death—namely in a nebulous future—looms the answer. His feminine relationships will fail again unless the hero, the individual self, can grow to where his feminine counterpart, his wife, or his *anima* is experienced as the fountain of youth which challenges continued growth.*

6. Whereas Heracles' ambivalent relationship to women is emphasized from the very beginning of the myth, his feelings toward men—though less obviously—are equally ambivalent. After accepting his wife's son, Amphitryon fearfully rejects the adolescent Heracles. Later the stepfather joins his son in the battles to free Thebes from the bonds imposed by a neighboring king, and dies while Heracles is victorious. Jolaos, the hero's best friend, is nearly murdered by him. Eurystheus is both a fearful, jealous cousin and a wise guide. Admetos is a friend whose wife he saves from the dead, and who, in psychoanalytic terms, is an

*After failing on earth to establish a lasting relationship with Gretchen and with Helena, and after entering a transcendental realm, Faust finally concludes, "The eternal feminine keeps drawing us upwards." In Goethe's *Faust,* Gretchen can be viewed as the personal, Helena as the collective *anima;* and in Jungian terms Mephistopheles is both Faust's guide and the *shadow* he has to deal with before a harmonious relationship with the feminine counterpart is possible.

excellent example of an internalized, hidden, conflictful father-figure: first Admetos has to die; however, this cannot be allowed to happen. Thus mother becomes the recipient of the death wishes. Yet she is too lovable and kind. So the guilt-ridden son-hero rescues her for the father. He saves the parents and then he becomes insane. He cannot as yet tolerate the desperate feelings of loneliness resulting from the solution of the oedipal triangle and the uncertainty of waiting for Jole. Had he successfully resolved the oedipal triangle, he would have had the inner strength or patience to wait.

The hero painfully remembers every injustice against him by any father-figure, and spends much of his later life in "getting even." In a deeper psychological sense this, too, is an intrapsychic process of establishing a greater inner balance and freedom. Thus Laomedon and Augeas who fail to pay promised rewards are slain; the two kings who refused to give him absolution for the murder committed during his second psychosis are exterminated along with their families; and, finally, even Eurytos is killed for hedging to give Heracles his daughter Jole, the price earned in fair competition. All the accounts are straightened, and the hero is now ready to die, leaving the son to marry the woman who could have been his mother. The oedipal triangle, and the struggle to free oneself from its entanglements, permeate this myth in manifold ways.*

7. The mountain is the place from which everything is visible. Inasmuch as the heroes—Elias, Moses, Heracles, or the Winnebago Wakdjunkaga—have gained an encompassing vision, their death and transfiguration on top of a mountain is a beautiful metaphor. The genuine experience on a sacred mountain is one of transcendence. Transcendence from the perishable world where "everything is but a symbol,"[54] where every greatest effort still proves inadequate; transcendence to a world where that which

*The hero is neither calculatingly selfish nor romantically humanitarian. He acts out of an inner necessity, a necessity to unfold his authentic fate.[136] His alternate choice is to refuse, with attendant negative consequences for himself and for his people. Heracles, like Faust, did not miss the call for adventure. Both failed at times, both became psychotic temporarily, both struggled on, and both had not reached perfection when death called them. But both had, again and again, expanded their world-design into new dimensions.

was started on earth will find achievement. And achievement here is not an end, but a new state that leaves room for the eternal becoming, for the eternal feminine, for youth. The earthly cycle is ended. It originated on Mount Olympus from which Zeus descended to meet Alcmene; it terminates on Mount Olympus to which Heracles returns to marry the goddess of eternal youth, Hebe. Or, to quote once more from the last lines of *Faust:*

Alles Vergängliche ist nur ein Gleichnis.	Everything perishable is but a symbol.
Das Unzulängliche hier wird's Erreichnis.	Here the unattainable is reached.
Das Unbeschreibliche hier wird es getan.	Here the undescribable is done.
Das ewig Weibliche zieht uns hinan.	The eternal feminine keeps drawing us on.[54]

PART III

Various Themes of Fairy Tales and Myths

CHAPTER XVIII

INTRODUCTORY REMARKS

Illustrated with the Story of Zlatovlaska

IN THE PRECEDING CHAPTERS we attempted to show that many fairy tales depict the essential features of *individual* human development from birth to adulthood. To this effect we chose-for a closer study some of the best known Grimms' tales which focus fairly specifically on different phases of childhood development. However, we were repeatedly led to realize that the growth of the individual is closely interrelated with the historical fate of the human race, and that the chosen tales contain numerous themes referring not only to the meaning of childhood development, but also to all aspects of human existence. The previous chapter on Heracles showed how the myth deals with the hero's development, leading beyond childhood and adolescence. The grown-up human being who has become aware of the continuous challenge for further development finds himself wedded to the goddess of eternal youth. Both for the individual and for his culture, growth appears as a never-ending process.

There is a complex, essential interrelationship between the growth of the individual and the progress of his culture. It would be incorrect to see the people of Sumeria, ancient Greece or Egypt as differing from those of modern Western civilization solely because their environments affected their development in different ways. It would be equally incorrect to view the individual of the twentieth century as incompatibly different in his basic psychosomatic makeup from his ancestors. Nevertheless, there seem to occur gradual changes in the basic structure of the human beings, changes which require a suitable environment to manifest themselves. It is primarily the Jungian psychology which clearly stresses this in its description of the archetypical images. These are seen as hereditary factors, acquired and rooted in preceding generations, and as powerfully active in structuring the individual's feelings, thoughts and actions.

In the following chapters we hope to shed some light upon several recurring fairy tale or mythic themes and images dealing with the meaningfulness of our world, with our historical development and our distant goals. Human life contains so many different significant aspects, such almost unfathomable depths and mysteries, that we shall be satisfied if we add but a little insight into the wisdom of folklore as effective portrayals of human existence and evolution. In order to gain a wider perspective and in order to avoid conveying the impression that the Grimms' tales are unique, we shall draw from a larger circle of stories, but limit ourselves mostly to fragments or brief summaries.

Before attempting a more thorough discussion of several basic fairy tale themes, I would like to review one of the many beautiful Czechoslovakian tales.[89] The purpose is to show how many aspects of human existence can find a simultaneous echo in one single story. This fairy tale tells of a young man, Yirik, who, after numerous challenging adventures, receives in marriage the princess with the golden hair, Zlatovlaska. Yirik, the old king's cook gains a kingdom thanks to his cleverness, his courage, his unselfishness and his compassion for others. However, the whole world seems to participate, in one way or another, in his evolution from cook to king. We recognize, among others, themes of heaven and hell, of deep Christian mysteries, of the three realms of the physical world, of the twelve constellations of the zodiac, of death and of resurrection.

The story first speaks of an old woman bringing the king a serpent. Whoever eats of this serpent will be able to understand the language of all animals. The king, wishing to hide the secret, asks the cook to prepare the serpent as a fish. However, Yirik recognizes the disguise, logically deducts that there must be some special power in the serpent, and therefore eats a little of it. There is in this episode a reference to the paradisiacal serpent promising new knowledge. The king's attempt to deceive Yirik clearly indicates that he tries to hide his continued allegiance to the luciferic serpent under the guise of Christianity, since the fish, *jchthys*,* has always been the main symbol of Christ. We can say that the king still eats from the gift of Lucifer, but pretends that it is a holy wafer. Yirik, too, partakes of the food which enlivens old talents, but without pretending that they represent an expression of Christianity.

Next we see that the king begins to suspect in Yirik a potential, powerful rival, and that he challenges him to fill the goblet without spilling one drop of wine. The goblet and the declining king can remind us of the Holy Grail and Amphortas. The old king senses in Yirik, as Amphortas did in Percival, an individual who eventually may be worthy of guarding the Holy Grail. Both Yirik and Percival fail their first test and are forced to wander into the wide world and to meet various new adventures. To Yirik the mystery of the transubstantiation, of the Holy Grail, is not yet meaningful enough and he allows himself to be distracted by the argument of two birds who are fighting over three golden hairs. As punishment he must find Zlatovlaska, the princess from whose head the three golden hairs came.

Here the fairy tale introduces in a most artistic way the theme of the three realms of the physical world: earth, water and air, which Yirik must befriend before he can hope to find the princess. And it is mostly his ability for sincere compassion,† along with complete unselfishness and clear reasoning, which leads him to success. By helping the ants in the earth, the goldfish in the water and the ravens in the air he gains their friendship.

Now Yirik is ready to meet the father of the golden-haired princess, the king of the crystal palace. Only one of his twelve daughters has golden hair, but she is in sad shape indeed: the pearls of her necklace are scattered in the lawn, her ring is lost

*Not only do the letters of the word *jchthys* correspond to the Greek *Jesus CHristos THeos Ymon Soter* (Jesus Christ our Lord and Savior), but throughout the New Testament the fish has been a symbol of the activity of Christ and his disciples.

†Interestingly, it was Percival's failure to experience and express pity which led to his being chased from the castle of the Holy Grail into the world. Here he had to develop the ability for compassion before he could find his way back.[57]

in the sea and her hair, like that of her eleven sisters, is hidden by a veil. We have already mentioned the number twelve in *Briar Rose* as indicating the forces shaping the human spiritual life, forces which in ancient times were seen represented in the twelve constellations of the zodiac. Here we find this world-embracing number in the twelve daughters in the crystal palace of whom Yirik has to choose the right one. Her spiritual treasures are lost or hidden, and only he who has befriended all the realms of the physical world can restore them. The earthbound ants help Yirik find all the pearls scattered on the earth, the fish help him to recover the ring in the water and the airborne ravens help him to detect under which of the twelve veils the hair flows golden. The theme of the golden hair is found in numerous fairy tales and we shall speak of it in greater detail in another chapter.*

The most significant theme in this story is that of death and resurrection, which recurs three times, and which—again with a deeply Christian coloring—points to an essential aspect of human evolution. The grateful ravens (we already encountered them in *Snow White and the Seven Dwarfs* as symbols of higher wisdom) have brought to Yirik, from far away, the water of life and the water of death. Taking pity on a fly caught by a spider, he uses a little of each of these waters to kill the spider and to revive the fly which gratefully helps him discover Zlatovlaska among her sisters.

Even the restoration of her spiritual assets, her pearls, ring and golden hair, is tied in, therefore, with the problems of the physical world and of death and resurrection. Indeed, before Yirik becomes king himself and can marry the princess, he, too, must go through death and resurrection. In fact, instead of keeping his promise, the old king has Yirik decapitated when the latter returns with the princess. Zlatovlaska first sprinkles the head and the trunk with the water of death, and this makes the

*There are many variations of this tale. The Grimms brothers have the story of *The White Serpent*, and Madame d'Aulnoy tells the tale of *Dawn, the Golden Haired*. Here the king's ambassador named Welcome is sent to woo Dawn. A fish, a crow and an owl he had helped assist him in achieving three "impossible" tasks. Eventually the king, jealous and desiring eternal youth, dies by mistakenly taking the poison he uses against his enemies, and Dawn marries Welcome, who becomes the new king.[6]

body whole again. Then she revives Yirik with the water of life. Death has to be accepted along with life before a true spiritual awakening can occur, before the wedding of the spirit or *animus* with the soul or *anima* can take place.

The old king, who has secretly hoped to marry Zlatovlaska himself, again fails because he cannot properly accept the Christian mystery of the resurrection. Wishing to be rejuvenated, he has himself decapitated also, ordering that the princess then pour the water of life upon him: nothing happens. Then Zlatovlaska pours the water of death upon him and his body becomes whole again. Now the flask with the youth-restoring water of life is empty, and so the old king remains dead. This can be taken as a beautiful image for the deadness of restored ancient wisdom, in contrast to the aliveness of any new, resurrected spirituality.

Thus goes the tale whose central theme deals with the human being's loss of the old spiritual powers, with his involvement with the earth and with his spiritual rebirth. The water of death is seen not so much as a destructive force than as a force which is able to integrate the head and the body—the brain and the heart, if you wish—which at the end of the adventures on the material earth tend to become separated. We have seen this separation between "spinning brain" and the rest of the personality beautifully portrayed in the old woman and Briar Rose, up in the top of the tower, spinning, separated from the rest of the castle by a door, locked with a rusty key. The spinning intellect, like the spider spinning her deadly net, has to be overcome. This frees the little fly which leads Yirik to the true princess. Through death a new and higher consciousness becomes possible, but it takes the water of life (again reminiscent of Christ's blood in the chalice) to bring this new consciousness to a spiritual awakening.

In fairy tales death has therefore two meanings: (a) The coming to nought of such destructive, negative forces which may have had some usefulness in the past, but which have been successfully overcome. (b) An experience which we human beings must cope with, which we have to face, before a higher consciousness can be awakened. This tale illustrates in sweeping, magnificent images the course of human evolution, starting in a remote, clairvoyant past, moving through a present in which the earth must be faced in all its aspects, including death, toward an indistinct future. Thus this tale is an excellent introduction to the following chapter. The theme of death, however, will be picked up in greater detail in two later chapters.

CHAPTER XIX

THE THREE EPOCHS OF HUMAN EVOLUTION AS PORTRAYED IN FOLKLORE

Any categorization of human development or evolution into clear-cut periods is bound to be somewhat arbitrary. However, in a large number of tales, three main phases are fairly easily discernible. On the one hand they are related to Joseph Campbell's distinction of *departure, adventure* and *return* of the hero.[24] The emphasis is laid upon the need of rejuvenation of the old order that becomes suffocating because of its radical conservatism. Here, the hero—defying and breaking down seemingly impregnable barriers (dragons, sphinxes, devitalizing commitments and obsolete taboos)—returns eventually with the boon that brings new life to his people. On the other hand they simultaneously correspond to a basic experience of the human being, telling him of a past, more spontaneous awareness of the meaningfulness of himself and the world of his despair in an existence caught up within a purely objective, alien, material-sensory world, and finally of his inkling that he will be able to find a new, profounder awareness of his role in a significant universe. It is the latter view of the three phases that we shall develop in this chapter.

In the simplest terms, the three phases are portrayed, one way or another (a) by a prematerialistic period (golden age, garden of Eden, etc.); (b) by a very long period during which humanity is oriented increasingly toward the material world with its sensory and spatial features; and (c) by a (future) post-materialistic period.

It may be proper to insert here that the careful phenomenologic analysis of the development of consciousness in the infant has shown what might be called a pre-formation or matrix of these three experiential phases. On the basis of observations by Spitz,[164] Klein[159] and others, Elkin has shown how critical the period between the third and sixth month of infantile development is in laying the foundations of self-awareness. Whereas the three-month-old child, at the dawn of what Elkin terms "primordial consciousness," experiences a paradisiacal, non-spatial, Nirvana-like consciousness, he is soon precipitated into experiences of alternating terror and bliss, of goodness and evilness, eventually shifting his trust, at approximately six months, to an all-mighty, external Being. Whereas the first phase is described by terms such as "garden of Eden," "satori," "Nirvana," or is portrayed in the magnificent *Mandalas,* the second is symbolized by the horror and bliss of the Indian goddess Kali or by apocalyptic, contending forces; and the third is depicted best in the image of the Madonna with her child, or in the heavenly Jerusalem.[39]

It would be a grave error to *reduce* all cultural phases as well as the rich experiences of the grown-up to these early terms. The latter should be seen as a first manifestation of the essential human potential which, through repeated cycles, aims at concretizing itself in the individual and in his culture. These ongoing cycles of loss of blissful harmony, existential anxiety or despair, and new integration seem to reflect the very pulsation of life and lead to new levels of consciousness.

In other words we may simultaneously envision: (a) a basic cycle of human evolution, beginning with the first emergence of awareness, continuing with the deepening knowledge of good and evil and of this earth's joys and sorrows, and eventually moving toward a blissful resolution (satori, new Nirvana, millenium, new paradise, or Teilhard de Chardin's "Merging in Point Omega");[170] (b) innumerable subcycles in which cultures and individuals repeatedly undergo this alternation between safely established structures, unstructuring or deconstitution, and restructuring of an ever wider world; (c) the original matrix for these experiences, laid in the period of the early awakening of the infant's consciousness; and (d) the new manifestations of this matrix in the successive developmental phases of the individual.

However, it is only by letting the images of myths and fairy tales speak *to* us, rather than by making them fit into rigid theories, that we begin to notice their multidimensional and colorful meanings. They are likely to reveal new aspects to different readers. If we do not impose our prejudices upon these insights, if we let them emerge out of the experience of the narrations, they will take on more and more convincing characteristics.

Let us focus, for the sake of clarity, concreteness and simplicity, upon the basic cycle of human evolution as it is reflected in many fairy tales. The central theme is the development of a spiritually self-aware individual during the course of the three mentioned epochs or phases. The variations of this motif in fairy tales and myths from all over the world are not simply trivial or accidental; they are mainly the indication of the richness and diversity of the meaningful ideas that underlie, shape and further our existence. Each people, each person, each period manifests this motif according to its own peculiarities. If to us in the twentieth century this central theme appears overly simple, it is because our thinking tends toward extreme abstractions. We describe—as I felt compelled to do in the preceding paragraphs—whatever deals with profound meanings in such a way that it appears overly general, vague or unreal. In fact, Western civilization tends to treat thoughts and things almost as entirely unrelated entities. It views thoughts and ideas as secondary to things, just as shadows are to objects.

When we contemplate man-made technical or artistic objects, it is easy for us to see that their physical substance is shaped by the underlying thoughts and ideas. Without ideas the physical substance would be worthless. In analogy to this it can be said that in the God-created world our five senses perceive the physical manifestation of creation (using this term in its very broadest meaning), while our thinking grasps the thoughts and ideas that led to this manifestation.[67,137] Physical objects are then seen as secondary to thoughts, as a form of apparition of ideas within the material realm. Consequently the thought-world, instead of remaining a realm of vague, dull shadows, becomes a creative, real world, filled with ideas whose contours are sharp, whose colors are rich, and whose variety equals or exceeds the infinite variety of things we experience with our physical sense organs. Thoughts become things; and truth becomes more than mere ratiocination; truth becomes revelation.[64]

Yet this world of ideas truly discloses itself to the thinking individual only when he is capable of love, since without love, without the capacity for a genuine intersubjective relationship he cannot maintain a feeling of identity or self-awareness. This is the conclusion of a modern fairy tale, in which the wise fox asks the Little Prince to tame him, to become his friend: "One only understands the things that one tames." And the fox continues: "Men have no more time to understand anything . . . it is only with the heart that one can see rightly; what is essential is invisible to the eye."[151]

May I add that the wealth and variety of the world of ideas has been impressed upon me also by the fact that when I have tried to recapture a thought I had previously, it was often lost in such a vastness of ideas, that I could not find it again. However, once an insight is really complete, we become aware of its exact location in the world of thoughts, and we can then find it easily whenever we need it. This has little to do with intelligence as measured by intelligence quotients. Intelligence is merely a tool, often clumsy and inadequate, but certainly not proportionate to the insights it may help us gain. The latter depend more on my interest, my sincere efforts and my love for them. They are beyond the intellect and especially beyond our corruptible memory which disappoints us so often. When insights and ideas are solely the result of intelligence, they become like the brilliant, prodigally scattered gold pieces in Goethe's *Fairy Tale*[53] which are worthless to the will-o'-the-wisps that produce them, and highly disturbing to the eternally moving river between the two shores.[67]

We become more and more aware of our apparent physical insignificance as science shows us that we are but one of three billion inhabitants on one of the smallest of billions of celestial bodies. We can find some compensation for our minuteness in the realization that our thinking can encompass the universe.

In this materialistic age we have become spiritually poor. We may still have a vague memory of a past golden age, but even in this respect the present natural-scientific viewpoint may cast doubts as to whether such an epoch ever existed. The term "golden age" certainly does not imply a romanticized belief in an early period when there was no cruelty, suffering, sickness and want. It refers to a stage of evolution of mankind where the individual experienced himself in harmony with the world around him; where everything was experienced as meaningful, whether bad or good, painful or gratifying; and where a person's feeling of selfhood was not sharply delimited, thus preventing the loneliness and anxiety that makes many of *our* pains and conflicts unbearable. Today we may still sense that there must be a meaning behind all that our physical senses reveal. We retain a glimmer of hope that the future will offer an explanation of our existence which—rather than making skeptics and nihilists out of us—will truly satisfy.

Whether they deal primarily with the development of the individual child or whether they deal with the evolution of humanity, fairy tales and myths always point toward this future. While there is a wide choice of tales in which the three epochs of humanity can be recognized, the story of *The Goose Girl*[58] (because it is another beautiful Grimms' tale), and that of *Jack and the Beanstalk* (because it is so well known) will serve here the purpose of illustration.[89]

The king-father having passed away, the mother sends the young princess off to the bridegroom prince. In parting she presents her daughter with a dowry, with the horse Fallada, with a maid and with a handkerchief on which there are three drops of her own blood.

This beginning of the story of *The Goose Girl* refers to a transition: the old king, as in many other stories, is the representative of the golden age which is coming to an end. The golden age was an almost prehistorical epoch in which the human beings communed freely with the gods and other supernatural forces, while their awareness of themselves as unique individuals was still only vague and undeveloped. Their *conscious* orientation was more toward spiritual things than toward the physical surroundings to which they responded instinctively rather than rationally.

In our story we see the human being, the princess, wander into this wide material world. Her golden hair bears testimony of her noble origin, the mother's blood on her handkerchief still ties her slightly to the past and protects her, the talking horse Fallada reflects a persistence in her of atavistic, intuitive powers. Such was shown by the old king and by Yirik in the story of Zlatovlaska, the princess with the golden hair, which we mentioned in the preceding chapter. The arrogant maid, however, represents a new facet of the human being which has no respect for its noble origin and selfishly wishes to usurp all the rights and possessions of the princess.

As they travel through the physical world, the pure human soul, deprived of the solace of her home, grows thirstier and thirstier.* And since the spiritual world no longer quenches her thirst, she is forced, again and again, to bend toward the earth in order to drink from a simple brook. But in doing so, she loses her handkerchief with mother's protecting blood drops. At this moment the noble soul becomes helplessly subservient to an arrogant maid, to a presumptuous materialistic consciousness, who, arriving at the prince's castle, pretends to be the rightful bride and sends the true princess to help little Conrad tend the geese.

Every day the princess goes out into the fields, guards the geese and combs her beautiful golden hair. Whenever Conrad teasingly disturbs her by trying to pull a few of her hairs, she asks the wind to blow away his hat so that he has to run after

---

*One of the most beautiful descriptions of this thirst in the material world is contained in the aforementioned story of *The Little Prince,*[151] a modern, at times a little too intellectual, fairy tale. Here the prince with the golden hair, who had owned a little planet all by himself, descends to the earth and finds himself in the midst of the Sahara desert, where he encounters the thirsting poet and consoles him: "What makes the desert beautiful is that somewhere it hides a well." And soon they find it. What seems impossible (or as Goethe would say "unreachable") in the physical realm, becomes possible in the spiritual sphere: "What I see here is nothing but a shell. What is most important is invisible."

it. Little Conrad with his *hat* (see Chapter XXII) as well as the honking geese seem to represent the silly, disorderly disturbances of everyday life which impinge upon the soul when it wants to rearrange its delicate golden threads. Finally, the prince's father begins to suspect that there is something peculiar about this goose girl, but she cannot tell him her secret. The human soul has to find its reawakening entirely within itself, harmonizing it fully with the warmth of the heart. Admirably and in perfect simplicity, this is illustrated by the image of the goose girl hiding in the oven to which alone she can confide her sorrow. However, the prince's father* listens in (old spiritual powers help us even when we do not know it). With the reinstatement of the true princess, the arrogance and the narrow, selfish, materialistic, false pride of the maid is exposed, and the fake princess chooses her own destruction.

In direct relation to this fairy tale I wish to mention a historical event which—though outwardly hardly noticed—turned out to be of the utmost significance for the evolution of philosophic and scientific thinking. I am referring to the mystical crisis of the young Descartes on the night of November 10, 1619, excellently documented and analyzed by J. Rittmeister.[149]

Descartes had lost his mother soon after his birth, received most of his education in the Jesuit Collège of La Flèche, obtained degrees in law and medicine in Poitiers and, at the age of twenty-one, entered the military service as a volunteer soldier for four years. He was twenty-three years old, far away from his country, constantly assailed by doubts in regard to the validity of the scholastic philosophy taught at La Flèche, when on the fateful night he retired to his abode which he called his oven, at the winter quarters of the army. Here he had three dreams: in the first one, fighting a tornado, he attempts to reach the chapel of La Flèche in order to pray. As he passes a person carrying a melon, his intention changes and he again has to fight the bad

*The old king in fairy tales and myths can have two connotations. Sometimes one prevails, sometimes both occur. He may be a jealous, hindering, cruel "holdfast," or he may represent a solid, enduring, calm principle that succors the human being.

spirit, namely the wind which is now trying to push him toward the chapel; he awakens.

In the second dream he experiences thunder and his room, the oven, is filled with sparks. The oven, here, has exactly the same significance as in *The Goose Girl:* it is the place where a spiritual rebirth takes place (with thunder and sparks), when the human being, alone, shaken in his innermost depths by doubt, cold and tossed around by the wind, turns into himself. The young volunteer soldier, on the eve of the Thirty Years' War which was to transform Europe, fights within himself to find the *universal key* to unlock the meaning of the world.

In the first dream he experiences as evil the force which interferes with his wish to return to the former, God-centered, source of spiritual knowledge, the chapel. But as he passes the fruit (of knowledge?) everything is suddenly reversed and it becomes evil to let one's self be pushed back to the chapel. True spiritual wisdom can no longer be obtained from tradition; it has to come from within; it starts with the ego (this he later expressed in his famous *Ego cogito ergo Ego sum:* "I think" or rather "I reflect upon myself, therefore I exist"). The third dream, then, reassures Descartes that it is permissible to doubt, and that eventually there will be a general science based, not on what God has revealed to others, but on our own ego.

Only nine years after this crisis to which the philosopher-scientist himself attributed the greatest importance, did he start publishing his ideas. From what I gather, the experts are still arguing as to whether Descartes was a devil who drew humanity away from God by paving the way for our present-day natural science, or a prophet who opened the door for an eventual spiritual rebirth of the human being on a more self-reflective level. I believe the latter, even though Descartes himself only experienced an inkling of this reawakening. After going through three epochs—spiritual training in France, soldiering and traveling all over Europe, and creativity in Holland—he died shortly after arriving in Sweden where he had been called to discuss the problems of love and hate with the young queen, and where he overdid himself taking loving care of a sick friend.

In the Cinderella stories we can also easily detect the three epochs, the suffering and slaving of the good girl representing, like the goose girl tending the geese (or Descartes' soldiering), the middle, materialistic epoch (see Chapter XI). Usually these tales end happily. But occasionally we find a story such as that of *The Turkey Girl* (see Chapter IV) which ends sadly. Having lingered too long at the dance, the poor Indian girl disappears forever from her village, as she looks for the escaped turkeys. This points out that the human soul, lost too long to the pleasures of physical existence, may never regain its original contentedness. This is most dramatically shown in the Greek epos of *The Argonauts* which ends in utter tragedy. The hero, Jason, who had the mission of carrying some of the spiritual treasures of the first epoch, namely the golden fleece* and the woman endowed with supernatural powers, Medea, into the second epoch becomes unfaithful. His new false bride and his children are destroyed by Medea, and he commits suicide.[158]

In one form or another, the three epochs can be recognized, in some respects, in many fairy tales and myths. So often they start with the mention of a beautiful, kingly, safe and loving home. But something occurs which destroys this tranquillity and happiness. Adventures, privations and sufferings befall the human being as he wanders through the world. Then, often when everything seems hopeless, comes the salvation, the vindication, the return to a happier home, the acquisition of a new kingdom, and often the marriage with the prince or the princess.

The story of *Jack and the Beanstalk*[89] shall serve us as a final, quite different example for this. Here the end of the first epoch is depicted by the drying up of the milk in the only cow† of Jack and his mother, necessitating the sale of the animal. Instead, he trades the cow for five beans. Sure enough, the products of the earth appear worthless at first, compared to the

*The fleece, referring to a former, instinctual wisdom, being both fur and golden, can be seen as an amalgamation of the theme of the golden hair and the themes in which the animal represents our instinctual life.

†The cow in this story can be compared to the heavenly cow of the Egyptians, seen as nourishingly outstretched as firmament across the earth. The early source of life is no longer adequate and is exchanged for new potentials in which the human being assumes an ever more active role.

heavenly riches of paradise. But these products grow to gigantic proportions and challenge the intelligent and courageous to outwit the giants of the past and to acquire again more durable heavenly goods. Jack's greatest danger and final victory, however, comes with the acquisition of the permanent and completely spiritualized gold, namely the golden harp. And since in his adventures, Jack's quick thinking was of such decisive importance, this story represents an excellent transition to the next chapter dealing with the human intellect and its relation with other soul forces.

CHAPTER XX

AMOR AND PSYCHE

WE MENTIONED THAT IN OUR TIMES the human intellect has had the tendency to develop itself in one of two directions. As a servant of the natural sciences it has been led far away from philosophic and religious concerns. It has been challenged to become more precise, since in the natural sciences any error in reasoning can soon be revealed by the experiment. Simultaneously, however, thinking is often viewed skeptically when it deals with values, meaningfulness or morals, as experimental proof is not available in the same way in these realms. As a servant to collectivistic, materialistic, political ideologies, the intellect frequently has been corrupted, thereby becoming the tool of the "reign of the lie"* which spreads its ominous shadow all over the earth.

Our increasing capacity to change our physical surroundings (vegetation, climate, configuration of the earth's surface, etc.) by technology, and the steady danger that we—and everything around us—will be destroyed in a nuclear holocaust, by chemical warfare or by pollution, are bound to impress us with the perishableness or transitoriness of everything material. Previously the

*The intellect, in its most common meaning, is but an abstraction which, however, is blindly accepted as a viable reality. It is this very intellect that has allowed us to abstract or create this concept. Thus this type of intellect is the abstraction of itself, revealing its predominant solipsistic or narcissistic aspects. It hides the fact that just because of its artificial separation from feelings, commitment and action, it is permeated by and controlled by drives, urges and impulses that prevent it from revealing the truth, from leading to *aletheia*.

Only when reason, on a more self-aware level, is again the result of the harmonious interaction of feeling-intuition, of thinking, and of creative commitment, can it lead to mutual understanding between human beings or—which is the same—to truth that is revelation.[64]

contemplation of the ancient temples* and pyramids, or the view of the unending flow of a river may have nurtured the feeling or the hope that certain things, at least, of our physical earth are timeless. Contrariwise, our present civilization calls out loudly reminding us every day of Goethe's conclusion in *Faust:* that everything transitory, that everything on this physical earth is only a symbol or a parable, that only in the world of the spirit the unattainable, that which here is inadequate, can be attained. In this world of the spirit, Gretchen, the young woman Faust had loved, seduced and plunged into utter despair, becomes or is recognized as the quintessence, the eternally feminine, which lends impetus, goal and meaning to a timeless existence. This is an existence where the experience of ongoingness is radically different from ours.

Tom Thumb, the fairy-tale tailor, Puss 'n Boots, represent an intellect which, though tied to the material world, eventually opens the door to a new, meaningful or spiritual world. Another aspect of this is given in the will-o'-the-wisps in Goethe's *Fairy Tale* whose tongues alone can open the golden lock to the mysterious temple that had been hidden for so long. Yet we see in the intellect also a potentially diabolical force leading to a greater, chaotic imbalance of our world. Similarly Eros (or Amor) who already in the myth of *Amor and Psyche*† was alternately visualized as an animal monster and as a radiantly beautiful youth, presents two aspects, one leading to sorrow, confusion, madness, imprisonment and death (as in the first part of Goethe's *Faust*), the other leading to salvation.

*Thanks to air pollution, the Greek temples have deteriorated more in the past fifty than in the preceding two thousand years.

†The poet Apuleius in the second century A.D. uses the Latin term *Amor* in conjunction with the Greek *Psyche.* However, since his story is firmly embedded in Greek and pre-Grecian myths and mysteries, we are substituting the name *Eros* (which designates better the essence of this being) except in the direct mention of the title of Apuleius' story. We follow in this Erich Neumann[130] whose book is a fascinating and learned interpretation of this mythical story from a Jungian viewpoint. Eros is largely identical with Phosphoros or Lucifer, the light carrier, the defiant fallen fourth archangel. Goethe's will-o'-the-wisps in his *Fairy Tale* again manifest this dangerous aspect of the sharp intellect, when their antics in the ferryboat threaten to disrupt altogether the link between the two shores.

An impressive fairy tale description of this can be seen in *Allerleirauh* (meaning literally "all kinds of rough things"), where the widowed king falls passionately in love with his own, beautiful, golden-haired daughter.[58,124] Aware that such a sinful, incestuous relationship would only bring disaster upon the whole kingdom, the princess acquires for herself a large coat, made of the skins of many animals. Hiding her beauty and her golden hair in it, she escapes. Even when tempted by the most sinful amorous passion, the truly human aspect of the soul remains intact, though it is covered by the animal skins. Lost in the woods the princess Allerleirauh is found by another king who at first assumes that she must be some strange animal. She ignores her noble origin and is given menial work, very much like Cinderella. Eventually she emerges as a real princess, modest and beautiful, with an ethereal star-studded dress which attests to her belonging to a heavenly world. Now she is worthy of the marriage with the new king.

Perrault's version[139] of this tale is *Donkey Skin*, where the widowed king promises to remarry only if he finds someone as fair as his deceased wife. Thus he ends up wishing to marry his daughter who tries to dissuade him by demanding a dress the color of the weather, then one the color of the moon and finally one the color of the sun. When he is able to produce them all, she asks for the skin of the king's donkey and escapes hidden in it. Like Allerleirauh, Cinderella, Psyche and Iron John, Donkey Skin must hide for an established period the finest spiritual germs of her soul.

Incest is the negative reflection, the misunderstood aspect of the highest love. A rather drastic reverse illustration of this was offered recently by a brilliant psychoanalyst who, in a well-documented talk, advanced the hypothesis that the crux of the Christ-Maria-Judas relationship consisted in an incestuous attachment between Christ and Maria for which poor Judas was made responsible.[147] If the spiritual significance of Christ is ignored, we end up seeing only a shadow of His relationship with the Virgin, a shadow which then spells out incest. Or let us look at the beginning of the wonderful prayer of Saint Bernard in the last song of Dante's *Paradise:*

Vergine Madre, Figlia di tuo figlio . . . Virgin Mother, daughter of your son . . .

With a bit of sophism, we conclude that this verse implies a double incest, namely between the father and the daughter, as well as between the mother and her son.

The human being, dressed in plain, shabby clothes and having lost contact with the true, loving mother, is forced to turn, like Cinderella, to the spent ashes. While being subjected to the selfish and cruel passions of other people (the stepsisters and the stepmother), the human being, alone and covered with the dirt of the physical world, still tries to separate the nourishing lentils and peas from the worthless ashes. Only temporarily can the genuine, unselfish soul free itself and go to the prince's castle, clothed in the most beautiful golden and silvery dress. This is in anticipation of the day when the individual, like Allerleirauh or Cinderella, having successfully experienced abandonment in a materialistic world, can in full consciousness (in ordinary, daytime clothes) meet the prince and find acceptance. Together they return to the castle which represents a meaningful world and body in which spirit and matter are integrated. The longing for this world which Cinderella had preserved in her heart, almost as a gift from her deceased mother, becomes now (because of her unselfishness and her demonstrated willingness to cope with the lowliest tasks of the physical world) a new, conscious ability to envision what truly counts. The stepsisters' soul, on the other hand, became corrupted by the selfishness of physical desires. They lost what vision they had: the white doves—always symbols of spiritual life—pick out their eyes.

Our reasoning moves on safe ground when it envisions natural-scientific data, as any error will usually show up soon and can then be corrected. When our thinking becomes part of our fantasies, it remains harmless, as long as we remain fully aware that our daydreams are unreal and serve primarily a need for emotional satisfaction or for playful exploration of options. However, when our thinking is directed toward the understanding of our world, including ethics, religion, philosophy and values, we may or may not be convinced of the reality or viability of our conclusions; yet we have no easy way of corroborating them with a tangible experiment. Whether our conclusions represent objective views of the wisdom of our world, or whether they are distorted images or projections of selfish desires and unresolved problems, will depend largely on how adequately we cope with the animal aspect of our personality. Albrecht Dürer's picture of Saint Jerome (see Fig. 5) in deep meditation over

his writing while the lion and dog are sleeping, his large hat hanging behind him on the wall, so that the rays of light from heaven communicate directly with his head, is a beautiful illustration of the human being exploring the significance of his world when the animal passions are quieted.

The human intellect has contributed greatly to man's separation from nature and has led to a gigantic technologic chain reaction causing human presumptuousness (hybris) and megalomania. On the other hand, the increased keenness of our thinking pitted against the problems of the physical world may also lead us forward to a new, more conscious spiritual awareness.

The dual aspect of the intellect (deadly and magnificent) and the challenge to integrate it harmoniously with our whole personality is portrayed in the story of *Amor and Psyche*. Here Psyche's sisters think of Eros as an animal monster, whereas to Psyche he appears as a beautiful god when she, prematurely, lightens the lamp (of knowledge). More prosaically, in our everyday experience, love—which is so closely associated with sex—encompasses everything from the most sublime longings to the filthiest perversions, from a feeling of unique individual experience to a common, ubiquitous and monotonous passion, from a yearning for beauty to a desire for security, from a meaningful human relationship with heightened consciousness to a reflex interaction which is largely unconscious, from an automatic or compulsive event to a freely and deliberately chosen behavior.

The sexual drives as well as the self-preservative drives are unique in the human being inasmuch as they carry an element of freedom of choice. This is also borne out in Campbell's[25(I)] excellent exposition of the fact that in the human being even the most basic instinctual complexes (defined as "Internal Release Mechanisms"—IRM's) are, at best, only vaguely delineated.

Other biological needs such as hunger, thirst and sleep are less subject to choice; they assert themselves and force the individual, even though he temporarily succeeds in suppressing them. Here, in extreme situations, the hero, the truly *human* being, may still be free, often at the risk of death.

All instincts appear only vaguely—and mostly through secondary manifestations—in our consciousness. In their subjective experience they are hard to describe, devoid of logic, and have a compulsive quality. Thus freeing one's self from their domination has often been considered a sign of self-mastery and of maturity. If it is not fully motivated by hidden, neurotic drives, the ability to renounce sex in chastity, and of disregarding the self-preservative drive in heroism and martyrdom, is seen as true human greatness. The ability to overcome even the instincts which appear more compelling or inevitable, such as hunger and the need for sleep, has frequently been taken as an indication of holiness. While the accounts of such instances usually appear exaggerated, morbid or incredible, we find that even chastity and martyrdom are often the result of morbid needs and inhibitions rather than of true greatness and freedom. Our ability to love and understand may miss an opportunity for further growth by blindly ignoring, condemning or denying the sexual instinct. Yet, in its association with the animal instinct, love also runs the risk of deteriorating into inhuman excesses and perversions; the human being then is "more animal than all other animals" (Mephistopheles in Goethe's *Faust*).

Tales such as those of *Amor and Psyche,* of *The Frog King* (Grimm) and of *The Löweneckerchen* (*Singing and Jumping Lion Lark*—Grimm) in which the lover appears alternately as an animal and as a beautiful male, can be seen, psychoanalytically, as illustrations of a process where guilt and fear because of the sexual desires are followed by sublimations of these wishes into something pure and fine. Usually, in these tales, the lover is human in the darkness of the night, yet returns to his animal form, or disappears altogether, in the daytime. When Psyche prematurely lights the flame of knowledge revealing the beauty of Eros, he disappears. Now she must seek him a long, long time.

In Apuleius' tale *Amor and Psyche*[4] we can recognize the development of the early ego-consciousness out of the original darkness of existence. Here, the youngest of three daughters who "was so strangely and wonderfully fair that human speech was all too poor to describe her beauty" is wedded to Amor or—to use his Greek name in deference to Psyche—Eros. This Eros has two aspects. Psyche's sisters experience him as a huge serpent, "blood and deadly poison dripping from his throat as he devours his human prey." But for Psyche, alone and blissfully unconcerned in the magnificent palace in the depth of a canyon, he is the anonymous lover who meets her only during the night. Her deed of lighting the lamp and of recognizing the beautiful young god corresponds to Eve's original sin. Both actions lead to the awakening of individual consciousness. Psyche, like Adam and Eve who are driven from the garden of Eden, loses her paradisiacal existence and is led through a series of difficult tasks and turmoils.*

In her desperate search for Eros, Psyche first approaches the sacred river, then she defies the horrible monsters and serpents in the river, and finally she is able to cross the river in order to bring back from the underworld the ointment of eternal beauty. Yet this ointment causes her to be overcome by a death-like sleep from which Eros eventually awakens her. We encounter this theme of the death-like sleep in numerous fairy tales—to mention but *Snow White and the Seven Dwarfs* and *Briar Rose;* and we find fragments of the *Amor and Psyche* story in many other folk tales: the separation of the lentils and the peas in the story of *Cinderella;* the danger of being devoured in a regressive paradise in *Hansel and Gretel;* the pricking of the finger in the tale of the *Sleeping Beauty* and of *The Juniper Tree;* the wind which carries the mourning girl to the land of her beloved in several Scandinavian stories;[85] the bad stepsisters, the water of life, the golden hair, the white bird, the three impossible tasks, etc., in fairy tales from many countries. It would be erroneous to see these recurrent themes solely as deteriorated parts of the old myths. Rather, these images constantly modify and rearrange themselves in order best to reflect the basic psychologic situations, configurations and goals of the particular cultural group; at the same time they achieve satisfactory compromises with the current traditional, social, religious and moral standards.

The crucial scene of the *Amor and Psyche* story, the awakening of the nightly lover by the hot drop of oil or wax falling accidentally from the lamp or candle, is also found in several fairy tales. The lover in a French fairy tale is *Green Snake;*[6] the Scandinavian *Prince Hat Beneath the Earth* is a monstrous beast;[85] the German-Swiss *Bear Prince*[167] is a brown bear; the hero in

*Erich Neumann offers an outstanding Jungian analysis of the story *Amor and Psyche,* pointing primarily to the origin of human consciousness in the soul's vicissitudes with the great mother, Venus, mother of Eros. We note here that the Greek distinguished the planet Venus as evening and as morning star. As morning star, it was called Phosphorus, Lucifer or Eros. Succinctly, then, Eros could also be seen as the masculine counterpart of the uroboric serpent, of which Venus, in the tale, would be the feminine counterpart, the *magna mater.*[130]

the Swedish *East of the Sun and West of the Moon* is a white bear;[92] a lion becomes the husband in Grimms' *Singing and Jumping Lion-Lark* tale; and *The Bewitched Prince* in the Swiss-Engadin tale appears at first as an ugly serpent.[22] Yet all these monsters appear as beautiful men when the young woman's light shines upon them. Slightly altered we find a similar theme in the English story of *The Beauty and the Beast,* in the Scandinavian *Prince Lindworm* who is half man and half snake,[85] and—with the sexes reversed—in the Yugoslav *Frog Wife*[32] and the Russian *Frog Princess.*[171] These tales can be seen, psychoanalytically, as illustrations of a process where guilt and fear because of the sexual desires are followed by sublimation of these wishes into something pure and fine. Only gradually can the growing human being become aware of the mystery of Eros, recognizing him, not as an animal monster, not as a diabolical force, not as a silly Cupid, but as a beautiful being. True chastity, indeed, may well require the prior recognition of this.

The development of an individual's independence and ego-awareness appears to be liveliest during adolescence when he matures also biologically. Now the confusion between his intensified sexual drives and his idealistic longings or his growing ability to love lead the soul to experiencing Eros alternately as a beautiful youth and as an ugly or ferocious animal which threatens to defile or devour what is most specifically human. While the various beasts and monsters designate, on the one hand, the negative aspect of Eros, it is particularly the serpent and frog which, on the other hand, portray also the need for a synthesis of the physical-biological and the ideological-emotional world. As amphibian (namely as one who lives in two realms), the frog is excellently suited to symbolize this. We saw him as a messenger with prophetic knowledge in *Briar Rose* where he announced to the queen that she would bear a child. As a link between the cruel world of the Czar and the "I know not where" world, we saw the Giant Frog capable of jumping across the fiery river.[35]

Sexually, then, the snake, the serpent or the frog symbolize both the taboo, unconscious or animal aspects of the instinct and the integration with those emotions and attitudes which are properly designated as love. Here again the two dangers are those of either abandoning one's self blindly in this quasi-unconscious instinctual world, or of one-sidedly completely rejecting the instinct. The story of *The Frog King,* in which the young princess loses the golden ball of her paradisiacal childhood and finally becomes able to accept the ugly frog prince as her beautiful lover and husband, is well known. The psychoanalytic interpretation of the serpent or frog as phallic symbols is, therefore, quite correct, though one-sided or incomplete.[163]

The story of *The Bewitched Prince,* originally narrated in one of the Alpine valleys, will illustrate an additional point. Here the young woman is forced to marry the serpent who guarded the bush with the midwinter roses. She, too, awakens her serpent-lover—who hides in the darkness of the night—with the dripping light and is, therefore, exiled into the inhospitable world. With three pairs of iron shoes she must walk in the droppings of the cows until all the metal has worn off.* Only then does she find a new palace where during a midwinter night she gives birth to a son who turns out to be her lost lover. This fairy tale reflects the influence of the Christian religion in the roses blooming or in the child born in midwinter; and it has adapted itself fully to the pastoral setting. Yet, in all its simplicity, it represents a stage of human development considerably more advanced than that portrayed in the story by Apuleius.

It should be stressed in this regard that in comparing related fairy tales, the apparently trivial differences are often more revealing than the similarities. The mention of two such details

*Let us compare these iron shoes in which the young woman must walk with the glowing red metal shoes in which Snow White's stepmother is forced to dance herself to death. This gives an excellent illustration of the correct and of the erroneous involvement with the earth. The Psyche-woman in *The Bewitched Prince* accepts willingly, humbly and patiently the task of treading the earth with the heavy shoes until they wear off in the cow dung. The bad queen, however, experiences this involvement with the material world as a phrenetic, consuming whirl which leads to her destruction. Similarly we have seen Cinderella's transition from the crouched, hard working girl with the heavy wooden shoes to the princess with the delicate dancing slippers which fit her perfectly. They portray the gracious balance between the freely moving, upright human being and the earth.

can illustrate this and show the greater inwardness or depth of the dramatic events in the story of *The Bewitched Prince.* In place of the golden apples guarded by the ancient dragon, or of the gold and jewels owned by Eros, we find here the luciferic serpent guarding the rosebush. The outward permanency of the gold of the earlier civilization has become the transitory rose, which can leave a permanent reflection within the human soul. While Psyche has a daughter named Pleasure or Joy, our farm girl gives birth to the lover who first appeared as serpent-husband. While this, like the midwinter rose, can be seen as influenced by the Christian mystery of the God born to God and the Virgin, it points more generally to the birth of a higher self in the human being. Therefore, while in the story of *Eros and Psyche* it is the beginning separation of the ego which is dramatized, we find that here the fairy tale points toward this higher ego or self, thus marking the end of an evolutionary phase. With the disappearance of the former serpent-husband, and after a lengthy test in humility and unselfishness, the soul finds the reborn lover.

The idea of self-creation, of self-development, which is beyond the logic of the natural sciences, underlies our evolution on earth. Nothingness or Chaos (such as the abyss in the beginning of the tale of *Amor and Psyche*) and the birth of a higher ego (especially well portrayed in *The Bewitched Prince*) are the two limits we vaguely perceive in this evolution. The creation out of nothingness as well as an unchangeable, blissful future appear somewhat irrational or senseless. They are two limits which our present thinking has difficulty understanding, but which may appear flexible in response to the further development of our own thinking.

To the child the following message is brought by the fairy tales, particularly in those themes which are related to the figures of Eros and Lucifer. The question concerning origins and goals is not senseless, though it may be difficult to find a satisfactory answer, especially in our present world. But neither must one shirk from this material world; rather, by patiently and humbly carrying the burden of this earthly existence, life will be meaningful. Eventually the frustrating distance between the two shores of the river separating the world of matter and the world of the soul can be bridged.[67]

In the animal-prince story from Scandinavia, *Prince Lindworm,*[85] the lover is a ferocious dragon, part snake and part man, who does indeed swallow the first two maidens to whom he is married; the third bride succeeds in forcing him to shed all his animal skins. When she reluctantly embraces the remaining ugly, slithering pulp, he suddenly turns into a beautiful human being.

In the fairy tale such ambivalences are not resolved by the removal of fixations, complexes or taboos which might have turned the young lady against sex, but by the cultivation of qualities which are specifically human, be it unselfishness, modesty, humility, courage, patience, sympathetic understanding or keen judgment. They all contribute to the formation of a strong, mature ego for which Eros loses the animal or monstrous aspects.

May I add a biblical parallel. The Greek god of love and beauty, Eros, son of Venus, corresponds in many ways to Lucifer, who was cast from heaven and who appears to Adam and Eve in the guise of a serpent. For Plato he is also the god of *beautiful ideas.* Lucifer (or Phosphorous, the name given by the Greeks to Venus appearing as Morningstar) is the carrier of light and spirit of beauty. Like Eros, he arouses Eve's curiosity. By him Adam and Eve are driven toward self-awareness which at first leads to shame, suffering and deprivations. From a dogmatic religious standpoint this has often been described as the original sin. The intuition of the fairy tale and myth, however, views it as a necessary, though painful, step in the maturation both of the cultural group as well as of the individual human being. They see the solution *not* in the escape from the monster or serpent, but in a process of evolution in which Eros or Lucifer himself is restored to his original beauty.

The above-mentioned typically Swiss variation of the Eros and Psyche theme describes this redemption of Lucifer. In the story of *The Bewitched Prince* we find images in the simple life of the cow herders as well as deeply Christian motifs. The young woman must give herself in marriage to the horrible serpent from whom her father has obtained the red rose in midwinter (a common symbol of Christ born on Christmas). Whereas in *Amor and Psyche,* written in the second century and partly based on the much older Grecian Eleusic mysteries, Eros eventually carries Psyche with him to the top of Mount Olympus; we find here that self-awareness is born within Psyche. The blossoming roses and the son born in midwinter bring to mind Praetorius' beautiful Christmas song, *"Es ist ein Ros' entsprungen"* (A rose has blossomed forth . . .). Now spiritual assistance and growth comes no longer from without, but from our own innermost being. To quote Meyer:

> The development of the oldest fairy tale motifs under the influence of deeply mystic Christian beliefs would constitute a significant aspect of research in this field. In the succession and alteration of the themes of certain tales we would then see a reflection of the evolution of human consciousness.[125]

Just as the physical world is meaningless without the intellect, so the sexual-instinctual experience itself is essentially unconscious without the human feeling of love. We know little about the origin of the sexual attraction between two beings. Yet it may seem absurd to claim that sex, as an instinctual phenomenon, evolves below the level of consciousness. Is not sex daily and abundantly being brought to our awareness by movies, radio, magazines, television, advertisements, etc.? On close scrutiny, however, you will find that the pleasures associated with sexual activities are mostly beyond the sexual instinct and linked to a variety of feelings: belonging, acceptance, sharing, security, worthiness, empathy, fondness and self-awareness without loneliness. To these feelings may be added numerous others which are not commonly associated with the idea of love, which often may denote immaturity and abnormality but which, nevertheless, have a human dimension: pleasure of defying taboos, possessive dominance, suffering submission, cruel aggression or wishes to degrade and defile or to be degraded. In psychotherapy we find that many disorders or perversions that are manifestly sexual turn out to be problems related to various human needs and conflicts, just as some seemingly nonsexual problems may have sexual roots.

Biologically, sex is an instinct which has to be shared with another being (the only one of this kind). Thus it is particularly suited to become linked with all the feelings we have in regard to another person. This is enhanced by the fact that Western culture has placed an enormous emphasis on sex and sexual taboos. It is further enhanced by the purpose of the sexual instinct which is to secure our continued existence on this earth, making it possible to pass on to our offspring, by education more than genetically, our ideals, feelings and values.

Amor, Eros, Love, Cupid, has so many facets that the preceding remarks should be taken only as a feeble attempt to understand love as it is portrayed in many fairy tales and myths and to find the reason for the frequent omission, especially in Western fairy tales, of any direct mention of the purely instinctual, animal or sexual attributes of Eros. I do not believe that such omission is due primarily to taboos.

Beautiful young Rapunzel, carefully guarded by the old witch, lets the king's son climb up to her room in the tower at night by lowering, as if it were a rope, her long golden hair. They love each other, marry and she conceives twins. The sexual aspect of the relationship is barely alluded to as a step in the human development of the lovers. We are first told of the danger, of the dire consequences of Eros. The witch finds out about their meeting at night. The punishment for sexual pleasure that is not yet fully integrated in a human bond affects both partners. The king's son not only is separated from his beloved, but he also loses his vision.* Rapunzel uses her long golden hair to allow the prince to climb up into her tower, rather than to reserve this privilege to the clairvoyant witch. Thereby she rejected an

*We shall point out (in connection with *Cinderella*) that in fairy tales the loss of sight often refers to the loss of spiritual vision, the loss of understanding the meaningfulness of our existence. The loss of vision as a result of forbidden sexuality brings also to mind the blindness of the King Oedipus which is the result of his incestuous relationship with his mother. In this myth, however, the blinding is also linked to the development of deeper insights.

atavistic insight into spiritual matters which inhibited her further human evolution. She loses her hair and is banned to a deserted, arid place. Only after wandering for years in utter misery does the blind prince find his Rapunzel with the two children. As the tears, probably of joy and pity, of his beloved touch his blind eyes, he regains his vision. They all travel to his kingdom and live happily ever after. Though the tale does not say so explicitly, you may be assured that Rapunzel's beautiful golden hair grew back while she waited for her prince.

In summarizing let me recall the two-fold meaning of normalcy, the two-fold aim of the intellect and the two-fold aspect of Amor or Eros. We may surmise a definite interrelation between these three concepts. When speaking of normalcy, we usually refer, in psychology, to the most conscious, *human* aspect of our personality rather than to its unconscious, biologic aspect. The same applies when we speak of Eros or love. And just as there will always be a tension-differential between biologic normalcy and human normalcy (much as we may try to lessen it by seeking an optimal harmony between the two), so there will continue to exist a conflict between the sexual instinct and human love. A return to complete biologic normalcy or to purely instinctual sexual functioning would imply giving up most of our human values.* Yet the continuing challenge to find new integrations between the two, rather than lessen or compromise, may heighten our human values and our ability to love. Only in this sense can celibacy become a manifestation of deep love. In analogy to this we notice how the intellect, on the one hand, endangers human existence by its involvement in the natural sciences and particularly in technology, and how on the other hand it can

*Any conscious satisfaction contains a human element, since our consciousness is always related to our view of the world (*Weltanschauung*). Any biologic satisfaction of which we become aware will depend qualitatively on the view of the world which is individually ours. This view of the world is beyond the biochemical and physiologic realm. It is not the outflow of these realms, and must not be confused with them. While the biochemical and physiologic processes are fairly uniform in all human beings, each individual has his own personal view of the world. And inasmuch as this colors his biologic satisfactions, these too can take on individual characteristics which in turn may show reverberations in the biochemical or physiologic realms.

derive from this involvement the criteria of sharpness and strength which eventually enable it to guide us forward to a more conscious experience of the beauty and wisdom inherent in our world.

There is in the present Western world a great interest in Eastern philosophy and religion. Thus a historic comment may be appropriate.[30,168] It appears that in the fifteenth century Japan went through a similar stagnation of philosophic thinking as did Italy and France. Having reached the highest degree of sophistication, this thinking became involved in trivial, hair splitting, abstract debates that satisfied no one. The two cultural centers, almost on opposite sides of the globe, solved the dilemma in opposite manners. In Europe man turned more interestedly toward the earth and led the way to a materialistic world separate from, and almost rejecting, a spiritual world. Examples of this trend are the interest in perspective in paintings, best illustrated by Mantegna; Galileo Galilei's discoveries of some basic laws of physics; Columbus' exploration of the New World and Copernicus' of the universe; and eventually Descartes' philosophic underpinning of the natural-scientific split of the universe.

Though the roots of Western rationalism can be traced back to the time when, in the sixth century B.C., Thales reasoned that water was the ultimate substance and source of everything, man retained until after the Middle Ages the feeling that the earth was God- or spirit-centered, that the world was *one*. Yet especially after Descartes the accelerating evolution of the natural sciences choked this feeling. The human being found himself alone in a world of *things* against which the world of ideas, ideals, values and feelings appeared illusory. Like Thumbling, the intellect, swallowed by the world of the senses, was doomed to become part of the beast, unless it could be rescued. We are again reminded of the cruel, destructive lamb-like beast of the Apocalypse.

Martin Elsner[41] noted that the first signs of such a rescue manifested themselves just before human intelligence entered a stage where it became the all-powerful ally of mechanistic and animalistic trends. Around 1500 A.D., when Galileo, Corpernicus, Kepler and others shook the customary conceptions of the universe, we find that in the hearts of many artists the images of the Madonna and child, of Christophoros, and of the adoring shepherds and kings became preponderant. The Madonna and Christophoros portray the pure human being carrying *a new consciousness,* a consciousness of the *self.* This self or higher ego represented by the Christ-child is also seen in the adoration of the kings (or Magi) and of the shepherds. The feeling side of the soul represented by the latter raises upward to this new consciousness, whereas the intellectual forces represented by the kings bow down to the young being who is to become the bearer of a more comprehensive and reflective understanding of the world.

Up to the time of the first Milethian philosophers human self-awareness could be described as "I feel, therefore I am." Subsequently, rationalism overshadowed this experience more and more until Descartes concluded "I think, therefore I am." But already a more intimately central self-awareness dawns in the magnificent pictures of the Renaissance. This new consciousness is portrayed in epos and fairy tales (see, for examples, our discussion of *The Bewitched Prince* and of the *Kalevala*). Many poets, to mention but Goethe, Novalis[134] and Rilke,[148] have clearly sensed this newly emerging consciousness; and from Kierkegaard onward it is mainly the philosophers with an existential orientation who are trying to grasp its essence and to find a newly alive language that will do it justice. "I am, therefore I am." It is "the self related to its own self and willing to be itself."[96] Kierkegaard's definition of the human being free from despair, authentic, refers to this highest consciousness that he illustrated by the knight of faith, Abraham. Yet this self-awareness is always integrated with the consciousness expressed in the "I think, therefore I am" and "I feel, therefore I am" which correspond to Kierkegaard's ethical and esthetic levels of consciousness.

In fifteenth-century Japan, Zen-Buddhism, that had been flourishing in China ever since the fourth or fifth century, was another solution, aiming at the experience of the unity of all, of subject and object, and at the recognition of Maya, i.e. the illusional nature of the physical world which to the fully enlightened became unnecessary, worthless. Zen-Buddhism, even nowadays, often appears either as a sophisticated intellectual plaything for the counter-culturists and for the cocktail crowd, or—as it always has been—as an attempt to reach wisdom by going backwards, by becoming a perfect, egoless being through which IT (the spirit) works. Nowadays, Zen can be a constructive force for us primarily because it reminds us of the one-sidedness, if not falseness, of many of our materialistic views, of the need of spiritual values, of heartfelt, personal morality; but we have to seek these by going forward, not backward!

Zen can then be viewed as analogous to the golden twin brother from the Grimms' tale who has never left home and who eventually will rescue the hero who has turned to stone. This becoming stone is a bewitching far more serious than that of Eros who is turned into a monster or ferocious animal. It can be characterized as a satanic (ahrimanic) influence in comparison with the diabolical (luciferic) aspect of Eros. Yet, just like Lucifer or Eros, Ahriman (the antagonist of the spiritual power in ancient Persia)* cannot simply be rejected, ignored or avoided, but ultimately has to be also redeemed.

Human normalcy, without ignoring biologic normalcy; human love, accepting the challenge of sexuality; and the human intellect, willing to explore the problems and possibilities of the physical world; these three may lead us through darkness, blindness and despair to higher values, deeper love and wider vistas.

*By ahrimanic we designate a complex of forces or gestalt that abrogates all subjectivity for the sake of establishing a purely measurable, deterministic world.

CHAPTER XXI

CINDERELLA

SINCE THE STORY of the lovely and patient, modest and rejected young lady who is forced to perform menial tasks while her stepsisters are spoiled, is one of the most widely known fairy tales; and since it contains themes closely related to the story of *Amor and Psyche,* we shall add here a few observations showing how the psychoanalytic interpretations can be widened by a predominantly phenomenologic approach. And we shall try to show that in *Cinderella,* just as in the tales based on *Amor and Psyche,* the specifically *human* problems rather than the *biological* developmental conflicts are emphasized.

While several hundred versions of the Cinderella theme have been found around the world, we shall consider here the one by the Grimms, not only because of its special beauty, but also because it is so generally known that the mention of a few details will refresh the recollection:

The narrative begins by telling that Cinderella's mother has died and that the father soon marries a cruel stepmother who has two haughty and heartless daughters. One day the father goes on a trip, promising each one of the girls a gift. While the two stepsisters ask for fine clothes and for precious jewels, Cinderella only wishes for a young twig of a hazel tree which, during his voyage, would push father's hat from his head. This twig she then plants on her mother's grave where it grows, nourished by Cinderella's tears, into a tree in the top of which some white doves live.

Then the story mentions the three-day celebration proclaimed by the prince which the stepsisters are allowed to attend. Cinderella's wish to go also is denied, even after she has twice met successfully the challenge of "separating the lentils from the ashes." When she prays underneath her hazel tree, the latter sheds upon her a fine dress and wonderful dancing slippers. Three times she attends

> the dance and the prince has eyes only for her; yet at night she always manages to escape and to return home before her stepsisters. When the prince comes looking for her, the father at once suspects Cinderella; therefore, with his axe he splits the bird house, and the next day he cuts down the pear tree, in which Cinderella had hid to shed her beautiful clothes before returning to her ashes; but fortunately each time he is a little too late. During her third escape occurs the loss of the slipper which gets stuck to the steps of the palace, because the clever prince had had them painted with black pitch. As you know, the prince identifies the true bride by finding that Cinderella's foot fits into the slipper perfectly. Before this, however, the stepsisters almost succeed in deceiving him, one by cutting off her toe, the other by cutting her heel, in order to be able to fit the foot into the slipper; but in both instances the white doves reveal the fraud to the prince. And the story ends with the wedding; on the way to and from the church the stepsisters receive their punishment when the white doves pick out their eyes.

One can point to several themes in this fairy tale bearing out psychoanalytic theories of childhood development. The frequently encountered theme of the good mother who dies when the child is an infant and is followed by the bad stepmother can be seen as a picture of the earliest ambivalence of the child toward the mother: The all-giving, all-loving, all-protecting, all-understanding and forgiving mother turns into the frustrating depriving, selfish, unfair and rejecting mother who makes unjust demands and accords more privileges to the two older stepsisters who—in the light of sibling rivalry—are seen as greedy, mean and cold.

The father appears also in an ambivalent light: weak at times, brutal at other times; giving and depriving, helpful and hindering. Furthermore it is not too difficult to recognize a phallic theme in connection with him. Is he not the one who brings Cinderella the young twig of a hazel bush which grows into a tree on which the white doves live and which is able to provide the young lady with everything she wishes? As if to stress the phallic significance of this twig, the tale points out that it is the one which pushes father's hat from his head, whereby hat and head could—psychoanalytically—be construed as symbols and representation by displacement, of the male genitals. Later, the father reappears as the cruel, and maybe jealous castrator, when he cuts down with an ax the birdhouse and the pear tree after Cinderella's return from the dance.

The dancing itself can be viewed as representing sexual arousal from which the young woman flees at first. Eventually Cinderella is able to confront her lover, and painlessly she lets the foot slip into the slipper. Her stepsisters, on the other hand, represent a prematurely arrested psychosexual development, since they see in marriage mostly a sadomasochistic relationship: The one who cuts off her toe portrays the castrating tendencies, while the other who cuts her heel displays the attitude which sees in female sexuality, including menstruation, a painful, suffering submission. And the story ends with contrasting symbolically the happy wedding with the loss of the stepsisters' eyes, which can again be viewed as a sexual loss or failure expressed in the form of displacement to the eyes. It might be added, at this point, that many American versions of this tale, derived from Charles Perrault's[139] French narration, carefully omit the blinding of the stepsisters and substitute a happier end when Cinderella forgives and even supplies the stepsisters with husbands. Instead of symbolization and displacement of the sadomasochistic problem we find, then, an attempt at repression and reaction formation.

A more phenomenologic approach, without preconceived hypotheses, may add to the psychoanalytic view of the Cinderella story. Even if we try to let the images of the tale speak for themselves, it is still almost impossible to avoid completely the injection of some personal convictions and prejudices, so that we must beg for the reader's indulgence. With this in mind, let us look once more at several themes of our story:

In many fairy tales we notice that, in contrast to the selfish, cruel stepmother, the original mother is pictured as loving, unselfish and ethereal. Often she is described as being surrounded by a wintery landscape: The forces of nature have withdrawn and all lies quietly under a white snow blanket which fell from heaven. The child may sense in this, almost virginal, mother a spiritual origin of his being; an origin which lies beyond the confines of the sensuous and often cruel material world into which he finds himself cast and which is like a stepmother to him. The physical mother is part of this material world—note the common etymological root of mother and matter (*mater* and *materia*)—and the two stepsisters represent those feelings or attitudes which see their exclusive origin in the material world or in the physical mother.

But while her stepsisters are seduced by material wealth and gay splendor, Cinderella does not shrink from joy nor from physical reality. In fact, hardly any task could be more down to earth than that of separating the lentils from the ashes. Yet, this menial task which she performs humbly and modestly seems to emphasize her ability to isolate even out of the spent ashes something which is nourishing and life-giving. The white doves help her in this. They appear in other fairy tales, such as *Hansel and Gretel,* and always seem to represent some sort of supernatural help or guidance. As a symbol of the Holy Ghost the white dove occurs in the New Testament, and to the present day it portrays the moral forces of peace. In our story the doves are clearly associated with the grave of the first, spiritual mother, since they live on the hazel tree which has been nurtured by the praying and mourning girl's tears. The young soul's ties with her spiritual origin have been broken. The one whom she experiences as her true mother lies buried; and only her humble, unselfish prayers help Cinderella to gain some help and comfort from a world she has lost.

At this point I wish to refer to a small detail in the narrative which further supports the idea that the doves, rather than being of physical help, portray spiritual assistance exactly opposite to the laws of the material world: We read that on the first day of the celebration Cinderella is challenged to separate one potful of lentils from the ashes in two hours, and that she accomplishes this—with the birds' help—in one hour. Yet when challenged the second time, she finishes twice this task in only half the time. From a spiritual viewpoint the physical tasks cannot ever become impossible; the greater the hardship, the greater the help.

This fairy tale underscores that only the young individual who willingly faces the challenges of our material existence, but who also is keeping faith with her noble origin, becomes capable of solving even those tasks which at first seem insurmountable. Thanks to the tree which has grown out of the twig her father had brought her, she can exchange her coarse grey dress and her wooden shoes for fine clothes, which at first are silken, then silvery and finally golden. But her first encounters with the king's son are only short, as if her young soul were not yet capable of tolerating the intensity of the relationship for a longer time. Only when she has further developed her finest qualities, can she stand before him in her coarse grey dress and reveal her true nature. The slipper, which fits her foot exactly, is the link between the erect human being and the earth, portraying once more the central theme of the story, namely that the human being who has lost the early paradise, the golden age, must find a harmonious integration of the spiritual longing with the earthly existence before the world can again appear meaningful. The two stepsisters who selfishly exploit the material existence and the prince's celebration do not achieve this integration, and are betrayed by the white doves, eventually losing their sight.

Cinderella's escapes from the festivities point to a commonly overlooked facet of human growth. Just as excessive impatience in the search for a lasting marital bond can lead to the stunting of the two individuals' personalities, so also a precipitous confrontation and acceptance of latent aspects of our personality may become harmful. It takes the most delicate sensitivities of the individual and of those who act as guides, if the proper timing is to lead to an ongoing, optimal, harmonious development.

The stepsister who cuts her heel must walk on her toes, and the other who cuts her toes must walk on her heel. The one reveling in gay splendor is insufficiently, the other, possessed by material greed, is overly involved with the earth. Thus the threesomeness of the sisters points to three different realms of the psyche. This threefold nature of the psyche is portrayed in innumerable mythic and fairy tale episodes. It seems appropriate to elaborate briefly on some of the common denominators of these episodes, stressing simultaneously that each one also has specific meanings that emerge only out of the context of the whole story. In the Cinderella tale the two older sisters cling to a nonreflective consciousness carried mainly by feelings and to an analytic, greedy consciousness supported by the intellect. Thus, like the two older sisters or brothers in many narrations, they discourage, disparage or counteract the emergence of the third sibling who aims for a higher, all-embracing, reflective awareness.

Indeed, Meyer[124] has shown how these soul forces can appear as masculine or feminine. In the Swiss-Engadin tale of *The Satchel, the Horn and the Cap,*[22] for example, we find that the youngest of three brothers has received the most inconspicuous gift, namely a cap which, however, has the miraculous quality of rendering its wearer invisible. This quality points to a higher degree of consciousness which allows him to overcome the deceit of the physical senses and to regain eventually also the gifts of his two older brothers. Versions of tales analogous to the Grimms' Cinderella (or *Aschenbrödel*) in which the two siblings are forgiven and obtain gifts and worthy husbands are not entirely the result of the wish to circumvent seemingly brutal scenes, but portray also another meaningful aspect of the development of the soul forces.

In another Swiss tale, *The Three Ravens,*[167] the three soul forces are viewed from a slightly different vantage point. Here the young maiden, innocently and unwittingly, has caused her three older brothers' transformation into ravens. Only when, after marrying the king, she has kept absolute silence for three years, are her brothers freed from the spell. During the three years she gives birth to three sons who are then kidnapped by the evil mother-in-law. The latter then accuses the queen of having killed her own children.

These three children can be viewed as renewed soul forces which ripen as the young queen goes through a threefold process of purification. Her silent, willing acceptance of the verdict that she must burn at the stake is the sacrifice of the last vestige of one-sided materialism. As she faces certain death for her three older brothers' sake, both her three brothers and her three sons are restored to her. Ultimately both are the same! The three brothers are the three soul forces that became bewitched into an animal existence and the three sons are the three soul forces after they are permeated fully by the higher ego, the queen. Only when the latter has proven her incorruptibility in the face of the dark forces (represented by stepmothers, mothers-in-law, witches, etc.) can she effect the rescue of the original and new soul forces.

In very similar tales the young woman's three abducted or murdered children are juxtaposed to seven or twelve bewitched brothers. The latter is the case in the Grimms' *The Twelve Brothers*,[58] while in the Swiss *The Story of the Only Daughter*[43] there are seven brothers. Here the stories seem to allude, as we have mentioned in regard to the good fairies of the Sleeping Beauty, to the need for a harmonious corresponding of intra-psychic or microcosmic processes on the one hand, and macrocosmic events portrayed by the number of planets or zodiacal constellations, on the other hand. But let us return now to Cinderella.

It has been claimed that fairy tales are poor fare for children, because of the extremely sadistic crimes and punishments occurring in them (see Chapter XV). Grimms' Cinderella story would be another good example of this: At the end of the tale we read that the stepsisters accompany the young bride on the way to and from the wedding. The white doves first pick out the left eye of one and the right eye of the other; and as they reverse their positions on the way back, the birds pick out their other eye. Quite contrary to the cruelties portrayed in some comic books, television crime stories and documentaries, the so-called sadism in fairy tales is so utterly absurd that even the child senses that it cannot be taken at face value. In the first place, it is hard to believe that the stepsisters could have walked to the church with their wounded feet, even if they had been invited. That they quietly attended the wedding ceremony just after a bird had picked out one of their eyes, and that thereafter they would stupidly expose themselves once more to these horrible doves, sounds even more absurd.

Whereas the psychoanalytic interpretation of the blindness quite correctly recognizes the psychosexual aspects of the incomplete development of the stepsisters, the narrative indicates a more comprehensive significance when we examine it phenomenologically. It tells us that those who become greedily involved in the material world, who lose faith in something beyond the physical senses, forfeit eventually the chance of developing the sense of seeing what is valuable, beautiful and meaningful, be it in marriage or in life in general.

A further comment about the two men, the father and the prince, may shed additional light on the meaning of this story. The juxtaposition of the father or old king and of the prince, the king's son or the young hero is a very frequent fairy tale theme with recurring characteristics: Usually the father-king possesses some valuable gifts with supernatural qualities which can be very helpful to the young soul. Whereas he possesses these gifts because of his link with a past where spiritual things were still experienced more immediately, he has little understanding for the present problems of the human being and soon becomes a force which hinders or opposes the maturation of the youth. In the Cinderella story this magic gift is the twig. The fact that it pushes father's hat from his head has a particular symbolic meaning which we can recognize in one way or another in many tales, customs, etc. While the slipper forms the transition to the earth, the hat shields the head from the heavens above from which spiritual forces are pictured as streaming down. The hat which hides the golden hair, the rabbi's cap, the Chinese thinking cap, etc., portray the development of an earth-centered, self-aware type of reasoning. Cinderella's father, then, is a human being who is still temporarily subject to spiritual inspirations which he can transmit to his daughter.

The prince or hero represents a new, growing force capable, after his marriage to the young woman, of taking over the kingdom. In a way this drama is repeated in the development of each child for whom the father, at first, is an essential furthering influence, but who, later, has to become capable of escaping the parent's destructive, hindering efforts in order to find his own, mature ego. We know the psychosexual reflection of this drama in the oedipus complex. And while the marriage, after numerous trials and tribulations, of the prince and the fine young lady represents on the one hand the ideal relationship between two matured human beings, it also portrays the acceptance by the soul, namely Cinderella, of a higher, independently reigning ego. And speaking to all people, the fairy tale stresses how this higher self-awareness or self-consciousness must be reached, if the vision for what is truly worthwhile is to be regained. It is characteristic for the myths and fairy tales born out of our Western culture, that they see any true spiritual maturation or growth as contingent upon the willingness to accept and include also the physical part of existence, whereas in most Eastern philosophies—including Zen-Buddhism, now so popular—the material world is always shunned or denied:

Numerous are the variations of a theme in which the eager student approaches a famous yogi in his search for the secret of Maya. The Yogi remains silent but indicates that he would appreciate a bowl of water. As he bends down to a nearby pond to fill the bowl, the student slips and plunges into the water. He emerges in another world where in the course of many years he achieves fame, riches and pleasures. He has many beautiful wives, children and grandchildren, but eventually loses everything through death or treachery. Yet when he reaches total despair he suddenly reaches the surface of the pond into which he had fallen. It all had been an instant illusion, and he brings to the yogi the waterfilled bowl, aware that he has been given a glimpse of Maya.

In addition to the Cinderella stories, many other fairy tales have incorporated some aspects of Apuleius' original narration. However it is the above-mentioned Scandinavian tale which depicts well the supernatural aspects of *Eros and Psyche*. In *East of the Sun and West of the Moon*[85] the girl who has lost her lover, a white bear, wanders through the meaningless world until she finds three crones who give her a golden apple, a golden comb and a golden spinning wheel. Then the four winds carry her through space, dangerously, to the place "East of the Sun and West of the Moon." Here she meets the three bad trolls with whom she barters, sacrificing to them her three golden gifts in order to see her lover. Only the third time is she successful in preventing them from putting the young man to sleep prior to her visit. Finally, she frees him and the three trolls destroy themselves. Here the ultimate victory is achieved because of the trolls' inability to wash out the three drops which had fallen on the youth's shirt "because they came from a Christian candle."

One sees here clearly the intrusion of a Christian motif in an essentially pre-Christian story.

It may be of interest to note that the *Eros and Psyche* theme may also be reversed. In the mentioned Yugoslav story of *The Frog Wife*, the third son of the czar is forced to marry a young frog-woman. His brothers and his father despise him, and he has to move out of the palace into a simple hut, so that he is forced to earn his living by hard manual labor. While he is away working during the day, his wife keeps their little house immaculate; and he grows curious. Hiding himself, he discovers that, when she believes herself alone, his wife sheds her frog-skin and becomes a beautiful woman. He therefore skilfully snatches the skin and burns it. But this leads to great hardships, as the czar and the brothers grow jealous and try to destroy him by giving him three impossible challenges. Contrary to their expectations, he meets them all successfully, overcomes his enemies, and eventually becomes the new czar.

Every step in development, each acquisition of a new depth, width or quality of consciousness goes hand in hand with defiance of previous taboos or rules. In the Cinderella tale most charmingly we find the proper balance and timing of modesty, of willingness to affirm the earthly, of escape from premature intimacy and of defiance or open confrontation. Only the person genuinely striving for authenticity senses when to bend, when to pray, when to defy, when to confront, and when to assert himself.

This confrontation, this risking is seen as evil by the overly rigid established order, even if it is genuine.* It implies "fear and trembling," to use Kierkegaard's expression,[96] as the protagonist is utterly alone in his fateful decision. In touch with

*"Genuine" is a term not to be used lightly, but of profound meaning. It implies a person's being in touch with his innermost being, with his self. This self is not to be viewed as an isolated kernel striving in isolation, but as a higher ego that is freed of all petty selfishness. It senses its harmonious interrelationship with the world and the spiritual principles pervading the world. It is Kierkegaard's self[96] that is free from despair and authentic, because it is "transparently grounded in the power that posited it"; it is Buber's "I"[16] able to relate to the "Thou"; it is Heidegger's authentic *Dasein*[63] (or self) that affirms the mutual relationship between world and man.

his deepest, creative moral impulses—but is he sure that they are not rationalized selfish desires or neurotic needs?—he is willing to go against not only evil outward demands (stepmother) but also seemingly well meaning, just and accepted instructions (father). In Freudian terms this has been described as the assertion of the ego that is in control of the instinctual drives (id) against all aspects of parental injunctions (superego). At one time these injunctions were blindly accepted, but later—good or evil—they are no longer commensurate or appropriate to the current reality.

Cinderella risks exposure and death in each of her courageous, independent excursions to, and flights from, the prince's castle. Eventually, like Psyche, she overcomes all challenges and her prince comes to her. With each excursion, Cinderella's consciousness is strengthened, until finally she is able to meet her lover in the light of day. Similarly we saw Psyche, after numerous trials, able to live with Eros in the splendor of Mount Olympus.

Only very gradually, after numerous confrontations involving "fear and trembling," after many relapses into inauthenticity and silent or overt despair, is the mystic marriage of *anima* and *animus*, princess and prince no longer a mere wish or hope, no longer a fleeting peak experience, but an achievement that will be the basis for a further step in development. Only then will the seeming split between the good archangels and Lucifer be healed, only then will the latter reveal his own meaning. In Goethe's *Fairy Tale* which we mention repeatedly this eventual achievement, this beginning of a new millennium is ushered in when the luciferic serpent (aided by the gold of the ahrimanic will-o'-the-wisps) becomes the broad bridge between the two shores.[53,67]

CHAPTER XXII

THE FROG AND THE RED CAP

IN THIS CHAPTER, based on two themes, the frog and the red cap, we add a few comments concerning the interrelation between a psychoanalytic and a phenomenologic interpretation. Thereby we hope to further explore the possibilities of integrating the two.

Simburg[163] once pointed out the phallic nature of the frog in some fairy tales. His most convincing example was the frog in the story *The Frog King or the Iron Henry* where the unbelievably beautiful youngest princess plays with a golden ball which accidentally rolls into a pond. A frog pities her tears and returns her ball when she promises to love him, to let him play, eat and sleep with her. However, the princess conveniently forgets her promise and returns to her castle without the frog. She is surprised when she finds that he has followed her and demands to sit with her at the dinner table. The king, hearing of her promise, insists that she keep it no matter how repelled she is by the ugly animal. But when the frog persists in his wish to sleep with her, she is overcome with anger and disgust and smashes him against the wall of her bedroom. In that moment he turns into a beautiful prince with friendly eyes, who, with the king's approval, becomes her husband. He explains to her that he had been bewitched. Now the princess loves and accepts him, and after spending the night together, he returns with her into his kingdom. The innocent young girl's fear of and repugnance toward the male genitals and the transformation of this disgust into happiness and sanctioned matrimony can hardly be symbolized better than by this transformation of the frog into a prince.

In the story *Briar Rose* the frog, according to Simburg, is furthermore a symbol of fertility, promising a child to the barren queen. Other details can be added to support these psychoanalytic views, such as the ability of the frog to enlarge himself, or—referring to the castration fears supposedly always inherent in the possession of a phallus—the tadpole's losing the tail, etc. Yet, as happens with any reductive interpretive approach, we may reach the point where additional ideas appear farfetched and overly sophisticated. Simburg himself offered a humorous example for this, by adducing as a further proof of the frog's symbolizing fertility, the frog-pregnancy test. True enough, the same can happen with phenomenologic interpretations, if one allows oneself to revel in fantasies or to be influenced by an unruly ambition to find new interesting meanings, instead of remaining objective and letting the pictures of the story speak for themselves.

To be sure, the phallic interpretation of the frog must not be separated completely from the one suggested in the preceding chapter. The challenge to the young woman to see male genitality not only as physical lust, but to accept even the phallus as a part of an integrated love relationship, can well be taken as a reflection in the erotic field of the process of human development outlined above.

With the beginning of puberty and the victorious self-assertion of the physical instincts, the spiritual aspect of the human being falls asleep. Even while having to go through a period of materialism, of one-sided sensuality, of lost paradise, of deathlike sleep, this spiritual self prepares for a new awakening where an integration of the human being's physical and spiritual aspects is achieved. In *The Frog King* the girl who has lost the golden ball, the golden world of childhood, of innocence, spontaneity and playfulness, at first rebels at the idea of having to integrate her awakening instincts with her spirituality. She wants to recapture the golden world while rejecting the ugly frog. The fact that eventually the phallic frog becomes a beautiful prince of a new kingdom further supports our previously expressed ideas concerning the *Briar Rose* frog, namely that he represents an intermediary stage, a being which partakes of a soul world and of a physical world.

The story of *The Frog King* ends with the happy couple riding off in a carriage, accompanied by the faithful servant, Henry, who portrays what remained unaffected by the spell that turned the king into a frog. Now, one by one, the three iron bands that Henry had forged around his chest as if to control the pain of seeing his master turned into a frog, crack with a loud noise. We are reminded of Rank's "character armor."[144] This creative student of Freud recognized in many persons a seeming constriction or rigidity of the chest that must be overcome, if a harmonious integration of the lower, middle and upper aspects of the human being is to be achieved.

The theme of the frog as intermediary between two worlds can be followed backward for some four to five thousand years. Thus we find, for example, the frog-headed Heket, goddess of beginning life who helps the birth of the child.

With the loss of the paradisiacal world and with the ascendancy in our world of the natural-scientific and technologic supremacy, genitality and sexuality become ugly, at least at first, because they enter the sphere of consciousness. Thus Adam and Eve covered themselves. This shame may disappear in personal relationships in which both partners have gained awareness of the reality of a spiritual, moral or human world in harmony with the material world, or in marriages where genuine love dispels the shame. However, we see all too frequently, even in apparently good marriages, a reemergence of the repugnance, when one of the partners, sometime as a result of the mate's attitudes, regresses to experience genitality as something purely physical, selfish, sinful and therefore ugly and wants to suppress or repress it.

The conscious awareness of, the exploration and exploitation of the physical world, has led to a dichotomy of spirit and body which reflects itself also in the erotic area. While the old Hebrew texts still sense the psychologic wholeness of the human beings in the expression "recognizing or knowing the wife" (which denotes a truly intimate marital relationship), the dichotomy is quite pronounced nowadays and calls for a new integration. Such an integration, rather than being a return to the original paradise, must be achieved on a new plane and in full consciousness.

Another example of the interrelation of the psychoanalytic and of the phenomenologic viewpoints is the red cap of Little Red Riding Hood which was seen by Freud[50] as a symbol of castration and of beginning menstruation. Such an interpretation is rather far-fetched and based on the opinion that a defense of displacement from the genital area to the head had been operative. Besides, the story, while not specifying the age, speaks of a "small, little girl" rather than of a girl who is entering puberty. This can then be seen as an additional attempt at hiding the sexual implications of the tale (see Chapter XIII).

However, if menstruation designates symbolically the time when the loss of the early childhood paradise is completed, when the human being experiences himself totally in the world of the senses and cut off from a spiritually conceived world, then the Freudian interpretation of the red color may contain a deeper meaning. The redness now points to the quality of blood that represents egoity or egocentricity; that quality which is captured by the devil when he asks the victim to sign his name with his blood, in turn for sensory satisfaction which will eventually make him forfeit a paradisiacal existence. In fact, the cap itself portrays this cutting off, this separation of the human being from the heavens. It is the direct opposite of the golden crown which opens up toward the skies and carries on its points the precious star-like jewels, thus symbolizing the bearer's openness for spiritual values. The cap, contrariwise, appears to separate the ego from the cosmos in order to further a development toward self-containment or selfishness. The halo, the golden crown and the princess' golden hair all indicate the openness of the human being for the nonphysical world, whereas the hat or the cap hides the golden hair and indicates a turning of consciousness (and especially of thinking) inward and toward the material world. This furthers an independent ego but carries the threat of choking the person off from the living world, just as Little Red Riding Hood was endangered when she was swallowed by the wolf.

This turning inward or earthward is a necessary phase of human development. We see it expressed strongly in the Hebrew culture where men carried their black cap continuously, or in the Chinese thinking cap. In a story such as that of *Iron John* (Grimms' *Eisenhans*) the young gardener hides his golden hair under his hat and refuses to uncover it until the time is ripe, until his ego has been strengthened by the encounters with the physical world, and until he is capable of a more conscious synthesis of material and spiritual existence.[124] The priest who bares his head when he speaks the revealed word and covers his head when he preaches his own sermon portrays the same basic idea.

A hat gives status, it points out our uniqueness, our importance, our rank or position in everyday life. This is clearly seen not only in the ladies' fashions, but also in the gold braided hats of officers and in such expressions as "being high hatted," "putting on different hats," "throwing one's hat in the ring," etc. Lastly, the saying "as long as I have a place to hang my hat" beautifully describes the need of the human being to free itself periodically from its too earthbound existence when returning to the home from the tasks of the competitive daytime world. If one does not have a place to hang one's hat, be it a hut or a palace, one is unable to open one's soul to wider and deeper emotional or spiritual experiences.

A psychoanalytic approach may also recognize the covering up, the inhibiting, the hiding aspect of the hat. Since in psychoanalytic parlance the head frequently (by what is called displacement) stands for the genitals, the wearing of a hat would be equated with covering up sexuality, with sexual denial. Taking off the hat would then represent acceptance of sexuality, sexual freedom or, in sublimated form, freer social intercourse. This ties in with the custom of greeting by taking off one's hat, and with sayings such as "I'm taking my hat off to you" and "they are under one hat." "Talking through one's hat,"* countrariwise, in-

*The imaginative language of myth and fairy tales finds many such reflections in our everyday language. Not only in folktales but also in our current expressions do people "lose their head," "turn to stone," "become monsters," "turn into pigs," "feel in seventh heaven or in hell," "become blind," "become fragmented," "swallow each other," etc. The German language is unusually rich in such expressions that reflect fairy tale images. Friedel Lenz[104] has tried to revitalize the understanding of myth and fairy tales by uncovering these analogies. Thus she

dicates inadequate communication and thinking. All this, however, is only a relatively one-sided manifestation in the instinctual and social field of the much wider meaning we tried to describe in connection with *Red Cap.* We can further illustrate this with an episode in *Cinderella.*

In Chapter XXI we saw that while her selfish stepsisters ask for expensive clothes and for pearls, Cinderella modestly asks her father to bring back from his journey the first young branch of a tree that would push his hat away. He fulfills her wish and she plants the twig on her mother's grave. Whenever Cinderella cries or prays underneath her hazel tree, the latter sheds upon her a fine dress and wonderful dancing slippers. When the unselfish human being is most alone in a materialistic world, when she nostalgically can turn to the grave of the first, loving mother and tearfully say her prayers; when the hat shields the intellect (represented here by father) from the heavens above as he takes his journey unaware of the narrow, cruel selfishness of his new wife and stepdaughters; when things seem most desperate, a new spiritual force (the young twig) awakens which can push the hat away. This force grows into a tree, as if nourished by the love of the buried mother; and from its top the white birds, always a symbol of the Holy Spirit, of new spiritual forces pouring themselves into the human being, drop delicate gifts upon the soul, upon Cinderella who has remained pure in spite of the ashes in which she has to work, and in spite of the stepmother and the stepsisters who represent one-sided or corrupted aspects of the personality. At first, the young lady can hold on to the gifts brought by her faith and by her prayers only for a limited period; but she grows in the esteem of the prince (representing a more perspicacious, higher ego than that portrayed by the father), and the prince is able to recognize the falseness of the selfish drives of the stepsisters. Now Cinderella can permanently leave her place near the ashes and marry the king's son.

Again the hat symbolizes here the required temporary restric-

---

is able to strengthen her thesis that the actions in these narrations portray intrapsychic rather than external events and that the concrete images are a pictorial language which nowadays is not as immediately understood as formerly.

tion of the human consciousness. By developing the skill of integrating the thorough knowledge and acceptance of the material world with strong discriminating moral forces (depicted excellently by the white bird's helping Cinderella separate the lentils and peas from the ashes), this consciousness can lead to a greater awareness of self, without which a new understanding of the wisdom of the world is impossible.

The relationship between the human head and the deeper wisdom of the world, often depicted by the golden hair, is such a frequent motif in fairy tales that we shall presently study it in more detail.

CHAPTER XXIII

THE GOLDEN HAIR IN FAIRY TALES AND MYTHS

MY INTEREST IN THE GOLDEN HAIR is linked with the observation—upon reviewing numerous fairy tales—that when the color of the hair of one of the protagonists is mentioned, it is almost invariably golden. Whether it is a narrative from the American folklore such as *The Monster of Leeds,*[110] an American Indian legend such as *Tis-sa-ack,*[163a] a modern French fairy tale such as Saint-Exupéry's *The Little Prince,*[151] a Czech tale such as *Zlatovlaska*[89] or a story by the brothers Grimm such as *Rapunzel, The Goose Girl, Allerleirauh* or *The Clever Little Tailor,*[58] we always find that the hair is not only blond, but golden. This golden hair occurs in fairy tales of nations where blond hair is commonplace, and of races where it does not occur at all; and it is not simply mentioned for an esthetic purpose. In fact, we find that, when the golden hair is mentioned, it often plays a significant role in the story. It is not a synonym for blond hair, but denotes something specially precious.

The Scandinavian story of *White-Toes and Bushy-Bride*[85] bears this out particularly well, since here the good daughter whose hair initially is "yellower than the primrose" is rewarded by her hair turning to gold. We may add the Swiss tales of *The One in the Bearskin*[22] and *The Dwarfs' Godmother;*[43] the Russian *The Death Watch, The Firebird, Fair Vasilissa and Baba Yaga;*[35] the Yugoslav *The Little Fairy* and *The Child and the Colt;*[32] the French *Down, the Golden Haired,*[6] etc. In some the hair is described as shining rather than golden, to mention but *Bluecrest*[6] and *Bright, Deardeer and Kit.*[171]

We have discussed the meaning of the golden hair hidden

by the cap in the story of *Iron John* and by a veil in *Zlatovlaska*, while in the story of *Rapunzel* we recognized a similar significance in the cutting off of the long, golden hair. Already in pre-Christian times we find an Egyptian tale explaining the greatness of Alexander by his descendance from a pharaoh-god, the Lybic Ammon with golden hair.[15] In marked contrast to the metallic, physical gold, the golden hair represents a live gold, delicate threads seemingly radiating from the human head—physical receptacle and main tool of our spirit—to a supernatural world.

How gold can become more and more spiritualized is beautifully shown in the previously mentioned story of *Jack and the Beanstalk:* first, Jack acquires a sack full of gold pieces, but soon they are spent; a little longer are the benefits derived from the hen which lays golden eggs; but Jack's ultimate victory over the giant occurs when he is able to bring down to earth the golden harp. The gold pieces represent the crude metal as having only a material value. In the beautifully shaped golden eggs, the metal alludes to the formative forces of life. However, both the full aliveness and the permanence of its value is established only when the gold is formed into a musical instrument yielding marvelous tunes which can be repeated and varied forever.

A most impressive portrayal of the reverse process, of the transition of gold from the spiritual to the material role is found in Wagner's *Rheingold,* where the diabolical, ahrimanic being, Alberich, renouncing love, steals the sun's golden reflection from the rocky slopes bordering the Rhein River, and forges it into a ring. This ring, in its circularity symbolizes the concentration and restriction of rational consciousness that threatens to smother any deep and loving concerns. The enormous power that this consciousness can wield, as well as the ultimate dehumanizing potential of it, is dramatically portrayed in Tolkien's trilogy of *The Lord of the Ring.*[175] Here the only hope is seen in the annihilation of the ill-fated ring: an expression of the twentieth-century author's sensitivity to the dangerous power of megalomanic leaders. Wagner, reviving and reinterpreting in the nineteenth century the old Nordic and Arthurian sagas, was still able to see the ultimate potential usefulness of the ring. Though it brings death to the Giants, the dwarf, Hagen, Gunther,

Gutrune, Siegfried and Brunhilde, and though it is linked to the death of all the old gods, it nevertheless is returned for safe-keeping to the Rhinemaidens. The fires that destroy the gods and heroes are analogous to the fire storms that ravage the darkened earth in the *Kalevala.* They are followed by the hopeful anticipation of a spiritual reawakening, portrayed in the *Kalevala* by the "child of Marjatta," in the Wagnerian operas by Parsifal.

This spiritualized gold recurs in many variations in numerous fairy tales: golden apples, golden feathers, golden furs, straw or clay turned into gold, etc. In the above-mentioned story of *White-Toes,* golden words fall out of the girl's mouth; and in a similar Swedish tale *Little Rosa and Long Leda*[92] the good girl's hair also turns into gold and a golden ring falls from her lips each time she smiles. In this tale the material gold and the spiritual gold are contrasted sharply; the envious stepmother uses gold to bribe the ship's captain who promises to drown the girl. This material gold of the stepmother almost achieves its goal, but the girl ends up shipwrecked on a lonely island. Her patience and compassion with a deer which has been killed by wild animals eventually help her, however, and she is found by a king. Love and pity can overcome even the forces of death: the deer's skull turns into a wonderful nightingale who keeps the girl from being lonely until the hero arrives to rescue her. Yet, after her marriage to the king, the deadly gold of the step-mother exerts its power once more. The latter sends the young queen a gold embroidered nightgown which turns her into a goose with golden feathers. Only after the magic nightgown is once more placed over her, the spell is broken. The garment is then placed, for punishment, on the stepmother and stepsister who turn permanently into wild geese. The story alludes to the fact that everyone must come face to face even with the physical gold. Rosa, pure and unselfish, can eventually integrate her spiritual nature with the physical world; whereas to those (stepmother and stepsister) who have not developed and harmonized their soul forces, this material gold becomes a seduction into permanent, wild animal behavior.

We noticed that the fairy tale frequently portrays the breaking away from the golden age, from the castle, from the kingly parents, and how this is necessary for the development of the human personality.* While in many fairy tales the color of the hair is not mentioned, it may be significant that the one Grimms' tale in which the beautiful girl's hair is black is that of *Snow White and the Seven Dwarfs.* Here the exception appears to prove the rule. Have we not seen that the central theme of this story is the latency period, the years when the soul has lost contact with its original home, when the human being learns to deal with the physical world, as illustrated by Snow White doing the household chores, and by the dwarfs' daily penetrating the earth to extract minerals?

Another seeming exception in the Grimms' tales, which may also widen our understanding of the golden hair, is the story of *The Devil with the Three Golden Hairs.* Here we must remember that the fairy tale, like the Greek myth, does not sharply separate its supernatural beings (be they dwarfs, devils, fairies, sorcerers or giants) into good ones and evil ones, beneficial ones and maleficent ones. Pluto in hell or Hades is not always bad just as Jupiter on Mount Olympus is by no standards always good; and Proserpina, Castor and Pollux are deities who alternate their sojourn between heaven and Hades. Heaven (or Olympus) is not all happiness and the Greek underworld—though seen as less desirable than existence on earth—is not all suffering. Our fairy tale devil has golden hair and soon he proves that he, too, has some deep insights into the meaningfulness of the world. In fact, with each hair that our young hero can obtain from the devil, the latter reveals a new valuable insight into a mystery which all the people, including the young man, had not been able to

*In many religious paintings the golden halo has the same meaning as the golden hair. It indicates that the saint is holy, or whole, that he has been able to achieve a harmonious integration of material and spiritual existence, that therefore he is ready to commune again with the supernatural world, and that, after his death, he is capable of entering directly into paradise. We already referred to the superb engraving of Saint Jerome by A. Dürer, where we see the saint in deep meditation, light rays streaming from his skull to the spiritual world he is inspired by, his large hat hanging on the wall as if to stress further his openness for the supernatural; the lion and dog quietly sleeping on the floor, indicating complete, harmonious control over the animal instincts: the "holy whole man" with an *aura aurea* or golden halo.

penetrate, since their everyday reasoning and their physical sense organs were not adequate for the task.

Hence even the supernatural beings who are seen as devilish assume in the fairy tale roles which can further the progress of the hero or heroine. They have an essential function in human evolution. Whether they are portrayed as maleficent or beneficial depends partly on whether they further evolution by challenging and tempting the people or by helping them, whether they represent past, atavistic spiritual forces or beings which are viewed as leading forward toward a new spiritual awakening. Just as the good Zlatovlaska was the one among twelve daughters with golden hair who helped Yirik to be revived with the waters of death and life, so we see the bad Judas as the only one of the twelve apostles with a black halo play an essential role in the greatest victory of Christ. His betrayal made possible the crucifixion and the burial of the highest spirit who thereby became part of the earth, penetrated the depths of the underworld and resurrected. In the American folktale *The Monster of Leeds,* the maleficent spirit has golden hair[110] and in the Russian story of *The Death Watch,* it is the flowing golden curls which prove that a certain woman is a bad witch.[35]

The human being meets two dangers during his journey and exploration of the physical world. On the one hand, he may fail by shirking from material reality, by denying matter, by abandoning himself to vague reveries and sweet, fanatic or sensuous religiousness. This danger has been described as the luciferic temptation. On the other hand, there is the danger of becoming too completely and permanently involved with the material aspect of existence. Snow White's beautiful but cold and selfish stepmother, Jason who becomes unfaithful to Medea, as well as the arrogant maid in *The Goose Girl,* represent this peril. All, like Judas Iscariot, end up seeking their own destruction. A materialistic or natural-scientific orientation, unless adequately balanced by unselfishness and deep ethical feelings, is able to maintain itself only as long as it can deceive itself with false promises of betterment and of final victory. The whirlpool in which such a selfish, amoral, satanic materialism destroys itself is portrayed excellently by Snow White's stepmother who—after hoping in vain that any competition with her beauty has been eliminated—chooses to go to the wedding of the prince and the reawakened young lady, and who dies dancing wildly in the red hot metal shoes. This peril of an irreversible materialistic orientation, which looms nowadays most dreadfully in the shape of the atomic weapons, has been called, by some, the satanic or ahrimanic temptation. In the Revelation of Saint John (18:21) the *Whore Babylon* is destroyed by the satanic power upon which she is riding. Her flesh is eaten and she is destroyed by fire.

A superb illustration of this double danger is contained in Homer's *Odyssey*. We already mentioned Ulysses as a representative of a new culture, without whose sharp intellect final victory over Troy, a city harboring an older culture, would have been impossible, and whose shrewdness outwitted the cyclops Polyphemos. In a later part of his long, wandering journey across the Aegean Sea turned into a mystical realm, we find him confronted by a quadruple danger: The Sirens, Scylla, Charybdis and the island Thrinakia. The simple diagram below illustrates the course of his ship. While the Sirens (1), with their seductive songs, want to render the sailor oblivious of the earth so that his ship will shatter on the cliffs, it is the disregard of the spiritual power and the absorption by physical needs which leads Ulysses'

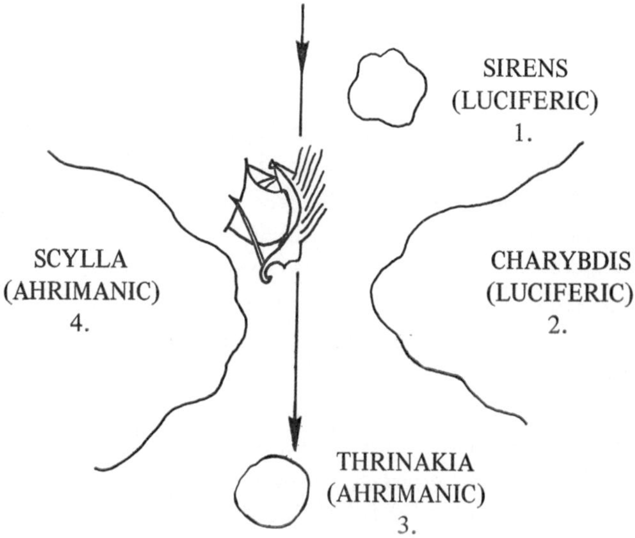

sailors to land on the island of the sungod and to slaughter sacrilegiously his animals (3). Similarly, in the narrow passage between two promontories, it is Charybdis (2) which pulls downward on the one side and the supernatural monster Scylla (4), devouring people from above on the other side, which represent the satanic and luciferic forces. It is the passage between the danger of intellectual infatuation or inflation and mystical confusion.

Thanks to his cleverness, his courage, his developing moral integrity and his burning desire to return to his home and wife in Ithaca, Ulysses weathers all these perils. Yet, in the process he loses everything: his ship with all his possessions as well as all his companions. As a lonely, poor, despised beggar he arrives in his palace. Ulysses' trip is indeed a path of growth and initiation, during which he is completely divested. Only thus is he able to integrate intellect and feelings, and to confront the triple aspect of the anima (Circe-Calypso-Nausikaa, or Aphrodite, Hera and Artemis). Then only can he return to Penelope, his wife.

Goethe described exquisitely the luciferic temptation which draws us away from the earth, when he had the mermaids sing this to the fisherman:

Ach wüsstest du, wie's Fischlein ist	Oh, if you knew how fishes feel
So wohlig auf dem Grund,	So cozy in the depths,
Du stiegst herunter wie du bist,	You'd climb way down just as you are
Und wuerdest erst gesund.[55]	And you'd grow healthy then.

On the other hand, we find the hopelessness of a world viewed as dominated entirely by the materialistic ahrimanic forces powerfully portrayed by Leopardi who admonishes his own heart:

Ormai disprezza	Now finally despise
Te, la natura, il brutto	Yourself, nature and the ugly
Poter che, ascoso, a commun danno impera	Destiny which insidiously governs to the common detriment,
E l'infinita vanità di tutto.	And the never ending vanity of everything.[106]

In our present everyday life we may recognize luciferic tendencies in those religious and philosophic orientations which deny evil, suffering and matter (Zen-Buddhism, Christian Science, etc.), whereas we find ahrimanic forces wherever human beings deride values as fictitious or arbitrary and would like to structure society so as to fit the model of an extremely complicated machine.

Even some of the best intentioned endeavors such as Skinnerian behaviorism can indirectly produce profound, dehumanizing effects while achieving important particular results. This must not be construed as an argument against a specific educational or psychotherapeutic technique, but as a warning not to let any technique obscure aspects of human existence that are more fundamental. Was it not that most behaviour therapists deny in their spontaneous, warm attitudes their own pandeterministic, mechanistic scientific presuppositions, the latter would lead towards an ever more dehumanized world.

CHAPTER XXIV

FOLKLORE MOTIFS

In the preceding chapters numerous mythic and fairy tale motifs are mentioned, and some are dealt with in depth. Thus we discussed the golden hair, the frog, the cap, etc. In later chapters some additional motifs are focused upon: the meaning of death, of sleep, of a person's name, of a person's shadow or reflection, of the forest, and others. Yet these motifs are always discussed primarily with the aim of exploring the comprehensive meaning of various narrations.

The enumeration and analysis of all the main mythologic images and motifs is beyond the scope of this book. The best known systematic collection is that of Steth Thompson.[172] A bird's-eye view of some of the main folklore images with fairly consistent symbolical meanings may, however, be appropriate. We shall group them, somewhat arbitrarily, in twelve categories, elaborating only on a few particularly important themes that are insufficiently covered in other chapters. Thus the reader's ear may become better attuned to a language that can be appreciated only gradually in its full depth.

1. Giants, centaurs, one-eyed or three-eyed individuals, sorcerers, witches, elves and sirens; stepmothers, ugly stepsisters, arrogant maids, dwarfs, orcs and trolls are beings combining human with *infrahuman characteristics.* As the protagonist, the hero or the individual progresses slowly and arduously on his path, he is helped and hindered, challenged and warned by these beings. Some of them clearly tempt him away from the solid, material world, promising bliss in a regressive, ultraterrestrial paradise. This role is often taken on by sirens, by "holdfast" kings, as well as by giants, witches, sorcerers and one-eyed be-

ings. Others try to imprison the striving human being in an unfeeling, hard, rigid, spiritless material realm. This is true of some dwarfs, of the arrogant maid in *The Goose Girl,*[58] of some stepmothers (*cf. The Juniper Tree,* Chapter XV), and of many orcs and trolls.

A sharp separation of forces leading to avoidance of the material realities and of forces fostering subservience to the material realities is not always easy, as one and the same being assumes, at different moments, either characteristics. For example, one stepsister of Cinderella is unable to foot solidly on the earth, while the other is footed too firmly. Similarly, in Goethe's *Faust,*[54] Mephistopheles takes on alternately both of these seemingly negative roles which at times have been designated as expansive-luciferic and rigidifying-ahrimanic, as devilish and satanic.[124]

The paradisiacal serpent, too, has both of these aspects: By means of the fruit of knowledge he provides the human being with the power to expand toward godliness; but simultaneously he deprives him of eternity, thus making him face the fact that he will return to dust. The paradisiacal serpent effectuates God's intention to create man in His own image, but he also brings forth the awareness of the finitude of human existence. It is this awareness of death which can prevent false self-aggrandizement in the human being's exercise of his creative potentials, and which also underlines the irreplaceable value of every moment. It is this awareness of the ever present possibility of death which makes possible—as the existentialists[63,99] have stressed so firmly—an authentic life. It now becomes clearer that the above-mentioned beings combining human with inhuman characteristics are never to be viewed as solely harmful or as solely helpful. Even the seemingly most rotten ones (Polyphemus, Hansel and Gretel's witch, Louhi in the *Kalevala,* etc.) become "a part of that force which always desires evil and always creates good."[54] Even the best ones (Briar Rose, Turandot or the virgin of the Northland) can cause death and failure when they are not sought at the right time and with the proper attitude.

Failure, pain and destruction are indeed not due to sadistic-punitive urges of the positive spiritual powers but to the human beings' inability to accept and integrate the blessings that can come from these powers. Thus, in *Faust,* Mephistopheles is eventually vanquished by the roses strewn by the angels who carry away Faust's immortal self. Similarly in the Apocalypse the seven vessels containing the gifts of the Supreme Being turn into vessels of wrath for those who carry the sign of the animal on their forehead and hands, who are still unable to cherish the gift that would help them cross the bridge towards a new millennium.[11a]

As is true of all folklore images and themes, the precise meaning of any one of these beings must always be seen as a function of the entire context of the narration. For example, the old king's role varies from that of the cruel "holdfast" (*cf.* the story of *Zlatovlaska*) to that of the sickly old man (Amphortas, or the king in Grimms' *The Water of Life*) and to that of the "ongoing self of the human being" (*cf. The Juniper Tree,* Chapter XV).

2. Entirely different meanings are conveyed in folklore by the representatives of various *professions.* Most frequent are the hunters, shoemakers, millers, goldsmiths, knights, weavers, blacksmiths, shepherds, tailors, cooks, gardeners, fishermen and robbers. Reflecting about these persons, we sense again the deeper meaning of symbolism. They are so thoroughly embedded in the macrocosm that their adopting a certain profession is but an expression of the deepest qualities or characteristics of this embeddedness. Thus the gardener is led to his occupation by his genuine ability to further the growth of all that is good, valuable and useful, while weeding out whatever is opposed to such growth. The shoemaker's innermost quality consists in his ability of reaching the proper balance between spirituality and material reality. In his work world he is, therefore, able to create shoes that help the human beings' harmonious, erect walk through life. He is sensitive to their destiny (German: *Schicksalswege* = walks of destiny) and is thus capable of heartfelt sympathy. The stories of *The Shoemaker and the Elves* and of *The Juniper Tree* (see Chapter XV) offer good examples for this.

Quite different is the fisherman who spends a great part of his life on the threshold between the solid earth and a fluctuating, liquid world from whose hidden depths he pulls what he needs for his existence. These treasurers which he tries to catch are evanescent like our dreams which so easily evaporate in the daytime. They are well exemplified by the golden fish in the story of *The Gold Children* whose benefits are lost again and again.[58]

Some characteristics of other occupations are mentioned throughout the book. Thus I shall add here only a brief remark concerning a negative profession, that of the robber. He represents a being who selfishly seeks to appropriate all the material goods or sensory pleasures of his world. It is this orientation that leads him to adopt his antisocial profession and to associate with persons who are dominated by a one-sidedly developed, amoral intellect (see Chapter XXXI). It is only because we no longer experience occupations or professions as spontaneous expressions of a person's inner stance, that we see their occurrence in folklore as meaningless, accidental, or, at best, as mere metaphors.

3. In moving from the human to the *animal representations,* we penetrate different levels of the human being. Adopting a Teilhardian[170] rather than Darwinian evolutionary view, we believe that folklore animals primarily portray quasi-instinctual qualities that the human being has integrated during a continuous evolutionary process of which the various species are but more or less fully developed branches. Thus all animals can become significant symbols in folklore. The lion representing overpowering courage; the cunning fox; the stubborn but hardworking and reliable donkey; the greedy wolf; the instinctually intelligent horse; the clever serpent; the powerful and fertile bull; the sensitive, restless and friendly deer; the helpful birds, bees, ants and fishes; the mouse, porcupine, bear, dog, and many others reflect these instinctual regions. We speak of them throughout this book.

In addition, animals can portray, especially in fairy tales, the three elements, earth, water and air, which the hero must befriend before he can make further progress. We saw this in the story of Zlatovlaska. In the Scandinavian tale of *The Giant Who Had No Heart in His Body,*[85] the hero in search of a golden-haired princess similarly gains the assistance of the wolf (earth), the salmon (water) and the raven (air). In the Swiss-Engadin tale *The Helpful Animals,*[22] the hero meets the lion who allows him to pull three hairs, the birds who allow him to pull three feathers, and the masons who give him a ring. The first gift shows the hero's control over his instincts and feelings, the second his mastery of his thoughts. The third, however, indicates that the hero has gained what the protagonists in the Siegfried sagas strove for, namely the ring representing a higher level of human consciousness. A similar theme is found in another Swiss story of *The Ants, the Ducks, and the Bees,* and in many other tales.[22]

In Chapter XVI we described the frog's role of mediator between two realms, between the physical and the soul world. A Russian tale, *I Know Not What of I Know Not Where,* portrays this excellently. Here the czar's archer can retain his beautiful, golden-haired wife only if he is willing to jump on the back of a giant frog across the river of fire into the "I know not where land" and by finding there "I know not what" who then helps him defeat all his enemies. In the Swiss tale *The Intelligent John,*[84] the frog, messenger between two worlds, brings to the youth the holy wafer (itself a symbol of the interpenetration of spirit and matter) by means of which the sick woman is cured.

At times we find that animals, especially birds, symbolize clearly superior forces. Thus we have seen the spiritual guidance and help of the white birds in *Cinderella* and in *Hansel and Gretel.* Similarly we find the raven often as a benefactor of human beings. Sketco, the raven[7] of the Canadian Indians, represents in a series of stories the wisdom which comes to the aid of the still primitive human being. As the intelligent friend of the Indians, raven defies various gigantic ancestral powers and outsmarts them. He helps his friends to enjoy the stars and the moon, to benefit from the sun, the tide and the fire, and he assists in their becoming successful hunters. Mysterious birds whose feathers have magic qualities become the central theme in various tales, to mention but the Swiss-German *Bird Greiff*[167] and the Swiss-Italian *The Feather of the Bird Greiff.*[95]

Most often, however, as we mentioned, animals refer to instinctual drives that become more and more humanized as they are confronted, or that become less important as new levels are developed in the process of human development. By way of examples I shall mention here but the lion and the horse. The latter is a particularly frequent and interesting symbol that we shall discuss at some length and to which we will return once more in Chapter XXVIII. In the story by the brothers Grimm concerning three brothers in search of the water of life, the successful prince must know how to quiet the lions guarding the castle before he can enter it. He harmoniously integrates their powerful courage that otherwise could be destructive. This quieting of the lions recalls Dürer's picture of Saint Jerome as well as the story of Daniel in the lions' den. The overcoming of the beast of prey in the two *Thumbling* tales (Grimm) precedes the little heroes' return home and seems to have a similar significance as the quieting of the lions.

In the early history of the human race the taming and use of the horse constituted an enormous step forward in the application of man's intelligence to the challenges of the material world: its exploration, conquest and cultivation. This may partly explain why in myths, epos, religious texts and fairy tales the horse often represents the evolution of this early intelligence, largely tied to subconscious instinctual needs. Usually seen as a boon, it becomes, at times, devilish.

Be it the horse of the Muses, Pegasus, born out of the trunk of Medusa (experienced as the destructive aspect of the original, archetypical great mother[131]), be it the clever intelligence expressed in the Trojan horse, or the malevolent cunning symbolized in the devil's horse hoof; be it the wise teaching flowing out of the centaur Chiron's mouth, or the deep, empathic understanding of the horse Fallada, we always seem to deal with an intelligence that is born of early stages of human consciousness. In the Grimms' tale of the *Iron John,* the integration of this intelligence in the feeling, thinking and willing aspects of consciousness is magnificently portrayed by the red, the white and the black horse on which the protagonist successfully approaches the princess until he is accepted by her in marriage. This is clearly a reference to the passage in the Revelation of Saint John which we shall discuss presently.

Quite often the horse must be sacrificed. In the Scandinavian tale of *The Seven Foals,*[85] the hero cuts off their heads, whereupon they turn into seven princes who had been bewitched. In a

Swiss fairy tale, *The Wandering Youth on the Fir Tree*[167] has to kill his white horse and wrap the ailing princess in its skin in order to cure her. In some narrations the horse appears only as the wise advisor. Thus the horse in the Swiss-Engadin tale of *The One in the Bearskin*[22] counsels the hero to rub a certain salve into his hair which will turn golden, and to hide his golden hair for some time under a bearskin. In the Yugoslav story of *The Child and the Colt*[32] the horse helps a young boy find the girl with the golden hair. Finally we saw the horse Fallada in the story of *The Goose Girl* continue, even after its decapitation, to give emotional support to the true princess. A similar combination of sacrifice and counsel is found in the Swiss tale of *Count Golden Hair.*[22] Here the count is first told by his white horse how to make his hair turn golden and how to cover it at all times with his hat; then the count must behead the horse which thereby turns into the twin brother who had been bewitched. In the Swiss story of *The Three Ravens*[167] the young man must clothe himself in his own beloved horse's skin. The helpful horse which brings the hero close to his final task, but which must be killed, occurs also in the Irish tales of *The Prince of the Lonesome Isle and the Lady of Tubber Tintye* and of *Conn-eda.*[24] In epic form we find a beautiful parallel in the story of Owain whose horse is cut in half at the very moment he enters the mysterious castle of the Lady of the Fountain, so that from here on he must face the future perils on foot.

In a grandiose way, and with slightly different meanings than in the above-mentioned tale of *Iron John,* the horses in Saint John's Apocalypse show the progressive development and reorientation of this intelligence: pure and unspoiled at first (white horse), it is followed by an intelligence serving lust and desire (red horse), then by one which is wholly oriented toward the constrictive blackness of matter (black horse). While these three horses reflect a potential harmonious integration of intuitive thinking, feeling and willing, they are succeeded by a selfish and self-destructive, death-bringing intelligence (the pale, fallow horse).* From this point on the central theme of the

*This fourth horse corresponds to Youkahainen in the *Kalevala,*[91] where Wainemoinen, Ilmarinen and Lemminkainen represent the feeling, the thinking

apocalyptic age unfolds with the punishment, destruction and death of all those who turned to unrestricted lust and tight material possessiveness. We then see those who have kept faith ride as a glorious army, following Christ on white horses. In the beginning the white horse carried a rider armed only with bow and arrow (what a beautiful image of the skill and precision of pure thinking!) and bearing only one crown. Now Christ arrives on a white horse, His eyes flaming, His tongue a sword (a reference to the power of the word, of the *logos!*), His head covered with many crowns and with a name which only He Himself knows (indicating the deepest spiritual insight, the rebirth of meaningful language, and greatest self-awareness arising at the end of the apocalytic era). Eventually each human being merges with Christ while retaining his identity.

In the previously discussed tale of *Zlatovlaska* or *The Princess with the Golden Hair* we see the early, intuitive intelligence associated with the horse on which Yirik rides in search of the golden-haired princess. Here, as in other tales, the ravens represent a considerably higher degree of intellectual development. This is portrayed by Yirik's willingness to sacrifice his horse in order to feed the starving ravens. These, later on, bring him the waters of death and of life which lead to the death of his former self, to his rebirth and to his coronation.

A related version combining the meaning of *wit* and the meaning of the *horse* is represented in the old Egyptian tale of *The Clever Masterthief* who is able to steal the horse of the king.[15]

As a last example I wish to mention the Russian story, *The Fire Bird,*[35] since it harmonizes beautifully the themes of an initial horse which must be sacrificed as well as of a later magnificent horse with the themes of the magic numbers (see below), of the golden hair, of the water of life and death, of the youngest of three sons, of the king, and of the tree with the golden apples, ransacked by the golden-feathered fire bird. The young hero suc-

---

and the willing aspects of human consciousness. In Youkahainen there is but a shallow mixture of these aspects. Proudly as well as selfishly he bears a deep grudge against the great singer Wainemoinen whose horse he shoots when he sees him travel toward the Northland in search for the beautiful virgin.

cessfully meets three challenges: catching the fire bird, stealing the horse with the golden mane and abducting fair Helen. He is helped by the wolf to whom he sacrificed his horse. When he returns with his treasures from the "Thrice-Ninth-Land" his two brothers slay him and he lies dead for ninety days. Then the wolf finds him, sends the crows to fetch the waters of death and life, they bring it after three days, and the wolf revives the youth.

4. In the above narration, as in numerous myths and fairy tales, the *tree* portrays the world navel or world axis.[24] Different species of trees convey additional meanings. Thus the oak may portray powerful, martial impulses, the birch gentle, youthful drives, and the juniper rejuvenating forces (see Chapter XV), etc.

5. *Fruits* (apples, pears, strawberries, nuts, etc.) and other foods (bread, flour, milk, eggs, salt, etc.) can refer to specific psychic functions that must be nourished. In the *Kalevala* we find a beautiful example in the Sampo, a mill that produces coins, salt and flour. Here the salt must preserve as memories all the perceptions that enter, foodlike, (flour) into the human organism.[123]

6. *Clothing articles* may refer to the invisible covers that are integrated with, that structure, and that sustain the physical human body. Thus the linen shirt frequently alludes to the vegetative life-forces, the dress may reflect various aspects of the human psyche, and the coat can portray the ego that encompasses soul and body. Indeed, various forms of divestiture can be observed in myths and fairy tales. Sometimes this is portrayed concretely as the giving up of a coat (*cf.* legends of Saint Francis) or of clothes (*cf.* the story of *The Star Ducats* or of the young man in *Puss 'n Boots*[58]). At other times the divestiture is shown as a relinquishing of previously acquired achievements or structures for the sake of a new and wider development (*cf.* Heracles myth, Chapter XVII and Odyssey, Chapter XXIII).

7. *Dwellings* (houses, huts, castles, towers or caves) commonly refer to the body that houses the human soul and spirit. A person can "lack foundations," may "feel at home," or is described as "not right in his upper story." When the young woman is bewitched in a dwelling situated in the midst of a forest,

this can be viewed as a radical disharmony within the human being. By removing all spells or dangers from this dwelling, the hero is able to reestablish on a higher plane the lost harmony. Laing and others[102] have described in psychiatric terms this alienation of the individual from his innermost self and from his body. While most of the buildings mentioned in this book can be viewed from this vantage point, it is our discussion of *The Dragon in the Black Wood* (Chapter XXVIII) that most clearly shows how the hero, Louis, reunited with Louise is able to take possession of the magnificent, disenchanted house, celebrate the (mystic) marriage and live happily ever after.

8. A broad spectrum of images refers to the *rhythmicity* of life: waters of death and life, winter and summer, spring and fall, day and night, sun and moon, life and death, drought and rain, sleep and wakefulness, dreams and reality, misty and clear landscapes, etc. They all convey excellently the various mysteries of the human being's harmonious integration within the basic cycles of his environment. As the summer looks to winter, or the day to night, so we look to sleep to refresh fatigue, and to dreams to uncover secrets beyond our conscious ability. Are Odysseus' experiences between the arrival in the land of the hallucinogenic Lotus and his awakening in Phaeacia, or is Dante's mystic voyage a dream? And what about *Alice in Wonderland*, *Peter Pan* and the events in Shakespeare's *Midsummernight's Dream?*

9. *Geographical items* are powerful symbols: the lofty glass mountain, the dividing (and yet uniting) flowing river, the bridge and the rainbow, the desert and the swamp, the world-encircling ocean, the nourishing springs, the valleys of toil, the enigmatic woods, they all reflect significant psychological and spiritual conditions. A very transparent symbolism, combining geographical items, religion and intrapsychic processes is found in the Yugoslav tale of *Bâs Celik.*[32] Here the reviving waters are brought from the river Jordan.

10. Past epochs have been identified with certain *metals*. The meaning of this transcends chronological references to the discovery and utilization of gold, silver, bronze, iron, etc. In fact, it is a legitimate question whether the search for and use of these metals is not just as much the result as the cause of new

cultural attitudes and trends. Allusions to these epochs are frequent in myths and fairy tales.

11. *Many man-made objects* become meaningful images in folklore. The spinning wheel or the loom appear in epos such as the *Kalevala* and the *Odyssey,* in Goethe's *Faust* as well as in many fairy tales and ballads. The oven as a shielded center from which heartfelt warmth radiates contrasts sharply with the barrel in which the diabolical false princess is imprisoned by her own counsel and rolled to death (see Chapter XIX). As one of the richest and most meaningful images we may mention the church bells. They summon to a God, serve as fertility charms, protect from evil spirits, become curative agents as well as prophetic voices, and can control storms as well as lightning.

One of the most powerful symbols among man-made objects is the ring, though mythologically it originates from super- or infrahuman beings. Zeus forced Prometheus (as well as mankind under the latter's protection) to wear an iron ring as a reminder of the sentence that chained the son of the Titans for thirty thousand years to the rocky walls of Caucasus. This sentence was reduced when Heracles was able to redeem him. In the Wagnerian *Ring of the Nibelungs,*[31] it is the satanic Alberich who swears off love and destroys the encompassing spiritual gold reflected from the sun on the rocks along the Rhine river. Carrying it into the depths of the earth, he converts it into a magic and deadly ring. Even more powerful and nefarious is the ring that Sauron forged, in Tolkien's trilogy, in order to gain absolute power. In myths and fairy tales the ring again and again refers to the historical emergence of a self-contained consciousness. The *Summum Bonum,*[99] the greatest boon of the human being, conferring freedom and creativeness, can also lead to hybris, to conceit, to a total loss of awareness of the spirituality of the cosmos, to the "Twilight of the Gods" (Goetterdämmerung). Yet in the depths of human despair and isolation, new impulses make themselves felt, offering hope for a new integration. Siegfried's ring, thrown into the Rhine by the dying Brunhilde, is guarded for a future epoch by the Rhine-maidens.

12. *Mirrors* could be placed in the preceding group. However, since their meaning is closely related to that of the shadow,

of the painted image, and—to a lesser degree—of the twin, they may be considered along with them. They all refer to the development and significance of a dichotomy in the human being which leads to the possibility of reflection. We spoke of the shadow as viewed by Jungians in discussing the Winnebago Trickster Cycle. Whether it is the painting of Dorian Gray,[184] the shadow that Peter Schlemihl sells to the evil one,[112] the missing reflection in the mirror, the twin brother left behind[58] or the shadow needed by *The Woman without a Shadow*[31] in order to become whole: again and again—though with differing connotations—we deal with the theme of self-reflection that is tied to the problem of individuation. The willingness to see ourselves the way we truly are leads to the experience of wholeness, whereas the consistent avoidance of one aspect of ourselves leads to stagnation (Dorian Gray), emptiness and sterility (*The Woman without a Shadow*), petrification (Grimms' twin brother tale) and loneliness (Chamisso's *Schlemihl*). It is particularly in Hofmannsthal's libretto for Richard Strauss[31] that the importance of the acceptance of the shadow becomes clear. It alone can lead to the development of a relationship to the contrasexual side of the personality. Only when the woman has courageously acquired a shadow does her interaction with her *animus,* with the emperor, open up deep creative potentials. Short of such an interaction the emperor would become petrified. It is the awareness of this that leads the empress to find the remedy, the shadow.

The meaning of *numbers* should be mentioned briefly. While they are not symbolical in the exact sense of the above groups of items, they, nevertheless, reflect hidden meanings and cultural beliefs. In addition they can be viewed as a stylistic element (see Chapter VII, C). The great predominance of the number three and multiples thereof in Western folklore is not universal. Thus we usually find in American Indian tales a predominance of the number four. In the Winnebago Trickster Cycle the foursomeness occurs about twice as frequently as the threesomeness. And in the Pueblo Indian myths this predominance of the foursomeness seems clearly related to their cosmogonic ideas, since the human being is seen as having emerged into the present world through three previous worlds, and since his present world is seen as delimited by the *Four Corners.*

Instead of scrutinizing the reasons for the frequency of the number three and its multiple in Western civilizations, I wish simply to cite as one of many excellent examples Grimms' story of *The Devil with the Three Golden Hairs.* Three times the old king tries to kill the hero: when the latter is a baby, when he is a child and when he has become an adolescent. The hero escapes each attempt and is subsequently sent out into the world to solve three riddles. All his adventures are tied in with his obtaining three golden hairs from the devil, which then enables him to overcome the old king and to marry the princess. Alternately and concomitantly the number three may refer to the three stages of childhood development (early childhood, latency period and adolescence), to the three main epochs of humanity, to the three aspects of the psyche (thinking, feeling and willing), to the three aspects of our organism which are necessary for our human existence on earth (physical, vegetative and animal), as well as to the oedipal triangle and its religious parallel in the Trinity. Whenever we scrutinize fairy tales, legends, myths or epic poems (*cf.* the comments concerning the marvelously harmonious structure of Dante's *Divina Commedia* in Chapter V[33]), we see, at times clearly, at times nebulously, reflections of these and other meanings of this number.

While the number four is rarer, as such, in Western civilization, it nevertheless occurs frequently in conjunction with the number three. Thus seven ($3 + 4$), twelve (3×4), and thirteen ($3 \times 3 + 4$) are common.

Other numbers in folklore can be interpreted as referring to the hours of the day, to the days of the week to the weeks or months in a year, to the number of planets or zodiacal constellations and to certain rhythms in the relationship of moon, sun and earth. Such numbers may secretly convey the protagonist's integration with his surroundings. Thus there are twelve, and twenty-four, and fifty-two, and twenty suitors around Odysseus' wife, Penelope. Except for the number twenty, the reference to months, hours and weeks is fairly clear. And if we see Penelope as a lunar heroine, the eighteen years of separation from the solar hero, Odysseus, corresponds to the period that elapses between the times these two heavenly bodies (moon and sun) rise from the same spot.

Hardly anywhere are the numbers of deeper significance than in the Revelation of Saint John. Yet, especially the numbers 144 and 666 have been interpreted entirely too literally by various sectarian groups. We have previously alluded to this magnificant work, and a broad view of its numbers will give further evidence of the depth of its message. The numbers we find here most frequently are seven (three plus four) and twelve (three times four). While the number seven refers more to our ordinary experience of time (related in ancient times to the seven classical planets), the number twelve refers more to space (e.g. the fixed position of the twelve constellations of the zodiac). And we may notice that the basic, overall movement in the narration is from the number seven (seven seals, trumpets, vessels of wrath, etc.) towards the number twelve (twelve times twelve thousand followers of the Lamb; twelve walls and portals of the heavenly Jerusalem, guarded by twelve angels; on the portals the names of the twelve hebrew tribes, and on the foundations the names of the apostles; the walls measure twelve times twelve yards, etc.). Bock sees in this an eventual shift in human experience where ordinary time changes into space and eternity. This, for example, is Percival's experience upon entering the castle of the Holy Grail: "Time here turns into space!". Sixhundred and sixty-six, then, is the fateful number which in a numerical system based on seven, on time, precedes the end of a basic phase of time. It precedes the millennium the way the number 999 would precede it in our decimal system.

After these very fragmentary remarks about folklore motifs, we proceed with the discussion of the meaning of the *name* in some narrations. Though the name is a frequent folklore topic, it is not a symbolical motif like those mentioned in this chapter. Thus it is treated separately and will lead into a detailed study of the libretto of Puccini's opera *Turandot.* Subsequently, because of their very great importance, two other central topics of myths and fairy tales will be covered in several chapters, namely death and the role of the intellect.

CHAPTER XXV

THE NAME

Rumpelstilzchen

sanctificetur nomen tuum "hallowed by Thy *name*"

IF YOU CAREFULLY question people in regard to what they consider "truly their own," you will find tremendous differences in opinion. A few will show great modesty and limit their ego to a small number of truly individualistic features. More people will take credit for traits, assets and qualities, as being truly their own, which have little to do with their ego. They remind you of a small nation wishing to annex surrounding territories under the pretext that a few of its citizens reside there.

The concept ego = "truly one's own" leads us to examine all our attributes in regard to their ego-quality, and we find that most of them are gifts, the possession of which we may humbly acknowledge, but which are not truly our own. This may apply to musical talents and intelligence, to a stable and pleasant disposition nurtured by a happy childhood environment, to physical beauty, etc. More careful scrutiny may lead to the recognition that such things as professional success or marital happiness, for which we readily accept responsibility and praise, are largely due to factors which have nothing to do with truly our own. Having to dismantle one's self of layer after layer of attributes which are neither our merit nor truly individualistic may prove dangerous to a person whose self-respect and pride reside entirely in being accepted and accepting himself for such peripheral qualities. Such a person may develop a severe depression when he begins to realize, indeed, how little he is himself. Yet, this dismantling of one's self can also further true humility,* tolerant understanding of other human beings, freedom and creativity.

What constitutes the uniqueness of an individual can never be expressed in general terms, cannot be weighed or measured, cannot be analyzed. General terms, analytic findings, extensive studies which recognize similarities between the function of our brain and man-made, complicated, self-regulating mechanisms (cybernetics) will teach us more and more about what man is not.[182] Cybernetics as applied to human psychology is only the ultimate, logical consequence of psychoanalysis rooted in natural science. The human being is seen as an unusually complex computer interrelating continuously with the environment. Self-awareness, then, is only a secondary by-product of these complex physicochemical processes and thus unworthy of serious scientific consideration. Any experience of freedom is a mere illusion due possibly to our inability to recognize the complicated innumerable forces (instincts, etc.) which determine our behavior.

Psychoanalysis—or any form of psychiatric treatment based on these foundations—would then aim at increasing the efficiency of this tremendously complex computer by changing some of the circuits within the person, or by changing the interaction between these circuits and the environment.

If we accept such a radical cybernetic formulation, the conclusion imposes itself that the differences between human beings are purely quantitative. Since subjective experiences, since the feelings of individual, qualitative uniqueness are discounted, a person deserves about the same amount of love and consideration as a machine, and humanity can, therefore, be destroyed as easily or with as little moral compunction as a pile of obsolete cars or as an ant heap. (Arthur Burton[23] has excellently described the effect of such a cybernetic orientation upon education in his analysis of the book *The Child Buyer* by J. Hersey.)

*The genuinely humble person rarely thinks of himself in terms of humility, since his actions and the ideas he expresses are more important to him than his appearing humble or not. The truly humble person is the one who hardly cares when he appears in the spotlight or if he gains prestige, as long as he feels that he does all that is in his power to further the ideals which to him seem paramount.

In psychoanalytic treatment the therapist may pay lip service to the respect for the individuality of the patient, while simultaneously reducing one by one all activities, beliefs, feelings (noble or ignoble) to instinctual drives. One way or another he communicates to the patient that these drives are biological (namely inherent in his non-individual, animal nature); that they result from complex biochemical processes; and that they are modified by the restrictions imposed by parents and society. Later, many of these drives turn up in the form of conflicts, physical symptoms or noble disguises (sublimations), because instinctual demands must adjust to the demands of the external environment by means of various types of compromises. Since, according to psychoanalytic theory, this adjustment is accomplished by a special group of instinctual forces that is designated as ego, the patient may be left with the feeling that his idea of his own qualitative uniqueness is fictitious. Thus the natural-scientific orientation, which in so many ways has been helpful, thoroughly monopolizes psychology and threatens to take away from man what he cherishes most. The story of *Rumpelstilzchen* deals with this danger.

We recognize in the daughter of the poor but braggart miller the soul of the man who, because of his technological achievements, feels unlimited power. Not only can he make flour out of grain, but he boasts that his daughter has the ability to make gold out of straw. Yet the miller's poor daughter, or the soul, needs the assistance of an ugly little dwarf, of Rumpelstilzchen, of a force which has tremendous power. The soul readily takes credit in the daytime for his accomplishments even though she does not know how Rumpelstilzchen—the keen intellect—operates and produces the gold (*cf.* with Goethe's will-o'-the-wisps in Chapter X). Then the soul becomes more heavily indebted to this helpful but diabolic power to whom she first sacrifices her natural, intuitive or spiritual wisdom of the past (she must give him first her golden necklace, then her golden ring). On the third night, when she has nothing more to give Rumpelstilzchen, she must promise him the first child which will result from her marriage to the king. This marriage represents the union of the soul with a new, powerful consciousness. It is possible only when the soul has divested itself of all its heirlooms and risks its most precious potentials for the sake of objective, brilliant thoughts.

Just as in our times the fantastic—and frightful—technologic achievements of man are clearly tied to forces and progressive events over which man is losing more and more control, so the miller's daughter achieves wealth and marries the king by becoming involved with a powerful force which threatens the child of this marriage. The new or higher ego, the new feeling of identity, the more fully conscious need for meaningfulness, is threatened with annihilation by the very force which led to so much progress and made possible its birth. Only by finding out the name of this powerful dwarf can the queen hope to save her child. But to know the name is to recognize the mephistophelian (or ahrimanic) nature of Rumpelstilzchen. While the beneficial effects of his activity can be retained, the soul can now free itself from the dwarf's desire to destroy the new ego; and with that, Rumpelstilzchen ends up destroying himself.

We noted that both the natural-scientific viewpoint and the candid self-evaluation tends, at first, to make the existence of a real ego more and more doubtful. No longer can we blindly take credit for all our assets; and while our natural-scientific efforts have led us to the conquest of space, to the power of controlling (and destroying) the earth, and to tremendous insights into the operation of the instincts in the human being, we must become clearly aware of the real nature of the force we have unleashed. The story of *Rumpelstilzchen* seems to tell us that instead of thinking of this force only as an abstract concept, we must try to see it as a concrete entity, a holon, a gestalt, a system or a spiritual being which has given us knowledge and self-awareness, but which will lead not only to our physical but to our spiritual destruction, if we are not able to recognize it and find his name in time.*

*This meaning of the tale of *Rumpelstilzchen* does not need to conflict with a more one-sided psychoanalytic interpretation which would see in the story a personal drama of the growing girl. This drama deals with the young woman's attempt to become truly independent from her father, the miller. Yet, while outwardly—or in her daytime consciousness—she becomes independent, wealthy and gets married, the father remains a strong unconscious (at night) influence

In the Bible we see this spiritual being appear as the tempting serpent who, promising self-awareness and knowledge, leads Adam and Eve to lose their paradisiacal world. Eventually, this tempting serpent must be sacrificed or must sacrifice itself. In Goethe's *Fairy Tale* we find the green serpent whose self-sacrifice leads to the building of the bridge between the two shores, and makes it possible for the youth and Lily to enter a relationship that is no longer deadly.

---

in the form of the Rumpelstilzchen-superego. This guidence by the superego is at first helpful in gaining a feeling of worth which enables the young lady to accept an outstanding husband (the king). Since she has simply exchanged her dependence upon the father with that upon the superego, she does not yet feel free in her relationship to the king and to her child. Only by freeing herself from the undue influence of this demanding father-superego-Rumpelstilzchen can she become the ideal mother, capable of offering her child a healthy environment. Insight (knowing the name) leads to the destruction and repression of the superego-forces: Rumpelstilzchen tears himself apart, stamps and disappears in the ground.

Similarly, the naming of Rumpelstilzchen can be viewed as the sexual maturation of the young woman who has to learn to make straw into gold, who must grow beyond seeing the male as a mere (though creative and powerful) sexual tool. Only by facing sexuality, can she integrate it into a deep human relationship. Naming Rumpelstilzchen (a term once used as a synonym for the penis), she destroys her former image of man as being merely a productive and exploitive genital, and is able to turn to her husband in a genuine intersubjective relationship that alone can safeguard the healthy growth of the child.[185]

Different interpretations do not exclude each other. They have separate validity and often they hiddenly validate each other. Indeed, it is the very one-sidedness of natural-scientific rationalism (required for the birth of a higher consciousness or new ego), that not only depletes the soul of the meaningfulness of all feelings, but also leads to a one-sided view of sexuality. Sexuality becomes impersonal, technical, exploitive. Only with the transcendence of this natural-scientific rationalism, can sexuality again be integrated into a higher, genuinely intersubjective relationship.

There is a charming Swedish version of *Rumpelstilzchen,*[92] *The Girl Who Could Spin Clay and Straw into Gold.* Here the girl's helpers, Mother Bigfoot, Mother Bigback and Mother Bigthumb are much less cruel and demanding than Rumpelstilzchen, since they are satisfied with being invited to the young lady's wedding. Noticing that their spinning has caused these mothers' large foot, thumb and hunch, the king-father forbids the girl ever to spin again, lest she lose her beauty. We find, therefore, in the place of Rumpelstilzchen's self-destruction, a skillful, gentle repression and modification of the superego forces. So the girl becomes a queen who "never demanded more of her subjects than she knew they were able to perform, and who was loved by everybody": a delightful description of the role of the mature ego toward itself and others.

The honest and humble individual will feel lonelier and more insignificant, as his material knowledge and his self-awareness increase. He may arrive at the point where—in spite of a great deal of erudition—existence has become meaningless and where he would drink the poison, if some vague recollection of a once-meaningful existence did not prevent him. Present-day humanity finds itself fairly much in this situation. In his interaction with the physical world, in his mastery of the natural sciences, man has developed his consciousness, but the meaningfulness of the world which in the golden age was never questioned, is escaping him completely. He becomes aware of himself as nothing; by his natural-scientific approach he is led to curse every aspect of his world. But this is also the moment for a new awakening, for a new beginning:

Weh, weh!	Woe! woe!
Du hast sie zerstört,	You have destroyed
Die schöne Welt	The beautiful world . . . .

So sings the choir of spirits to Faust who has cursed the world.[54] Then they continue:

Mächtiger	Powerful
Der Erdensöhne,	Son of the earth,
Prächtiger	More splendidly
Baue sie wieder,	Build it again,
In deinem Busen baue sie auf!	In your own bosom build it anew!
	—W. GOETHE, *Faust I*

Man, lonely, powerless in an empty world starts to question his existence. Sustained by the nostalgic reminiscences of a golden age, he retains in the disillusioned present a continued and inescapable need to value things and to see things as meaningful. Unfortunately, nowadays some of the promises, be they expressed as an expectation of a Messiah, of a second coming of Christ, of a paradise on earth, of a new Jerusalem, of a Mohammedan heaven, etc., are often interpreted in an overly materialistic, sectarian or primitive way. Their symbolic language is no longer understood, and thus they are rejected as false or silly.

Similarly the significance of the name is rarely experienced in our days. The name of the person in our technologic society is sharing the fate of the ego, becoming merely an abstract, though necessary, concept. Its importance in designating uniqueness is maintained only in trivialities, such as in the re-naming of movie stars, in the attempts of salesmen to remember the names of customers whose ego they hope to bolster thereby, or in commonly used expressions such as "making a name for one's self." Tradition combines the naming of the child with the baptism, but the celebration of the name day is all but forgotten.

In earlier times the meaning of the name as standing for the uniqueness of a being was much better known. A text that is over three thousand years old relates how Isis cured the oldest and greatest of the gods, Re, from the bite of a serpent.[15] She accomplished this by getting him to reveal to her his most secret name, which gave her some exclusive power over him. This is a magnificent mythic tale in which a wealth of common themes are combined. Isis, her heart trickier than that of a million humans, outranking millions of gods, and with deeper insight than millions of spirits, creates by means of witchcraft a serpent that poisons Re. This god who created himself out of Nun or Chaos, despairs and finally yields his secret which Isis now shares exclusively with Horus, her son. We thus see Re, the original, uroboric unity, divided in male and female, mother and son, who share his name. Osiris, Horus' father, is in the netherworld; he represents a longing and hope for an eventual, new integration on a higher plane.

God answered to the prophet who inquired about His name: "I am the 'I am.' " The knowledge and possession of the powerful name of God was the attribute of the "Baale-Schem," the "masters of the name," among whom Baal-schem-tow (1700-1760), the founder of a deeply spiritual Jewish movement, was the most prominent and influential.[17]

In the beginning of the Lord's Prayer the first invocation "hallowed by Thy *name*" can be recognized as a counterpart to the seventh and last "but deliver us from evil." With evil is meant more than the trespasses of the fifth invocation, more than the temptations of the sixth, but the ultimate destruction of our spiritual nature by the satanic aspect of Goethe's Mephistopheles who speaks of himself:

So ist denn alles, was ihr Sünde,	Therefore, everything you call sin,
Zerstörung, kurz das Böse nennt,	Destruction, or in short, evil,
Main eigentliches Element.	Is my proper realm.[52]

While God stresses the *name,* humility and the need for individuation, the devil who aims at collectivization and ultimate destruction emphasizes rank and pride. Goethe illustrates this dramatically in the "Prologue in Heaven" (*Faust I*) where Mephistopheles boasts that he would be able to alienate Faust from God:

God: "Do you know Faust?"	(God stresses the name.)
Mephistopheles: "The doctor?"	(The devil cannot grasp the individuality. He recognizes the rank, the title, whatever is not individual.)

Mephistopheles can understand all about Faust, but he never can understand Faust. We share Mephistopheles' attitude when we look at the human being as solely an organism which can be measured, comprehended or clearly defined. And once human beings are likened to computers, the idea of mass destroying them whenever this appears expedient, does not seem any longer horrendous.

In the tale of the *Three Little Men in the Forest* (by the Grimms) we see the human soul, the little girl rejected by her stepmother, dressed in a thin paper dress, with only one piece of stale bread, wander alone through the ice-cold forest. She is given the seemingly impossible task of finding strawberries, even though the ground is covered with snow. Only in her utter loneliness and rejection the soul may find her truest self, provided that her search is combined with a continuing, loving unselfishness. It is the girl's willingness to give her bread to the three little men and to sweep the snow off their back yard which leads her to the discovery of the strawberries and to the eventual marriage with the king (representing both the finding and assertion of her higher self). Her lazy half-sister who enters the forest well provided with food and clothed in fur, who is unwilling to share with the three little men, perishes at the end.

While for the young, immature and insecure human being protective love and moral support are necessary, loneliness becomes a challenge for the maturing soul; and while acceptance by a group represents encouragement to the doubtful, rejection may become for the pure in heart the basis upon which he can penetrate the meaning of the world. "Purity of heart is to wish one thing."[97]

We end up with an apparent paradox. The human individuality must find its unique self in deep loneliness, but for his existence the human being needs to be related to another human being.[16] Maybe it is the interaction, the tension between these two requirements for self-realization which contributes to spiritual growth.

The tale of Turandot centers on the possession of the name. Since Puccini's beautiful operatic version of the story portrays this theme in relation to the gradual attainment of a true intersubjective or "I-thou" relationship, we shall devote the next chapter to it.

Mentioning the story of *The Star Ducats* (Grimms' tales) may be a fitting conclusion to this chapter. In it we see the human soul in the shape of a young girl who has lost both parents (namely the link to a meaningful past), who has no home and no bed to sleep in, and who wanders through the world, poor, with only a piece of bread and the clothes on her body. One by one she gives away her bread, her cap, her dress and her shirt. The soul of the charitable and honest human being, wandering through the material world, after giving away the bread she has left after losing the parents, sheds one by one the garments which she recognizes as not being essential to her nature. Divested of everything that links her to the past, she finds herself, cold and nude, in the nocturnal forest. Just when the situation appears hopeless and she is completely lost and deprived of everything, the golden stars begin falling from the heavens. The young girl collects them in the wondrous white linen shirt which suddenly clothes her, and she is wealthy for all her life.

This beautiful short tale stresses that only the humble and unselfish soul can find a new relationship to a spiritual world (represented by the golden stars from heaven) which is able to sustain and strengthen it when it is hopelessly lost, weak and alone, in a dark and cold world. Lack of charity and humility in this world lead the soul to amass material goods and to pride itself on attributes which are not truly its own, thereby blocking any opportunity for a renewed spiritual growth.

The story clearly points to the future: our future. We are still in the cold, dark forest. But, without false pride, we may already sense that one day we shall experience our ego otherwise than nude, deprived or—as we mentioned early in this chapter—reduced to an abstract concept. We may surmise that our uniqueness is not so much a part which can be dissected out of our body and soul, but something which penetrates these; that our individuality not only gives a specific coloring to our feelings and actions, but influences and configurates to a certain extent everything we are connected with: our bodily health, our relationship with other human beings, and our career. Therefore, we may learn to appreciate, to comprehend a person's individuality not so much in this or that trait or ability, but mostly in his biography from which we learn how his ego has shaped—coping with innumerable situations and events—its own history. We begin to recognize the meaning of Kierkegaard's self[96] or Jung's self[82] or of Goethe's Higher Ego or of Husserl's Transcendental Ego, hidden behind the everyday, ordinary or empirical ego.

CHAPTER XXVI

TURANDOT

THE THOUGHTS IN THIS CHAPTER evolved principally from the text of the libretto of Puccini's last opera which I heard a few years ago and which became an important factor in the growth of my interest in the meaning of fairy tales. While this libretto of *Turandot* was actually written by Giuseppe Adami and Renato Simoni,[1] it was Puccini who chose the story and who carefully selected and shaped every detail of it by himself.[68]

The story of Turandot first appeared in an ancient collection of Persian tales. These became available in Western Europe toward the end of the seventheenth century in a French translation. This was shaped into a play (or *opera comica*) by Carlo Gozzi in the eighteenth century, and into a drama by Friedrich Schiller at the beginning of the nineteenth century.[132] One hundred years later Giacomo Puccini became fascinated with the plot of the story. His own intuition into its basic meaning induced him to change and add several essential parts of the narrative, while the adaptation to the operatic form made additional changes necessary.

In all probability, Puccini's fascination for an intuitive understanding of the story was largely the result of the drama of his own life.[115,160] He was born into a family with several past generations of musicians of note, and very early it became apparent that he combined true musical genius with inherited talent. Yet there is a marked characterological disharmony between the delicate artistic perceptiveness in his operas and the rather meager understanding for his fellow human beings in his everyday life. Somewhat vainglorious and rather selfishly avaricious, he spent much of his time seeking the applause of the opening nights of his operas, indulging in rather meaningless affairs with women and driving various sport cars which seemed to be his main hobby. Relatively little time was devoted to composing, and only in a few of his operas does his deepest musical genius fully blossom out.

His adult life was overshadowed by the unsatisfactory relationship with a wife who left her first husband because of a passionate sensuous attraction between her and the young composer. She had no deep understanding for his musical career, and her jealousy, often fed by Puccini's various little amorous adventures, by his frequent lack of consideration for her, and probably also by her guilt over her own previous unfaithfulness, grew to be plainly pathological. Verbally attacked and persecuted with letters oozing jealousy, Puccini rather weakly tried to navigate with the currents. Finally, the wife's jealousy led to tragedy, when a simple servant girl drowned herself right in the main fountain of the town because of Mrs. Puccini's bitter delusional accusations. Yet, rather than assist his spouse, the composer, most cowardly, stayed away from home and from the lawsuits in which his wife became involved on account of this suicide. Only after the slander suits were settled, did he and his wife get back together again. The marriage appears to have been calmer from then on until Puccini's death a few years later. In an atmosphere of resigned or fatalistic discouragement over his own family and over the post World War I world, Puccini created his last, and probably most beautiful opera.

The plot centers around Turandot, the beautiful young Chinese princess. Determined to take vengeance for a severe tort done by the king of Tartary to her maternal ancestor Lio-u-ling, she has made a vow to reject and destroy all her suitors. The story leaves us in the dark concerning the nature of this cruel tort, until toward the end of the opera when Turandot discloses that this king had forced Lio-u-ling into submission to his passionate love. The memory of this shameful humiliation spurs Turandot to combine her rejection of men with cruel revenge by means of her tempting but deadly promise to marry whichever prince would be successful in solving her three riddles. Yet, all the princes who, lured by her reputed beauty and by her challenge, come to China from faraway places, fail and lose their heads.

We are told in the libretto that all this occurs in Peking in legendary times. We quickly begin to sense that the eerie, grotesque, yet fantastically beautiful Chinese setting was chosen not with any intent of alluding to the real China, but solely because the vast magnitude and distance of this Far Eastern country contained the elements necessary to represent the soul-world within which the story unfolds. When Puccini, about fifty years ago, composed this opera, China still appeared to most people as a political nonentity, vaguely better known for its past artistic, philosophic and religious splendor than for its present existence. In the opera everything conspires to avoid any identification of either the scenery or the action with our daytime reality. The city is named "the violet city of the celestial empire," and the weird architecture with its sculptured monsters, unicorns and phoenixes, the odd—only partially Chinese—costumes of the populace, the music, everything removes us beyond the confines of our commonplace world.

With the coming of the night, when outward reality becomes shadowy, the human being's attention can turn inward and the inner, the soul-world may come to light, if only in our dreams. Many fairy tales, for example *The Dance-Worn Shoes* (Grimms' tales) in which an intensive and rich life unfolds after sunset, use the night setting to portray this soul-world. Similarly we find in this opera that the plot begins at sunset, and that soon the full moon shines upon Turandot's imperial palace, in front of which are impaled the eleven heads of princes who, during the preceding year of the tiger, had accepted the deadly challenge. These heads are a dreadful warning, whether seen as the expression of the young woman's envy of men, or of Turandot's loyalty toward her maternal ancestor ravished by a man; whether they are interpreted, psychoanalytically, as penis envy and castration wishes, or as a portrayal of the dangers inherent in trying to solve prematurely and too superficially the mystery of the man-woman relationship. Be that as it may, the psychological paradox that any normal man could even conceive of marrying a cruel, cold murderess, leads us again to seek the meaning of the story in an area beyond our ordinary daytime consciousness. We then find that this is the story of the inner development of the adolescent, namely of Turandot and of Calaf, the unknown prince.

> The sun is setting, and the picturesque crowd in front of the imperial palace is clamoring for the decapitation of the twelfth suitor, the delicately youthful prince of Persia. Just then Calaf, the "unknown prince," finds in the midst of the populace his long lost father, Timur. Dethroned as king of Tartary, Timur became separated from his son while wandering around in exile, accompanied only by Liù, the faithful, unselfish slave girl. Soon the full moon rises, and the loving reunion is disturbed by the executioners who bring along the extremely beautiful Persian prince. Seeing him, the populace feels pity for him, and Calaf, enraged at the cruelty of Turandot, loudly protests and demands that the princess show herself. And with the crowd begging and Calaf protesting, Turandot, illuminated by the moonlight, almost ethereal, like a vision, appears on the balcony of her palace. Her proud bearing at once stems the tumult, and the unknown prince is so overcome by her divine beauty that he completely forgets her cruelty. While the young Persian prince dies in the background with Turandot's name on his lips, the more mature and forceful Calaf becomes involved in a most painful struggle between his sudden intense longings for the princess and the heartbreaking pleas of the newly-found father and Liù, not to be foolhardy and risk almost certain death for the love of Turandot. Yet, he wants to tear himself away from Liù who tenderly takes his hand to lead him away; he wants to rush by the three imperial ministers who try to stall him off, and to ring the big gong which would announce his willingness to accept Turandot's challenge.

In translating the foregoing events into our less colorful psychiatric language, we can first point out that the lost kingdom represents Calaf's early childhood during which Liù, the eternally young, unselfish, virgin-mother grew to love her boy simply because he smiled at her. Subsequently, the early childhood kingdom is lost. Not unlike Snow White who at seven years lost her castle and became acquainted, far away, with the tasks of our daytime world, Calaf was separated from his parents during the latency period between early childhood and adolescence. With the beginning of adolescence, the normal development leads to a short, attenuated recapitulation of the early relationship between parents and child. Only then can the adolescent's maturing love turn to a person outside his family. So we see in the story how the adolescent, for a short time, enters again in close contact with his parents. For both parents and child the problem arises, whether to hang on to each other and enjoy the former mutual dependence, or whether to let go so that the child not only becomes acquainted with the physical world surrounding him, but also starts entering a new, deep human relationship which to the parents appears as a terrible danger, to the adolescent as a great but terrifying challenge.

Of particular interest and importance in this opera are the three imperial ministers, named Ping, Pong and Pang, whom we saw quarreling with Calaf. These odd looking characters originate, historically, in Gozzi's comic opera where they are a sort of masked clowns. In Puccini's opera they take on a lengthy and major role. While they are in the service of the emperor, they obey Turandot and deal primarily with Calaf. Their reaction to Turandot's continued cruelty and to Calaf's strong love varies extremely from one moment to the next. They are alternately sarcastic, sentimental, sadistic, silly, serious and intuitive. Since they are incapable of grasping either the meaning of Turandot's cruelty or the essence of Calaf's love, they are inclined to consider the whole affair a great nuisance which is likely to lead to the ruin of China.

Ping, the most intelligent and powerful of the three, quite mephistophelian, can see only the sensuous side of Calaf's love. He cannot understand why the unknown prince would be crazy enough to risk his life because of Turandot, when there were women galore to be had:

> Demented youth!
> Turandot is non-existent!
> Nothingness alone exists
> into which thou wilt be annihilated!

And so Ping, Pong and Pang, while at times enjoying the cruelty of Turandot, vacillate between delicately beautiful daydreams in which they long for the old small home on a little lake surrounded by bamboo, and vague hopes that someday China, which—before Turandot—had slept "culled in seventy thousand centuries," will see a day in which love can undo terror.

It is not difficult to recognize in these ministers of China the awkward, alternately delicate and crude soul-forces of the adolescent, where Pong and Pang reflect the sentimental, and Ping the rational aspects of these soul-forces. However, their sentimental, impulsive and rational roles are not clearly defined, and this is one reason for their utter confusion. Only at the end of the opera we find them more dignified and in their proper place in the imperial court. In fact, it may be considered one of the essential steps in human maturation, to separate our emotions, our impulses and our reasoning while maintaining a harmonious integration of the three.

Because of the fact that nowadays these rational forces more than ever have been monopolized by the materialistic, natural-scientific, anti-spiritual philosophies, it is in Ping that this mephistophelian-satanic aspect is more clearly evident. We recognize these troubled soul-forces so often in our own adolescents, when they appear inconsiderate and cruel one day, then exquisitely sentimental, then again discouraged, pessimistic and longing for their early childhood, only to be happily hopeful on the following day. One moment we see these soul-forces enter an alliance with the blind sexual or aggressive instincts, only to despise and disparage these in the next moment in favor of some overly idealistic sublime feelings. Never resting, they can irritate and annoy us, then charmingly appeal to us; they courageously reject us and then again they beg for our love and support; and so they often appear tragicomic in their changing varied appearance.

We have previously tried to explain that fairy tales can be interpreted from several viewpoints; each interpretation, rather than contradicting, enriches the others. A subjective interpretation, such as is frequently stressed in Jung's psychology, would see in "China" the central adolescent figure. China, then, is the adolescent who, in his drive for maturity, suddenly feels himself tormented by the challenge of finding the right inner balance between masculinity and femininity, or between *animus* and *anima*. In this struggle, China's soul-forces, Ping, Pong and Pang push forward and backward, aiming at quick solutions; quite often they look back upon their earliest childhood which loses itself in the infinity of time, chanting nostalgically:

When I might go back to Tsiang,
And I might return to Kiu
To enjoy my lake so blue,
All surrounded by bamboo.

And it is again Ping, the most conscious of the three, who best describes this adolescent turmoil by saying:

Oh China, Oh China,
Now astounded and confoundedly restless!

It is characteristic of such a subjective interpretation to stress the fact that *all* the personalities in a tale (or dream) are viewed as different attributes of *one* central individual, in this case China. And so the soul-forces are able to reminisce about China's childhood which they trace back seventy thousand centuries, a subjectively experienced infinity of time. Then things were quiet and happy until after Turandot was born and until the various suitors began to appear. Besides the soul-forces and besides the emerging feminine and masculine aspects of the adolescent, we have the populace representing the more instinctual, aggressive and libidinous drives.

Finally, this adolescent China is also subjected to the influence of feminine and masculine, kind, stern, forbidding, loving, wise and helpful parental forces. It is important and interesting to note that Calaf's old, powerless, kind and feeble father, Timur, and Turandot's venerable, wise and god-like emperor-father, Altoun, are originally the same personality. Is not the cruel king of Tartary who ravished Turandot's mother Lio-u-ling, a faraway early childhood memory of the passionate side of this emperor-father; and is not Calaf's father also the king of Tartary who lost his kingdom when the unknown prince was still a child? But if, from this viewpoint, Timur and the emperor Altoun are originally the same father figure, then the empress, Lio-u-ling who was ravished and the virginal slave-girl-mother, Liù are equally two manifestations of one and the same personality, as is already indicated by the similarity of their names.*

*The skeptic reader may object that in the opera Liù is described as a "girl" and with Newman[132] he may feel that she was younger than Calaf who did not remember her because she was just a small child when he "once smiled

This illustrates quite clearly the fact discovered and analyzed in modern psychology, that each parent leaves in the child's soul several reflections of his personality, reflections which vary greatly, often appear completely separated and can be contradictory. In analogy to what we discussed in regard to the *Hansel and Gretel* tale, we can surmise that Lio-u-ling represents the old (ancestor) witch-aspect of mother, in that she, too, is cruel and demands human sacrifices. Liù, on the other hand, represents the pure and precious pearls of the witch, the never-aging treasure left by the young mother in the child's heart, treasure which, though consciously little cherished and often ignored, is always ready to help and support the growing child in his most serious struggles.

Of the father we have three representations in China's soul: the young passionate king of Tartary, the loving but powerless Timur, and the father ideal, namely the emperor Altoun. Of these the first is frightening to the feminine aspect of the soul, as he appears so ruthless; the third is a lofty goal for the masculine (*animus*) apsect of the adolescent soul. Between the

---

at her." Such a viewpoint is too one-sidedly technical and overlooks the fact that Liù, simply because of her protectiveness, her unselfishness and her pure love for Timur and Calaf, represents ideally what the human being longs for in a virginal mother. Nowhere do we see this more beautifully portrayed than in Michelangelo's sculpture of the *Pietà* in the Cathedral of St. Peter, where a virginal Mary, seemingly about sixteen years old, supports the body of her thirty-three-year-old son. This youthfulness of the mother is eternal and manifests the beauty of purity, love and chastity. Similarly, one might at first question the assumption that the maternal ancestor, Lio-u-ling, actually best represents Turandot's mother or at least one aspect of this mother. Aside from the factors already mentioned, there is one time reference to Lio-u-ling's ordeal which quite directly supports our contention: "Thousands of years ago . . . , at a time which everyone remembers, the cry of despair of the vanquished Lio-u-ling took refuge in my soul," says Turandot. Only the mother, among the maternal ancestors, could have been young enough in Turandot's childhood ("Thousands of years ago" being a purely subjective time indication, describing both the experience of length or distance, as well as the feeling of permanent loss of childhood) to be engaged in such a struggle with a man. Thousands of years ago, at a time which even Turandot remembers, the sweet and serene Lio-u-ling (this description again reminds us of Liù) defied the domination of man, "and now she lives in me." Lio-u-ling, the mother's attitudes, prohibitions, values, become part of Turandot's. They become internalized, or psychoanalytically speaking, they form the child's superego.

two, Timur, most clearly represents the real father, appearing old and weak. The adolescent cannot draw any longer from his strength which at one time he thought boundless and for which he now has to substitute his own force and initiative. However, let us return to the narrative of the story:

> Calaf, the unknown prince, finally succeeds in repulsing his pleading parents and the three imperial ministers and loudly rings the fatal gong which awakens the castle and the city. Right away, Ping, Pong and Pang try in a lengthy tragicomic discussion to prepare themselves for each eventuality; for the wedding, should Calaf win, for the funeral, should he lose. Finally the court, including the wise men, the emperor, and the populace gather to hear the three riddles of the haughty Turandot, read by the eight wise men. They see the princess defeated and humiliated by the "unknown prince." The three answers are: "Hope," "Blood" and the princess' name "Turandot." But the princess is not able to take Calaf's victory gracefully, and—in spite of the emperor's admonishments—pleads with him not to accept her as a victim who would always hate him. And to the consternation of everyone, the unknown prince renounces his victory by declaring that she can take his life, if by daybreak she has been able to find out his name. Without delay Turandot sets out to discover his name, mobilizing for this purpose the whole population, and particularly Ping, Pong and Pang, while threatening to destroy everyone if the search should prove unsuccessful.

The three answers, "Hope," "Blood" and "Turandot" reveal the essence of three phases in the princess' development. At the end of the first period of the child's development, when the paradise-castle has been lost, when one no longer lives at the "blue little lake surrounded by bamboo," when the witches have been relegated to the unconscious and the gingerbread house has been left behind, then only "hope" is left: a dreamlike hope which carries the child through the latency period up to the frightening awareness of puberty symbolized by "Blood." Here blood represents the beginning of puberty not only because the onset of the monthly periods coincides more or less with the end of the latency period, but also because blood stands both for the greater forcefulness of the instincts and for the innermost nature of the human being (as indicated in those stories in which the devil demands a drop of blood; to quote Goethe's Mephistopheles: "Blood is a very special liquid"). However this innermost nature requires time for its harmonious development, and only at the end of adolescence can the true individuality, which finds expression in the *name* "Turandot," blossom out and awaken, as we have clearly seen in the tale of the Sleeping Beauty.

The name, be it Turandot's or Calaf's, stands for the unique nature of the person, and knowledge of the name can lead either to true love or to the power of destroying this person. We saw the latter aspect of this knowledge dramatically portrayed in the fairy tale *Rumpelstilzchen* in which the little, partly helpful and partly harmful, dwarf tears himself to pieces when the princess finally discovers his name (see Chapter XXV). Whether the revelation or the discovery of the name proves beneficial or disastrous depends entirely upon the degree of development of each personality. In Wagner's *Lohengrin,* Elsa,[31] overcome by false suspicion, asks prematurely for her bridegroom's name, and this forces Lohengrin to leave her and to return to the castle of the Holy Grail. The knowledge and the use of the name entails a profound sense of responsibility and requires the previous personal achievement of trust and unselfishness. The greatest example for the fact that the name represents the essence of a being is seen in "The Lord's Prayer" in which the worshipper, turning to God, at first states: "Hallowed be Thy name."

Growing up cannot be forced. In the regressive and progressive vicissitudes of human development, the proper timing of each step is of utmost importance. The anxiety of waiting and uncertainty may predispose to rash decisions. In our present story this is brought out quite well by the attitude of the frightened ministers, Ping, Pong and Pang:

> While the night air is filled with dread because of Turandot's terrible threats, Ping, Pong and Pang approach Calaf, tempting him to give up his quest for Turandot and to accept in her stead quick sensual pleasures, riches and glory. The temptations and mounting threats of the ministers, as well as the panicky fear of the populace, engulf Calaf with a veritable nightmare against which he struggles desperately. Just when the crowd pushes to overpower him because of his obstinacy, or rather fortitude, his old father and Liù appear on the scene, as if to indicate that at this stage Calaf's strength alone is still unable to dispel the nightmare. Ping with his guards

arrests Timur and Liù, since he recognizes in them the two people who talked with Calaf the evening before, and since he hopes to extract from them the unknown prince's name. Turandot, also, appears on the scene, and just as she is about to order Timur's torture, Liù, the virgin-mother, steps forward and, by declaring that she alone knows the name, unfolds her truest nature, that is, completely unselfish love. This love leads her to sacrifice her own life, both to protect her husband and to avoid the possibility of weakening under torture and thereby revealing the unknown prince's name. At first sight, her voluntary death might appear senseless, inasmuch as Turandot soon afterwards yields to Calaf's passionate embrace, and inasmuch as the "unknown prince" spontaneously reveals to her his identity, giving her thereby the choice of either destroying him or of accepting him of her own free will. In fact, however, Liù's death operates a deep change in the bystanders, a change which makes the subsequent positive developments possible. Timur, in his bottomless sorrow, senses this first: "Liù, it is the golden hour of the awakening, it is dawn, Liù, open thy eyes, my dove. . . ." The violent populace turns quiet, terrified lest the soul of the dead woman take revenge for the perpetrated injustice, and the three ministers sense that for the first time they are capable of genuine, deep feelings of compassion.*

Turandot no longer can maintain her fierce pride by remembering the fate of Lio-u-ling; she is vanquished by Calaf's tender and passionate affection, and has genuine tears in her loving eyes. Her pride is rekindled briefly once more at dawn, when Calaf unexpectedly reveals his name, thereby leaving it completely up to her to destroy or to accept him. But in front of the court and the populace, reassembled in plain sunshine, Turandot becomes one with Calaf, declaring that his *name* is *love*. And the opera ends with the crowd praising the sun, the light of the world, which is love.

And so we see the victory of the higher ego over the egoistic drives, of the sun over the goddess of the night, which Mozart portrayed with such beautiful music in his *Magic Flute*, which is another fairy tale.

The personality of Liù was introduced into the story by Puccini himself. While some critics have been inclined to dis-

---

*Using Jungian terminology, we may say that here the shadow-nature of the ministers reveals itself fully (see Chapter III). Only when the shadow is no longer an obstacle in the human psyche, can the *animus* and the *anima* meet in harmony.

count her significance in the opera, attributing Puccini's choice mostly to his predilection for cruel torture scenes, there can be, at closer observation, little doubt that Liù plays a very essential role.

While she was alive, Liù's love and devotion were often more hindering than helpful to Calaf and Turandot. Her dying makes possible the successful further development of the two. Calaf achieves another degree of independence and courage, whereas through her death Liù's ability for self-denial and unselfish love penetrate Turandot, thereby overcoming the forbidding, witch-like forces of Lio-u-ling which had dominated the princess. Calaf, now, can no longer conceive of love as conquering and dominating. True unselfishness is born also in him (again by taking into himself the corresponding aspect of the dead Liù), and now he can accept love only as a relationship between free human beings.

Turandot, on the other hand, overcomes her hatred and envy of men, born of early, misunderstood childhood experiences. If we use a predominantly psychoanalytic vantage point, we can say that she no longer has to fight her adolescent femininity, overcompensating for the terror of each monthly period by impaling, each full moon, the head of a suitor in front of her palace. True maturity is not avoidance or denial of physical realities, whether these realities are pleasant, indifferent or distasteful, but consists in seeing that which is meaningful in (or despite of) the physical realities. Once she obtains the unknown prince's *name*, Turandot can no longer transfer upon him a vague, painful childhood memory; she must now confront him and accept him as a unique individual.

I hope that no excessive confusion was created by interrupting the narrative of the foregoing story with interpretations and comments which at times viewed the persons in the story subjectively as projections of the struggles between various components within the adolescent (named China), and which at other times treated the tale as an objective description of the gradual development of an ideal relationship between the opposite sexes. In both the subjective and the objective interpretation we can distinguish several additional viewpoints. Some may sense in the story the struggle of the human soul (Turandot) who has lost its relatedness to the ancient happiness and wisdom during its struggles with the material realities, and who finds this relatedness again—on a higher, more conscious level—in its union with the unknown prince who has overcome the temptations of power and passion, who is willing to assume the karmic (or fateful) consequences of leaving his parents behind and of seeing Liù die for him ("We will have to expiate this! The troubled soul —of Liù—will seek revenge."). He must assume and carry this existential guilt and responsibility, because only in complete freedom can the higher ego be born:

Lange hab ich mich gesträubt, Endlich gab ich nach; Wenn das alte Ich zerstäubt wird das Neue wach.	Long have I resisted, Finally I yielded: When the old Ego disintegrates the new Ego awakens. J. W. GOETHE[55]

According to Jung, human fate consists in the establishment of a harmonious integration or unification of the various dichotomies within the human being: personal unconscious vs. collective unconscious; *animus* vs. *anima;* ego vs. self; outside world vs. inside world, etc. The experiencing of the opera would then activate in the spectator or listener those forces which would lead to his own maturation. But for Jung as well as for some existential philosophers[63,109,162] the ultimate limit of maturation is death; and whether the meaning of human growth has validity in terms of something beyond subjective experience is just as unanswerable as the question whether God is only an ubiquitous, unavoidable subjective experience or whether He has an objective existence. Jung opens our eyes to the colorful depths of the soul-world, only to leave us somewhat disconcerted by his agnostic conclusions. He does not even give us the vague consolation which Goethe expresses so beautifully:

Es kann die Spur von meinen Erdentagen	The trace of my days on this earth
nicht in Aeonen untergehn.[54]	cannot disappear in the endlessness of time.

An objective interpretation of the narrative can equally use various viewpoints. The orthodox, conservative psychoanalyst would see in the decapitation of the princes an expression of the woman's distress over her monthly periods and over her lack of a male organ. In Liù's death he would tend to see the successful repression of the superego which to Turandot (in the guise of a memory of Lio-u-ling) emerges from her unconscious in form of the cruel rejection of feminine and male sexuality, and which to Calaf appears as the eternally young, virginal, self-sacrificing, protecting and loving mother. The executioner, Pu Tin Pao, would represent the instinctual id forces put at the disposition of the cruel superego, whereas the populace—ready to enjoy happiness and cruelty alike—would symbolize the original instinctual id forces.

A realistic objective interpretation would, as we have pointed out, stress the irrational and utterly unpsychological as well as illogical aspects of the story in which Calaf would appear as an infatuated fool who chases—disregarding completely the extreme hurt and harm inflicted upon his parents—a good-looking feminine monster. However, the tale can also be looked at from an objective romantic viewpoint, namely as the actual development of a mature relationship between a young man and a young woman, where the irrational aspects are not so much psychoanalytically explained symbols, but powerful metaphors illustrating with overemphasized colorfulness what the poet wishes to express.

Undoubtedly, other interpretations using other viewpoints and abstractions might illuminate other meanings. For example, we can see the opera as an appeal to humanity to overcome feelings of fear and pride (represented by Turandot), to abandon needs for conquest and domination (represented by Calaf); only such inner victories (rather than outward social laws and reforms), leading to true unselfishness would bring peace to our troubled civilization, symbolized here by China. Helpful interpretations do not attempt to translate symbols into an original meaning, but express the meaning of the phenomena of the fairy tale in terms which are more familiar to our modern, rationalistic thinking. The story simply deals with human adolescence, as experienced in its essence by the authors of the libretto. Whether this adolescence is seen as that of the individual or—in a more sweeping view—as that of modern humanity may well be of secondary importance.

By not judging whether this or that interpretation is better, by experiencing each interpretation as a true expression of some of the meanings of the events, by this passive receptiveness we may better sense the depth of the story. Ordinarily, the stage setting, the narrative and the music find direct access to deeper experiential levels within us. The possibility that our analysis of the story enlivens our understanding is not so much due to the unmasking of symbols, but to our inability, as modern adults, to experience the message of the story as spontaneously and as deeply as many children would. It appears to me that it is this more immediate, contemplative rather than analytic, understanding which the phenomenologists strive for. The phenomenologists and existential analysts, in their profoundest efforts, seem to aim at reassigning to meaningfulness the first place among human values. They do not simply long to return to the past, rejecting the natural-scientific achievements, but they hope for a synthesis of the past and of the present into a deeper, spiritual concept of our universe. And they endeavor to find this synthesis by a maximally presuppositionless approach that will let the things reveal themselves, showing their essential qualities and relationships. This endeavor, admittedly, is but a way toward a distant goal.

CHAPTER XXVII

CHILDREN'S RESPONSES TO FOLKLORE

THE CHILD, before his mind is strongly patterned by our contemporary, technological thinking which concentrates on quantities and on causes and effects, usually enjoys and accepts fairy tales without many whys and wherefores. In particular, the healthy small child tolerates without difficulty even the most horrid cruelties in these stories, sensing that the fairy tale belongs to a special world which, in a way, is just as meaningful—if not more—as our daytime world, but which must not be confused with it. Only as he gets more sophisticated may he start to be bothered by some of the apparent incongruities in the narrative.

I cannot think of any better way to illustrate how a child subconsciously understands and elaborates a fairy tale than by telling this anecdote concerning my older son who at the time was eleven years old:

One evening I was reading to my wife a paper I was going to present the next day, the main theme of which was the above story of *Turandot*. Our boy was quietly listening while pretending to sleep. The following day he made the—for him quite unusual—declaration that he had had a dream and, at my request, he wrote it down as follows:

> I dreamed that my brother and I got to have a stone that if you let it touch something, you could wish for something and you would get the thing you wished for right on the place the stone had touched. One of the things I wished for was a few golden rings, but instead I got some pearls. I started picking them up, but something made the pearls go away. After a while the golden rings appeared that I had wished for. They appeared in the same

place the pearls had appeared. I was very delighted and began to put them on. I said to myself that when I was older I would give one of the rings to a girl I would like.

When I woke up, I was kind of sad because I did not really have the rings. I would really have liked this dream to come true, but I was sad that it did not come true.

While we do not recognize any of the objective details of the *Turandot* story, we see in this dreamed fairy tale a tender echo coming from the soul of the preadolescent child. We recognize in it the three periods of development, with particular stress placed on the third period which to the eleven-year-old child is something far in the future, something which he cannot hold on to as yet. The earliest period is indicated by the magic stone which at first does not produce the wished for rings, but creates pearls. They are analogous to the pearls of Hansel and Gretel, the pearls of infancy, the treasure we retain from this earliest phase of magic and omnipotence. Then, with the latency period, they disappear altogether. Yet later, exactly in their former place, the rings emerge, which here become the symbols of the most precious and purest feelings between the young man and woman. The golden ring expresses the willingness to permanently belong to somebody; it is a fully conscious commitment to be linked to another person. While the gold refers to spiritual values and permanence, the roundness symbolizes the self-contained, conscious ego. The ring, therefore, can symbolize the mature, free, self-aware ego which is faithful to another, not because of social conventions or instinctual necessity, but by its own decision. The eleven-year-old boy awakens, nostalgically realizing that he is too old to see and to hold on to the pearls, and too young to wear the golden rings. But it is a pleasant nostalgia which carries the promise of future beauty and love, and which thereby encourages the child to cope healthily and conscientiously with the tasks of the present.

When the tales are narrated sympathetically in their original version, they will not only be entertaining, but they will also exert a doubly beneficial effect upon the development of the child. In the first place, the fairy tale awakens the feeling of participation with other human beings, with people not only of the child's immediate environment, but of all nations and races. (It is indeed surprising how easily folktales cross even the borders of enemy nations.) He begins to sense that he is not alone with his, at times horrid and violent, fantasies, and that the latter are meaningful and valuable sources of strength for useful sublimations, as long as they never become confused with the outward reality. Furthermore he feels understood in his most tender longings, in his highest wishes and ideals.

In the second place, the fairy tale communicates to the child a dim, intuitive understanding of his own nature and of his future positive potentialities. And he starts to sense that he became a human being primarily because in this world of ours he is meant to meet important and wondrous adventures. And so the fairy tale nourishes the child's courage to widen his horizons and to tackle all the challenges successfully. Then only, like some of the fairy tale heroes, he can hope to become a king within whose realms spiritual wisdom will harmonize with power over earthly things.

If we rely on our psychologic terminology, we may see that any offering, at the proper time, of a gradually wider and deeper understanding of the world in and around us contributes to the growth of the ego, and that therefore fairy tales have both an educational and therapeutic value. The narrator's understanding of their meaning furthers the sensitivity for selecting those stories which are most appropriate in various phases of the children's development and for stressing those themes which may be therapeutic for specific psychological difficulties. Furthermore, our sensitivity to the tale's hidden language will enable us to find suitable answers to the doubts which children will justifiably voice. At times the grown-ups may skeptically see in the fairy tale nothing but entertaining, silly or moralistic stories, or they may use the fierce aspects of them in order to intimidate and control, or in order to morbidly enjoy the gullibility of the child. We then may find that the child later on goes through a rude awakening, when he realizes that he was fed a bunch of lies; and this may permanently undermine his ability to trust properly his fellow human beings.

Fairy tales are most effective when told from memory by a

person whose heart is responsive to the tale and to his listeners. As said before, explanations are unnecessary, superfluous and can weaken the effectiveness of the tale, especially with children. However, explanations may be meaningful and advantageous for several reasons in high school and college classes dealing with folklore; and they may help the overly rationalistic adult to unlock the doors in his scientific walls that obscure or obstruct his vision for what is more profoundly significant: for qualities, feelings, values, meanings and hopes.

Before being told a fairy tale, saga or epos, the listeners—not only children but also adults—must often be familiarized with concepts and objects occurring in the narration that are no longer used in the same context as in our present world. Many children have never seen a spinning wheel, a wolf or an old-fashioned mill on the side of a brook; few have seen the type of feather pillows and bed covers Mrs. Holle shook in order to make it snow or, for that matter, an old-fashioned well such as the one through which the children fell into Mrs. Holle's realm. The tight vest that squeezed life out of Snow White or the grandfather clock in which the littlest goat hid may be but vague concepts to most children, and few will know what an old-fashioned oven (*cf*, the story of the *Goose Girl*) looked like. When reading ancient Egyptian tales (*cf.* that of *Ni-noferka-Ptah*[15]), few will have an idea of the complexity and purpose of a rich sarcophagus; and when the epos (*Kalevala, Odyssey,* myths of Jason, etc.) refers to the important ships of its heroes, not many listeners will have a clear image of these early boats or galleys; and when the tale of Solomon and the Queen of Sheba[15] speaks of the column on which all the knowledge of the world is engraved, it may be very useful to show pictures of the remnants of ancient columns that portray history. Finally, since the fairy tale, even more than the myth, tends to objectify interpersonal relationships, it may be advantageous to explain beforehand to the listeners that an action like delousing was for ages an expression of care, tenderness and love, devoid of any unpleasant connotations. Such elements, then, lost partly behind the curtains of our civilization, should be presented, illustrated and discussed before the telling of the story.

If this is done skillfully, it may enhance the attention and the feelings of anticipation of the young listeners.

The healing value of fairy tales can best be seen in children who, often because of parental influences, have prematurely grown skeptical and thereby bored, discouraged, listless or depressed, as well as in children who, quite early, have become withdrawn and insecure, fearful and distrustful because of too many hurts. Here the fairy tale, offered lovingly and delightfully, can become a fountain of youth, reviving the courage and the interest to meet the future. However, fairy tales can lead to increased confusion and psychopathology in some very disturbed children whose ability to separate inward and outward experiences is already seriously impaired. Treatment of these children demands highly specialized psychiatric skills which might still include, here and there, the use of well selected fairy tales.

As if to make quite sure that it speaks directly to the inner soul-world, the fairy tale makes use of various devices to avoid confusion between its own world and everyday reality, between Tolkien's secondary and primary world. This may be accomplished by remote and fantastic settings, such as we noted in the Turandot story, by the avoidance of historical time (through expressions such as, "Once upon a time") or by very vague references to the location of the plot (such as, "Near a big forest lived . . ."). Occasionally a slightly bizarre terminating sentence underlines the separation of the fairy tale from the daytime world (see Chapter VII).

Finally, the physical impossibility as well as the very monstrosity of the events help separate the two worlds. How could a wolf ever swallow six goats whole, how could they continue to live in his stomach, how could his stomach be cut open and sewed up without his noticing it? Equally absurd are: Jack climbing up the beanstalk into an upper world of giants; the witch planning to roast and eat Gretel; the bad queen having to dance in red hot metal shoes until she drops dead, and innumerable other similar incidents.

This is equally true of many mythologic images. While some could possibly be interpreted as mere metaphors or explanations of cosmic events (*cf.* Phoebus sun wagon, or Atlas supporting the earth), there are a great number that are so strikingly absurd from our everyday vantage point, that they appeal directly to whatever sensibility we may still have for the world of meaning, of being, of creative forces, called "secondary world" by Tolkien.

In the *Kalevala*,[91] for example, the mysterious tale of the origin of iron is sung by an old man in order to stop the flow of blood from the wound Wainemoinen accidentally inflicted upon himself with his ax, while building—without ever touching it—a marvelous ship out of the splinters of a virgin's spindle. After telling of the god Ukko's creating three fair daughters, "Mothers of the rust of iron," by rubbing together his mighty hands and then pressing them on his left knee, the song continues:

> Strolled the maids with faltering footsteps
> On the borders of the cloudlets,
> And their full breasts were o'erflowing,
> And their nipples pained them sorely.
> Down on earth their milk ran over,
> From their breasts' o'erflowing fulness,
> Milk on land, and milk on marshes,
> Milk upon the peaceful waters . . . .
> Where the black milk had been dropping,
> There was found the softest iron,
> Where the white milk had been flowing,
> There the hardest steel was fashioned,
> Where the red milk had been trickling,
> There was undeveloped iron.
>
> *Runo IX*

In primitive folklore we often find even more outrageous departures from everyday reality. The extremely interesting and beautiful African tale of *Mrile* speaks of a young man who raises a child from some bulbs. When his mother kills the child, he elevates himself spontaneously into the skies, there to become a culture hero in search of the moon king. Eventually he returns on the back of a bull. However, when the father kills the bull and Mrile unwittingly eats of the fat that mother mixed with flour, he sinks deeper and deeper into the ground until he disappears altogether.[46]

The meaning of such images can be taken as literally as that of picturesque expressions of our everyday language such as, "he is dissolving in tears," or "she is floating on cloud nine." Yet, while we recognize immediately the experiential meaning of the latter expressions, we have largely lost the understanding for the full meaning of the former.

In our modern, at times overly rational and one-sidedly materialistic, world some fears arise therefore, lest the monstrous and cruel episodes may frighten or misguide the children. Because of this we find many attenuated and rationalized versions of these narrations. The effect of such watering down, however, is often just the opposite of what was desired. Without the bizarre incongruities and with less impossible cruelties, the tale becomes more like a story taken out of our everyday life. Because the child now has much less of a clear sensation that the events of the tale belong to a special world, he may more easily become frightened or he may be encouraged toward unhealthy identifications (see Chapter XV).

We have described how the fairy tale often tries to furnish the meaning of three main periods of the individual's development. The first of these is the period of early childhood when the human being still lives in a world in which his delicate experiences of beauty and ugliness, love and hatred, far outweigh any natural scientific logic. Then comes the latency phase where these intuitive abilities are lost, or rather suppressed, for the sake of learning to adjust to our material world. In the third period, adolescence, the human being seeks to achieve a new spiritual height, which he approaches consciously and freely and which transcends materiality. Yet the meaning of these tales, both to children and adults, always goes beyond the narrow limits of the single individual's destiny, thus manifesting simultaneously where mankind is culturally or spiritually. As indicated fleetingly above, a more profound sense can be discovered in numerous tales, to the effect that, in many ways and from various viewpoints, they show how humanity has lost the golden, paradisiacal world, how it has become bewitched, petrified, lost in a wood or has fallen into a death-like sleep, and how it hopes to reach a newly meaningful existence on a higher plane.

Our present, spiritless times are far from meaningless. On the contrary, it is only by going through and overcoming the petrification (materialism) that this higher plane, often described as the marriage between the princess and the king, will be reached. Therefore a story such as *Turandot* can offer a feeling of consolation and hope also to the adults, when they experience its meaning not so much in terms of a description of two adolescents who find the ideal love relationship, but in the description of humanity (China) itself. The most spiritual part of the human being has become an "unknown prince," while death reigns in China under the leadership of Turandot. The soul-forces have become disorganized, confused, partly longing for the paradisiacal past, partly enjoying the cruelty of the present, and partly hoping that the dreadful spell of Turandot's three riddles will finally be broken. Only the sacrifice by Liù can create that unselfishness in the unknown prince, and that willingness in Turandot to overcome pride and tradition, which can lead to the harmonious union of *animus* and *anima,* of prince and princess, which becalms Ping, Pong and Pang as well as the masses, and which "gives back peace to China."

As we are caught up in egotistic self-aggrandizement, in escapist addictions to race cars, television programs or drugs, and in the pursuit of superficial sexual adventures, we may find ourselves empty and dissatisfied like Giacomo Puccini. The genius of the composer, however, reached out for the new spiritual integration and harmony portrayed in the last scene of *Turandot* by the emperor of China again reigning benignly, while the soul-forces (Ping, Pong and Pang) are harmonized and the united Turandot and Calaf are acclaimed by a happy population.

CHAPTER XXVIII

THE MEANING OF THE FOREST MOTIF IN *THE DRAGON IN THE BLACK WOOD*

Illustrating Additional Motifs Alluded to in Chapter XXIV

"IN THE ENGADIN tale of *The Dragon in the Black Wood* we first meet a father who is returning from a fourteen-day trip. As presents he brings for his eighteen-year-old son, Louis, a white horse, and for his sixteen-year-old daughter, Louise, a rose bush. The latter has the mysterious property that its red roses will turn pale when someone of the family is in great danger, and that they will wilt when he has died.

One day the young lady, Louise, walks into the forest to pick cranberries for the family; but she does not return. Instantly the roses on the bush turn pale, yet all the searching for the girl remains fruitless. Two entire years elapse, when her brother, who meanwhile has gone to a foreign land, is startled by a most unusual dream. As a result of this, he decides how he can rescue his sister.

After hurrying home, he lets his white horse carry him into the forest which soon becomes thick and almost black; everything appears familiar to him on account of that prophetic dream. As it carries him through the dark wood, the white horse suddenly steps upon a red Alpine rose; with a loud noise a nearby tree splits open, and a fiery red man steps out of its trunk. The apparition tells him:

> Your horse has stepped upon the flower queen of the forest, upon this Alpine rose; and he who crushes this rose at the time when the sharp horns of the moon look upward has also the power to disenchant this dark wood. At dusk, you will arrive upon a green meadow in the center of which stands a marvelous building surrounded by a high wall. You must spend the night inside this building, and the following morning proceed toward the courtyard, in the middle of which you will notice a magnificent fountain. On one side of this fountain the earth is loose. Take this roll, which will turn into a heavy stick when you unravel it; with it you must hit three times upon the loosened ground to kill the magic dragon who is beneath.

Our young hero follows the red man's advice. As he strikes the soil three times with the heavy stick, the dragon inside the earth explodes into a thousand pieces; Louis' sister and another bewitched young lady, whom he subsequently marries, are freed from the dragon's witchcraft which held them captive, and the beautiful building becomes the possession of Louis' family and the place for a happy celebration."

The house in the middle of the woods where extremely significant events take place is well known to us from the stories of *Little Red Riding Hood, Snow White and the Seven Dwarfs, Hansel and Gretel, Jorinde and Joringel, Percivale,* the *Magician Merlin* and many, many other sources. In contrast to the home from which the hero or heroine departs, it contains, it houses something mysterious, be it the wolf-grandmother, the seven little dwarfs, the bad witch, the Holy Grail, or the bewitched magician. In our tale it houses the two mute young women, clad in black, and held captive by the dragon. As all fairy tale themes, the image of the house in the forest can be interpreted in somewhat different ways, which, to a degree, compliment each other. We shall gain a better understanding of it, as we focus on the three items closely associated with it; namely, the forest, the fountain and the dragon.

First, however, we must consider the central human theme of the tale, the relationship between Louis, the young hero and the bewitched sister. This is the well-known, universal theme, recurring in many variations, of the courageous young male who rescues the young woman who has been bewitched or stolen, has gone to the underworld, or was offered as ransom to a monster. Perseus who frees Andromeda from the sea monster, Orpheus who tries desperately to bring Eurydice back from Hades, Sir Lancelot who rescues the abducted Queen Guinevere are but a few epic examples of this theme which refers much more to an inner developmental process than to an external event. A common denominator of this theme is the portrayal of a split which occurs within the growing individual and which eventually must be bridged or healed, if disaster is to be averted and if evolution is to continue. We can say that this split occurs between the human intellect, mind, or spirit and the less rational aspects of the human being, often, though inaccurately, described as the soul. In Jungian terminology this would roughly correspond to a split between the human being's *animus* and *anima.*

In our fairy tale we see Louis, the intelligent, adventurous young man, leave the harmony of his home and settle in a foreign city, while the sister is left behind. She represents that delicate aspect of the adolescent's soul which is neglected, repressed if you wish, while his intellect matures, and his adventurousness drives him into independence. She seeks nourishment, namely the cranberries, in the forest which soon becomes black and imprisons her. The soul-forces represented by her are lost to the daylight; they are, one could also say, hidden in the darkness of the unconscious. And here they remain for two years; no one can find a trace of them.

Just when hope wanes, these soul-forces become alive again, only at night, in Louis' dream which shows him what he has neglected, what he has lost, and how he can recapture it. Most of the subsequent details of the fairy tale are illustrations of the path and of the trials by which the hero can find a new, harmonious integration with the hidden, temporarily bewitched, feminine soul-forces. This adventure is not a fully conscious, deliberate undertaking. Rather, the young man must admit that his intellect alone, his daytime consciousness, would never have led him back home. It is his unusual dream which opens up the blocked avenue to the unconscious, to the dark forest; once he arrives there, it is not his own, deliberate ingenuity, but his white horse which finds the way into the very core of this forest. He must let the white horse guide him through this mysterious region which appears familiar to him on account of his dream.

Both in myths and in fairy tales, the horse, and especially the white horse, appears frequently as an image of those instinctual, wise intuitions, which, at times, can guide us more securely than our abstract intellect. In portraying human development, the fairy tale often refers with the image of the horse to an early form of reasoning which, in a later period, must be left behind or sacrificed (see Chapter XXIV). Thus his white horse leads our hero first to the Alpine rose and the red man, then to the castle-like building in the woods. From here on, however, the young man must continue on foot toward the courtyard with the magnificent fountain and with the subterranean dragon.

This association of the fountain and the building surrounded by a wall points toward the deepest meaning of the tale. The fountain, spring, well, pond or lake, frequently situated in an unusual forest, is a common theme alluding to the single, nourishing source of all life or all existence. A legend describes this forest-surrounded spring where Saint John Chrysostom, living in a simple hut in the middle of a forest, battles through gravest sin toward mature perfection.[24] We are again reminded of the Arthurian epos of *Sir Owain, the Knight with the Lion,* as well as of the pond into which has rolled the golden ball of Grimms' princess in the story of *The Frog King.* In another Grimms' tale, *Mrs. Holle,* the good and the nasty girl descend through the well into a mysterious realm from which they eventually return with their deserved rewards. Again it is a well where the benevolent Irish prince, Niall, far out in the wilderness, obtains life-giving water, because its guardian, the monstrous looking old woman, was turned into a graceful, fair lady when he did not shirk from having to kiss her ugly features.

The meaning of these wells is similar to the well in the deep tower where the Arabian Nights prince, Kamar-Al-Zamon is imprisoned, anxiously waiting for his beloved, or to the fountain near which Mary stood to fill her pitcher when the angel of the

Lord appeared unto her announcing that she had conceived the Christ child (The gospel of pseudo-Matthew, Ch. IX[24]). Of the stories on our continent we may mention the tender tale of the young Pueblo hero, *Water-Jar-Boy,* who, after a long search, finally finds his deceased father who lives inside a spring in a remote region; his father then takes the boy with him inside the spring.

The fountain with the water of life is removed from our everyday world. This separateness may be indicated by the allusion to fantastic, astronomic distances as in the Hawaiian tale of *Au-Ke-Le, the Seeker;* or the fountain may be hidden in a tower or located in a desert, or, very frequently, it may be surrounded by woods. To equate the significance of all the heroes who rescue a lady, of all the fountains or of all the forests in myths and fairy tales would obviously be fallacious.

However, when we look at the forest motifs, we may recognize one meaning which they all have in common, namely the reference to a threshold toward another aspect of human existence, or toward a new phase of development. Any genuine change or development implies the abandonment of the habitual, everyday consciousness, the entering into something which is still obscure, the risking of non-being, or, in more psychological terms, the confrontation with the forces from the unconscious. The black, fearsome forest of our tale differs greatly from the enchanted forest in which the magician Merlin, bewitched with his own sorcery by his beloved, lives on eternally; it differs from the frightening woods with the ferocious animals through which Snow White flees toward the little hut of the seven dwarfs, as well as from the joyful, sun-drenched forest in which Red Cap (Little Red Riding Hood) deviates from her path in order to gather some flowers for grandmother, or from the lonely woods through which Hansel and Gretel wander, guided by a white bird toward the gingerbread house of the witch.

Quite different again is the forest of despair in which Dante, in the middle of his life, sees himself lost and confronted by three wild beasts until Vergil arrives to lead him through hell and purgatory to paradise.[33] This forest resembles somewhat the one through which Sir Lancelot must travel in search of Queen

Guinevere who has been taken by Prince Maleagant to the land of the departed. There are qualitative variations from the forest in the Buddhist tale of *Prince Five-Weapons,* who overcomes Sticky-Hair, to that forest of the King Arthur cycle in which Owain confronts Woodward of the Wood and the Black Knight before conquering the Lady of the Fountain; from the woods where the Greek Actaeon spies the goddess Diana bathing, to the grove of trees in the midst of which Ramakrishna beholds a beautiful woman ascending from the river Ganges.[188]

Yet we find that in all these myths and fairy tales the hero's, i.e. the human being's, entering into the forest represents the willingness or need, the challenge or the possibility of a new phase of development. This can be illustrated with the three just-mentioned Grimms' tales by using a somewhat simplified and restricted psychological viewpoint. In the *Hansel and Gretel* story we would recognize the child's first struggle against dependence upon a most ambivalent mother. The child experiences this mother not so much in his daytime consciousness, but at night, in his subconscious, in the middle of the forest where she appears all sweet and friendly, all cruel and devouring. Red Cap, still of preschool age, is already more independent than Hansel and Gretel; the peril which she faces and overcomes is that of becoming too fond of being ensnared and swallowed by the sensory world. Snow White's flight through the forest is the seven-year-old child's final emancipation from the early infantile family ties.

Louise, in our fairy tale, is sixteen when she is lost in the dark woods, and her brother is in his twenty-first year when he sets out to find her. In several respects his deed corresponds to that of the prince who awakens Briar Rose who fell asleep on her fifteenth birthday. Her sleep corresponds, in various ways, to adolescence, and her awakening signals the attainment of maturity. Her prince must also penetrate a dangerous wood, namely a wood of rosebushes, in order to remove the all-paralyzing spell from the hidden castle. Like the brother in our story, Briar Rose's prince is impelled to act exactly at the right time (namely when the hundred years are up), and like the prince, Louis is told the details of the fate of the castle by a man whom he meets on his adventurous journey.

The venture into higher, wider levels of existence thus leads across thresholds; at the threshold the true hero usually encounters some sort of guardian who warns and guides. This guardian appears under many different guises and with varied attitudes. At times he cautions against, at times he encourages the undertaking; at times he turns out to be one of the bewitched, at times he belongs to the negative, bewitching forces. Thus our red man who alights from the bursting tree when the white horse, at the right time, steps upon the red Alpine rose is a most remarkable apparition. His intimate association with the tree, his explosive appearance, his redness and maybe even the reference to the "sharp horns of the moon pointing upward" confer upon him a devilish, luciferic connotation, in spite of his helpful advice. Like the luciferic serpent in the Garden of Eden he brings knowledge. All this becomes more plausible when we view him as a counterpart of the subterranean dragon near the magnificent fountain who explodes when our hero, again at the right time, hits the ground with the heavy, miraculous stick.

Remembering that this story focuses upon the threshold from adolescence to adult life, we may see the red man as a reference to the impulsive, instinctual drives which puritanically have been designated, at times, as devilish. In the adolescent these drives are rather chaotic and can become harmful if they are not controlled, our tale says bewitched, by other forces. However, once the supremacy of the ego is established, the soul can become free, and these instinctual drives then constitute a normal asset of the grown human being. The controlling force, the dragon, now represents a deadlier, satanic element which wishes to separate the soul permanently from the spirit. By furthering the repression of the instinctual urges, he would also suppress the access to our soul and to the fountain of life. We would be grown, intelligent and probably prosperous, but only at the cost of being estranged from our own soul.

This loss of communication, of dialogue, with the soul is beautifully portrayed in our tale. It is in the evening that the sister and her friend, draped in black, unrecognizable and mute, appear to the young hero for the first time. Silently they share the evening meal. Then at ten, eleven and twelve o'clock, frightful noises can be heard, but the youth remains steadfast in his goal. Only after a silent breakfast with the two mysterious women, when he unravels the roll given him by the red man and with the resulting heavy stick destroys the dragon in the courtyard, do the young women regain their recognizable features and their speech.

This magic roll which can turn into a large, heavy stick, and which was offered by the red man with helpful, instinctual and devilish connotations, is suitable for an additional comment about so-called Freudian interpretations of fairy tale symbolism. By seeing the object which is first soft and then becomes hard and straight and large, as a male sex symbol, a psychoanalytic interpretation may point out two complementary aspects of the hero-dragon relationship. On the one hand, the latter would indicate the final overcoming of that part of the parental superego which interferes with the development of a mature, integrated personality; on the other hand, it would also portray a last, symbolical approach to and relinquishing of the mother-dragon. Only with this climactic dissolution of the last oedipal tie, can the young man turn his interest toward women of his own age. The fact that, beside the sister, there is another bewitched girl whom the youth eventually marries, would thus underline the transition from an earlier, incestuous to a mature, nonincestuous relationship. In psychoanalytic parlance one can say that the hero's libido is first transferred from the mother to the sister, and then to his wife.

The penetration into the darkest part of a mysterious forest hiding the unrecognized virgin guarded by the destructive dragon can also be interpreted psychoanalytically. It becomes a symbol for sexual penetration, for sexual recognition. The forest in English, and equivalent terms in other languages, has long been used, mostly by inquisitive youngsters, as a metaphor indicating the pubic hair that covers the female genitals, that hides the innocent young woman's virginity. One may then speculate whether the horse stamping upon the "queen of the Alpine roses" at the entrance into the dark forest, the Alpine rose, and the explosive appearance of the red man are other, more detailed symbols referring to the sexual act. The reference to the proper phase of the moon can be adduced as further evidence for this. The horse alludes to the spontaneous male sexual drive; the rose can stand both for virginity and for the sensitive sexual responsiveness of the woman; while the male emerging from the tree would be related to the joint climactic experience.

In our tale, then, we can see Louis depart from the narrow world of his home and penetrate the wider world with its spatial dimensions, with its mysteries and darknesses, with its sexual dangers and challenges.*

It has remained my conviction that psychoanalytic interpretations, as long as they are not too far-fetched emanations of a playful mind, are correct. However, they very frequently represent but a shadow of a more comprehensive interpretation. Such an interpretation does not content itself with abstract, intellectual formulations and is, therefore, more difficult to grasp and to express: Maturation is more than just getting rid of the dependency and erotic ties to the parents. Rather, this emancipation during adolescence goes hand in hand with the loss of the God-given, natural creativeness and spontaneity of the healthy child, leading at first to a certain degree of disintegration of the harmonious balance between his thinking, feelings and actions. All this has to be regained on a different plane if the grown-up human being is to realize many of his potentialities.†

*Phenomenologically the penetration into a wider world occurs in several modes: The spatial separation from the parents is followed by a penetration into one's own psychic darkness which lightens up in a dream. It is the discovery within ourselves of a mysterious realm that seems to be a precondition for our finding the right way to the "other," to the object of our love. Now we are willing to risk ourselves in an encounter with the other in which we lose and find ourselves. This is a penetration of the "other" of which sexuality is but a facet and which must always go hand in hand with an awareness of our physical surroundings and of our own potentialities. In existential-analytic terms, then, the maturation of the adolescent implies a simultaneous widening of his *Umwelt* (or awareness of the physical surroundings), of his *Mitwelt* (or capacity for human relatedness) and of his *Eigenwelt* (or self-awareness). Thus a descriptive-revealing approach based on the phenomenologic method provides a wider scope within which the psychoanalytic interpretations achieve their proper relevance.

†This, alas, is a lengthy process which to the suffering, loving and patient

The blossoming capacity to appreciate independently, to assert and to defend our own identity or uniqueness; the growing ability to build our own world with our own dimensions, while strengthening a meaningful relationship with our physical environment and our fellow human beings; the courage to face our existence with all its unknown "whens," "whys" and "wherefores" including even the cryptic problem of nonexistence; all these are aspects of this much more comprehensive, arduous and perilous task of human maturation.

In regard to this task the dragon assumes a wider significance. He now refers to the nourishing source, to the fountain of life of which he has been a universal symbol in the form of the serpent biting its own tail, the uroboros. Its circular form points to the same meaning as the Chinese symbol Wu-Gi, a perfect circle which portrays the unitary source of everything. The self-generating aspect of the uroboric dragon-serpent is reflected in the familiar Chinese symbol Yin and Yang, where darkness and light, below and above, left and right are seen creatively interacting within the circle. In the Bible, the uroboros becomes the serpent slung around the tree with the forbidden fruit, promising Adam and Eve knowledge of good and evil. In the old Sumeric myth it is the monster-goddess Thiamat, slain by Marduk.[52] We can thus state that, in our fairy tale, Louise represents that aspect of the developing human being which, in its search for spiritual food (the cranberries), is overwhelmed by the desire for returning to the impersonal unity, the quietness and darkness of the original source of *All*. Eventually that other aspect of the human being which, through Louis, adventurously sought independence by moving far away from home, finds a new contact with its deepest, wise impulses, faces courageously the power of the dragon and overcomes it.*

---

parents may well seem as long as Briar Rose's hundred years sleep. Yet, any effort to speed up this process, such as occurs, for example, with our numerous teenage marriages, is bound to lead to a great deal of crippling of the soul-forces, to a considerable loss of *human* potentialities.

*The roll which becomes a strong stick has many connotations in this regard. It makes one think both of the roll which leads Theseus to the Minotaurus, and of the spear with which Saint George or Saint Michael slay the dragon.

Only now a new integration with the lost soul-forces becomes possible, and a new phase of human development sets in. The fountain, the building and the walls surrounding them, which had been a horrid threat and a prison, now are owned by the hero and his family. The pale roses on the rose bush resume their lively color and the red man is freed. The dark, frightening gloom inside of the building gives way to a most happy and gay celebration with which the story ends.

With the mention of this joyous feast, I wish to conclude this discussion. Several themes of this fairy tale were deliberately omitted, such as the themes of the father, of the father's trip, of the gifts, as well as the themes of the treacherous fruit, of the rose bush and the Alpine rose, and the hidden theme, death. However, I hope that the discussion has shown that fairy tales and myths can convey magnificent images of what is most genuinely human in us, and of the most significant challenges in our development. Thus we sense what an indispensable nourishment these tales represent especially, but not only for the growing child.

CHAPTER XXIX

DEATH IN THE FAIRY TALE AND EPOS

Genuine fairy tales release us not only from time and place, but from mortality itself.

HERDER

THE TOPIC WHICH existentialism and fairy tales are preoccupied with and share, more than anything else, is the significance of death.

To the agnostic, natural-scientific researcher death is of little import, since it represents only a negation, an absence or an end of life-processes he may be focusing upon. On the other hand, death is all-important in those religious orientations which portray it either as a transition to some form of eternal individual existence, or as the ultimate victory over the illusion or maya of our ego and of our entire earthly life. Thus death could portray an end, a passage toward an eternal, unchanging individual life, or the merging with the undivided unity of *All,* with Nirvana, which alone is recognized as real.

In the following paragraphs I hope to show that neither the fairy tale nor the existential outlook on life view death primarily from these vantage points. The meaning (and even the meaninglessness) of death in the fairy tale and in existentialism consists in the portrayal of crucial steps of development. It is mainly because of this that both the proper existential-philosophic attitudes and the offering at the right age of suitable fairy tales are of paramount importance in the raising of children.

By way of introduction, I wish to draw attention to an apparently contradictory combination of symptoms which every therapist has encountered frequently. This is the enormous fear concerning death of the hypochondriacal patient who, simultaneously, can be quite suicidal. Some of these unfortunate patients cannot endure the feeling that they are being made fools of by everyone, since no one is able or willing to tell them "the truth." They want to kill themselves, as they prefer certainty over continued, extreme doubt. At times, they become keenly aware of the emotional and financial drain they are upon their relatives and friends; and thus they wish to relieve them of this burden by ending their lives. These are superficial and—at best—only partial answers. A more profound, psychoanalytic view may see the intense hypochondriac fear as a last, desperate attempt to confine self-destructive (or thanatos) impulses resulting from deep guilts; however, it is unlikely that even this explains fully the contradictory emotions of the hypochondriacal person.

Let me, therefore, submit an additional hypothesis, based largely on clinical observations. It often seems as if both the hypochondriacal fear and the suicidal impulses are pathologic attempts to evade authenticity, to avoid human growth. Such genuine growth can be characterized by the individual's willingness to abandon patterns of life which he is accustomed to; to abandon them without yet knowing what—if anything—will take their place. In fact, if a certain way of life were exchanged for one which is fully known ahead of time, this would not represent human growth in the above sense. Genuine growth occurs in the experiencing of, understanding, dealing with, suffering from and even despairing over something new, something that had been totally unpredictable. This uncertainty in the prospect of required growth can, at times, reach terrifying proportions. It has then been called "existential crisis." The following is a vivid description of such a crisis.

> I walked along a perilous bridge very high in the starless night. The path was scarcely wide enough for my feet. It had been broader. It became narrower . . . . Behind me the bridge was crumbling away to nothing. And the path became narrower and higher . . . . And then there was no more bridge. I stood on a tiny point in the inky night . . . . If only there had been a star, but the stars were all gone . . . . If a vague firmament had promised only to smash my falling form

> beneath, but the firmament had disintegrated . . . . If another figure could hold my hand as we plunged, but no other clasp met my groping fingers . . . . There was nothing; nothing but my terror, my aloneness, my emptiness . . . . And so I leaped . . . .[19]

What life with cancerophobia, what death even, could be more terrifying than this? Has the hypochondriacal patient gradually, imperceptibly, reached the narrow path, the tiny point, without daring to leap? Is he avoiding the choice of something new, since all true choices harbor a certain amount of contingency? Is he blindly trying to preserve his identity by his quest for absolute certainty which then prevents his human growth?*

We may illustrate this with two other descriptions of "existential crises," one couched in fairy tale, the other in epic style:

In the romance of Sir Lancelot we find an episode which is quite strongly reminiscent of the dramatic existential crisis quoted above: Searching for Queen Guinevere who has been abducted by Prince Maleagant (representing death), Lancelot arrives, after many battles and trials, at the river which he must cross in order to succeed. Here he is confronted by the sword-bridge. It stretches across the swift, raging, black, dangerous, diabolic stream which is so bottomless, "that anything falling into it would be as completely lost as if it fell into the salt sea." At the other end of the sharp sword-bridge he sees two fierce lions. "And the water and the bridge and the lions were so terrible to behold that anyone standing before them all would tremble with fear."[188] Yet the hero, Sir Lancelot, with bare hands and feet, braves the bridge, the waters and the lions. In this undertaking, which appears so utterly hopeless, the hero is quite alone. No one is there to console him, to stretch out a kind, helping hand; no one is present with whom he can share his despair.

The fairy tale portrays this despair in its own characteristic

*Growth means change. It may seem paradoxical that in order to strengthen our identity we must be willing to accept change, and that our identity wanes, if we try to strengthen it by avoiding any change within our make-up. The atmosphere in which the person develops during early childhood has unquestionably a profound effect upon the ways he later experiences change. However, the problem of the interrelationship between etiologic factors and phenomenologic data is beyond the scope of this chapter.

style, as is shown in the following example taken from a Scandinavian tale:

In order to regain the human form for her seven brothers who have been turned into wild swans, the young queen must maintain complete silence for three years. Even when, clandestinely, one by one her three children are murdered and she is accused of their deaths, and when, eventually, she finds herself tied upon a burning pyre, she cannot speak. Just when all hope is lost, the three years are up, the seven brothers return in human form as rescuers, the innocent young queen is freed in the nick of time and her three children are miraculously restored to life.

Death, such as Guinevere's abduction by Prince Maleagant to his castle, or the slaying of the young queen's three children in the Scandinavian fairy tale; *near death,* such as Sir Lancelot's venture or the young queen's extreme peril on the burning pyre; and *symbolic death,* such as the bewitching of the seven brothers into seven wild swans, reveal a very definite, novel meaning. These portrayals of death point to the need of discarding what has become obsolete or inauthentic, and of replacing it by what may be newly authentic. Death becomes the door to the mysterious—often seemingly forbidden—room with the golden atmosphere, with the promise of new adventures.

Since in the fairy tale physical existence becomes transparent, there is no longer a radical distinction between the passage from one developmental level to another, and the passage from physical life to physical death. The developmental crises during infancy, the shift from early childhood to the latency period, from the latency period to adolescence, the change from adolescence to adulthood, the acceptance of parenthood, the transition from the first to the second half of life and so on, including the step from old age to death: all these passages become somewhat analogous. The fairy tale, even more limpidly than the epos and myth, portrays these passages with similar images.

Both in the epos and in the fairy tale the image is often that of the protagonist's descent to Hades or hell. In the epos or in the saga the hero, though able to return to the surface of the earth, does not often achieve untroubled bliss: Gilgamesh forfeits in the last moment the chance of eternal life, after having penetrated courageously to the world beyond; Ulysses meets many profound tragedies after his return; Orpheus fails to bring back his beloved Eurydice; Theseus comes to a tragic end; and even Dante, after his voyage through hell, purgatory and paradise, views with considerable apprehension his remaining life on earth. What counts is that for all these heroes the descent into the underworld is not the anticipated one-way trip which is announced on the gates of hell ("You who enter here, abandon all hope"). Rather it becomes an unavoidable threshold toward further growth.

This is equally true of the fairy table hero who descends into hell, yet his return leads always to complete, unmarred happiness. We can see this in Apuleius' *Amor and Psyche* tale, written in the second century after Christ, where Psyche's last trial consists in a descent to Hades. She brings back an ointment which later causes her to fall into a death-like sleep. She is awakened from this near-death by Amor who then transports her to Mount Olympus. Here they dwell perpetually in complete bliss, after Jupiter has succeeded in calming the jealous rage of Amor's mother, Venus.

In the saga, or epos, the paradoxes of existence often persist painfully and frightfully; in the fairly tale they are resolved. The young hero in Grimms' *The Devil with the Three Golden Hairs* is at peace with the devil's grandmother; and though the devil himself smells human flesh and threatens with total destruction, he nonetheless yields the three golden hairs. These golden hairs enable the youth to solve the three paradoxes by which he had been puzzled beforehand, and to acquire the princess as well as the kingdom.

The experience of confrontation with, or of going through, death is slightly more veiled in those numerous stories in which the hero travels to the fountain yielding the water of life. Here he may have to overcome the Green Knight, whose color alone already stamps him as a representative of death, in order to marry the princess of the fountain, or to fetch some of the miraculous nectar.[188] The Grimms' tale of *Mrs. Holle* combines excellently the trip to the underworld motif with the voyage to the fountain motif when it portrays how the unselfish girl is driven by the evil stepmother and stepsister to fall down into the deep well. She emerges in the world of *Mrs. Holle* whence—because of her receptive attitude toward spiritual values—she returns greatly enriched. A similar amalgamation of the image of the fountain and the underworld is found in the aforementioned charming fairy-tale-like Pueblo Indian story of *The Water-Jar-Boy* who seeks his deceased father and eventually finds access to him through a spring.

The supernatural reality of the water of everlasting life is beautifully portrayed in the Hawaiian tale *Au-ke-le, the Seeker.* Here the hero must face, during his long voyage, the most fantastic perils before he can find this miraculous nectar in a mysterious, enormously distant, cosmic region. He overcomes his adversaries by knowing their *name.* "What can we do," they say, "with this man who knows even our names!"[29]

This story, like most folk narrations from the non-Western world, has both fairy tale and epic characteristics: It contains the free dialogue with the spiritual world, as well as the tragic note of the soul's captivity in the physical world.

The fairy tale, as well as the myth, experiences the origin of life and death as one. Where the water of life is, there is also the water of death, the death-bringing dragon or the knight of death who must be overcome. Analogous is the tree of life beside the fountain, contrasting with the tree of knowledge and the deadly serpent.

One of the most impressive epic portrayals of the fountain, tied in with the picture of the need of the confrontation of death, stems (like the above story of Sir Lancelot) from the cycle of King Arthur.[188] It is the tale of Owain, *The Knight with the Lion* who overcomes the Black Knight guarding the Fountain of Life. He takes on the latter's role of guardian and thus becomes the new mate of the Lady of the Fountain.*

*This heroic epos illustrates the gradual development of the hero who dies and returns repeatedly. In fact, some time after his marriage to the Lady of the Fountain, Owain becomes homesick for his companions at the round table, and is allowed to take a year's leave; but then he forgets his lady, and as punishment he must wander, alone and helpless, across the wide world. Gradually he degenerates to an animal-like existence, and he is in a death-like condition

In many tales the allusions to the kingdom of death are much less obvious. The fountain of life may be replaced by the tree of life, the guardian is often depicted as a dragon, and the realm of the dead may be a castle in which the human beings, abducted from the earth, are imprisoned. Here they exist as shadowy creatures or are bewitched into animal forms. A beautiful example is the Grimms' tale of *Jorinde and Joringel* where the girl is captured in the form of a bird in a cage inside of a bewitched castle, in the middle of the forest, until the lover-hero, risking his own existence, comes to free her. In the fairy tale the heroes invariably achieve complete success, though often only in the last moment (as in the above-mentioned tale of *The Wild Swans*). In fact, the stress upon the very last moment is a way of emphasizing that, "only he who risks everything without any guarantee of a favorable outcome can truly progress."

Yet this statement creates a paradoxical situation. It spurs us on to risking more and more, by promising a most blissful denouement; on the other hand it tells us that this blissful resolution cannot take place if we count on it at all. Probably it is by protraying the hero in an utterly desperate plight, when no help whatsoever appears possible, that the fairy tale conveys the idea that no amount of intellectual understanding can help us avoid the complete despair necessary before any genuine growth can occur; that no rational foresight can cushion the leap into apparent nothingness which characterizes the existential crisis or the Kierkegaardian leap into faith. In fact, intellectual understanding only accentuates the above-mentioned paradox. However, this should by no means make us shy away from the intellectual achievements of our age; rather we may sense that their acceptance and integration in our life will deepen and strengthen the paradox which then can become an even richer source of new forces which we do not and cannot as yet recognize at this time.

---

when rescue arrives in the very last moment. Braving seemingly insurmountable dangers, he then finally finds his way back to the fountain. Now he has grown spiritually to the point where he is able to take his lady along with him to the round table of King Arthur. Thus the rigid barrier between life and death has been overcome.

If we are right in assuming that the vantage point of the fairy tale is so lofty that physical death becomes here of lesser importance than failure in human growth,* then we must ask ourselves: "What does the complete, permanent physical death and destruction in the fairy tale mean? What is the meaning of the lasting mutilation of some of the personages we encounter. Why does it affect the old king, the stepmother, the stepsisters, the witch, the sorcerer, the malevolent dwarf, or the giant?" But have we not already formulated the answer in the way we arrived at the question? Does the fairy tale not tell us that the only complete death is the failure of risking death, despair, poverty and loneliness for the sake of a true ideal, for the sake of further development? Implicitly or explicitly this complete death or permanent mutilation—in the fairy tale—is usually portrayed as self-inflicted, self-chosen. In the story of *The Goose Girl,* the false bride freely determines her own punishment: to be put naked into a barrel with sharp nails pointing inward, and to be rolled and rolled until she is dead. Or, in Grimms' *Cinderella,* the stepsisters expose themselves, without offering any resistance, to the beaks of the white birds which pick out their eyes. Yet, to be exact, the stepsisters are not blinded by the doves; they were blind already, since they had become "inauthentic," dishonest, insensitive, in their quest for a better life. And, similarly, the false princess in the story of *The Goose Girl,* the stepmother of Snow White, or the witch in *Hansel and Gretel* destroy only that which had become arrested in its development, that which was already dead. Thus these mutilations and physical annihilations in the fairy tale are, in the last analysis, but an external confirmation of what has happened spiritually before. Even here death does not exist, since that which does not meet (sooner or later)the challenge of change, is not alive in the first place; since that which has renounced the full flow of life with its

*Yet we encounter opinions such as those of Adah Maurer[117] who, on the basis of excellent clinical observations, concludes that religion, values and "altruistic choices" are sublimations of death anxieties. Her clinical material fully supports a diametrically opposite interpretation; that the preoccupation with death in adolescence is the expression of a particularly strong challenge toward growth. Those who for one reason or another do not respond to this challenge will thus be more likely to feel hounded by continuing fears.

choices, torments, sins and joys, cannot be considered alive, and thus its death is but an illusion.

Growth is characterized by a series of crises, each one carrying some of the connotations of death. The fairy tale views these crises in the very young individual and allows no doubt regarding the eventual success. Contrariwise, the saga tends more to view these crises in the grown hero, and the outcome of these crises is not uniformly blissful. In the folk-saga, physical death is tragic; in the epos, heroic; in the legend, a symbol of spiritual victory. But in the fairy tale, whose vantage point offers a much wider and penetrating view, complete physical death is usually senseless self-destruction of what is no longer alive in the true, human sense. The stepmother who portrays that aspect of matter (*materia*) which blinds us to spiritual values and growth shows, finally, her true nature when she turns to matter herself. Otherwise, any simile of death in the fairy tale is but a signal of a crisis which offers the opportunity for a further step in the human development.

CHAPTER XXX

EXISTENTIAL CRISIS AND CHANGING WORLD-DESIGNS IN MYTHS AND FAIRY TALES

What the law of cause and effect is in the material world, that the paradox is in the spiritual.

THERE IS BUT one view of physical death which is able not only to ignore it as a problem, but also to deny its great importance in determining the meaningfulness of life. Occasionally it appears in fleeting fantasies of healthy individuals, in playful philosophical speculations and in profound preoccupations of severely troubled persons. This view is derived from the hypothesis that physical death—at least as it refers to "the death of myself"—does not exist except in the form of a fearsome anticipation, since every moment of our life is but a fragment of a dream which creates for itself an imaginary past and future. Even if you walked to your certain death at a determined time and place, even if—as the condemned hero—you saw the fire from the guns of your executioners, even then all this would be but an instant of life followed immediately by another (related or unrelated) instant with its own past and future. All existence would thus have reality only in the present moment, and all speculation concerning the past and future would be meaningless. It could be shown that our dream life largely resembles this far-fetched hypothesis; in the dream we exist markedly in the present, changing arbitrarily and incongruously the preceding events to fit the current ones, molding the future events without regard to logic, and never allowing ourselves to die.* We shall notice later that in folklore the devilish or demoniacal beings frequently approximate this form of deathless existence, and that their destructive, inhibitory, gloomy, dreadful and other connotations are a direct result of it.

All other views or attitudes must find in death a most crucial determinant of life's meaning or meaninglessness (which still is an assigned meaning). This remains true even if one should not agree fully with those who have stressed that the basic significance of death, as far as the conduct of our lives is concerned, is not altered appreciably by the particular religious, metaphysical, agnostic or atheistic convictions of an individual.[98] These thoughts have been formulated excellently by such diverse authors as Kierkegaard,[96] Heidegger,[63] Nietzsche[133] and several younger philosophers and therapists.[20,26,45,155] They all agree in pointing to the paradox that the human being tends to lose what is most specific for him, that he becomes inauthentic, because of the dread of death. This inauthenticity, then, can find expression in "silent despair" when the person—as a complete conformist or as a fraud—runs through a meaningless life, or in "overt despair" where symptoms of depression and anixety hide the real dread. Yet, if the human being becomes capable of facing courageously the absolute certainty of his death, he grows more authentic and begins to imbue his life with new meaning. In fact there is a close correlation between this courage to face the unavoidability as well as the implications of one's death on one hand, and, on the other hand, the ability to look in an unbiased way at all the surrounding world, at ourselves and at our fellow human beings. This unprejudiced, phenomenological, constantly fresh approach reveals new meanings, opens new doors to un-

*Even in the worst nightmare the dreamer never dies either "factually" or in the sense of "losing consciousness." One might think that a logical termination of a nightmare, in which the dreamer is either shot, falls down a precipice or is otherwise confronted by certain death would be the transition into deeply unconscious sleep. This, however, never seems to occur. Instead, the subject either awakens, or he experiences in his dream a "life after death," or—more or less aware of "cheating"—he may refuse to die when, for all intensive purposes and even within the logical framework of the dream, he should have died.

suspected dimensions, thus allowing a widening of one's world-design.[71]

Of the three brothers who go out into the world in order to accomplish three impossible feats, the older two—usually—are both somewhat cowardly in the face of death, and unable to confront their surroundings with an open eye and heart. Thus, when the unsightly dwarf, the hungry fox or the greedy monsters along the path ask to share their bread, the older brothers can only follow their accustomed, conventional, practical reasoning, and therefore refuse.[58]

The unwillingness to feed the animal, semi-human or other guardians at the threshold to a new world parallels the avoidance and repression of one's own hidden potentialities, lofty, ugly, frightening or impulsive as they may be. This leads to the progressive narrowing of one's world.* Whereas in our psychologic idiom we may speak of the problem of confronting (ours and the others') unconscious, the myth and fairy tale speak of confronting the underworld. Thus the willingness to see the world around us without bias, the willingness to look into our own darkness, the willingness to descend into the underworld, and the willingness to face death coincide to a large extent.

The hero knows that identity wanes in the absence of change or growth, that the monster would eventually sap all the creative

*Hart[60] has pointed to this meaning in his interpretation of Grimms' story of *The Water of Life,* where two older brothers—having spurned the dwarf's request—end up captives in a narrow canyon. In another Grimms' tale, the spoiled, selfish daughter of the stepmother starts out, well protected by warm clothes and richly supplied with food, to find the dwarfs' mysterious hut in the middle of the woods, but fails in the end. The unspoiled, genuine girl, however, faces cold, hunger and night with hardly any protection; willingly she shares with the dwarfs her few possessions, and she responds to their wishes with spontaneity and cooperation. Thus "the impossible" (hidden, unconscious, yet beautiful and nourishing) becomes manifest to her: the red strawberries buried underneath the winter's snow.[58] And in his *Fairy Tale* (of the *Green Serpent and the Beautiful Lily*) Goethe[67] portrayed how abstract thinking leads to the shrinking of the human being. In this story the guardian between the two worlds is the River who must be appeased by the fruits of the earth before he allows some communication between his two shores: he would wildly rebel and become impassable if he were fed only the glittering gold-pieces, namely the abstract or superficial thoughts of the will-o'-the-wisps who shrink as they scatter them.

vitality from the city which continues to appease it daily with ten maidens,[158] that he must confront the dragon even if all the odds seem to be against him, that he must proceed even if—utterly alone—he seeks the Minotaur in the depth of the dark labyrinth (made by Daedalus, representing the human intellect). The hero thus faces an existential crisis; and though loneliness, isolation, emptiness, guilt as well as impending pain and destruction are aspects of it, death is its background. Yet, in the fairy tale, death as viewed tragically in one's everyday world is of little weight; the tasks which the hero or heroine perform never kill them permanently, and their eventual physical death is considered of very little importance: "And if they have not yet died, they are still alive."

This belittling of physical death, however, is not the type of denial of death mentioned earlier, or sought by the inauthentic person. Rather, it is the attitude toward physical death of the individual who has faced death fully and deeply. While in many sacred myths we find a similar attitude, death is seen as dreadful, as failure and doom in numerous heroic epos or sagas; to mention but the tragic death of Gilgamesh,[52] of Phaeton, of Orpheus and Icarus, or the heroic death of Achilles,[57,59,158] of Siegfried and his Nibelungs,[179] of Roland, of Winkelried or of Jeanne d'Arc.

One of the most impressive examples showing how authenticity, how being true of one's self, is linked to facing death is the story of *Sir Gawain and the Green Knight*.[188] Gawain, on an agreed-upon day, compelled by his dedication to the perfection of chivalry, must face the Green Knight, representing death, at a certain place in the dark woods. Here he will let the mysterious challenger cut off his head. On the way to this dreadful rendezvous Gawain spends three nights in a magnificent castle where the most charming hostess thrice attempts to seduce him. His valiant resistance is tarnished by only one minor flaw; and because of this flaw the Green Knight (who turns out to be the temptress' husband) nicks Gawain's neck slightly when he swings the ax upon the fearless hero. All the previous men who met with the Green Knight had not been able to maintain their integrity in the face of death, and had therefore lost their heads.

The ability to face death, of being true to one's self, of seeing things with an open eye and heart, leads into a new world. This world with changed dimensions may be most dreadful, since we meet it alone, and since former concepts and yardsticks prove utterly inadequate in coping with it.

As Campbell,[24] Zimmer,[188] Meyer,[124] Hart[60] and others have excellently shown, the essence of the dramatic plot of the epos as well as of the fairy tale consists often in the fact that the old world reaching into the current existence has grown sterile, boring and stale, and thus begins to disintegrate from within. The fairy tale may portray this in the figure of the old king who is growing weak and whose three sons go out into the wide world to find the remedy for his ailment. In the epos we similarly see Amphortas' wound smart as he is waiting for Percival to mature and to assume the leadership. This need for renewal is not always spelled out quite as clearly. What is an ubiquitous element in fairy tales and epos, however, is the challenge by a dreadful, overwhelming danger, or the suffering from an unbearable fate, neither leaving much hope for the promised bliss. The dreadful danger may be portrayed by a monster which the hero must slay, or by three seemingly unsolvable riddles. Failure in the face of these challenges, then, would lead to a catastrophe, usually portrayed as death, not only for the hero, but often also for his people. The suffering from a miserable, hopeless fate finds expression in the infinitely variable theme of being reduced to a servile state; and in this state the protagonist, be it Cinderella, Heracles or Psyche, is usually challenged to perform what seem impossible tasks. Here it is the courage to endure one's fate patiently and to try even in the face of hopelessness, which leads to a happy denouement.

In the heroic and self-sacrificing deeds of sagas, myths and fairy tales one encounters a breakdown of the existing world-design. The protagonist in these narrations is able to partake of a wider world where the habitual concepts of time, of space, of materiality, of causality, of subjectivity and objectivity, as well as of self-identity are no longer fully applicable. It can be argued that any genuine human growth goes hand in hand with a changing world-design,[74] and that, therefore, most worthwhile literary products must reflect this. However, the epos, and—even more—the fairy tale portray these changing dimensions of human existence in a very concrete way. They emphasize the need for the perfect movement for the maintenance and unfolding of human identity which disintegrates in its absence, and which is threatened by its imperfection. Movement, here, is meant as "change toward something new," as adventure, not unlike Kierkegaard's use of the term when he speaks of the movements of faith and resignation. A series of five brief examples may give perspective to this concept.

1. *Inhibition of Movement Leading to Loss of Identity.* In the epic poem *The Minstrel's Curse,*[177] we see the aged harpist and his youthful singer wander to the court of the cold, cruel king, hoping to move his heart with their music. And as they put their deepest feelings and finest skill into their performance, the queen melts and throws to the charming youth a rose of appreciation. The king, however, becomes irate at the show of emotion by his soul's companion and flings his sword at the youth who almost succeeds at influencing his rigid and merciless reign. And then we hear the aged minstrel, alone with the boy's corpse, outside the beautiful castle, throw his annihilating curse, predicting the drying up of the beautiful fountains, the disintegration of the majestic colonnades and utter oblivion. And the poem concludes:

Des Königs Name meldet kein Lied, kein Heldenbuch; Versunken und vergessen,— das ist des Sängers Fluch.	No song nor book of heroes the king's name does disperse; All's lost in deep oblivion,— this is the minstrel's curse.

L. UHLAND[177]

2. *Failure of Movement Leading to Annihilation.* The grandiose movement of the temerarious Phaeton who perishes in his unskillful attempt to guide the sun wagon across the sky.

3. *Success and Failure of Movement.* The fate of Oedipus who solves the riddle of the Sphinx but who is almost totally crushed as a result of his courageous wish to know the truth about himself and Jocasta.

4. *Temporary Failure of Movement.* Suffused by the hope of eventual success exemplified in Wainemoinen, the great Finnish *laulaia* (singer) who fails in his quest for the beautiful virgin

of the Northland sitting on the rainbow. Embittered and discouraged, he retreats to the furthest horizon, there to wait for the opportune time when his people will be ready to receive him and his songs again.

5. *Movement and Success.* Found in some myths and in most of the typical Occidental fairy tales. Among the many thousand narrations, the tale of *I Know Not What of I Know Not Where* (see Chapters XXIV and XXXIV) illustrates this most graphically, when the young hero jumps upon the back of a giant frog across the river of fire into the land of "I know not where" to fetch "I know not what." His unswerving willingness to confront absolute uncertainty makes his movement perfect; he eventually overcomes all his enemies and regains his golden-haired wife.

Whereas this concept of movement involves all the abovementioned dimensions which establish a given world-design (time, space, materiality, causality, objectivity vs. subjectivity, self-identity and others), we find that different fairy tales and myths lend themselves particularly well to the illustration of one or another of these dimensions.* Note that these narrations emphasize the basic developments having occurred, occurring or about to occur in their respective cultures. Whereas the saga is inclined to focus upon the tragic, negative aspects of these developments, we find that the popular Occidental fairy tales view these same events so as to emphasize primarily their necessity and usefulness in a great and glorious plan.† All this is easier

*That any movement requires space and time is obvious. However, it also requires a moving thing the materiality of which can be experienced in different ways. In addition, each movement brings forth the question of causality, the answer to which becomes another determinant of the world-design. That in every movement the problem of subjectivity vs. objectivity (i. e. to what degree is it objective, to what extent is it merely a subjective experience?) is implicit, and that answers to this problem equally shape the individual's world-design, may be less obvious. This is so because usually we blindly assume to know whether "I" or "the other" is moving (Galileo Galilei almost lost his head because of this!). Finally we take self-identity for granted, even though in our dreams, for example, we often experience ourselves as simultaneously observing and observed identities.

†Alberich in the German saga,[179] the *Old One from Pohjola* in the *Kalevala*[91] and the clever devils in many a folktale reflect the negative aspect of the sharp intellect which leads the human being away from paradise toward unhappiness, death and hell. Ulysses represents also this cleverness which overcomes the less

for us to observe by focusing upon the folk narrations which have been nurtured and transmitted by our Western culture. The movement which occurs in them departs from a world-view, a world-design, that is familiar to us, whereas the oldest and remotest myths and the most primitive folktales describe movements in cultures whose basic world-designs are utterly foreign to us. The fact that in these narrations the laws of time, causality, self-identity, etc., are most different from ours to start with, becomes an obstacle to their full comprehension. Contrariwise, our own fairy tales and the myths we inherited from our closer ancestors evolve on a background which is similar to the world we are accustomed to:

1. "A queen and a king are unhappy that they have no children. One day the queen bathes in a pond." All this is fairly commonplace, but then we see the introduction of a new dimension—the eruption of a new world—when the frog approaches the saddened woman, announcing that she will have a child.[58]

Compare this, for example, with the beginning of an American Indian tale,[101] which offends immediately our sense of logic:

2. "Long before the first human beings lived on earth, there lived an old woman and her grandchild on the shore of a large lake."

Thus, restricting ourselves largely to myths and fairy tales of our Western culture, we shall try to examine some of the fundamental dimensions of world-designs, as they undergo changes in these narrations:*

---

abstract thinking portrayed best in the Trojans and in Polyphemos. His fate is better. In the typical fairy tale, however, this abstract thinking—most often expressed by the clever little tailor or by the thumbling—uniformly leads to a blissful end, even though it had to go through some of the lowest aspects of human existence.[124]

*The movements that are portrayed may be occurring between a preceding and the current culture. This is exemplified by the previously mentioned narrations describing the successful and fateful ascendency of abstract thinking: the story of *The Trojan Horse,* of *Ulysses and Cyclops,* of *Puss 'n Boots,* of *The Clever Little Tailor,* of *Thumbling,* to mention but a few. Or, the narrations may describe a movement away from the present situation which is found ailing because of its reluctance to change.

A. *Measurable time* is but a limited, though—especially in our technologic era—practically very useful, aspect of the whole phenomenon of time. Only rarely does it correspond to experienced time where a second may seem to last hours and an hour may fly by like a second. Nor does it often allow to determine the proper time (or appropriate time) which may occur in a minute, or in a year, or never, depending on a complex constellation of attitudes and events. When mentioned in myths and fairy tales, reference is usually made to experienced and proper time. If, for instance, the beautiful young queen must refrain from talking or laughing for three years; and if this time is up at the very moment when she stands on the pyre and when the flames begin to approach her; then we can sense that the three years refer to the experience of a very long, painful and frustrating period, and that the end of the three years represents the proper time. (There is a large group of narrations with many variations of this theme.) It is the proper time not because of the passage of a measurable period of time, but because this is the moment when the young queen has completed a necessary inner development and is able to confront certain death in order to remain true to herself. Some old myths transcend completely the dimensions of the measurable time in human life, and attempt to communicate the experience of wider aspects of the phenomenon of time by grandiose and fantastic images. Thus Brahma sits in absolutely motionless, meditative contemplation of one single point for a period of 36,000 years in order to find contact with maya.

A different portrayal of the relativity of our everyday time concepts is found in the group of numerous narrations in which the protagonists (Rip Van Winkle,[110] Urashima[171]) or heroes (Evo, Erpho,[112] the twelve apostles,[58] Oisin[24] and others) submerge in a different world where the experience of the passage of time is quite different from that in the physical world. However, once the human being returns to and touches the physical world, he responds as if he had been governed by its laws all the time; thus he suddenly finds himself aged, or he may turn into a skeleton several hundred years old.

Oisin has met and married the beautiful, mysterious princess with whom he lives in the Land of Youth. But he becomes homesick for his own people in Erin, and eventually his supernatural bride gives him a white steed on which to visit Erin, warning him never to touch the soil of his land. Yet in a moment of forgetfulness his foot touches the earth, the steed disappears and Oisin lies on the ground a blind old man.

B. *Measurable space* is only one aspect of the total phenomenon of space. For thousands of years it was measured anthropomorphically by multiples or fractions of the length of the foot, in other cultures by multiples or fractions of the length of the thumb, forearm, pace, etc. Only relatively recently did abstract measurements become prevalent: metric system, light years, etc. Yet, our heart can feel close to people miles away, and our mind experiences no difficulty whatsoever embracing much of the infinite universe.

In *Puss 'n Boots*,[58] the youngest of three sons inherits only the seemingly worthless tomcat, while his brothers get all the earthly riches. He is ridiculed by them; and yet he accedes to the cat's wishes and buys him, with his last pennies, a pair of boots. Surprisingly, these boots allow the cat to travel miles in seconds, and the young hero is driven by the animal's speed and cleverness toward an entirely novel existence. Having shed even his last former possession, his clothes, he meets the king. And with the cat's help he gains the hand of the king's daughter as well as a kingdom. Transcending the common spatial attitudes, relinquishing traditional material security, he finds a new, wider and meaningful world.

A similar transcendence of space is found in several Scandinavian fairy tales when the hero is carried by the winds to the castle *East of the Sun and West of the Moon*.[85] Again, abandoning the earth and conventional human space, the hero—at extreme risk—gains a newly meaningful existence. The story of *Six Can Cope with the Whole World* also leads to a successful denouement, mostly because of the transcendence of conventional spatial concepts. Here the embittered soldier, who was unfairly discharged, associates himself with five companions. Each one has a miraculous talent which transcends the physical laws. But it is the one who runs faster than the wind when he attaches his second leg, who wins, against all odds, the crucial race with the princess.

Whereas these and analogous fairy tales always have a happy ending, the epos dealing with the transcendence of space quite often ends tragically. Both Icaros and Phaeton who are attempting to escape a depressing and confining existence by flying through space, fail as they too quickly aspired to the highest regions and thus were drawn back prematurely to the earth.*

Time and space are so intimately related that their above, separate discussion is somewhat artificial. One of the simplest and yet most beautiful examples of this interrelationship of the transcendence of space and time is the previously mentioned Egyptian tale concerning Solomon who, challenged by the Queen of Sheba, is able to produce from a far away region and in the short time between inhaling and exhaling, the mighty column on which all the knowledge of the world is engraved.† This story also alludes to the transcendence of materiality by portraying the absolute ease with which the heavy column is transported.

C. *Materiality.* The most fantastic and grotesque deviations from our own everyday conceptions of matter are prevalent in

---

**Au-ke-le, the Seeker* is a Polynesian tale in which the hero also transcends space, traveling to the very limits of existence to the water of life in the land of the everlasting sun. But—as in many other primitive tales (see above)—the basic setting of the tale is in spatial dimensions which are foreign to us, "in the land which is now lost, Ku-ai-he-lani, the country which supports heaven." The tale, then, even though the hero transcends successfully the most fantastic distances, ends on a discordant note, as it is reminiscent of a lost world where heaven and earth were experienced as one.[29]

†This is a magnificent portrayal of the power of human thinking which is not limited by measurable time and space. The human soul, certainly, has its own dimensions, as Emerson pointed out long before existentialism became fashionable: "The soul circumscribes all things. As I have said, it contradicts all experience. In like manner it abolishes time and space. The influence of the senses has in most men overpowered the mind to that degree that the walls of time and space have come to look real and insurmountable; and to speak with levity of these limits is, in the world, the sign of insanity. Yet time and space are but inverse measures of the force of the soul. The spirit sports with time—can crowd eternity into an hour, or stretch an hour to eternity."[42]

May I add that one of the aims of existential psychotherapy is the awakening of this Emersonian soul, the furthering of authenticity. Unawakened, the soul remains captive in an overly rigid world-design forced upon it by a self-deluding collectivistic culture, or established in reaction to certain family—or group—interactions. Such a rigid world-design may then conflict with changing conditions in the environment or with hidden potentials of the soul itself.

primitive folk narrations and in ancient myths. Weight, mass and density may be treated with a disconcerting nonchalance. A black bear steals sun, moon and the stars in a satchel;[101] a young Indian boy destroys his enemy and causes a great flood by means of a cuttle-fish which inflates to enormous proportions; he saves himself and his mother by holding onto a bird whose beak eventually hits against the sky, remaining stuck therein for ten days; when the flood has receded, the boy and his mother let themselves drop down on the earth.[101] In a Polynesian tale,[109] the inhabitants of an island descend to a world where they can walk through the walls of houses and through tree trunks, a world not unlike the world of the shadows in Grecian mythology. When a bracelet has sunk to the bottom of the lake, one half of the water can be folded over the other half, thus exposing the bottom and the lost object.[15] The mass of a being can change spontaneously, and the smallest part of a being can reconstitute the whole. This is excellently portrayed in the ancient Egyptian tale of *The Two Brothers*, (discussed in Chapter II.) where Bata turns into a large bull; then, the bull is killed, two drops of his blood turn into two large Persea trees, and when these are chopped down, a splinter of their wood flies into the mouth of the treacherous woman who thus becomes pregnant and eventually gives birth to—Bata![15]

In the typical fairy tale the everyday concepts of materiality are also transcended, though usually in a more discreet way, which indicates that beyond the conventional there are wider meanings.[109] Bread and wine which never exhaust themselves, magic wands which allow to go through closed doors, coats which make a person transparent, sorcerers who can shrink to the size of a mouse or grow to the size of an elephant and other examples are found in the Grimms' and in other fairy tales. The hero can squeeze water out of a stone or he can carry away in a sack all the enormous treasures of the king.[58]

D. The extreme distortions of accepted logical sequences of *cause and effect* are again found in primitive tales. Coyote, charged with ordering the earth, destroys the cruel Ice-people by carrying the sunshine under his coat until he gets close enough to destroy them with it.[101] A young African boy flies to the moon on a chair simply by wishing to do so.[46] A swallow takes revenge on the sea by carrying it drop by drop into the desert and filling it grain by grain with the desert's sand.[15] While our own culture is too far removed from the origins of these tales, we find in the Western fairy tales discreet deviations from everyday logic in which we more easily surmise a hidden wisdom. The old, jealous king, for example, to be rejuvenated, has himself decapitated after ordering that the water of life (of everlasting youth) be then poured upon him; and he remains dead. His young rival, however, achieves the goal. He, too, is decapitated, and his beloved pours upon him first the water of death which makes him whole, then the water of life. Only he—the tale seems to say—who transcends everyday logic, only he who faces the paradoxical aspects of death, can attain a new kingdom. (See Chapter XVIII.) Another delicate use of illogicity in the service of transcending ordinary reasoning was seen in Grimms' *Cinderella* where the white birds achieve the task of separating the lentils from the ashes much quicker, when the task becomes twice as large; as if to indicate that the spiritual assistance can never be decimated by the increasing magnitude of the problem—cannot be measured by the physical measures of time and quantity.

E. We are living in a common, contemporary world, and we have been taught carefully the rules concerning what is to be considered *subjective* and what *objective*. All in all, we have accepted these rules without questioning them. In fact, there is so much security to be derived from the blind acceptance of these rules, that it is generally considered dangerous to doubt them. Those among us who—for unclear reasons—are unable to abide by these rules are termed neurotic or psychotic; while those who deliberately question these rules pertaining to subjectivity vs. objectivity are frequently pegged as unrealistic philosophers who are attempting to upset the applecart.

We need not always take recourse to subtle phenomenologic procedures or philosophical speculations to be aware of the vagueness of the boundaries between our subjective and objective world. Where is the charm of yonder pretty girl, and where the beauty of this tune? Is it in the object before me or in my soul? And if my sister has died, and I miss her, is she not missing in my soul more than in the hustle and bustle of the everyday world which barely noticed her disappearance? What we see in our surroundings is profoundly influenced by our own make-up and past experience, and the thoughts which we so often pride ourselves of as *our* productions are far from purely subjective.

The myth and the fairy tale transcend quite freely the accepted limits between objectivity and subjectivity. The most impressive way by which this occurs is the interesting correlation between the hero's development, his dream and his outward experience. The youth in a Swiss tale (see Chapter XXVIII), having dreamed in all details what he must do, enters the dark forest in which his sister was lost two years before. The outward path of the hero closely parallels his descent into the hidden, dark depths of his own soul; and his finding the young maiden becomes one with his discovering the eternally creative aspects of his being, located in the castle near the fountains with the waters of life and of death, but guarded by the frightening, evil and ugly dragon.[70]

Very similarly in the Grimms' tale of *The Wild Swans*[58] the young maiden first dreams of her journey into the forest where she finds her twelve brothers who, in the daytime, are bewitched into swans: a beautiful portrayal of the totality of the soul-forces which, unfortunately—in the light of our present daytime consciousness—appear only in their subhuman, animal form. And in a Scandinavian story it is a plain soldier who is led by his dream to the deep cave wherein the king's three daughters are imprisoned. In such tales we find that the habitual view of the objective world is suddenly widened, enriched by a revelation arising in the individual's subjectivity. And as the individual innovates the external world he also takes another step in his own development.

F. Probably the most extreme distortions of the habitual world-design are found in regard to the idea of *self-identity*. Though in many dreams self-identity is put into question by the fact that the dreamer may be, simultaneously, onlooker and several participants, our culture generally sees the conscious person's doubts regarding his identity as a sign of insanity. This appears to have been different during the early Indian culture which was imbued by a profound belief in the ultimate identity of everyone and everything. In one of the famous Indian tales, a most dangerous fight between Shiva and Brahma is stopped by Vishnu who is able to demonstrate the meaninglessness of the argument, since all three of them are in reality identical, namely one and the same. In primitive tales and early cultures the identity of an individual was rarely defined sharply, but often included the individual's totem-animal, his ancestors, his descendants, etc. With the development of human consciousness, however, such deviations from self-identity became rare and alluded—then—to exceptional dimensions of existence transcending the everyday world-views.

In one ancient Egyptian story we are told that the son and wife of the famous scribe Ni-noferka-Ptah exist simultaneously in two locations. In the Egyptian tale of *The Two Brothers,* part of Batu's identity, his heart, is hidden in the umbrella-pine, not unlike the heart of the giant in several fairy tales. Here it is usually concealed most carefully in a faraway region, and only he who can find this heart, can kill its owner. The giant-monster's, Bas Celik's strength, for example, is concealed in a bird which exists in the heart of a fox on a high mountain within a large forest.[32] Or, in a Scandinavian tale[85] the giant's heart is hidden in the egg within a duck in a well, underneath a church on an island in the middle of a lake surrounded by a large forest.* Whereas in the narrations of the primitive ethnic groups the vagueness of identity is part of their everyday world-view, we find here—again—that the fairy tale hero's transcendence of the narrow, accepted identity concept leads him to a victory which yields new powers with which to renew the old kingdom.

With these few and fragmentary examples of the transcendence of various basic dimensions of the accepted world-view or

*It would be easy to elaborate this symbolism (egg, well, church, lake in the forest) to the effect of seeing in it a parallel to the ancient Indian reduction of all identity to the one and only, all-containing Identity. The "strength", the "heart" is here the ultimate, creative reality of the individual. Philosophers might describe it as the *transcendental ego* or the *higher self* that constitutes and structures the manifest, empirical person. This structuring, "enheartening" self is usually experienced as related to the center of *All* which can be portrayed as island, forest, well, egg, or church. It is only when this self is mastered that the empirical person which is supported or enlivened by it loses its power.

world-design, we may now proceed to some conclusions. We pointed out that this transcendence in myths and fairy tales could be seen as a movement which entailed an unavoidable risk, and we indicated that the paradigm of this risk was death.

In a most scholarly recent dispute between Koestenbaum[98] and Bugental,[20] the latter questioned the inference that all existential anxiety was linked to the certainty of one's own death. Rather, he felt that besides (a) fate and death other sources of existential anxiety had to be recognized, such as (b) guilt and condemnation; (c) emptiness—meaninglessness; (d) loneliness and isolation; and (e) pain and destruction. It appears that the philosopher and the psychotherapist viewed death in slightly different ways: Death and physical death, as anticipatory experiences, are not necessarily quite the same. Physical death can be anticipated, e. g., as a release from pain and unhappiness, as a transition toward eternal bliss, or—neurotically—as prolonged suffocation and dreadful, conscious disintegration within the buried coffin.

In a wider sense death is viewed as an end, as closure of whatever may have been meaningful in our earthly existence. Thus the awareness of the unavoidability of our death forces us to face both the farce of our inauthentic attitudes, and the fact that there are potentialities within us which we failed to express. Fate and death, then, pierce unmercifully through our disguises and reveal us to ourselves. We may, like Dorian Gray, avoid the true image of ourselves, refusing to accept our inevitable fate. In this case we do not want to see ourselves the way we are, since this would challenge us to change, to risk, to explore the depth of our own dark forest with its dragon and captured maiden.

For the same reason loneliness and isolation may be avoided, since they would lead us into our inner self. Such avoidance of authenticity may create guilt and self-condemnation in him who still harbors some awareness that he is failing himself. He then experiences existential anxiety in face of an empty and meaningless life. The fear of pain and destruction is to be added to the above as a very special aspect of existential anxiety, since it is in pain and when physically mutilated that we most convincingly find out what we are: whether the self-confident and courageous, kind and unselfish front we had been presenting when we were whole and hearty corresponds to something authentic, or whether pain and destruction will expose us as phonies.

The fairy tale and myth refer to all these facets of existential anxiety described in ontoanalytic literature: The young queen faces certain death on the burning pyre; Oedipus is haunted by fate until his death; Psyche is left utterly alone;[4] Orestes is plagued by his guilt; the girl of the Star Ducats finds herself completely deprived and empty; Osiris is cut up into pieces;[15] and Prometheus suffers continued, untold pain while still defying Zeus for the sake of his and the human beings' identity.[158] Death looms behind all this turmoil, a death which appears imminent or unavoidable—but which does not occur.

Yet the turmoil was avoidable: The young queen did not need to keep her silence; Oedipus could have easily avoided finding out the truth about himself and Jocasta;[153] Psyche did not have to light the lamp which revealed and removed her lover; Orestes could have murdered only his uncle and spared his mother;[57] the kind girl of *The Star Ducats* was in no way forced to give her food and clothes away until she stood bare and cold and hungry in the midst of the forest; Osiris could escape his mutilation and Prometheus was in no way committed to bringing the heavenly fire to mankind.

Thus we find in all these narrations the basic theme of free choice; of a choice—however—between remaining arrested, and daring what appears hopeless; of a choice which is neither shrewdly calculated nor masochistic. The hero confronts death, hopelessness, loneliness and pain not because he figures that he will be saved in the last instant, and triumph; nor because he relishes the admirability of his demise. His existential crisis is the movement of faith in the presence of utter hopelessness which Kierkegaard so powerfully and poetically extolled in his portrayal of Abraham about to sacrifice his son, Isaac.[96] This paradox, more or less obvious, is a basic theme in the classic myth and fairy tale.

The turmoil was avoidable: The questions advanced by the past can be ignored at the cost of devaluating the past, and the challenge of the future can be shunned by adhering to the *status quo*. Thus we would choose a monotonous, deathless existence in which we may or may not be aware of our despair. The improper confrontation with the challenges of life leads to such existences as portrayed by Tantalos or Sisyphos in the saga, or by the demons and condemned in Dante's *Inferno*. Tantalos, Sisyphos and Ixion[59] are condemned to a meaningless, futureless, and thus hopeless and painful, eternally present existence, because they attempted to reach greatness and immortality by outward ruse rather than by inward development. While self-development is viewed with favor by the gods, trickery and purely outward increase in wealth and power leads to the eternal frustration of the true self.

On the physical plane, the principle that a more complex mechanism cannot arise from a simpler one dominates and is based on the law of cause and effect. On the other hand, the meaningfulness of our existence as human beings is based on the conviction that we can develop and better ourselves, that we can reach beyond our present limitations. This implies that we are not only able to add to our knowledge and experience by taking in from our environment, but that we are also capable of some sort of self-creation. This somewhat paradoxical concept of self-creation is linked to the idea of freedom. Thus it is tied to another apparent paradox; on the one hand we may view our fate or evolution as being determined by outward rules or forces; genetic laws, culture, or divine providence. On the other hand, the idea of freedom implies not only the active participation on our part in the creation of an ever more meaningful world, but also the possibility of ultimate utter failure. Yet, if the outcome is failure, then the entire plan of evolution would have been senseless, and existence would have been meaningless for all.

Thus it appears—and myths or fairy tales express this in their own characteristic language—that the physical development of more complex structures requires an outside mind, and is based on ever more complex causal interrelationships; contrariwise, spiritual self-development (the widening of our world-design) can be spontaneous and resides in some profound paradoxes (leading to existential crises) which give rise to the energies for human growth.

Probably no human faculty has been viewed more ambivalently than our intellect. Its development and emphasis has been hailed as the ultimate boon to humanity and has been blamed for all the dehumanized aspects of modern human existence. Since fairy tales and myths are keenly aware of the crucial importance of its proper role, we conclude this part with a chapter discussing in greater detail the human intellect portrayed in folklore.

CHAPTER XXXI

THE INTELLECT

IN SWITZERLAND, when, a little over a hundred years ago in 1844 (England's first train was inaugurated in 1825), the first train drove from Zürich to Baden, the farmers rose in protest against the devilish monster which frightened the cows by its speed and noise and which threatened to burn down their homes with its sparks. Not too long before this, the last witch had been burned publicly in a nearby town (Glarus, 1782).[187] Meanwhile, the naive remarks of the peasants have become a part of the amusing ancedotes concerning the first motorized vehicles; and the last burning of a witch has come to symbolize the end of a dark era full of superstitious beliefs.

No doubt, the farmers were ignorant and unquestionably the beliefs in witchcraft and devilish possession had led to horrible abuses. However, the two events can also be seen as two symbolic cornerstones in the evolution of the human race. The witch burning, unfair and cruel as it was, represented a degenerated remnant of a belief in a live, real, spiritual world. On the other hand, while its sparks were quite harmless, the steam engine sparked off a chain reaction of mechanization and automation in which the human being, previously seen as easy prey to devilish forces, becomes a slave of the machine. He hardly perceives that the devil has gone underground, that the destructive forces which mankind superstitiously or maliciously projected into some poor insane individuals are now leading the human race into a spiritual obscurity and confusion of which the Apocalypse of Saint John gives a fairly accurate picture.

To be sure, the chain reaction had started long before the first steam engines. Whatever the length of time human beings have toiled on this earth, it seems reasonable to assume that at first there was a period during which they were fully and harmoniously integrated in the mineral, plant and animal kingdoms. There seemed to be a natural, biological balance between the various living beings; and while man had his sorrows and satisfactions even then, there could simply not exist any thought of something better or different. Or, maybe, there was even then some degree of striving, some slight progress, but so little and so insignificant that it passed unnoticed. Thus the golden age was certainly not without pain, cruelty and suffering; but these were humbly accepted as part of the harmony of nature. The motto would have been: "Happiness is to know no better."

Be that as it may, at one point the ball of human civilization started rolling, first slowly, then faster and faster, as if following an impulse of destiny which no one could ever stop, as if in the earliest beginnings was already contained—like in a seed—all our modern technology, including the nuclear chain reactions with all their implications. In biblical terms, we could say that the fall of Adam and Eve and the expulsion from the apparently never-changing Paradise already postulated the apocalyptic era toward which our present civilization seems to be driven.

The serpent promised Adam and Eve that he would help them to think, to understand. And with this the human intellect put itself outside of—and often in opposition to—the paradisiacally perfect natural laws and balances. (The pain of this dysharmony was keenly felt. Rites and religions came into being to compensate for it.) But the thinking human being started to use these natural laws and forces for shortsighted, selfish goals.* Lacking moral magnitude and an all-encompassing view, the human mind very often overlooked the fact that any interference with the laws and forces of nature could create apparent prosperity and progress only at the cost of unbalancing nature more and more.[150]

Up to the present date we have been fairly successful in

*In Greek mythology this is depicted as the gift of fire brought to mankind from heaven by Prometheus; this gift angered the new gods and consequently led to another gift, namely that of Pandora's box, which was to bring untold sorrow and suffering to all the human beings.[158]

counteracting any disturbing evidence of nature's imbalance (draughts, overpopulation, exhaustion of various natural resources, epidemics, pollution, etc.) by drawing on untapped forces and resources of nature. Yet this offers only a brief respite and will, sooner or later, lead to more catastrophic manifestations of the disturbances created by the human intellect interfering with the laws of nature. We obviously cannot remedy this by renouncing our intellect which, anyhow, is not the only nor even the main culprit. If we could develop an unselfish morality which could use this intellect for the sake of *all* human beings, present and future, then and only then some healthy counterbalancing forces could be created. In Goethe's *Fairy Tale* (see Chapter X) the sacrifice of the green serpent represents such a purified intellect which eventually spans the river between two worlds for the sake of all mankind.

Most people, however, remain blinded by the spectacular signs of temporary progress. Even if they were capable of recognizing the logic of thoughts such as we just tried to express, they have learned to ignore them, since they have become geared more and more to the things which are immediately demonstrable, considering all other thoughts as abstract or nebulous. Part of this is due to people's changed experience of time.[75] Time either is seen as merely measurable quantity—and thus meaningless—or as "here and now," and thus unrelated to past and future. This makes long-term commitments for the sake of future generations almost impossible.

Yet, there are many persons who are becoming progressively more aware of the problem; even if they are not able to stem the tide of the technologic chain reaction, they at least represent a group who is gaining insight into the beginning chaos and who deliberately and intelligently tries to promote the moral forces which would have a reharmonizing effect. They stand apart from the larger group who continues blindly and selfishly to seek temporary benefits by adding to the disequilibrium. I was truly amazed when I realized that Saint John the Evangelist had pictured in his Apocalypse this future chaotic world in which people would be divided in two groups, that he was aware of an evolution which already at his time was well established, but the outcome of which no one sensed as clearly as he did.

The spirit of the Tower of Babel has reached tremendous proportions, but most people remain stricken with blindness. The few warning voices, such as the former pleadings of Cassandra,* are mostly misunderstood, ignored, ridiculed or refuted with superficial arguments. Those who cannot bear rejection, ridicule or ostracism will end up following the collectivistic trends where truth is equated with what the majority believes and where a distorted concept of democracy proclaims the relativity of all values and ideas. In *The Enemy of the People,*[81] nearly one hundred years ago, Ibsen portrays the tragic fate of a concerned, farsighted and mature physician confronted with the arguments of the masses that are totally governed by unintegrated and barely acknowledged selfish instincts and impulses. Realizing that only the strong and harmoniously balanced persons can be truly objective, the frustrated protagonist exclaims, "The solid majority is always wrong!"

Only moral strength allied with the sharpened intellectual forces can truly counteract the continuously increasing imbalance created, even within man himself, by his departure from the original, unconscious, instinctual, biologic integration with nature. Suicide can be a manifestation of this imbalance; and it is not surprising that, for example, in the United States the suicide rate in the white population, so much better off as far as physical comforts are concerned, is three times as high as that in the black population.†

In Goethe's *Faust,* Mephistopheles, who is incapable of ap-

*Cassandra, loved by Apollo, was given the gift of prophecy; but having been rejected in his amorous advances, and not being able to retract the gift, the god punished her with the fate that no one would heed her words. However, Thyresias who developed the gift of seeing the future when he was blinded by the offended Hera, did not fare much better in terms of being believed. Soothsaying must be a frustrating profession.

†There may be a number of reasons for this. However, it is noteworthy that not only do psychiatrists have the highest suicide rate, but also among the psychiatrists the psychoanalysts' rate is highest. It is not unlikely that this is due to the fact that the psychoanalysts subscribe generally to a reductionist theory of man and his world, which widens even further the breach between measurable and experiential data. The latter, in fact, are considered irrelevant, illusory or epiphenomena.

preciating the moral forces in the human being which can render valuable the intellect, derides God:

Ein wenig besser würd' er leben	A little better would he (man) live, though
Hättst du ihm nicht den Schein des Himmelslichts gegeben;	Hadst thou (God) not given him some light from Heaven;
Er nennt's Vernunft und braucht's allein,	He calls it reason (intellect), using it,
Nur tierischer als jedes Tier zu sein.	To be more beastly yet than all the beasts.[54]*

Fortunately, there is another aspect of the human intellect which stresses its role of delivering us, of freeing us, of achieving for us a new and more conscious spiritual awareness. This aspect is portrayed in numerous fairy tales in which the human being's loss of the golden age is shown in the form of expulsion from the castle, of not receiving an inheritance or of losing the mother and having to contend with a stepmother. This loss of helpful ties with the past, this impoverishment and aloneness are seen as the introduction of a fateful phase of human evolution, during which the intellect may play a major helpful role. But the intellect can fully assume this role only when the individual has shed the last blind dependence on the past, willing to substitute for vague spiritual awareness the clarity of precise thinking.

A story which illustrates this quite well is *Puss 'n Boots* mentioned in the preceding chapter: while his two brothers inherit the house and the useful donkey from the father, the youngest son gets only the apparently worthless tomcat. However, this animal is able to talk and displays such a sharp wit that it pro-

*The devil is quite right, here, if he point out that by departing—by means of his intellect—from his biologic nature, man has become biologically abnormal. The concept of normalcy in human beings can be confusing, because modern man is biologically always abnormal. We may end up with two concepts of normalcy, one biological and one human. The latter is much more difficult to define. Biologic normalcy transcends the individual and stresses the healthy functioning of the species which requires a stable balance with the animal, vegetable and even with the mineral kingdom. Human normalcy is individualistic and of the degree to which a person is able to create, experience and live his own ideas and ideals. There are strong interrelations between biologic and human normalcy, but since the first is referring to functions we share as human animals, while the second indicates a never-ending individual striving for meaningfulness, this interrelation is quite complex.

cures new wealth. The tomcat makes gigantic strides: he wants his master to marry the king's daughter and eventually become the new king. He arranges for the old king, as if by coincidence, to meet his master who is bathing in a pond and whose clothes (a last remnant of his past!) Puss 'n Boots has skillfully hidden. Only alone and nude can the human being meet a new kingdom. The king offers him kingly clothes, and with these our hero can begin to woo the princess. Meanwhile the tomcat demonstrates his master's worthiness by outwitting the great sorcerer. After cajoling him carefully into showing off how he can turn himself into a mouse, Puss 'n Boots swallows him and thereafter the castle and the lands of the sorcerer belong to the young man who then marries the princess.

There are two details in this story which help to characterize the healthy intellect. In the first place we must accept that our intellect (Puss 'n Boots) is inherited, that we cannot take credit for its acuity, only for the way we treat it, use it or follow its guidance. In the second place we have to be willing to give our intellect a good footing on the earth, even if this "being down to earth" may require some sacrifice. The youngest son is willing to sacrifice his last money to get a pair of respectable boots for his tomcat.

Past methods of gaining spiritual knowledge, by sorcery, magic, tradition, superstition and spiritism, etc., have to be done away with if we truly wish to gain new spiritual insights. Some of these methods were appropriate in their times, some were but decadent remnants of what once may have been appropriate. *The Spirit (or ghost) in the Glass Bottle,*[58] or the giant of the *Courageous Tailor,*[58] e. g. represent atavistic, powerful beings with supernatural gifts, but easily overcome by the keen intellect. We can find references to the victory of the modern intellect or reason over the plump sorcerers and giants all the way from Russia (*The White Mountain*[181]), to Hawaii (*The Boy Pu-Nia and the King of the Sharks*[180]) and up to the remote mountain valleys of Switzerland. Here we found *Tredeshin,*[21] the thirteenth child, for whom the poor parents could not even find a name, leaving his home and acquiring a princess and a kingdom with his courageous self-confidence and his superior cleverness.

Not only in fairy tales but also in myths do we find the same theme. Ulysses, whose sharp wit had helped the Greeks to conquer Troy (representing an earlier, glorious civilization), also overcomes the one-eyed giant Polyphemus by means of his sharp intellect. And David, too, with self-assurance and cleverness, kills the clumsy giant Goliath. Many ghosts and sorcerers, old kings and powerful giants represent a much dimmer form of awareness, characteristic of earlier cultures.

The number of stories dealing with this transition from a magic to a reasoning period is very great. Here I would like to point out just two types of themes which we frequently encounter and which will illustrate further this dramatic transition. I am referring to the theme of the Clever Tailor and the theme of Little Tom Thumb. Especially in the Grimms' tales, the tailor, frail, skillful, self-confident, measuring everything, cutting the cloth with his sharp scissors and sewing the pieces together according to his own plans, becomes an excellent representative of the keen intellect. The latter, by analyzing, cuts the world into parts, measures everything and rearranges the pieces to its own advantage.

The reasoning of earlier civilizations was much more concrete. The superiority and usefulness of cleverly used abstract thinking is, for example, shown by the courageous little tailor who, having killed seven flies with one swat, proudly stitches on his belt the words: "Seven in one stroke." The giants, the old king and his warriors, naive and rather dull in their reasoning, can only conclude that the tiny tailor is capable of killing seven *men* with one stroke. The little tailor's quick intellect is characterized by his agility and lightness which permit him to hide in small corners, to jump quickly from one thing to another when the going gets rough, just as we all may be inclined to do when, with some fast tricky reasoning, we try to outwit somebody. Our tailor, for example, has to overcome two dangerous giants in the forest, before he can marry the princess. Sneaking up on them, he finds them sleeping and climbs up into one of the nearby trees. Hidden by the foliage, he alternately drops stones on each of the giants. Naively, unable to reason that there might be an ulterior hidden cause, each one assumes that he is being harassed by the other. Gradually they become so enraged at each other that they start to fight. They finally kill each other with the trunks of the trees which they pull out of the ground, while the tiny tailor carefully watches, ready to jump to another tree if they should choose to pull his.

Another excellent example of the use of abstract thinking in outwitting the duller, concrete reasoning of the giant is Ulysses' telling Polyphemus that his name is "Nobody." When the giant is blinded by Ulysses and calls for the other giants to help him against Nobody, no one shows up. The Russian tale of *One-Eyed Likho*[35] is a fairy tale version of this theme, in which the hero in search of *evil* finds Likho, the one-eyed cannibalistic witch whom he tricks repeatedly by his cleverness and from whom he finally manages to escape after killing her. Somewhat analogous is the American Indian tale of *The Boy Who Overcame the Giant.*[113] However, instead of marrying the chief's daughter who is "too old and fat," the boy-hero asks for many good traps to catch fish, and lives happily by himself in a far away country.

In another tailor story we see the clever little tailor overcome the heavy, dangerous bear with music and with an intelligent ruse. Yet, in this fairy tale we are also shown that wit alone is insufficient if one wants to conquer the princess, if one wishes to find one's soul, one's *anima,* in a meaningful world. The intellect must learn to reach beyond the close material surroundings. When our young tailor and his equally clever older brothers are challenged by the princess to guess the two colors of hair which she is hiding under her hat, only the youngest, with a fantasy extending way beyond his everyday existence, guesses correctly: "silvery and golden." The other two mention colors familiar to them from their daily, material life. Cleverness alone is not enough. The young tailor is aware that the ultimate goal of the intellect is to find again, with self-confidence as well as with clarity of reasoning and perception, the golden and silvery strands which link the spiritual world through our intellect and soul with our physical existence.

The proportion between the tiny tailor and the giant corresponds approximately to that of little Tom Thumb and the ordinary human being. In Grimms' *Tom Thumb* the little fellow is extremely clever, tricky and fearless, and his adventures beautifully portray the fate of the human intellect. Separated from his loving parents, Tom Thumb first accompanies two men who hope to make money by exhibiting him. Then he joins two thieves who hope, with his help, to get the parson's gold and silver. There is, however, no easy way to acquire true wealth by means of the intellect, be it by exhibiting it or by trying to regain ancient treasures (namely the gold and silver) by mere cleverness and stealing. So Tom Thumb has to go through great tribulations. Yet he harbors a constant, deep longing to return to his parents. After having been associated with selfish men and thieves, he falls prey to the animal desires, being swallowed first by the placid cow, then by the greedy wolf. However, he never despairs and with his sharp wit he manages to lead the wolf to his parents who kill the animal and deliver their son.

Never had he let himself be completely corrupted by the temptations of the earth, though he could not avoid becoming enslaved and swallowed by the greedy forces in this world. Similarly, the intellect cannot escape becoming a tool of our natural-scientific and greedy civilization. Yet, when things may appear most hopeless, the intellect's, or Tom Thumb's courage and self-confidence will help him find a new freedom and a permanent home, if he has not allowed materialism to corrupt his own core. Only the surface (Tom Thumb's clothes) has been spoiled. The parents who greet their son happily provide him with new beautiful clothes, and he lives with them, enriched by his former adventures in the wide world.

In another Tom Thumb story by the brothers Grimm, *Thumbling As a Journeyman,* the similarity of the fairy tale roles of the tailor and of the thumb-sized little man is underlined by Thumbling being a tailor's son and becoming an apprentice tailor. Again, in his journey through the world, he first becomes associated with thieves. His exhibitionistic arrogance has led to his being chased away from his apprenticeship. In the deep forest he encounters the thieves whom he helps to steal the king's treasure.*

*This intellect that steals the old king's treasures is at first utterly amoral. We see this already in an Egyptian tale transmitted by Herodot (fifth century

When they ask him to be their captain, he declines and departs, taking with him only a small coin, a *Kreuzer* (named thus because it bears the sign of the cross).

The young, curious intellect, eager to learn, at first, like a thief, wishes to arrogate everything to itself. This reminds us also of that aspect of the human being represented by the arrogant maid in the story of *The Goose Girl.* Thumbling, however, leaves the thieves, tries to use his insights for moral goals, goes to work for various masters, and carries his heavy *Kreuzer* (cross) with him wherever he goes. But he comes into conflict with the selfish, animal drives in the human beings and—like Tom Thumb—he is first swallowed up by the cow (probably representing the sensuous, gluttonous desires) and then, almost, by the beast of prey, the fox (symbolizing the cruel, sadistic impulses). Thanks to his clear and quick thinking, he is able to save himself in the very last moment and soon find himself back at home with the overjoyed father. To him he hands the *Kreuzer,* almost as a token of the basic significance of his journey through the world: the deepest wisdom of Christianity, represented by the cross, can only be grasped if we allow ourselves to penetrate, to face the physical world, its temptations and turmoils; this involvement with our material existence is an essential step in our human evolution. Thus thumbling carries the sign of the cross. Though he cannot avoid the involvement with the world in which the animal reigns (see previous references to the Apocalypse), he does not assume the sign of the animal on forehead and hand, but remains one of the 144,000 that eventually surround the true lamb, one of the mysterious number of individuals that has been able to cross the gate leading into a new realm where *time becomes space* (see Chapter XXIV).

Thumbelina, by Andersen,[3] born in a beautiful tulip which grew from a seed sold by the sorceress to the childless woman,

---

B.C.)[15] where the clever thief in order to avoid identification cold-bloodedly cuts off the head of his brother who has been caught by the king. Later, when sleeping with the king's daughter who is given the job of trapping him, he lets her grab in the dark his dead brother's arm while he escapes. Eventually his shrewd cleverness so impresses the old king that he is forgiven and allowed to marry the princess.

emphasizes the need of completely unselfish love. Like Tom Thumb, this little girl gets swallowed up more and more by the earth as she goes from one adventure to another. Eventually she lives with the mouse underneath the ground, and is promised in marriage to the blind mole. This would mean that she would never again see the golden sun, the silvery moon, the stars and the flowers. Yet under the earth she finds the swallow who has missed its trip to the south and has almost frozen to death. Unselfishly she nurses it back to life and sadly bids it good-by when spring arrives. But on the day of her wedding to the mole, the swallow reappears just as the little girl is about to disappear into the earth forever, and carries her off to the flower-filled southland where she meets her little flower king.

In summary, let us mention three important features of the modern intellect as it leads man on an adventurous excursion through the physical world:

A. We can see the modern intellect as the force which tends to unbalance nature toward chaos. It strengthens our self-awareness in its exploration of the material world, but becomes easily a slave to selfish, greedy, bestial desires.

B. The danger of being engulfed by chaos is also augmented by the gradual decline of spiritual or religious experience, experience which still was very profound and real in pre-Grecian cultures. The human intellect can have a beneficial role here and carries the hope and the promise of a new, more conscious experience of the significance of the world.

C. This can only be accomplished, as we have seen and as we shall see further below:

1. If we do not let our intellect be corrupted during its servitude, but rather continue to sharpen our wit, as Tom Thumb did;
2. If we are ready to feed our reasoning with our finest fantasy, as the clever little tailor did; and
3. Above all, if we can develop in our soul charity and unselfishness, as we saw in *Thumbelina.*

Utter conscientiousness, openness, and charity—only the love of truth and the unselfish love of others can provide the basis for a presuppositionless openness, for *aletheia.*

PART IV

CONTEMPORARY USEFULNESS OF FAIRY TALES AND MYTHS

CHAPTER XXXII

FOLKLORE, WESTERNS AND CRIME STORIES

With Comments on the Effect of Television

THE DIFFERENCE IN EFFECT between the cruelties, longings and heroic achievements in folklore and the brutalities, desires and exploitations in so-called realistic stories is very crucial. Indeed, their effects upon the child's soul may be diametrically opposite. This has considerable importance, since many parents are inclined to justify their children's watching the most sadistic murder mysteries on television by saying that these are no more gruesome than many folktales or myths, and that they afford an opportunity for draining off excessive aggressive drives. The trouble with this justification—as with many harmful assertions—is that it is partly right. Mentally fairly stable children very often succeed in transforming the realistic stories into fantasy stories with the essential characteristics of folklore.

W. Schramm, J. Lyle and E. Parker,[157] studying the effect of television upon the lives of children, arrived at the following five main conclusions:

1. To date there is little convincing evidence as to whether or not television stimulates undesirable, primitive aggressive or sexual impulses in the *average* child.

2. Nor is there convincing evidence to the effect that television can render an *average* child either overly passive or withdrawn.

3. However, there is abundant reason to believe that all the undesirable effects mentioned in *1* and *2* do occur in children

who are predisposed to such a reaction to television either characterologically or as a result of an unsatisfactory family environment.

4. The authors stress repeatedly that much of this unfavorable influence can be prevented if the parents choose to give the child love and security, to show him interest and friendship and to regulate his television time wisely.

5. Finally, the authors admit that all the up-to-date research has covered too short a time span to allow any conclusions in regard to some long-term effects of television, especially the effects on values, on awareness, on response patterns and on individual behavior.[157]

These interesting findings and conclusions are questionable from a psychiatric vantage point. If we concur that television has an undesirable influence upon unstable children as far as primitive aggressiveness, tendency to withdraw and passivity are concerned, we can hardly accept a sharp limitation of this influence to the severely disturbed child. All children show various degrees of instability at various times and no child has an ideal family environment. The difference between the "unstable" and the "average" child would then consist mainly in the latter's successfully repressing the undesirable effects of television. However, we know only too well that repression is rarely achieved without some secondary symptom formation, without some barely perceptible personality change, and that under particularly stressful situations it will fail altogether.

In experiments conducted by Dr. Bandura of the University of Stanford, children of nursery school age were shown movies of adult models who interacted in a novel and aggressive way with a set of play materials. After being subjected to a frustrating experience, one child at a time was led into a room that contained the same play materials that had been depicted on the screen, as well as other materials. In all, the movie-exposed children exhibited approximately twice as much aggressive behavior in this test situation as the children who had not seen the film. Thus these results are contrary to the claim that filmed aggression has an effect only upon children who already have strongly deviant tendencies, since this experimental group of children had been randomly selected from a normal nursery school population.

Even if it should prove to be true that only unstable children with inadequate parents show *lasting* adverse reactions to watching television, this does in no way justify the conclusion that television is essentially harmless in its present setup. The suggestion that much of its harm would be avoided if parents offered their children love, security, good interpersonal relationships and adequate controls, seems naive inasmuch as it overlooks the fact that most parents' attitudes are firmly and deeply rooted in their own characterologic makeup and in their own past, so that they cannot easily change. Such naive views, supported by commercial interests, derive from an all too common philosophy in the United States to the effect that evil is a rather minor accidental occurrence that melts away in the face of positive thinking and unconditional love.

Indeed the influence of the parents' attitude toward their own television viewing—including their ability to regulate it—is very important. A great influence on the child's attachment and response to television is exercised also by the family members' views on aggression, sex, creativity and passivity.

Research has probably not yet established clear-cut effects of television on values, on cultural assets and on individual awareness, partly because of the need for a longer observation span. The changes in values and behavior, the increased passivity and the lack of wholehearted and lasting commitments among the young (and not so young), are undoubtedly due to numerous factors among which television viewing has not been established as the essential one. However, we cannot remain complacent and let things drift along until demonstrable, permanent, serious side effects are undermining the health of the population. We must try to formulate some helpful hypotheses and guidelines in regard to this most important problem.

Television is a fare which during the school years absorbs almost more time than school, which is geared to a low intellectual level and which predominantly gives a "realistic looking" distortion of reality with an excess of violence and sadism. It is a fare which more than any other medium (including books, radio, theatre, games) demands complete passivity, absorbs hearing and visual attention, and offers no active group participation. Such a fare will have some influence even upon the healthiest child, though he may successfully repress its most disturbing impressions. The more delicate, subtle, long-term influences are less likely to be repressed adequately, not only because of their insidiousness, but also because repression serves primarily the immediate needs for social functioning which do not appear threatened—at least for quite a while—by the flattening of values, by the loss of the sense of selfhood and by collectivism.

All through the previous chapters we have seen how folklore stresses the need for a harmonious, gradual human development; how growing up cannot be rushed without serious consequences to the spiritual aspects of the human being. The child who is being presented with an overabundance of adult-life conflicts and desires, and who thereby is being pushed toward grown-up ideas and attitudes, tends to become afraid of growing up and is therefore stunted in his maturation process.[104]

The small child, especially, is likely to confuse fantasy and reality when viewing television.[157] At first he learns that there are no real people behind the television screen; then he must find out that some of the things he sees on the screen are really happening somewhere, that others are enacted by real people, and that others again are animated cartoons. Then he has to learn that some of the acted things are true to real life while others are not. These distinctions can be very difficult at times, especially since some fiction programs aim at being as realistic as possible. The impact of *viewing* real people adds another dimension of reality to the scenes that is not contained in *hearing* a tale in the cozy presence of a sympathetic and interested adult.

The healthier a child is mentally, the more accurately he will be able to evaluate the reality content of a program. He may drain off some aggressive drives healthily by transforming some of the overly realistic, cruel detective and crime stories into fantasy stories with epic or fairy tale character. If this transformation is incomplete, the child experiences the story as appertaining —to a certain extent—to his everyday world. The sadistic scenes may then become too frightening and lead to repression, anxieties (including nightmares) and obsessive-compulsive symptoms, or identification. Unfortunately, identification is not always with the "good guy." Children want to be like the television character who is successful; they want to be the strong villain rather than the weak hero. The fact that the "bad guy" usually attains so much more primitive instinctual satisfactions can add to such consequential identifications. The realistic sadistic or sensuous story not only fails, in these cases, to enrich the colorfulness and productivity of the child's inner, personal, fantasy world, but dwarfs it.

The values found in the heroic achievements and the satisfaction of justice of myths and fairy tales are absent in the frequent themes of television stories which reveal the exploitation of men by other men and relish violence for the sake of violence. Or if in these stories the villains lose out at the end, it often leaves us with the impression that the author is making a superficial and meaningless concession to the demands of moralism and law, after having focused constantly on the extreme satisfaction of lust and sadism.

The difference in the effects of folklore and realistic television plays can occasionally be seen in the way children act them out. Fairy tales and epos are acted out playfully and joyfully, whereas with the crime and passion stories there is a tendency toward overly realistic, uncontrolled, asocial or antisocial acting out. Emotionally quite healthy children can act out even these realistic stories *almost* as if they were fairy tales, and derive thereby some beneficial cathartic effect.

To the modern adult, geared to the outside material world, the language of the fairy tale has become foreign, and he tends to take the images and descriptions to mean material rather than psychologic and spiritual happenings. They then seem to him so sadistic, farfetched and cruel that he feels, well-meaningly, that the tales have to be "adjusted" to the sensitivity of the modern child, mostly by eliminating the too bloody scenes and by injecting some "goody-goody" moral precepts.

I mention here as an example the *Bedtime Stories* by E. Graham adapted from Grimms' *Cinderella* and *Snow White and the Seven Dwarfs*.[56] The original story of Grimms' *Cinderella* ends with the stepsisters and the stepmother getting their eyes picked out by the birds. One stepsister cuts her toe, the other her heel, in order to fit the foot into the glass slipper. None of all these gruesome features occur in the adaptation, which takes on the characteristics of a harmless detective story, with a convincing clue and a good moralistic ending. The fact that Cinderella's foot fits the shoe is no longer a sufficient proof of ownership for the modern mind trained by crime stories. Cinderella must produce the other slipper; and as if to show what a good girl she is, she forgives her stepsisters and even helps them to find husbands of their own.

We see the same attenuation in the tale of Snow White, where, at the end, the stepmother is no longer driven by her own envious curiosity to the wedding where she is forced to dance in red hot metal shoes until she dies. No, she simply disappears and is never seen again. The well-meant, though sickening, pseudo-philanthropic distortion of the story hides or destroys much of its deeper meaning. At the same time it becomes harder for the child to recognize the fairy tale language as a language of the soul-world. This will lead to confusion.

We can see an almost diametrically opposite process in the development of the classic Western. The original historical happenings are converted by the needs of the human being's inner world into a tale which, while less and less true to history, reveals more and more of this inner soul-world. The historical fragments become only symbols to express inner, psychological events. As the course of time removes us farther and farther from the period in which cowboys and scouts fought their adventurous battles, the Western story tends to take on more and more the characteristics of the epos and fairy tale.

The good, almost inhumanly perfect hero with his alternately silly, violent, clumsy, swearing, drunk, angry, slightly dishonest, but always delightful traveling companion might easily remind us of Calaf and the three ministers in the Turandot story. Together with other rather stereotyped figures such as the "bad guy," the "murdered father," the murdered father's daughter who falls in love with the hero, etc., they begin to assume roles which reflect inner soul functions and conflicts of the human being.

From a psychoanalytic viewpoint we often see in the Western a constant, partially successful, coping with the oedipal situation: the father figure is murdered; the "good" hero avenges his death, but he cannot marry the young woman and moves on to new adventures (here the commercial needs of keeping the hero unmarried and the sexual taboo help each other).

The more stereotyped the Western becomes, the more it appears separated from our everyday outside world. The towns in which the events take place have disappeared or have become ghost towns; often they are not designated by name. Thereby all references to time and place in the Western are either immaterial or missing, and frequently the hero, capable of unbelievable feats, is a rather mysterious person, coming from nowhere and, at the end of the story, leaving for nowhere. While historically the cowboys and scouts were looking for a possible existence in the wild West, now they become symbols of a language which, often in a rather simple or primitive way, attempts to touch upon the meaning of human existence as such. The almost ritual violence shown in these stories (the barroom brawl, the gun duel, etc.) does not frighten the children excessively, because children sense that these stories portray inner soul-processes and conflicts rather than outward events. The typical Western cowboy story exerts an effect similar to the one of the fairy tale (though it does not have, usually, its spiritual depth and delicacy) and is therefore not prone to create excessive anxiety in the normal child.

In ballads, almost every notorious American outlaw (Billy the Kid, Jessie James, etc.) has been glorified. The original, real and usually unsavory individual is turned into a Robin Hood type hero, committing his offenses only for the greater good of the poor and oppressed. Persecuted by selfish and cowardly, hypocritical and greedy people, he usually dies in an ambush. These ballads illustrate a population's deep need to mobilize ever again hidden, inchoate, creative drives that are in opposition to cultural rules, taboos and restrictions that have become stifling. Of the true history of the outlaw only the fact of his opposition to the established order is preserved. Otherwise he becomes but a name for those hidden, broader, turbulent and rich potentialities—designated by Jung as "shadow"—which battle the everyday, narrow ego (see Chapter III dealing with the Winnebago Trickster Cycle).

A. Maurer cites the story of the *Gingerbread Boy* being eaten by the wolf as having been the cause of a fifteen-month-old boy's fear of death and of eating. She points out that parents sometimes present these stories to a child in order to force him to conform, thereby often creating great permanent harm. Her article brings out quite well the possible dangerous effects of fairy tales, effects which exist only if the tale is used improperly.[118]

There can be little doubt that the offering of a fairy tale to a fifteen-month-old child would easily pose a threat, as he could hardly separate its content from the events of his everyday world. It is unwise to narrate fairy tales to children much below four or five years of age. The years from five to twelve are those during which the child both enjoys and learns from the fairy tale, just as the adolescent years can be enriched by legends, epos, ballads and myths. A rejecting or insecure parent may use the cruelties in folklore for his own sadistic or controlling needs which in the absence of fairy tale material would undoubtedly find other equally effective and equally harmful expressions. I would also suspect that disturbing factors in his family atmosphere influenced the above-mentioned small child to experience the Gingerbread Boy incident in a very traumatic, personal way. Whether the fairy tale is cherished by the child will depend upon the narrator's own feelings about the story; the kindly, loving grandmother who tells the tale to a happy child sitting on her lap will surely communicate something else than an agnostic, frustrated parent who dutifully reads the story to his bored children.

The experience of active participation is an essential or indispensable feature of our existence. It entails an affirmation of one's individuality as well as a relationship to one or more human beings. This active participation can be manual, such as the plowing of a field; it can be personal and psychological, such as the work of a teacher; or it can be quite unobtrusive, such as listening to a symphony concert. The entertainment business, and television in particular, seems to be well aware of this need for *active* participation. Since television cannot provide such active participation, it offers in its stead an *illusory* participation. By offering more and more realistic images in color and soon, probably, with three dimensional quality, by adding applause and laughter from a magnetic tape, as well as by other means, it enhances this illusion of being there. We almost believe that we participate as a live audience, but deep down we know that we do not. We may laugh, but we do not applaud; and as human beings longing for active participation we are left empty, cheated, worthless. We may make an ultimate effort to be included by writing fan letters, but even here we are usually deceived; the innumerable fan letters of the spiritually starving from all over the country are barely read and must be answered impersonally.

Television is valuable in various respects. But much of it we cannot accept without damage to our humanity, to our true self; and we ought to guard constantly against this deceptive seduction aiming at lulling us into a belief of active participation where there is really none at all.

Participation has not only to do with "being together," "partaking," "sharing," "doing for" and alike, but also with the depth of experience. Yet there are subtle, widespread, corrosive influences undermining it. Consider only the use of good background music in homes where human beings sip their drinks, chat, joke and munch, while Beethoven turns over in his grave since—in order to be able to maintain some social interchange—the people are learning *not* to listen to the divine music they hear.

CHAPTER XXXIII

A PERSONAL FAIRY TALE

THIS BRIEF CHAPTER will serve as a transition to the subsequent comments concerning the use of mythologic and fairy tale themes in psychotherapy. It focuses upon a beautiful tale written by a student who took my course on mythology. It illustrates that such narrations can emerge spontaneously and almost compellingly from the psyche of modern man, and that they exert an effect upon their creator.

Especially Jung and his followers have emphasized that, in order to further his growth and maturation, it may be quite helpful for a person to learn to paint some of his fantasies and dream-images. In terms of affirming deep feelings and experiences it may be even more helpful to learn to write down spontaneously emerging daydreams or fairy tale-like fantasies. Once these are confronted without excessive fear, they can evolve toward a harmonious integration in a growing personality. For most people it may be particularly difficult nowadays to express themselves in the imaginative language of folklore. The following brief fairy tale, however, is an excellent illustration of its potential. Written by a mother to whom the two younger children epitomized supreme light, love and beauty, while her older daughter had been her object of destruction, it had a profound and beneficial effect upon her coming to terms with her problem.

Of her previous attitude toward her eldest she wrote,

> I felt darkly powerful in my hatred, bent on destruction, and drawing on all of my resources to reduce the girl to nothing, or, at best, to a state of total inner confusion. I was then dwelling in darkness, possessed by demon consorts of the bad witch. Perhaps my extreme negative feelings for my daughter may be dismissed as pathological (if aspects of a person may be so "dismissed") because

> it was my wish to make her as broken as a child as I was as an adult. But it was still a power play; she a target for the projection of all my inherent terribleness, using negation of love to render her incapable of achieving autonomy or independence.

Gradually this young mother was becoming aware in herself of the great mother with its life-giving and life-destroying connotations: Shakti, embodying all that is good, and her counterpart Kālī, the black one, dramatically representing eventual annihilation. Such oppositions are not resolved rationally; yet if they are experienced and faced, they can become powerful sources of strength.

A Tale Fairy

Once upon a time there lived in a little cottage in the middle of a dense forest a young woman, her husband and their three children. The trees were so thick in that part of the forest that the house stood always in shadow, except, of course, when the sun was at its zenith. A roof of thatch covered the snug, humble house, and inside there was but one large room with a huge stone fireplace in the center. The mother always kept a fire blazing as it was the sole means of heat; but the corners of the room always remained chill. Beds for the family lined one wall, each in its own alcove.

Above the hearth hung a large wooden cage. It was in this cage that the mother kept the oldest girl. For you see, while the mother was a kind and loving mother to the younger children, with the older she became a wicked witch. In her evilness she had placed a curse on the girl that she would die before she would grow up. The only way that this curse could be dispelled would be for the girl to live in constant light. Each day the witch looked upon the girl huddled in the cage and was pleased to see her looking more pale and sickly than the day before.

The girl spent most of her time watching the family activity from behind the wooden bars; but, occasionally, she was let out to play with her brother and sister. At such times a long chain attached her to the cage lest she should try to get free. When the girl was out playing she began to take on the beginning of life's bloom. When the witch saw this it made her very angry and she would grow darker and darker and plot anew the destruction of the child. In her rage she would yank on the girl's chain until she was again inside the cage, and then slam and lock the door. Only then would the evil powers within the witch withdraw, and she, once again, could become a kind mother.

Now the two younger children were rosy and glowed with good health, and enjoyed much freedom. They spent their days frolicking with the elves and the fairies of the forest, and shared the secrets of all the animals and the trees. Thus, their days passed happily, and each day when they returned to the dim cottage they were more rosy than the day before. They knew that their mother loved them very much; but yet, when she tucked them into their snug beds at night, and bent to kiss them, they would often get a chill and feel a restless fear pass through their bodies. So they would snuggle deeper into their warm beds and dream of their forest friends.

So the days passed without event, and the family knew neither happiness nor unhappiness.

Then one day when the little boy and girl were playing at the base of a huge, old tree, they saw in a pile of dead leaves, the broken, crumpled body of a small brown bird. They took it for dead, but when they bent down to take a closer look, they saw the bird's beak open ever so lightly as though in an effort to say something to them. The boy gently picked up the frail bird, all the while chanting soothingly to it, and placed it in the little girl's outstretched apron. They carried it in to their mother. The children were not at all sure the mother would want to bother with the bird, but they knew that they could not renew the bird's life by themselves, and that they must ask her.

But the mother was of a kind disposition that day, and quickly got a small box, put a soft pillow in it, then gently placed the bird on the pillow and placed the box on the warm hearth. She taped the broken wings, and fed the bird, with an eyedropper, a special healing solution made of herbs. The three children watched the bird anxiously each day, talking to it softly and sweetly.

In seven days' time the bird showed marked improvement, and was able to hop up and perch on the edge of the box. By the second week the mother was able to remove the bandages from the wings, and the bird began to fly, clumsily at first, about the hearth. And by the end of the second week it was quite well and would fly restlessly about the room, stopping occasionally to perch on the shoulders of the children.

On the last day of the third week, the bird was in its box apparently resting and the children were gathered round watching it. They were feeling sad as each one knew that the time had come when their little friend must be set free.

But then their reverie was interrupted as they noticed the fire had suddenly begun to grow higher and higher until it threatened to leap out and lick at the floor. Soon all the corners of the room were lit up from the great blaze. Then the fire began to take on brilliant colors that sent weird flickering patterns about the room.

The children drew back afraid, and when they stooped to move the bird's box to a safe distance, to their astonishment, they saw not the tiny drab bird that had been their friend, but a huge golden eagle. It was magnificent to behold, and as they watched, the bird's plumage took on the brilliant hues of the fire.

Now the parents had joined the children and they stood huddled together in awe and in fear. At that moment a great draught swept through the house, fanning the fire yet higher. The cage swung wildly in the breeze and then, suddenly, fell upon the hearth, breaking some of the bars. It rolled into the great fire and burned. The girl knew an older fear just then and instinctively looked up to her mother. But, instead of the mother she knew so well, she saw a beautiful fairy queen whose radiant smile drove the fear out of the girl and into the fire.

The draught had blown open the door, and with that, after three graceful swoops about the family, the great bird flew out into the forest. The children ran in pursuit of the great bird, calling to it, and the parents were close behind. And it happened that as the older girl went through the doorway, the chain that was trailing after her caught on the door sill, and she was wrenched free. All the forest folk were rejoicing and a soft breeze whispered in the trees, which only the children heard.

The family found that the great, beautiful bird had disappeared over the horizon. Its flight was marked by a dazzling shaft of light that penetrated the dimness of the forest.

At last when they returned to the cottage and went inside, they found it bathed in pure, pale light. The table was laid with a banquet, and that evening there was much merriment and laughter. When at last the children fell asleep, the parents tucked them into their warm, snug beds. As the mother bent and gently kissed their flushed cheeks each child smiled softly in his sleep.

Since that time the cottage was always suffused with light, and the witch, who could not stand constant light, fled, and the family lived happily ever after.

CHAPTER XXXIV

MYTHOLOGIC AND FAIRY TALE THEMES IN PSYCHOTHERAPY

THE IMPORTANCE OF THE ANALOGIES between the events in myths and fairy tales on the one hand, and of the psychodynamic features in individual human development on the other, has been recognized since the early days of psychoanalysis. Freud not only turned the Oedipus myth into a notorious tale, but he also commented on the meaning of the well-known tales of *Rumpelstilzchen*, of *Red Cap* and of *The Wolf and the Seven Goats*. Therapists, such as Rank, Fromm and Jung, have made scores of fine contributions concerning the significance of various fairy tales and myths. They, undoubtedly, must have incorporated some of their insights derived from these narratives into their therapeutic endeavors.

However, with the exception of Jung and his followers, there have been few relatively recent attempts to use fairy tale and mythical themes more systematically in order to enhance therapeutic effectiveness. Erich Berne and his group have begun to explore the usefulness of some of the well-known fairy tales for illustrating to the patient his basic life script, the games he is involved in, and his predominant transactions. Thus we may find patients who are caught repeatedly in the role of *Little Red Riding Hood,* carelessly seduced by the splendor of the world and by the cunning wolf, who expect again and again to be rescued from the wolf's stomach. Others may linger, like *Cinderella,* near the ashes of the fireplace, wishing for the magic tree to shed fine clothes upon them, while their more earthy sisters are going to the prince's ball. Or, like *Rapunzel,* a girl may let her parent lock her into an ivory tower until she finds herself pregnant by the first, ignorant encounter with a lover.

Especially in his posthumously published book Berne[9a] demonstrates a delightful skill in linking the pathetic roles he recognizes in various fairy tales and myths with the problems of his patients. These tongue-in-cheek comparisons may be quite effective in helping a person gain distance, and a certain amount of freedom, from his problems. However, Berne destroys much of the deeper meanings of these narrations by seeing in them only painful scripts made up of unsatisfactory games or manipulative interactions. Recognizing more and more clearly that he is living but one of several possible scripts, the patient now feels that he is permitted to exchange some of his most stressful interactions for more spontaneous ones. This alone can prove to be of great help; yet spontaneity and creativeness are more than simply freedom from playing dangerous compulsive games.

Graf Wittgenstein's use of fairy tales in psychotherapy,[185] though slightly reminiscent at times of Berne's approach, is more flexible, varied and profound. He shows how fairy tales can help the human being cope with his life, point to the goal of human existence and portray failures in the search for this goal. Avoiding dogmatic interpretation, he makes use of these tales by stressing, as psychoanalysts do in regard to dreams, the overarching importance of the patient's own comments or associations to the fairy tale themes. The patient thus may come to see his problems mirrored in certain stories that can also point the way for him. It particular, Wittgenstein uses the technique of asking the patient to narrate some of the common fairy tales he remembers from childhood. The distortions that these tales have undergone in the patient's mind are seen as an indication of the specific, individual shape of the general human problem portrayed by the tale.

The problems, challenges, and goals reflected in myths and fairy tales can also be found in dreams. Yet the dream portrays these only in terms of the individual dreamer. Because of the latter's frequent need to conceal numerous unresolved conflicts or forbidden urges, the dream shows many distortions of the underlying theme. As has been mentioned, such distortions are less likely in those folk narratives from which the overly personal and the neurotic elements have been painstakingly removed by the passage from one storyteller to another. As long as the storyteller was faithful, and as long as a culture was receptive to the meanings of its folklore, fairy tales and myths showed few of the omissions, displacements, substitutions and reversals that Freud has made responsible for the formation of the manifest out of the latent dream.

Only with the advent of the *âge de la raison* in the eighteenth century, and with the consequent loss of receptivity for the full meaning of imaginative language, was the stage prepared for the distortions, analogous to those in the dream world, of these tales. This has continued to the present, and consists mainly in the removal of cruelties and seemingly illogical events in order to avoid harm to the child. Fortunately, especially since the seventeenth century, a few men, aware of the danger that the folklore of the more civilized world might get lost forever, became interested in collecting and faithfully publishing the fairy tales, sagas and epic runos of their countries. Basile in Italy in the seventeenth century, Perrault in France in the eighteenth, the Grimms in Germany and Loennrot in Finland in the nineteenth, combined an intuitive appreciation for these stories with modern literary interest and salvaged some of the finest treasures.[73]

Nonetheless, the average person has become more impervious to the message of these narratives, since his adult world has become more restricted to the dimensions of natural science. The world of science, constituted by measurable space and time and ruled by the laws of causality or determinism, can see in myths and fairy tales only remnants of ancient superstitions, stories with which to scare children, or playful, immature fantasies. The myth of science, promising health and prosperity for all, has been able to keep alive the hopes and longings of the human race. But gradually, and appallingly quiet despair manifests itself, as former cherished illusions are dispelled, and our finest feelings are reduced to complex biochemical or instinctual reactions. Yet, out of this despair, a new but often still confused search for wider worlds emerges.

For the child, whose world is not yet as rigidly structured, the fairy tale still discloses some of its secrets. Similiarly, the adolescent can be fortified by the power of myths and sagas, unless he is prematurely forced to accept the rigid limits of the technologic age. Offered at the proper time, fairy tales and myths can become an irreplaceable nourishment to the growing human being. We can learn this by observing without bias the child who raptly listens to a tale; but so often we dare not question the supremacy of the lifeless scientific world to which we are geared.

In psychotherapy, the patient finds a situation where he dares to scale some of the walls of his self-made prison. His irrational urges, his feelings, his esthetic values, and his moral ideas are seen as meaningful by the therapist, and this creates an open, tolerant atmosphere in which the patient can become newly responsive to the images and themes of myths and fairy tales.

These introductory remarks provide a background for the following sketches illustrating ways in which fairy tale and mythical themes were introduced in the dialogue between patients and myself.

Case 1. A young man who had been in therapy for some time brought me the following dream: "I was a guide of a tour, leading a group of girls from the office on horseback deep into the woods to the site of an old temple. Near the temple was a pool. There I clapped like a seal and everyone laughed. Maybe I was just doing a trained seal act to keep them happy. I knew the way to the temple, or what the temple would be. But then I didn't know how to act when I got there. I certainly didn't belong there. The temple was round with solid walls. One couldn't see what was inside, and since we were at the back of it, we couldn't see the door."

This dream led us to discuss the fact that in many fairy tales and myths one finds the portrayal of a castle or temple in the midst of a forest, often beside a body of water. In these narratives it is the hero's task to enter the temple, to discover the numinous secret and to get the water of life. It occurred to us that in these tales the quest for wholeness is the basic theme. This quest requires an integration with one's other, hidden side that is often represented by the bewitched maiden, captive in the mysterious edifice. She expresses the unawakened and so far unrealized life.

Now the young man began to see how, even in his dream, he was avoiding authenticity by pretending (though well aware of the importance of the temple) to be a boy playing at being a guide or executive who ended up a trained seal. In his daytime existence this sort of play-acting was performed with such skill and humor that it lent him a special charm. Yet it also interfered with his more serious endeavors at finding closeness and wholeness. A trained seal is other-directed. He who covers up his genuine feelings and intentions with witticisms never needs to reveal himself, not even to himself.

> Shortly thereafter, this patient brought another dream in which he found himself in a hotel in Mexico. He met a brassy, yet, attractive, blonde, whom he had known a long time ago. She was mad at him for something and started for him with a funny threatening stare. When he tried to evade her by outwitting her, she cornered him by throwing knives that confined him, thus blocking his escape. The young man commented that he had the feeling that a long time ago he had done something lousy to the woman: that they had loved each other, that he had pulled out of the deal and that she had always held it against him. Going over the border into Mexico represented escape and avoidance.

The reference to a once-loved woman, attractive and repelling, threatening and deadly, led me to mention the mother of Hansel and Gretel who turns into the witch-mother in the house in the woods. I stressed that the dream not only reflected old feelings of ambivalence, but also alluded to a deep guilt of the dreamer for having persistently avoided a deeper commitment to a woman. The patient then elaborated on this by remarking that he still felt like Hansel who must outwit the witch by presenting a false front. Here he referred to Hansel's offering the witch a thin bone through the trellised gate in place of his finger: a beautiful portrayal of the arm's-length participation that characterized the patient's life at that time.

Gradually this young man became more aware of the need to commit himself openly to another human being, even if this implied a risk, with the other human being at first appearing in the guise of a witch. Perseus confronted (at least in the mirror) Medusa before he could rescue Andromeda. When Niall, in an Irish fairy tale, did not disdain kissing the horrid features of the old woman guarding the desert well, she turned into a beautiful young girl.[24]

Case 2. Another young man was obsessed by thoughts concerning artificial legs. He cherished illustrations of various prostheses, studied them, designed better ones, read whole books about them. They alone allowed him to achieve full sexual satisfaction through masturbation, whereas he felt panicky, choked up and impotent whenever he grew fond of a young woman. Though very bright and quite successful professionally, he never received a word of appreciation from his father. His mother used him seductively for years to tell him hours on end about her unhappy sex life with his father.

The unappreciative father, the seductive mother-woman who hated men and the interest in prostheses reminded me of a famous Grimms' tale, *Six can cope with the Whole World,* referred to in Chapter *XXX*. A soldier was discharged by his ungrateful captain without any reward. Eventually he gained the hand of the princess whose previous suitors were all put to death since they could not meet her cruel challenges. The characteristic of the principal hero is his being one-legged. With his one leg he walked at a normal pace. When he attached the other leg, that he carried with him at all times, he could easily outrun any svelte princess. This fairy tale's images communicated more meaning to the patient than any abstract psychoanalytic interpretation focusing upon oedipal fears or castration anxiety.

Case 3. A middle-aged woman related a most disturbing dream in which she saw herself drift precariously between a frightening triangle and a seductively appealing, golden ball. Neither of these objects was reached in the dream.

She was a capable, self-supporting, intelligent individual whose marriage had failed many years ago, and whose friendships usually ended in disappointment, mostly because she would feel abandoned as soon as she discovered that her friend was also genuinely interested in other people.

Any triangular relationships in her childhood home were frought with pain and disaster, since she grew up with an extremely sadistic grandfather, who ruled the family; a schizophrenic, fanatically religious mother; and a father who was basically or defensively ineffective. The triangle in the dream reminded her of the picture in her family's home of God's eye enclosed by a triangle, hanging between two other pictures showing a punitive God threatening with his fist.

The fear of the triangle and the longing for the golden ball reminded her of a fairy tale. She pictured herself as Jack, the frail human being, confronting the giant in heaven. In him she recognized all her childhood nightmares, all the people who so powerfully and sadistically dominated her, particularly her grandfather. He was a physician who operated on her many times without anesthesia because she suffered from a chronic tubercular abcess.

Triangular relationships were intolerable in her world. Periodically she reached out for a unidimensional, dependent relationship, and when this, too, failed, she began to long for the golden, zero-dimensional, original, paradisiac world. The golden ball evoked the image of the fairy tale princess who was happily playing in the garden. She, too, had a golden ball that eventually fell into the pond and which was returned to her by a frog. Yet for our unhappy patient there was no noble frog who turned into a charming young prince, once he was openly and courageously confronted. Human beings, especially men, remained ugly frogs or threatening kings. To follow the seductively pleasant, golden ball meant her disappearance in the pond, loss of identity, death, oblivion; yet to turn toward the triangle with the intention of resolving the utterly confused oedipal situation appeared both dreadful and impossible.

Yet she realized only too well that one cannot completely avoid one's childhood, no matter how difficult it may have been; that one must salvage something from it in order to support one's present existence. Thus Jack had to climb three times up to the archaic world of the giant and his wife.

I commented that this triple return was most meaningful. The gold pieces, the coarse material treasures brought back the first time, were passively received and quickly spent. The goose that laid the golden eggs, obtained during the second trip, already demanded active care by the owner who wished to obtain her gifts. It is the golden harp, however, that represented the eternally creative gold that revealed its value only in the ability of the owner to play the instrument. Now that the golden treasures from one's childhood—and I compared them to the precious stones that Hansel and Gretel brought back from the witch—became an instrument on which the individual expressed his own creative ability, the giant could no longer survive, and Jack could live with ever new satisfactions for the rest of his life.

Our patient who longed for the golden ball rarely got more than a few gold pieces. Again and again she had some profound insights into her childhood dynamics, but soon the feeling of satisfaction and worth derived from these insights vanished. It began to dawn on her that she had not yet learned to convert the gold of early childhood into more permanent, internalized and creative gold. Her brief but powerful dream led her to sense that she needed courage to integrate the search for what was most positive in her past with an ever more open confrontation of her fellow human beings.

Case 4. A thirty-five-year-old man arrived at the office in complete despair because his wife had left him. He could not live without her; he pestered her constantly, and repeatedly became so abusive that she called the police and he was jailed. He could not leave her alone, that is, free. He did not know the true meaning of free choice, of genuine love. He only knew possession and dependence. Since he could not grasp the idea of free relatedness, and since, like all human beings, he required for his continued existence some form of intimacy with another, the very idea of not possessing nor being possessed "for absolutely certain" became a horrid threat to his identity and he thought of destroying himself. Since he had shown interest in opera, I asked him to read the libretto of *Turandot.*

As we saw in Chapter XXVI, beautiful, cold-hearted Princess Turandot confronted all her suitors with three riddles. None could answer, so they were all beheaded. With the approval of her indulgent father, she did this in revenge against the cruel slaying of a maternal ancestress. Among the crush of spectators at the thirteenth beheading is an old man and Liù, his slave maiden. The old man is in danger of being trampled and Liù's calls for help bring a stranger—Prince Calaf—to the rescue. He recognizes the old man as his father, a dethroned king, and Liù as a sweetheart who played with him in his earliest childhood. Calaf's outrage at the beheading turns to love at a momentary glimpse of Turandot. On the heels of the execution, he declares himself a suitor. And Calaf, his wits sharpened by deep love, answers the riddles.

This fairy tale opera is one of the most impressive portrayals of the adolescent's struggle from a position where intimacy is seen as possession and being possessed toward a relationship in which each partner chooses the other freely. The princes are like men who easily lose their heads when they fall in love with a woman, unless they have attained at least a modicum of maturity. Losing one's head is losing one's identity. While the princes die, Turandot leads an empty existence in her palace surrounded by the impaled heads.

Identity cannot be maintained by treating the other as an object, as the patient did prior to his divorce. He provided well for his family, but stayed away from them every evening and never shared his feelings with his wife. Nor can identity be maintained by unconditionally submitting to the other, as he attempted to do after the divorce, when his wife, vaguely sensing her need for a genuine encounter, chopped off his head again and again. Losing his head over her, he would get drunk, end in jail or make a suicidal attempt.

Love is, to use a term derived from Heidegger,[63] a "dual mode of existence." The boy who is still tied to his mother, as Calaf is to Liù, or the young woman, Turandot, who, under the pretext of revenging her mother, clings to the forceful, admired and feared father and excludes any other man, cannot develop new dual relationships. When these early ties are loosened or broken, various degrees of duality become possible.

Calaf tears himself away from the eternally young, loving mother image, Liù, and challenges the princess successfully. Now he possesses her. Many fairy tales and many a human life story end here. Turandot, however, revolts bitterly against that which she herself has brought about—against being possessed; and Calaf recognizes that to insist on his price might be an empty victory followed by continued unhappiness. Thus, risking everything, he offers Turandot another chance: discovering his name before the next sunrise so that she can still claim him as victim.

Her only accomplishment is to drive Liù into a sacrificial suicide. The unknown prince, his loving bonds to Liù broken forever, confronts Turandot again. Liù no longer stands in the way of this confrontation. For the first time, through the pain and sorrow of losing her, Calaf fully appreciates his own name, his identity. Instead of triumphing again and claiming Turandot, he realizes that his name, his identity would mean little in a relationship where he would only possess the beloved. He gambles for a relationship of a higher order, for a dual mode of existence that at first presages certain extinction of his identity, by freely telling the princess his name. The last step of these dramatic developments, that take place in a realm not illuminated directly by the light of consciousness, is the freeing of Turandot from her own fixations as a result of the heroic risk taken by her lover. Thus, when she must give her answer at daylight in front of the assembled court and populace, she declares that the unknown prince's name is "Love."

For a modern young man such as our patient, living in a world replete with infidelity and divorce, manipulation and ambition, yet unwilling to renounce the wish for a genuine human relationship, the steps necessary to achieve a true encounter, an ideal dual mode of existence, may appear impossible. Indeed, from the materialistic, natural-scientific viewpoint the dual mode of existence of two people, who fully respect each other's freedom and nonetheless remain responsibly united, must be seen either as unrealistic or paradoxical.[114]

The patient came to recognize more and more that he was avoiding a genuine encounter with his former wife by either throwing himself into purely mechanical relationships with women who were seen only as objects, or by desperate attempts to reestablish a meaningful relationship with his wife by possessing and being possessed. However, both of these maneuvers would ultimately leave him empty and dissatisfied. He had to learn to risk leaving his former wife alone, even though he experienced this risk as a threat to his very identity. Once he was able to leave her alone, to avoid spying on her, to give her a measure of freedom, she became able to see him more objectively, to appreciate his positive assets, and to resume the marriage.

The preceding discussion, focusing upon the respect due to the other's freedom, can be expanded. With the lessening or weakening of broadly accepted standards or values, the human being is more and more challenged toward personal, independent moral decisions. In the quest for meaningful goals, such decisions can be most frightening, since they often must be reached in the complete absence of outward indices. We make and we feel challenged to make decisions without knowing clearly what or where our goal is. We no longer can rely on a wise and loving parent, nor on the injunctions of our social groups.

Case 5. A Protestant minister consulted me because of marked feelings of guilt and depression. These were somehow tied in with his being faced by an important choice between returning to an academic career or accepting a more remunerative post with a prominent public relations firm. While various personal and unselfish motivations were involved in his inner conflict, he was further plagued by the fact that the future of either job was most unclear. If he chose the academic job, he deprived his church of a person who had helped its expansion; if he decided against the academic job, he let the students down and could not develop his potential of a good scholar. He was guilty wherever he turned. He did not know where to turn, nor did he know what the eventual goal would be. He faced an existential crisis, a leap into nothingness.

All this became clearer to him through the images of the previously mentioned Russian fairy tale (see Chapter XXX),[35] *I Know Not What from I Know Not Where,* which alludes to a mysterious "something" that the young hero must fetch from the "I know not where land" in order to fend off the lustful czar and to retain his golden-haired wife. Not knowing what nor where, he risks being carried by a giant frog across a river of fire. He lands in a strange country and eventually returns with "I know not what," who helps him defeat the czar and all his enemies. What a magnificent portrayal of a man who not only retains fearfully what is most precious to him, but becomes certain of it. He easily repulses all the assaults of the external world (czar) because of his courage to face absolute uncertainty and because of his willingness to seek a goal, no matter how unclear its nature and location.

The above condensed fragments of the treatment of five patients may give an inkling of the varied usefulness of mythical and fairy tale themes in activating healthy growth potentials. There is not one human condition, not one human problem, not one human hope that cannot be found meaningfully expressed in numerous myths and folk tales. However, these stories will begin to reveal their power only when the relationship between therapist and patient aims for the dual mode of existence, where two human beings, sharing in the basic uncertainties of life, can be with each other, tolerating each other's differences without need to criticize or feel guilty, without need to control or be controlled.

By means of the story of Cinderella I have conveyed to several patients a variety of insights: into their ambivalent feelings towards mother; into the need to be properly footed on earth; into the significance of the loss of meaningful vision; and into the necessity of gradually and sensitively decreasing emotional distance in order to maintain identity while developing a deep, lasting relationship with another human being. The tale of the king's page mentioned in chapter XI lends itself to underlining the difference between an unfree reaction and a free response; and the Iron Henry in "The Frog King" with three iron bands around his chest conveys excellently the experience of Rank's character armor:[144] In the story of the frighteningly lucky king Polycrates who—in order to appease the jealous gods—throws into the ocean his most precious ring, only to recover it again accidentally, a patient may see reflected his own avoidance of happiness; and the tale of Thesus can illustrate the dangers and advantages attending the overly cerebral hero. However, the tales which I mention to a patient are never selected methodically, but arise within myself spontaneously in response to the immediate situation. More often than not I bring forth but fragments of folklore; and I may then compare a patient's purposeful self-denial with Ulysses' cunning escape from Polyphemus by naming himself "Nobody"; or a man's dream of entering a lion's cage will bring up the story of Daniel and the need to accept one's most powerful psychic resources.

The therapist who is honest with himself resembles a character in Thurber's beautiful tale of *The Thirteen Clocks,* Golux, whom the young prince must trust, though he is bungling and full of uncertainties. Together they try their best to meet the utterly impossible and inexorable demands of the Cold Duke, whose realities are coldly materialistic. Against all odds and logic, they eventually overcome many obstacles. Life can blossom forth again. The thirteen clocks that had stopped at ten to five begin again to tick and the young prince delivers the princess.

At various points during therapy the therapist, sometimes the patient, introduces mythical and fairy tale themes that seem to be germane to the problem under discussion. In the uncritical, respectful atmosphere of the therapeutic relationship, the patient's rigid world design yields to his own potentials which are strengthened and guided by the images of the stories. While having the character of universality, the stories adapt themselves easily to the particular situation of the patient. In the undogmatic discussion between therapist and patient, the latter will formulate his own insight into the meaning of the various themes.

How frequently fairy tale and mythical examples are introduced during therapy naturally depends on the number of stories familiar to the therapist, on his ability to recognize some of the many meanings portrayed by the tales, and on his experience with, as well as enjoyment of, the method. The patient's ability to recollect numerous fairy tales or myths and his own interest in them may also be a factor influencing the use of this procedure. It has been my experience that most of my patients have rather warmly opened up to this approach, as if they were thirsty for the nectar of these wondrous images that prove to be more nourishing than many abstract formulations.

Mythologic and fairy tale themes can be used effectively in psychotherapy. The rationale for this procedure evolved largely from a more comprehensive study of the origins and meanings of myths and fairy tales. These narratives portray at different stages of human development the various predicaments and goals, as well as possible solutions and failures. They convey their messages in rich images rather than in abstract formulations. Although in some respects they are comparable to dreams, they are free from the dream's secondary distortions caused by the dreamer's individual problems.

The effectiveness of the introduction of mythologic and fairy tale themes depends on the existence of a therapeutic relationship in which the patient feels unreservedly accepted. Here he can allow himself to become immediately responsive to imaginative language and is not unlike the normal child for whom these narratives can be of considerable growth-promoting value. Also, the effectiveness depends upon the therapist's experience, intuition and skill in selecting suitable themes at the proper time and in introducing them, not so much as an interpretation, but as a part of his dialogue with the patient. Finally, though most patients respond warmly to this procedure, it must never be rigidly used. The proper introduction of fairy tale and mythologic themes can be most helpful in reducing the inner distance between understanding and experiential owning that often remains unaffected by mere intellectual insight. It is this experiential owning that leads to basic change or growth.

CHAPTER XXXV

FOLKLORE IN EDUCATION

IN RECENT YEARS we find an increasing interest in folklore among the young and some of the not so young. This interest extends into and is related to interest in science fiction, mysticism, satanism, astrology and Oriental philosophies. While some of these endeavors appear disorganized, unintegrated, escapist or faddist, they nevertheless must be viewed as a basically significant individual and collective response to a one-sidedly rational, materialistic, causalistic world view. Though potentially harmful when distorted by various regressive or selfish motivations, they are nevertheless the expression of a deep longing of the human soul that has been reduced to molecular or instinctual interactions by modern science and which finds itself in a vast, unfathomable but essentially meaningless universe.

Especially the growing child likes to avoid the rigidity of a seemingly rational system that defines institutions, values and knowledge. The child equally rebels at a view of his psyche as a chaotic mixture of largely ephemeral epiphenomena (feelings, impulses, thoughts) without structure. The child, better than the adult who may be excessively conditioned by a scientific world view, senses that his self presides over a psyche that is integrated with the world around him, and which is made up of harmoniously interacting systems (or holons) and subsystems.[100] The child, furthermore, senses that the interactions within himself and between himself and the world are ongoing creative processes, and that these processes cannot be comprehended by the rigidified language of natural science.

If given freedom of experience, the child recognizes in fairy tale and mythic themes a portrayal of this world that is excluded by science and which nevertheless is more real, more meaningful than the atomistic world. Later, the adolescent or the adult may find in Eastern philosophies, in esoteric movements, in existential writings, etc., important openings that promise a new awareness of the significance of self and world. Even the classical Western, or a great amount of science fiction (Merritt,[122] Bradbury[14]) has gained its appeal through this promise of transcending the rigid limits of a mechanistic-deterministic world. The Western has taken on many characteristics of the fairy tale, but is largely hampered by the commercial interests that affect its form. The science fiction stories all too often give only an illusion of spirituality, while ultimately attempting to find physicalistic explanations for the most mysterious phenomena occurring in them.

The American ballad of the villain-hero who, Robin Hood-like, is the victim of a rigid, moralistic, unfeeling society, comes closest to that function of folklore which reveals the potentially beneficial aspects of those irrational elements (shadow) that are excluded by a strict cultural canon (Jessie James, Billy the Kid, etc.) (see Chapter III on the Winnebago Trickster Cycle).

The interaction between a child and various folk narrations and epos appropriate for his age not only affirms his self-awareness and self-respect, but simultaneously opens up the paths for his further growth. The tale helps the child to overcome overly narrow definitions and to experience an inner and outer world that is infinitely richer and more meaningful than that of pragmatic everyday life. The possibilities in education for furthering such interaction are unlimited. Whether the children are exposed in various ways to different forms of folklore, or whether the children are encouraged to create their own stories out of their own store of imaginations will depend on their age, their cultural environment, the ability or bent of their teacher and on several other factors.

As an isolated sample of what can be done, I will briefly discuss a fairy-tale play written entirely by eight students of an average sixth grade class. Preparation for the writing of this play consisted in reading several folktales and in a lively discussion of some of the characteristics and stylistic elements of these tales. The participation by the children was enthusiastic, and equally enthusiastic was the reception of the play when it was presented to several student and PTA groups.

The Guinea Pig Elves

NARRATOR: Once upon a time there was a palace in the land of Twinkleton. There were trees and grass all over; it was a land of beauty. Animals roamed the land. The king that lived in the palace was a kind old man and loved animals of all types. But most of all he loved guinea pigs. He raised all kinds of guinea pigs. He even took in strays! He had a beautiful daughter named Mary. She had hair of brown and every prince that saw her fell in love with her. But she had one bad fault; she was very lazy. For her fourteenth birthday her father gave her the most beautiful guinea pig in the land. But she didn't take care of Jerry, her guinea pig.

Scene One: Palace

KING: "Mary! You told me you would clean Jerry's pen. But, of course, like always, you didn't!"

MARY: "All right, all right! I'll clean his pen tomorrow."

KING: "Tomorrow, always tomorrow!"

NARRATOR: Then it happened. Jerry got sick! They called the family doctor. He came in a hurry.

KING: "Can you do anything for my daughter's guinea pig?"

DUMB DOC: "Boy! What's a guinea pig?"

MARY: "You don't know what a guinea pig is? What a dumb doctor!"

KING: "Mary! Don't smart off to your elders! You ought to be lucky he even came here."

DUMB DOC: "I'm afraid I can't do anything about him; I don't know anything about guinea pigs."

GUINEA PIG: "Help! Help! Don't let me die!"

MARY (*crying*): "I'm sorry I didn't mean to do this! Please Jerry, don't die! Don't die! (*crying more*) Oh, no! He kicked the bucket." (JERRY *kicks a bucket.*)

KING: "Mary, just look what happened. He's dead, and all because of your laziness!"

MARY (*runs off stage*)

NARRATOR: Mary comes back to Jerry's grave the next day to beg for forgiveness.

MARY (*crying*): "Oh, please forgive me, Jerry! I beg of you. If only I had another chance!"

(ELVES *appear on stage*)

MARY (*looks startled*): "Why, who are you?"

FIRST ELF: "We are the three guinea pig elves!"

SECOND ELF: "We watch over all guinea pigs."

THIRD ELF: "We saw how you took care of Jerry."

FIRST ELF: "We saw, and we didn't like what we saw."

SECOND ELF: "We think you should do a very good deed to make up for what you did."

MARY: "Oh, please, I'll do anything to make up for my laziness."

THIRD ELF: "To get your guinea pig back you must prove you are worthy; you must acquire the Ruby of Darkness."

MARY: "But where will I find it?"

FIRST ELF: "In the heart of the Forest of Darkness."

MARY (*gasps*): "Is that the place where the ogre lives?"

SECOND ELF: "Yes, but a word of caution. The ogre strikes at anything, so watch out. There is but one thing you can do to defeat the ogre. No one else knows about this secret weapon."

MARY (*excited*): "What is this secret weapon? Tell me! I must know!"

THIRD ELF: "First you must promise not to tell a soul."

MARY: "I promise."

FIRST ELF: "Say this to the ogre when he is ready to attack, for it only works once. Say: 'Poofy doofy, zippity zapp, run away and never come back.' It will keep the ogre away, but only for one hour. Quickly, for the sooner you go, the sooner your guinea pig will return to you."

(*Curtain closes*)

NARRATOR: One hour later Mary finds herself in the Forest of Darkness.

(*Curtain opens*)

MARY: "So this is the Forest of Darkness. It sure is scary! I'd better hurry. No telling what could happen next."

NARRATOR: So Mary was going deeper and deeper into the Forest of Darkness until—

MARY: "What's that noise? (*shaking bushes*) Oh. It's a wild animal." (*She hides.*)

TIGGER: "Hello, I'm Tigger. T-i-double g-e-r. Oh, the wonderful thing about tiggers is that I'm the only one!"

MARY: "Will you help me acquire the Ruby of Darkness?"

TIGGER: "Oh, I'd love to!"

MARY: "Well, let's go."

NARRATOR: Five minutes later.

OGRE: "AH HA!" (*roar*)

MARY (*screams*): "Oh, oh,—Poofy doofy, zippity zapp, run away and never come back."

(OGRE *runs off stage*)

MARY: "Whew, that was a frightening experience! Tigger, where are you, Tigger?"

TIGGER: "Hello. I'm Tigger. T-i- - - - -"

MARY (*interrupting*): "I know, I know, we met before. We'd better get going. We don't have much time."

MARY: "There's the stream." (*groaning*)

NARRATOR: As they reach the ogre's cave- - - - - -

MARY: "It sure looks spooky around here."

TIGGER: "D-d-don't worry. I-I-I-I'm here."

(*Two guys fighting* OGRE *in the background. He beats them and they run off. One of them he rips into pieces.*)

MARY (*after the fight*): "What's that?" (*The ruby shines inside the cave.*)

TIGGER: "I think that's the ruby. Let's go see."

MARY: "It's the ruby! It's the ruby!"

TIGGER: "Wow, what a shine, what a shine."

(OGRE *comes back, the spell wears off.*)

OGRE (*deep voice*): "Now I got you!"

MARY (*whispering to* TIGGER—*makes whispering noise*): "Got it?"

TIGGER (*nods his head*): "Okay."

MARY (*groans and moans*): "Ogre, will you let me get a drink of water? I feel sick."

OGRE: "Well, okay."

MARY: "Come on, Tigger (*still groaning*).

(MARY *and* TIGGER *walk out of the cave with the* OGRE.)

MARY: "There's the stream." (*groaning*)

(MARY *throws water in the* OGRE'S *face.* MARY *and* TIGGER *start to run.*)

TIGGER: "Here's the ruby, Mary. It's time for me to go." (*panting*) "Good-by."

MARY (*sadly*): "Good-by."

NARRATOR: After her long adventure she found her way home.

KING (*runs on stage*): "Oh, Mary! I'm so glad to see you. Where have you been?"

MARY: "I've been on a long adventure in the Forest of Darkness!"

KING (*leaving*): "I'll announce to the servants that you're back so they can make you some nice, warm broth and get you some clean clothing."

(ELVES *appear.*)

FIRST ELF: "Well, Mary, have you learned your lesson?"

MARY: "Yes, I sure have! You can count on me, I'll never be mean to any animal again. And I brought the ruby; here it is."

SECOND ELF: "We think you deserve a reward, since you were so brave. The trees told us all about it!"

MARY: "Oh, I don't really deserve a reward."

THIRD ELF: "Well, we still feel you should have a reward."

(ELVES *leave.*)

MARY: "Where are you going?"

(JERRY *appears on stage.*)

MARY: "Oh, Jerry, you're back; you're my reward! I'll never treat you badly again!"

(*Curtain closes.*)

Written by: July, Paul, Tobi, Mike, Joy, Jeff, Susie, Tim

Meyerholz School
Cupertino Union School District
Miss Vincent's Sixth Grade

This play is not only a charming, witty, entertaining and

moving tale; written by eight twelve- to thirteen-year-old children, it is a magnificent projection of the preadolescents' inward psychic structures, problems and goals. But it must be stressed immediately that the effectiveness of the images, themes or events in the tale is in no way dependent upon their being grasped intellectually. Indeed, neither the children nor their teacher were consciously aware of the meanings to which I shall presently point. Any premature awareness of these meanings by the children would have only hampered the creative process and weakened the psychologic effectiveness of the story.

Many of the elements in this tale are easily recognized from our previous observations. Significantly, the protagonist, Mary, is said to be fourteen, namely one to two years older than the children who created the play. Thus we suspect that the story deals with their anticipations, anxieties and goals. We might say that Mary is the individual who must come to terms with an aspect of the psyche represented by Jerry, the guinea pig. The latter portrays something ambivalent, something that is loved and yet neglected. It is Eros in Apuleius' tale, both beautiful youth and repulsive animal. It is—in Jungian terms—the *animus* which is abandoned to die by the *anima,* by Mary, just as the youth in the tale of *The Dragon in the Black Wood* abandoned his *anima,* his sister Louise, in the dark forest. Yet both, Louis in the latter tale, and Mary in the present tale, come to the conclusion that they must find again, recall to life, what they neglected.

Though not having acted with malice aforethought, Mary—like Magdalen in Grimms' *The Juniper Tree*—experiences intense regrets at the grave of the one who was neglected; and the genuine tears bring forth helpful powers. The three guinea pig elves can be compared with the three artisans who succor the young boy turned into a bird in *The Juniper Tree* tale; they are the three complexes of soul-forces that commonly are designated as feeling, thinking and willing.

The Forest of Darkness is so much like the black wood or many other forests; it is the realm of the unconscious. Penetrating into it, Mary must confront the crudest, most primitive drives that are housed in this vegetative realm. Her promise to the three elves, to the soul-forces, is a genuine commitment. Yet the trip inward is a private affair. Whoever wants to find the "Ruby of Darkness," the "jewel in the lotus" that can metamorphose the *animus,* revive the guinea pig, is not allowed to speak about it.

On the way to the deepest unconscious the protagonist meets the guardian at the threshold, an ambiguous figure that can become helpful, even though he may be partly under the spell of the opposing forces. Like Golux in Thurber's *The Thirteen Clocks,* he is on the side of the good "by happenstance," and represents a mixture of poorly organized impulses. Jung calls this figure the "shadow"; it corresponds to the Trickster figure (see Chapter III) and he is appropriately called "Tigger" in this play. There is a feeling of uniqueness about the Trickster, expressed in Golux statement: "I'm the only Golux in the world!" Indeed, a person first begins to sense his or her uniqueness in the confrontation with the shadow which cannot be negated but must become an ally.

The ogre itself is not eliminated. He remains a meaningful soul power, but the ability to face him leads to the "Ruby of Darkness." He is easily outwitted; and while he, like Polyphemus, the Titans and many other giants, represents deep unconscious powers, he is no match for the young intellect.

The "Ruby of Darkness," then, is also "the other side" of the guinea pig, the transformation of what is not yet fully human into something life giving and enduring.

Seeing thus the various personages of the play as significant, integrated parts of Mary, we sense that the palace in which she lives can best be viewed as her body, and that the father-king (analogus to the father in *The Juniper Tree*) represents the enduring essence, the entelechy, of the protagonist. The doctor, finally, reflects our narrow, everyday thinking that has no understanding or knowledge of the true meaning of psychic life; he does not even know what a guinea pig is! (What a perceptive irony expressed by children who have experienced that the intelligent, scientific physician often is quite dull when it comes to responding to the finest, innermost disturbances of the growing and maturing young individual.)

Seeing this play as the expression of profound intuitions of the preadolescent on his path toward maturity, does in no way negate the light, silly or even somewhat clumsy features of the story. But we must not overlook that the seemingly trivial, witty and entertaining surface hides—as in most folklore—depths that we often cannot fathom completely.

CHAPTER XXXVI

THE NEED FOR MEANINGFULNESS IN OUR PRESENT WORLD

THE BRIEF COMMENTS concerning the Western in Chapter XXXII lead us to mention other modern literary products qualitatively somewhat akin to folklore. We frequently hear questions concerning the future of mythologic and fairy tale language or imagery. The answer to these questions is not simple. On the one hand, we may look at the fact that progressive generations, in spite of their proud advances from one achievement to another, have to begin anew as infants. And since the infant must recapitulate again basically similar stages before he can partake of the achievements of his culture and before he can hope to add to these achievements, it can be said that the style and the images of the tales that speak of the essential qualities of these basic stages will forever continue to be meaningful. They can continue to be meaningful not only to the developing child but also to the grown-up person who finds in them a confirmation and affirmation of his origins and goals, who recognizes in them basic blueprints for his own evolution (see Chapter I). We, therefore, find modern art-fairy tales and myths that do not differ radically from the style and content of older fairy tales and myths (*cf.* Thurber's *The Thirteen Clocks,*[173] Sendak's *Where the Wild Things Are,*[161] Saint Exupéry's *The Little Prince,*[151] Tolkien's *Leaf by Niggle*[176] and *Lord of the Ring*[175] to mention just a few). Similarly, fantasy tales written by some individuals as portrayals of their intrapsychic struggles will often assume the basic characteristics of the traditional tales (see Chapter XXXIII).

However, we encounter narrations with epic and fairy tale characteristics that depart considerably from the traditional stories. James Bond may well be compared with Beowulf[142] as a culture hero, representing fertility and protecting humanity from utter disaster; but the style of the James Bond series of novels is certainly altogether different. Ray Bradbury may introduce into his science fiction stories mythologic themes (water of life, golden apples, etc.) and characters (for example, Daedalus and Icaros), and yet the morale in these narrations is largely an extreme extrapolation, an exposition, of the future of technology and natural science. The same can be said of most science fiction novels (for example, *The Moon Pool* and *The Ship of Ishtar* by Merritt[122]).

Finally, there are narrations dealing with the inner world of man, with the "secondary world," with the world of meaning (or meaninglessness) that are breaking radically with the traditional styles, themes and images of myths and fairy tales. They aim to express the spiritual in elevating our everyday language, that has become so depreciated, to new heights. I have contrasted Goethe's efforts to achieve this in his description of the secondary world at the end of *Faust,* with his use of traditional folklore images in his *The Fairy Tale.*[67] The attempts to communicate meaning in Albee's *The Zoo Story,*[3] Beckett's *Endgame* or *Waiting for Godot,*[9] in *The Trial* or *The Castle* by Kafka,[90] in *The Flies* by Sartre[155] or in *The Glass Bead Game* by Hesse,[65] etc., are, in my opinion, genuine expressions of modern myths in the profoundest and most realistic sense. They are attempts to see God without needing the images or masks that can mediate a limited awareness of Him, to elevate our consciousness beyond the ordinary, everyday world, and to lead to the merger of primary and secondary worlds of which Tolkien speaks prophetically.[176]

As an example we may mention the legend of Josephus Famulus in Hesse's last great work. Here the gentle hermit despaired after many years in the desert during which he fervently prayed and consoled the penitents that were seeking his kind, tolerant and patient ear. Barely avoiding suicide, he fled from his hermitage in order to find a far away, famous, temperamental healer, Dion Pugil, God's boxer, who is also a hermit. On his way he met an old man who eventually turned out to be Dion Pugil himself. Yet only years later, shortly before his death, the old hermit told Josephus why they had met on that lonely road to Ascalon. He too, so he explained, had lost all hope and had therefore resolved to find the quiet and gentle Josephus of whom he had heard. However, when he realized that the despairing man in search of Dion was the healer he was seeking, he knew that he could not burden him with more hopelessness. Returning with Josephus to his own dwelling, listening and sharing his work, Dion not only saved his own friend, but found again his own inner peace.[65]

I hope that throughout this book it has become more and more evident that in our present time we are placed in the very center of the necessary, materialistically oriented human evolution; that figuratively speaking we find ourselves in the cold midwinter, with only scant, rare hopes for a new spiritual awakening.

The brothers Grimm, in spite of all their respect and love for the German fairy tales, were not completely aware of what enormous spiritual treasures their stories contained. However, they sensed this need for a reawakening of the human spirit and recognized that the disclosure of many spiritual truths was still reserved for the future. So they placed at the end of their fairy tale collection the story of *The Golden Key*. It is the story of the poor youth who, in midwinter, goes with his sleigh into the forest to gather some wood. Almost frozen from the cold, he tries to start a fire and in the process he find under the snow a little golden key. As he digs deeper, he finds an iron box which can be opened by the key: "And now"—so finishes this tale—"we must wait until the box is unlocked . . . then we shall find out what marvelous things are in it."[124]

This story reminds me to be modest, patient and humble. I regret that my accounts of various fairy tales and epos have not always reflected the richness of my inner experience and that this experience often has only been able to grasp a small part of the variegated meaningfulness of these narrations. I could take some consolation from Dante, whose insights into the spiritual worlds (though patterned by his strict Catholic beliefs) were so much richer and deeper, and who nonetheless again and again had to grope for words to describe what he saw:

O somma luce, . . .	Oh supreme Light, . . .
. . fa la lingua mia tanto possente,	. . give my tongue power enough
Ch'una favilla sol della tua gloria	that it might leave at least one spark of Thy glory
Possa lasciare alla futura gente.	to the future generation.

Divina Commedia, Paradiso[33]

In our grandiose era of technological progress we find ourselves lost as far as the meaningfulness of human existence is concerned, lost in a cold, wintery forest. And like the poor youth we may, at times, see a golden key; at times we may even recognize the treasure box. But the contents of the box remain largely hidden from our vision which is so much more accustomed to the material, measurable objects around us. Yet we can conjecture the wealth of its marvelous contents, if we recognize that it must be more plentiful and varied than everything we have seen and explored in our outside, physical world, because this material, measurable world is but a one-sided aspect of the "world of meaningfulness."

The spiritual wealth contained in folklore is beautifully shown also in the variability of the stories. The fairy tale is not static, is not a rigid image of an immutable situation. It is subject to all kinds of modifications which depend on the psychologic make-up of the narrator as well as on his cultural environment. Our *Turandot* story was a good example of this: Originally a Persian fairy tale, it became an Italian comedy in the eighteenth, a heavy, moralistic drama in the nineteenth and finally the famous opera in the twentieth century.

In shaping the text of this opera, Puccini seems to have sought and visualized a solution to his and his wife's own inner dilemma which caused them so much bitterness and idle unhappiness. The climax to their frequent misunderstandings and incompatibility was the death of their young, innocent servant girl who drowned herself in the fountain in the center of the town, when Mrs. Puccini, pathologically jealous of her husband (not without cause), accused her again and again of having an affair with the composer. The suicide of this simple maid could be viewed as the concrete, simple model of the sublime self-sacrifice of Liù in the opera. It was a tragic result of Puccini's immature relationship with his wife, not a free sacrifice born of unselfish love; and certainly it occurred too late. Her death may have contributed indirectly to becalming the stormy marriage, but it did not lead to the happy climax which we encounter in the opera; instead, Puccini died from a painful cancer before finishing the music to the last act, as if the populace's warning after Liù's death had come true: "Horrendous crime! We all shall have to pay for it! The offended soul will take revenge!"

Yet, Puccini also appears to have sensed that the dilemma of his marriage was partly rooted in the nature of our present epoch in which problems of human relationship cannot any longer be dealt with by means of pride or cruel firmness, as Turandot attempted to do, nor by means of conquest and seduction, as Calaf first depended on, but only by means of unrestricted respect for the freedom of *the other:* respect which is born out of the loving unselfishness portrayed by Liù.

The ability to show unreserved consideration for the freedom of choice of the *other* person becomes here a *value* which transcends instincts of passion, needs for power and desires for revenge. Both Calaf and Turandot become truly human only in the moment they surmount the influences of tradition, of their environment and of their own inner drives. Instead of being determined (by their impulses, etc.) and instead of trying to force the other, they begin to recognize that real human existence is found "in the realization of *values* and in the fulfillment of *meaning* potentialities which are to be found in the world rather than within themselves."[48,64] This quote from a paper by Frankl points to the great dilemma into which the human being has been led on the path of modern natural science. This dilemma is best seen in the trend which psychoanalytic theory and practice has followed. Frankl stresses that the psychoanalytic assumption that everything in a person's feelings, actions, thoughts, etc., is predetermined (pan-determinism), is far more questionable than the tendency to reduce most psychic manifestations to modified sexual and aggressive instincts.

Freud's psychoanalysis is firmly rooted in the natural-scientific frame of reference of the past century. At that time natural science triumphed because of its rapid tremendous contributions to our knowledge, physical well being and comfort, and because of the continuous decline, in most communities, of a deeply felt religious orientation. The natural scientist limited his interest to measurable quantities and to their causal relationships. In psychoanalysis this exclusive interest in measurable factors was reflected in the emphasis of the dynamic interrelationship of drives, both within the individual and between the individual and his environment. The *essence* of a psychologic experience, be it a feeling, a sensation or a value, usually did not fall within the scope of the psychoanalytic viewpoint and was therefore neglected. Hence the tendency, for example, to confuse the reasons for choosing a certain value with the value itself.[72] The psyche was reduced to what could be objectivated, the human being became a complicated mechanism with predictable reaction patterns, whereas values were considered as subjective entities devoid of any objective meaning.[48]

Yet this physicalistic concept of the structure of the human psyche retains its full importance and validity as long as we remain aware that it represents only a restricted, one-sided viewpoint. However, if we forget that there are other ways of viewing the psyche, we shall eventually be dismayed to see that even the individual freed by psychoanalysis from disturbing, irrational, unconscious conflicts, is losing more and more the ability to *act* as a free human being. Experiencing himself as a mechanism, he finds himself "self-less" in a "goal-less" and meaningless world. Out of a continuing need to see the meaning—be it even the "lack of meaning"—of one's self, of the world, of one's own world, have flourished the various new schools of thought stressing the equivalence of subjective and objective experience.

Thus we discern nowadays two important orientations toward the world in general and the human psyche in particular. One is analytic, genetic and mechanistic, the other is explaining-revealing. The first seeks what is measurable or calculable, the second deals with the meaning of things. The first has been leading to progressively more spectacular successes and accomplishments at the risk of unbalancing the totality (of nature) more and more and of ever greater meaninglessness.[72] The second is always meaningful, but risks to appear primitive, vague or illogical, because our language, geared more and more to the events of the material world, has become inadequate for this explaining-revealing orientation which furthermore requires a far greater accuracy of thought and perception than the mechanistic orientation.

Our contemporary civilization has grown so proud of and satisfied with its natural-scientific achievements that we have become more like the "man with the stone heart" in Hauff's beautiful tale.[62] He has everything he wants, but it has no meaning. And with him we share a vague hope that our knowledge that at one time things were different may lead us to again experience them as significant.

Frankl[44] describes with great clarity how the mechanistic (dynamic) orientation of psychoanalysis turned the human being into a complex, supposedly predictable, object, while any values voiced by this object or automaton became purely subjective. But "if meanings and values were just something emerging from this automaton, if they were not something . . . from a sphere beyond man . . . they could no longer be a real challenge to man . . . ." We see here one of the leading European psychiatrists, while conceding that we may try to predict the mechanisms of the human psyche plead that "man is more than psyche; man is spirit," that man has an ability to determine (at least to a certain degree) whether he is going to yield to the conditions influencing him or not.

The agnostic, the atheist, the materialists may well agree that meaningfulness and values are necessary for human existence, yet still question whether these are not simply useful illusions. They may point out that the incomplete predictability of human behavior is due to our not knowing *all* the dynamic factors behind this behavior, and that, therefore, the feeling of "freedom" is a purely subjective experience of something which does not exist. They usually remain unaware of the fact that their reasoning is patterned or confined by having deliberately embraced the natural-scientific viewpoint which automatically and by definition excludes the reality of those extremely rich and variegated aspects of all psychic processes which cannot be measured or objectified. They have become almost incapable of sensing that the explaining-revealing approach *pre*cedes the mechanistic-analytic one and, in a way, contains it.

The natural scientist, the materialist, the atheist forget that even they derive their experience of existence (as well as their ability to function as human beings) from the *meaning* that they connect with their work and with their ideas, even though they are inclined to deny the reality of any meaningfulness. They cannot, however, be discounted or ignored, since they play a very essential role in the journey of humanity through the "wintry forest." In the fairy tale we have seen this orientation toward death (and away from values and meaningfulness), toward animalism and materialism in the guise of some sorcerers, witches and dwarfs, of stepmothers and stepsisters, of the haughty maid and other apparently maleficent beings. They laugh about God, but they serve His purposes. Goethe has made this the principal theme of his *Faust* where the devil Mephistopheles is:

Ein Teil von jener Kraft, Die stets das Boese will Und stets das Gute schafft.	A part of that force which always desires evil and always creates good.[54]

CONCLUSION

Let us enumerate succinctly the main points discussed in this volume:

1. Myths and fairy tales can be seen as reflections or portrayals of the basic events in human phylo- and ontogenetic development.

2. These events can be viewed from psychoanalytic, Jungian, existential and other vantage points, each one contributing to a fuller understanding.

3. Myths and fairy tales may reflect the past (that is still with us), the present (with its challenges) and the future (for which they supply some important blueprints).

4. The focusing upon the deepest meanings and origins of these narrations must not blind us to the more superficial purposes (entertainment, moralizing, political parody, etc.) simultaneously contained in them.

5. We should never accept the fact that we have grasped the entire and ultimate meaning of these narrations. This is doubly true since our present-day psychic organization is not adequate to this task.

6. Indeed, a progressively deeper and more accurate insight implies a simultaneous inner development. The interaction between the narrations and ourselves promotes this development.

7. Models, concepts and presuppositions such as are supplied by various psychologic and anthropologic orientations may accelerate and further some insights. The phenomenologic method which urges us to become aware of the limiting and distorting effect of presuppositions and to "let the things themselves speak" is more likely to lead toward the essential meanings of these narrations. However, the phenomenologic method must be used with great patience and self-discipline, or we are drawn toward unfounded observations and speculations.

8. Just as the phenomenologic method underlying the existential view of man can lead to a deeper grasp of fairy tales and

myths, so the latter lend themselves beautifully to illustrate the main existential ideas. Thus we illustrated the essential temporality of man and the development of body awareness with the Winnebago Trickster Cycle. Thus the Heracles myth lent itself to portray the gradual, periodic expansion of the striving individual's world-design. Thus the risks freely accepted by many mythic and fairy tale heroes portray the existential crisis. And finally we find a moving example of the theme of the existential encounter in the legend-like tale of Josephus Famulus in Hesse's *The Glass Bead Game.*[65]

9. These illustrations, images or symbols are *not* metaphors; nor are they to be experienced as *physically* concrete as the corresponding objects or persons in the everyday world. Even their analogy to the images in dreams and hallucinations is only a tenuous one. Their shapes and colors very indirectly convey the true, deeper meanings. Nevertheless, they are infinitely more effective than our present day attempts to objectivate the nature of man and his universe by means of reducing everything to basic, measurable units and to clear-cut causal interrelationships.

10. The growing current interest in myths and fairy tales can be seen as a reaction originating in the despair engendered by a one-sided natural-scientific outlook. This reaction—seen also in the emphasis on experiencing, on Oriental philosophies, on criticizing technology and material values, and on fundamentalist religiosity—is not automatically constructive, healthy or good. It can lead the human being towards escapist self denial and denial of the world, which is the opposite danger we must avoid. Frequently contaminated with the very evils that it is directed against, or strongly motivated by neurotic needs or attitudes, this reaction can also become hindering or harmful.

11. It is here where comparison of dreams, fantasies and hallucinations with folklore can be helpful in recognizing the meaning and potential usefulness of spontaneous productions of the human psyche.

12. Only when we have at least an inkling of the deeper meanings hidden in various myths and fairy tales, as well as of their origin and function, we can properly appreciate their possible roles in education and in psychotherapy. These roles are

important and varied. We limited the discussion of the use of folklore in education and psychotherapy to a few remarks and fragmentary illustrations.

13. Comments concerning classification, style, origin, transmission and variations of myths and fairy tales were restricted to the bare minimum necessary for the development of the main themes of this book.

We did not intend to leave the impression that the typical Western, the existential novel and most science fiction stories should be considered on a par with the fairy tale, myth, legend or epos. Yet the Western and science fiction tales show clearly that in the midst of our technologic epoch the human soul still seeks for every opportunity to verbalize and visualize its problems and destiny. While it is characteristic for the truly human aspect of our existence to find its clearest expression and its strength in the *word,* the struggle for some meaningful grasp of one's self and one's world is so desperate today that it spills over into art, into preoccupation with Oriental philosophy, into various forms of meditation, into the desire for intense religious experiences, as well as into renewed interest in astrology. The manifestation of these longings, unfortunately, is frequently linked with extremely primitive drives, with regressive behavior, with radical rationalism and scientism, and with cold commercial interests. Thus constant, growing self-discipline, vigilance, authenticity, thoroughness and patience are required in order to separate the chaff from the precious grains that promise to grow and nourish us in the future. I personally believe that in the times to come the classic fairy tale, myth and epos, along with ballads, legends and fables, will retain a most meaningful role. In addition, however, we will develop a newly alive and increasingly rich language suitable not only for the world of business and natural science, but able also to portray with greater precision and with a minimum of symbolic images all matters of the psyche or spirit. And as human beings grow in their ability to experience and describe these matters of the soul and spirit, we shall see come into focus a more fascinating, hierarchically structured secondary world, more variegated and rich than the primary world which eventually will become but a special facet of this secondary world.[176]

> Just as a hand held before the eyes conceals the greatest mountain, so does petty earthly life conceal from view the vast lights and mysteries of which the world is full; and he who can withdraw it from his eyes, as one withdraws a hand, will behold the great light of the innermost world.
>
> —Rabbi Nachmann in Buber's *Narrations of the Hassids*[17,131]

We are frightened lest we lose sight of the beautiful hand for the uncertain vision of the mountain. Yet, in the moments we are able to overcome our fears and shift the hand, we stand astonished to see that the hand, unchanged, remains a minuscule part of an infinitely wider picture.

BIBLIOGRAPHY

1. Adami, G. and Simoni, R.: *Turandot* by Puccini. New York, Ricordi and Co., 1926.
2. Albee, E.: *The American Dream* and *The Zoo Story*. New York, Signet Books, 1961.
3. Andersen, H. C.: *Fairy Tales*. New York, World Publ. Co., 1946.
4. Apuleius: *The Metamorphoses*. Translated by H. E. Butler. Clarendon Press, 1910.
5. Arbuthnot *et al.*: *Children and Books*. Glenview, Scott, Foresman and Co., 1967.
6. d'Aulnoy, Mme.: in *The Fairy Tale Book*. New York, Simon and Schuster, 1958.
7. Ayre, R.: *Sketco, the Raven: Folk Tales of Canadian Indians*. Toronto, The Macmillan Company of Canada, 1961.
8. Basile, G.: *Il Pentamerone*. 1637, (translated into modern Italian by B. Croce).
9. Beckett, S.: *Endgame* and *Waiting for Godot*. New York, Evergreen, 1968.

9a. Berne, E.: *What Do You Say After You Say Hello?* New York, Grove Press, 1972.

10. Binswanger, L.: In J. Needleman: *Being-in-the-World*. New York, Basic Books, 1963.
11. Bleuler, E. and Bleuler, M.: *Lehrbuch der Psychiatrie*. 7th ed., Berlin, Springer Verlag, 1943.

11a. Bock, E.: *Apokalypse*. Stuttgart, Verlag Urachhaus, 1951.

12. Boss, M.: *Der Traum und seine Auslegung*. Bern, Hans Huber Verlag, 1953.
13. Boss, M.: *Psychoanalyse und Daseinsanalytik*. Bern, H. Huber, 1957.
14. Bradbury, R.: *The Golden Apples of the Sun*. New York, Bantam Books, 1967.
15. Brunner-Traut, E.: *Altägyptische Märchen*. Düsseldorf-Köln, Eugen Diederichs Verlag, 1965.
16. Buber, M.: *Between Man and Man*. London, Routledge and Kegan Ltd., 1947.
17. Buber, M.: *Die Erzählungen der Chassidim*. Zuerich, Manesse Verlag, 1949.
18. Buber, M.: *Introduction to the Kalevala*. Translated by Anton Schiefner. München, 1914.
19. Bugental, J. F. T.: Existential Crisis. Mimeographed manuscript, 1964.

20. Bugental, J. F. T.: *Journal of Existentialism,* V 20:433, 1965.
21. Bundi, G.: *Engadiner Märchen.* (two volumes), Zürich, Polygraphisches Institut A.G., n.d.
22. Bundi, G.: *Märchen aus dem Bündnerland.* Zürich, Rascher Verlag, 1955.
23. Burton, A.: Review of J. Hersey's *The Child Buyer. Journal of Existential Psychiatry, II* 6:243, 1961.
24. Campbell, J.: *The Hero with a Thousand Faces.* New York, Meridian Books, 1956.
25. Campbell, J.: *The Masks of God.* (four volumes) I. Primitive Mythology; II. Oriental Mythology; III. Occidental Mythology; IV. Creative Mythology. New York, Viking Press, 1959.
26. Camus, A.: *The Rebel* and *The Stranger.* New York, Vintage Books, 1946 and 1956.
27. Carroll, L.: *Alice in Wonderland.* New York, Washington Square Press, 1969.
28. Cassirer, E.: *Essay on Man.* New Haven, Yale U. Press, 1966.
29. Colum, P.: *Legends of Hawaii.* New Haven, Yale U. Press, 1937.
30. Coudenhove, G.: *"Du".* p. 47, December, 1961.
31. Cross, M.: *Great Operas.* New York, Doubleday, 1952.
32. Curcija-Prodanovic, N.: *Yugoslav Folk Tales.* London, Oxford U. Press, 1957.
32a. Curtin, J. *Myths and Folk-Lore of Ireland.* Boston, Little, Brown and Co., 1890.
33. Dante, Allighieri: *La Divina Commedia.* In *I Quattro Poeti Italiani.* Paris, Presso Le Fevre, 1833.
34. Dockstader, F. J.: *The Kachina and the White Man.* Bloomfield Hills, Cranbrook Institut of Science, 1956.
35. Downing, C.: *Russian Tales and Legends.* London, Oxford U. Press, 1956.
36. Duerckheim, K. G.: *Durchbruch zum Wesen.* Zürich, Max Niehans Verlag, 1954.
37. Elkin, H.: Return to Foundations. Mimeographed manuscript, 1971.
38. Elkin, H.: Freudian and phenomenological approaches to the emergence of individual consciousness. *Humanitas, V*: 1970.
39. Elkin, H.: On selfhood and the development of ego structures in infancy. *Psychoanalytic Review, LIX* 3:389, 1972.
40. Ellenberger, H. F.: *The Discovery of the Unconscious.* New York, Basic Books, 1970.
41. Elsner, M.: Der Dummling und die Bewusstseinsseele. *Die Christengemeinschaft, XXXVII*:43, 1965.
42. Emerson, R. W.: The oversoul; essays. *M.D. Magazine, IX* 8:43, 1965.
43. Englert-Faye, C.: *Von chlyne Lüte.* Basle, 1941.
44. Fabry, J.: *The Pursuit of Meaning.* Boston, Beacon Press, 1968.

45. Feifel, H. (Ed.): *The Meaning of Death.* New York, McGraw-Hill, 1959.
46. Feldmann, S.: *African Folk Tales.* New York, Dell Publishing, 1963.
47. Ferreira, A.: *American Journal of Psychoanalysis, IX* 1:91, 1961.
48. Frankl, V.: J. Existential Psychiatry, *I* 1:5, 1960.
49. Freud, S.: *The Basic Writings.* New York, Modern Library, 1938.
50. Fromm, E.: *The Forgotten Language.* New York, Grove Press, 1951.
51. Galdston, I.: Prometheus and the gods. *Bulletin of the New York Academy of Medicine, XL* 7:560, 1964.
52. Gaster, T. H.: *The Oldest Stories in the World.* Boston, Beacon Press, 1952.
53. Goethe, J. W.: *Goethe's Werke.* Stuttgart und Leipzig, Deutsche Verlagsanstalt, 1898.
54. Goethe, J. W.: *Faust.* Berlin, C. Schuddekopf, n.d.
55. Goethe, J. W.: *Gedichte.* Leipzig, Bibliographisches Institut, n.d.
56. Graham, E.: *Bedtime Stories.* New York, Wonder Books, 1946.
57. Graves, R.: *The Greek Myths.* Baltimore, Pelican Books, 1967.
58. Grimm, J. and Grimm, W.: *Grimms Fairy Tales.* New York, Grosset and Dunlap, 1945.
59. Hamilton, E.: *Mythology.* New York, Mentor Books, 1969.
60. Hart, D. L.: The Problem of Evil in Fairy Tales. Mimeographed manuscript, 1964.
61. Hartmann, H.: Comments on the formation of psychic structure. *Psychoanalytic Study of the Child.* New York, International U. Press, vol. II, 1946.
62. Hauff, W.: *Das kalte Herz.* Zürich, Hallauer Verlag, n.d.
63. Heidegger, M.: *Sein und Zeit.* Tübingen, Niemeyer Verlag, 1960.
64. Heidegger, M.: *An Introduction to Metaphysics.* New York, Doubleday Anchor Books, 1961.
65. Hesse, H.: *Magister Ludi.* New York, Bantam Books, 1970.
66. Heuscher, J. E.: Language, authenticity and human growth. *Confinia Psychiatrica, XIII*:193, 1970.
67. Heuscher, J. E.: *The Green Serpent and the Beautiful Lily.* Book manuscript, 1972.
68. Heuscher, J. E.: Turandot. *Confinia Psychiatrica, V* 3:146, 1960.
69. Heuscher, J. E.: Lucifer and Eros. *Confinia Psychiatrica, VII*:151, 1964.
70. Heuscher, J. E.: The meaning of fairy tales and myths. *Confinia Psychiatrica, XI*:90, 1968.
71. Heuscher, J. E.: The use of existential-philosophic concepts in psychotherapy. *American Journal of Psychoanalysis, XXIX* 2:170, 1967.
72. Heuscher, J. E.: Patterns. *Diseases of the Nervous System, XXII* 1:1, 1961.

73. Heuscher, J. E.: Introduction to myths and fairy tales. *Existential Psychiatry, I*:196, 1966.
74. Heuscher, J. E.: *Journal of Existentialism, V* 20:371, 1965.
75. Heuscher, J. E.: The temporal experience today. *American Journal of Psychoanalysis, XXXI* 2:192, 1971.
76. Heuscher, J. E.: What is existential psychotherapy? *Review of Existential Psychology and Psychiatry, X* 2:158, 1964.
77. Heuscher, J. E.: *Schweizer Archiv für Neurologie, Neurochirurgie und Psychiatrie, LXV,* 1950.
78. Heuscher, J. E.: Vocation, celibacy and authenticity. *Comprehensive Psychiatry, XIII* 5:445, 1972.
79. Hollowell, L.: *A Book of Children's Literature.* New York, Rhinehart, 1950.
80. Husserl, E.: *Ideas.* New York, Macmillan, 1958.
81. Isben, H.: *Four Major Plays.* New York, Signet Classic, 1970.
82. Jacobi, J.: *Die Psychologie von C. G. Jung.* Zürich, Rascher Verlag, 1949.
83. Jaspers, K.: *Reason and Existence.* New York, Noonday, 1955.
84. Jegerlenert, J.: *Was die Sennen erzaehlen.* Switzerland, 1907.
85. Jones, G.: *Scandinavian Legends and Folk Tales.* London, Oxford U. Press, 1956.
86. Jung, C. G.: In P. Radin: *The Trickster.* London, Routledge and Kegan Paul, 1956.
87. Jung, C. G.: *Welt der Psyche.* Zürich, Rascher Verlag, 1954.
88. Jung, C. G. and Kerényi, C.: *Essays on a Science of Mythology.* New York, Harper Torchbooks, 1963.
89. *Junior Classics.* (The New Junior Classics.) I. *Fairy Tales and Fables.* Patten William, n.d.
90. Kafka, F.: *The Trial.* New York, Modern Library, 1964.
91. *Kalevala:* German translation by Anton Schiefner, Munich, 1914. English translation by W. F. Kirby, Everyman's Library, 1969. Also translated by T. P. Magoun, Jr., Cambridge, Harvard U. Press, 1963.
92. Kaplan, I.: *Swedish Folk Tales.* London, F. Muller Ltd., 1953.
93. Kaufmann, W.: *Goethe's Faust.* New York, Doubleday, 1961.
94. Kazantzakis, N.: *Report to Greco.* New York, Bantam Books, 1966.
95. Keller, W.: *Am Kaminfeuer der Tessiner.* Switzerland, 1940.
96. Kierkegaard, S.: *Fear and Trembling* and *Sickness unto Death.* Garden City, Doubleday, 1954.
97. Kierkegaard, S.: *Purity of Heart Is to Will One Thing.* New York, Harper Torchbooks, 1956.
98. Koestenbaum, P.: *Journal of Existentialism, V* 20:437, 1965.
99. Koestenbaum, P.: *The Vitality of Death.* Westport, Greenwood, 1971.
100. Koestler, A. (Ed.): *Beyond Reductionism.* New York, Macmillan, 1969.

101. Konitzky, G. A.: *Nordamerikanische Indianermärchen.* Düsseldorf-Köln, Eugen Diederichs Verlag, 1963.
102. Laing, R. D.: *The Divided Self.* New York, Pelican Books, 1965.
103. Lang, A.: *Fairy Tale Collection.* New York, Dover Publications, 1968.
104. Lentz, F.: *Bildsprache der Märchen.* Stuttgart, Verlag Urachhaus, 1971.
105. Leopardi, G.: *An Antology of World Poetry.* Translated by L. De' Lucchi, Albert and Charles Boni, n.d.
106. Leopardi, G.: *Poesie.* Milano, Casa Editrice Sonzogno, n.d.
107. Lévy-Bruhl, L.: *Die Geistige Welt der Primitiven.* München, F. Bruckmann Verlag, 1927.
108. von der Leyen, F.: *Die Welt der Märchen.* Düsseldorf-Köln, Eugen Diederichs Verlag, (Bd. I), 1953.
109. von der Leyen, F.: *Das Märchen.* Heidelberg, Quelle und Meyer Verlag, 1958.
110. Life Editors: *American Folklore.* New York, Time Inc., 1961.
111. Lorenzini, C. (Collodi): *Le Avventure di Pinocchio.* 1883.
112. Lüthi, M.: *Es war einmal.* Göttingen, Vandenhoeck und Ruprecht, 1964.
113. Macmillan, C.: *Glooskap's Country (and Other Indian Tales).* Toronto and New York, Oxford U. Press, 1956.
114. Marcel, G.: *La Dignité Humaine.* Paris, Aubier, Editions Montaigne, 1964.
115. Marek, G. R.: *Puccini (A Biography).* New York, Simon and Schuster, 1951.
116. Maslow, A. H.: *Toward a Psychology of Being.* New York, D. van Nostrand, 1962.
117. Maurer, A.: Adolescent attitudes towards death. *Journal of General Psychology, CV*:75, 1964.
118. Maurer, A.: *Journal of Existential Psychiatry, II* 6:193, 1961.
119. May, R.: *Existence.* New York, Basic Books, 1958.
120. May, R.: *Love and Will.* New York, W. W. Norton, 1969.
121. May, R.: *Man's Search for Himself.* New York, W. W. Norton, 1953.
122. Merritt, A.: *The Moon Pool* and *The Ship of Ishtar.* New York, Collier Books, 1967.
123. Meyer, R.: *Das Geisteserbe Finnlands.* Basel, Rudolf Geering Verlag, 1940.
124. Meyer, R.: *Die Weisheit der Deutschen Volksmärchen.* Stuttgart, Verlag der Christengemeinschaft, 1935.
125. Meyer, R.: *Die Weisheit der Schweizer Märchen.* Schaffhausen, Columban Verlag, 1944.
126. Minkowski, E.: *Le Temps Vécu.* Paris, d'Artrey, 1933.
127. Natanson, M.: *Essays in Phenomenology.* Introduction. The Hague, Martinus Nijhoff, 1966.

128. Needleman, J. (Ed.): *Being in the World.* Introduction. New York, Basic Books, 1963.
129. Needleman, J.: *The New Religions.* Garden City, Doubleday, 1970.
130. Neumann, E.: *Amor and Psyche.* New York, Harper and Row, 1962.
131. Neumann, E.: *Art and the Creative Unconscious.* Princeton, Bollingen Series, 1971.
132. Newman, E.: *Great Operas.* New York, Vintage Press, vol. II, 1958.
133. Nietzsche, F.: *Thus Spake Zarathustra.* New York, Dutton, 1933.
134. Novalis: *Gesammelte Werke* (I. Bd.) including *Gedichte* and *Heinrich von Ofterdingen.* Zürich, Bühl Verlag, 1945.
135. Nusbaum, A.: *Zuni Indian Tales.* New York, Putnam's, 1926.
136. Ortega y Gasset, J.: *Triptico. Espasa-Calpe,* 1962.
137. Ortega y Gasset, J.: *Meditaciones del Quijote.* (Ideas sobre la novela). Espasa-Calpe, 1964.
138. Ortega y Gasset, J.: *El Tema de Nuestro Tiempo.* Espasa-Calpe, 1938.
139. Perrault, C.: *French Fairy Tales.* Paris, Didier, 1945.
140. Pfister, O.: Kryptolalie, Kryptographie und unbewusste Vexierbilder bei Normalen. *Jahrbuch für psychoanalytische und psychopathologische Forschungen.* Leipzig, vol. V, 1913.
141. Radin, P.: *The Trickster.* London, Routledge and Kegan Paul, 1956.
142. Raffael, B.: *Beowulf.* New York, Mentor Books, 1963.
143. Raglan, Lord: *The Hero.* London, Oxford U. Press, 1952.
144. Rank, O.: *Psychology and the Soul.* Philadelphia, U. Pennsylvania Press, 1950.
144a. Rank, O.: *The Myth of the Birth of the Hero.* New York, Basic Books, 1952.
145. Rapaport, D.: *Organization and Pathology of Thought.* London, Oxford U. Press, 1951.
146. Raphael, A.: *Goethe's Parable.* New York, Harcourt and Brace, 1963.
147. Reider, N.: The Judas Myth. Paper read at the Northern and Central California Psychiatric Meeting, 1960.
148. Rilke, R. M.: *Duino Elegies.* New York, W. W. Norton, 1963.
149. v. Rittmeister, J.: *Confinia Psychiatrica, IV*:65, 1961.
150. Rusch, H. P.: *Naturwissenschaft von Morgen.* Küsnacht (Zch), E. Hartmann Verlag, 1955.
151. de Saint-Exupéry, A.: *The Little Prince.* New York, Harcourt, Brace and Co., 1943.
152. Sandage, A.: *Astrophysical Journal,* 1965. Quoted in the San Francisco Chronicle, June 13, 1965.
153. Sarro, R.: *Journal of Existential Psychiatry, I* 4:578, 1960.
154. Sartre, J.-P.: *Existentialism and Human Emotions.* New York, Philosophical Library, 1957.
155. Sartre, J.-P.: *Théatre.* Paris, Editions Gallimard, 1962.
156. Schiller, F.: *Schiller's Werke.* Stuttgart und Leipzig, Deutsche Verlagsanstart, n. d.

157. Schramm, Lyle and Parker: *T.V. in the Lives of Our Children.* Stanford, Stanford U. Press, 1961.

158. Schwab, G.: *Sagen des klassischen Altertums.* Stuttgart, K.Thienemanns Verlag, n.d.

159. Segal, H.: *Introduction to the Work of Melanie Klein.* New York, Basic Books, 1964.

160. Seligmann, V.: *Puccini among Friends.* New York, Macmillan, 1938.

161. Sendak, M.: *Where the Wild Things Are.* New York, Harper and Row, 1958.

162. Serrano, M.: *C. G. Jung and Hermann Hesse.* New York, Schocken Books, 1968.

163. Simburg, C.: The Sleeping Beauty. Paper read at the Northern and Central California Psychiatric Meeting, 1961.

163a. Smith, E. S.: *Po-ho-no and Other Yosemite Legends* (copyrighted).

164. Spitz, R. A.: *The First Year of Life.* New York, International Univ. Press, 1965.

165. Starbuck, E. D.: *Fairy Tale, Myth and Legend.* New York, Macmillan, Vol. I, 1928.

166. Steiner, R.: *Die Pforte der Einweihung.* Switzerland, Phil.-Anthrop. Verlag, Dornach, 1935.

167. Sutermeister, O.: *Kinder und Hausmärchen aus der Schweiz.* 2nd ed., Switzerland, 1873.

168. Suzuki, D. T.; Fromm, E. and De Martino, R.: *Zen Buddhism and Psychoanalysis.* New York, Harper and Bros., 1960.

169. Sydow, J.: *Die Edda.* Hannover, Buchvertrieb der Christengemeinschaft, n.d.

170. Teilhard de Chardin, P.: *The Phenomenon of Man.* New York, Harper and Row, 1959.

171. *The Fairy Tale Book.* New York, Simon and Schuster, 1957.

172. Thompson, S.: *Motif Index of Folk Literature.* Folklore Fellows Communications 106-109, 116-117; 1932-36. Also *The Folktale.* 2nd ed. New York, 1953.

173. Thurber, J.: *The Thirteen Clocks.* New York, Simon and Schuster, 1950.

174. Tolkien, I. R. R.: *The Hobbit.* New York, Ballantine Books, 1965.

175. Tolkien, I. R. R.: *The Lord of the Rings.* New York, Ballantine Books, 1965.

176. Tolkien, I. R. R.: *The Tolkien Reader.* New York, Ballantine Books, 1966.

177. Uhland, L.: *Uhlands Werke.* (Bd. II) Zürich, Hallauer Verlag, n.d.

178. Waters, F.: *Masked Gods.* New York, Ballantine Books, 1950.

179. Weitbrecht, R.: *Deutsche Heldensagen.* Stuttgart, Union Deutsche Verlags-Gesellschaft, n.d.

180. Wheeler, P.: *Hawaiian Wonder Tales.* New York, Beechhurst Press, 1953.
181. Wheeler, P.: *Russian Wonder Tales.* New York, Thomas Yoseloff, 1957.
182. Wiener, N.: *Cybernetics.* New York, Wiley, 1948.
183. Wilde, O.: *Lord Arthur Sevile's Crime and Other Stories.* Baltimore, Penguin Books, 1958.
184. Wilde, O.: *The Picture of Dorian Gray.* Washington Square Press, 1972.
185. Wittgenstein, G.: *Märchen, Träume, Schicksale.* Düsseldorf-Köln, Diederichs Verlag, 1965.
186. Wolfram, E.: *Die Germanischen Heldensagen.* Stuttgart, Der Kommende Tag, A.G., 1922.
187. Zilboorg, G.: *A History of Medical Psychology.* New York, W. W. Norton, 1941.
188. Zimmer, H.: *The King and the Corpse.* New York, Meridian Books, 1960.
189. Zimmer, H.: *Myths and Symbols in Indian Art and Civilization.* Bollingen Series, Princeton U. Press, 1946.

INDEX